RICKSHAW BEIJING

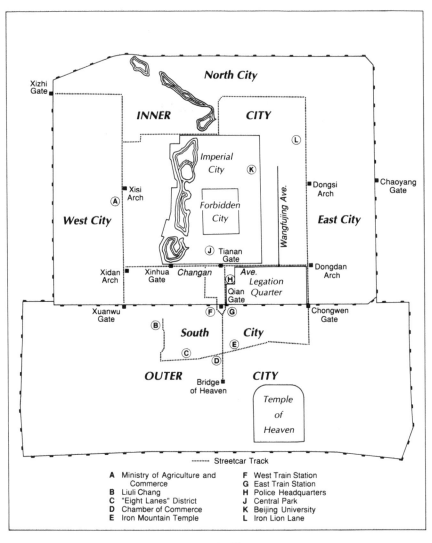

North City

Xizhi Gate

INNER   CITY

Imperial City

Ⓛ

Ⓚ

Dongsi Arch

Chaoyang Gate

Xisi Arch

Ⓐ

Forbidden City

West City

Wangfujing Ave.

East City

Ⓙ Tianan Gate

Xidan Arch   Xinhua Gate   Changan   Ave.   Dongdan Arch

Ⓗ   Legation

Qian Gate   Quarter

Xuanwu Gate

Ⓕ Ⓖ

Chongwen Gate

Ⓑ

South   City

Ⓔ

Ⓒ

Ⓓ

OUTER   CITY

Bridge of Heaven

Temple

of

Heaven

·········· Streetcar Track

A Ministry of Agriculture and
    Commerce
B Liuli Chang
C "Eight Lanes" District
D Chamber of Commerce
E Iron Mountain Temple

F West Train Station
G East Train Station
H Police Headquarters
J Central Park
K Beijing University
L Iron Lion Lane

Map 1. Beijing.

RICKSHAW BEIJING

City People and Politics in the 1920s

DAVID STRAND

University of California Press
Berkeley   Los Angeles   London

University of California Press
Berkeley and Los Angeles, California

University of California Press, Ltd.
London, England

© 1989 by
The Regents of the University of California

LIBRARY OF CONGRESS
Library of Congress Cataloging-in-Publication Data

Strand, David.
    Rickshaw Beijing: city people and politics in the 1920s /
    David Strand.
        p.   cm.
    Bibliography: p.
    Includes index.
    ISBN 0-520-06311-2 (alk. paper)
        1. Peking (China)—Politics and government.   2. Peking
(China)—Social life and customs.   I. Title.
DS795.3.S82 1989
951'.156041—dc19   88-15571
                                                               CIP

Printed in the United States of America
9 8 7 6 5 4 3 2 1

For Ceceile

Contents

Illustrations

Preface

When I arrived in Beijing in September 1982 for a year of research, the city was hosting the Twelfth Congress of the Chinese Communist Party (CCP). On a first visit to the Palace Museum, I stood on the terrace of the Hall of Supreme Harmony, at the center of the old Forbidden City, looking south, as I imagined emperors had done on great ceremonial occasions. Against the red and gold line of walls and roofs I could glimpse the red-flagged outline of massive public buildings rising like a farther range of hills: to the right the Great Hall of the People, where the CCP was in session, and to the left the Museums of the Chinese Revolution and of Chinese History. Invisible from my vantage point, in the space framed by the remains of empire and the heavy architectural signature of state socialism, lay Tiananmen Square, a paved expanse broken by the obelisk dedicated to the People's Heroes and by the Mausoleum of Mao Zedong. (Tianan *men*, or Tianan *Gate*, is the outer, southernmost entrance to the Imperial City and the Forbidden City within; the square runs south from the gate.)

Imperial Beijing (ending in 1911 with the abolition of the Qing dynasty) and socialist Beijing (beginning in 1949 with the founding of the People's Republic) are clearly visible in the sprawl of Ming- and Qing-vintage palaces north of Tianan Gate and the Stalinist behemoths parked to the south. In this gathering of monuments Republican Beijing, the transitional city that is the subject of this book, is harder to detect. On one side of the Monument to the People's Heroes, a white marble frieze depicts the eruption of student protests outside Tianan Gate in the May Fourth Movement in 1919. The students' nationalistic indignation, represented by heroic poses frozen in stone, was directed at their government's apparent willingness to accept treaty provisions, ratified at Versailles, that gave German concessions in nearby Shandong province to the Japanese. Inside the Museum of the Revolution photographs of the 1919 demonstrations are on display, along with the gallows on which CCP founder Li Dazhao was executed in Beijing in 1927.

Republican Beijing is inscribed on contemporary monuments as a footnote to a revolutionary past and is passed over briefly in museum exhibits. Away from the city center it is possible to find the physical remains of the Republic in period buildings, like the former cabinet offices on Iron Lion Lane. Iron Lion Lane itself was the site of the March 18 Incident in 1926 in which unarmed protesters were machine-gunned and bayoneted by the bodyguards of warlord politician Duan Qirui. There is no plaque of remembrance. But in the northwestern suburbs of the city, not far from the new campus of Beijing University and on the grounds of the Old Summer Palace, stands a monument to those killed at Iron Lion Lane. The small obelisk, erected in 1929 and one of the few Republican-era monuments to be found in Beijing, suffers from neglect except on the anniversary of the incident, when school children and their teachers bring wreaths to commemorate the dead.

Understanding Republican Beijing requires attention to the monumental projects of empire and socialism which bracket the period. But an eye for life-size detail is required if one is to reconstruct the days when Chinese subjects became citizens, modern ideologies such as nationalism and communism first seized the imaginations of citizens, and politicians and officials first wrestled with vexing problems of popular sovereignty and modern government. The reader will find the larger-than-life figures ordinarily associated with the Republican period, like Sun Yat-sen, Chiang Kai-shek, and Mao, either missing from these pages or viewed from the perspective of the crowds who revered, reviled, or ignored them. I have concentrated instead on the collective and individual biographies of ordinary and obscure individuals who lived in the shadow of great architecture and great men. I hope that this approach will allow the inner, natural light of city life and

lives to dispel some of the shadows that obscure the true dimensions of the Republic as a popular and local as well as an elite and
national creation.

Convenient to this style of interpretation, Beijing in the 1920s
projected a double image of the monumental and the miniature:
great avenues and narrow alleyways, grand palaces and modest
courtyard residences, the central spectacles of national politics and
the eccentric ceremonies of guild and neighborhood. I have
selected as an organizing conceit the miniature rather than the
monumental—hence "Rickshaw Beijing"—both because the small,
single-passenger vehicle was a commonplace of Beijing life in the
1920s and because its mixing of old and new, manual and mechanical, and Chinese and foreign elements is suggestive of China's
and Beijing's predicament in the Republican period. In both a
temporal and a spatial sense, Republican-era Chinese were caught
between worlds: between China's imperial past and its national
future and between Chinese culture and that of the rest of the
planet.

Republican Beijing provides a backdrop to several fine studies
of elite and national-level politics.[1] However, the meaning of the
urban scenes glimpsed in these accounts is less well defined. Sharply
etched portraits of presidents, ministers, warlords, and intellectuals hang against a background recognizable in silhouette as the
old walled capital. The city itself appears as so much masonry to
be marched through and around, an ancient prop employed to
deepen through contrast the colors of modern politics or to blend
in with the atavism of those intent on reestablishing the monarchy.

Illumination of the city's physical and human dimensions forces
a shift in perspective. In the 1920s itinerant political contenders
with armies and parties in tow arrived and departed in a blur of
activity. National politics, not local society, lacked clarity and
coherence. City residents reacted to this disorderly procession with
interest and with understandable concern for their livelihoods and
safety. By 1923 the Republican regime headquartered in Beijing
had been debased through corruption.[2] The provinces were
beyond the capital's administrative reach or in open rebellion. In
the political wreckage of the Republic, warlords and imperialists
clutched bits and pieces of authority: a functioning ministry or
government-owned railroad here, a foreign customs service there.

Meanwhile, local residents expressed in mass rallies their continued commitment to the idea of a sovereign republic, and local elites struggled to preserve social order. These elements formed parts of the unfinished puzzle of a modern Chinese political order. While the expectation that someone would soon be able to seize the political center and arrange the pieces in an orderly manner was strong in many Chinese, the parts could not wait for the reconstitution of the whole. As is described in the chapter-length portraits of "city people" (*shimin*) included in this study, policemen, merchants, capitalists, workers, civic leaders, and political cadres fitted themselves and their organizations into the corner of the puzzle occupied by local politics. In the process, piecemeal political and social development continued, despite the fact that the identity of the final victor and the nature of the completed polity remained a mystery.

The following chapters weave portraits of city people into a chronological treatment of the rise of political consciousness and participation in the ten years following the May Fourth Movement. Chapter 1 outlines the central theme of the study, which is the city's eclectic response to social and political change. New organizations, such as the police, political parties, chambers of commerce, and labor unions, appeared and evolved, while old institutions, such as guilds, volunteer fire-fighting and militia corps, charities, labor gangs, and elite mediation, survived and prospered. In this rich mélange of old and new practices, the repertoire of political strategies and tactics available to city people rapidly expanded. Chapters 2 and 3 offer the rickshaw as an emblem for a disordered age and as a concrete example of how Beijing functioned as a society divided by class and uneven rates of development and drawn together in a common urban culture. Despite the peculiarities of their trade, rickshaw pullers can be seen as representative of the urban laboring poor, the city's not-so-silent majority.

Chapters 4 and 5 focus on the police and the chamber of commerce, arguably the two most important order-keeping bodies in the city. Both the police and the chamber experienced considerable inner turmoil as they sought to reconcile competing and conflicting values and interests related to the issue of what kind of "order" could and should be maintained. Chapter 6 examines the effects of technological change on city life. A new streetcar system, promising progress and profits, sparked political opposition organized around the idea of "people's livelihood" (*minsheng*).

Despite the existence of spectacular anomalies, like the streetcar, most of Beijing's economy was preindustrial in nature and therefore most workers had little direct contact with modern machines or relations of production. The strikes, fights, and feuds discussed in chapter 7 suggest the ways in which conflict and cooperation in the tradition-bound workplace by turn inhibited and encouraged the emergence of modern unionism.

Poverty, a new impulse to police city life, enhanced group and class consciousness, and the transformative promise and threat of capitalism gave city residents reasons to engage in politics. The emergence of a new public sphere associated with the accelerating power of mass nationalism provided the means. Chapter 8 traces the development of the May Fourth style of mass politics from student beginnings to a far broader, distinctively urban phenomenon.

If mass nationalism periodically opened the city up to politics, warlordism just as frequently threatened to shut down and cut off the normal functions of city life. In chapter 9 the manifold effects of warfare on urban society and politics are outlined. These states of siege are examined for the evidence they provide of citywide leadership in response to military crises.

Toward the end of the decade another round of warfare brought the possibility of a reorganized city politics. The Nationalist party, deeply divided between right and left wings, began an intense program of mass mobilization in 1928 led by left-wing party cadres in uneasy alliance with a right-turning political center in Nanjing and rebellious warlords in north China. Chapter 10 focuses on how these external pressures, combined with internal, factional disputes, propelled and then derailed the city's labor union movement. Finally, a decade that began with the idealistic, elite-bound fervor of the May Fourth Movement is brought to a close with a wild riot in which rickshaw men nearly destroy the streetcar system. In the streetcar riot of 1929 all the elements highlighted in earlier chapters—rickshaws, the city poor, policemen, merchant politicians, streetcars, public opinion, soldiers, proletarians, and political cadres—come together in the company of additional actors, including Buddhist monks, to suggest the complexity and vitality of modern urban politics in Republican China. The Luddite tone of the climactic scene provides an opportunity to reflect on both the power and the vulnerability of China's distinctive contribution to urban modernity.[3]

Acknowledgments

Michel Oksenberg suggested Republican-era Beijing as a topic, and I remain grateful for that idea and his subsequent advice and support. My greatest debt is to Andrew Nathan, who provided invaluable aid, criticism, and counsel from the dissertation's beginning to the manuscript's end. Chen Yung-fa, Joshua Fogel, Susan Mann, William Rowe, and Richard Weiner provided much-needed help and insight at critical moments and over a period of years.

Comment and reaction to drafts and chapters from Guy Alitto, Richard Bush, Ming K. Chan, Helen Hettinger, Philip Kuhn, Laurel Kendall, William Muir, Evelyn Rawski, Tang Tsou, Frederic Wakeman, Harry Weiss, Roxane Witke, Bin Wong, and several anonymous readers were of critical importance in the researching, writing, and editing of this study. Joseph Esherick's comments and advice on revision of the manuscript were especially valuable. Professor Chen Qinghua of Beijing University offered generous assistance during my sojourn in Beijing. Sheila Levine of the University of California Press skillfully guided me through the editorial process. Gladys Castor expertly copyedited the manuscript. I also wish to thank Betsey Scheiner for her editorial help in the final stages of the book's production. I am grateful to *Modern China* for permission to quote from my "Feuds, Fights, and Factions: Group Politics in 1920s Beijing" (vol. 11, no. 4 [October 1985], pp. 411–435).

A Fulbright-Hayes Dissertation Research Fellowship and support from the East Asian Institute of Columbia University made the early stages of research possible. I am also grateful for the financial assistance and other support provided by the National Endowment for the Humanities' Modern China Project at the University of Chicago, the Center for Chinese Studies at the University of California, Berkeley, the Committee on Scholarly Communication with the People's Republic of China, and Dickinson College.

Ceceile Strand, to whom this book is dedicated, gave sound editorial advice on numerous occasions and contributed immeasurably to the pleasure of the work and travel that went into this project.

A Note on
Romanization and Currency

With the exception of two names (Chiang Kai-shek and Sun Yat-sen), I have used pinyin romanization. Accordingly, and reflecting current usage with regard to Chinese place names, I have titled this book "Rickshaw Beijing" instead of "Rickshaw Peking." In June 1928 the city's name was changed to "Beiping" by the Nationalists. For events after that date (and up until 1949 when the city was given its old name back by the Communists), I have used "Beiping."

Unless stated otherwise, all monetary units in the book are Chinese. In 1926 the Chinese silver dollar (yuan) was worth 345 coppers (China had a bimetal currency system determined by market prices), .72 taels (the old Chinese silver unit), and .49 American gold dollars. (Source: John S. Burgess, *The Guilds of Peking* [New York: Columbia University Press, 1928], pp. 63–64.)

One

A Twentieth-Century
Walled City

Wobbling Pivot and Armature of
State Power

Broad avenues, parks, and public squares open up the contemporary urban world to the mass assemblies essential to modern commerce, culture, and politics. By contrast, early-twentieth-century Beijing, as a physical entity, remained a city stubbornly defined by walls, walled enclosures, and gates.[1] The fifteenth-century Ming plan of the capital decreed boxes within boxes and cities within cities. The habits of vernacular architecture extended this principle into neighborhoods and residences.[2] Towering walls of tamped earth with brick facing formed the square Inner City (*neicheng*) and, adjacent to the south, the rectangular Outer City (*waicheng*; fig. 1). (The Inner City was conventionally divided into East, West, and North "Cities" or districts. See map.) The Inner City enclosed the walls of the Imperial City, which, in turn, framed the yellow-roofed, red-walled Forbidden City and the emperor's throne room. In his memoir of Republican Beijing, newspaper man Li Chengyi, quoting a line spoken by an emperor in a Beijing opera, remembered a cityscape composed of circles within circles: "In the midst of a great circle lies a small circle. Within the small circle stands a yellow one."[3] Within the compass of these great walls and a grid-work of imperial thoroughfares lay a mosaic of walled enclosures containing the mansions of the powerful, the smaller courtyard residences of the monied, propertied, and degree-holding classes, and the courtyard slums of the laboring poor.

I

Fig. 1. The wall separating the Inner and Outer Cities. Qian Gate and the western branch of the central railway station are visible in the distance. In the aftermath of the Boxer uprising in 1900, the portion of the wall pictured here was placed under foreign jurisdiction as a means of guaranteeing the security of the Legation Quarter immediately to the north. From Heinz v. Perckhammer, *Peking* (Berlin: Albertus-Verlag, 1928).

The hard symmetry of Beijing's monumental plan was softened by the random, mazelike wanderings of alleyways (*hutong*) typical of most neighborhoods and, seasonally, by nature. In the late fall and winter, the "special blueness of the sky, intensity of the sun and brilliance of the moon" placed the city's unique architectural ensemble of palaces and walls in brilliant relief.[4] In the spring north China's famous dust storms obscured the composite order of these elements, as did tree foliage in the summer when Beijing became a "forest city."[5]

In the late-Qing and Republican era, change directed toward the physical and social transformation of Beijing stirred and developed. Beginning at the turn of the century, reformers and

Fig. 2. On this modern Beijing avenue, a mule-cart driver has ignored the prohibition against narrow-tired vehicles using the paved, center section. Note the presence of gutters, street lamp, and flanking lines of young trees marking the borders of the unpaved side roads. Pedestrians naturally preferred the macadam to dusty or muddy mule-cart tracks. Courtesy of the Library of Congress.

entrepreneurs introduced inventions and institutions intended to make the city a fit capital, first for a modern empire, and then for a republic. As a physical space, Beijing seemed alternately to invite and to resist change. Strips of macadam could be laid without much trouble down the centers of wide, Ming-vintage avenues. But in order that narrow-wheeled country carts, which ruined pavement, could continue to travel in the city, the sides of the roads had to be left unpaved.[6] Alongside the new pavement, work crews installed water pipes, street lamps, postboxes, public latrines, and telegraph and telephone poles and lines. A new, uniformed police force built kiosks and deployed its members beside the thoroughfares. The tasks of the police included keeping mule drivers off the pavement and protecting postboxes and utility equipment from vandalism and pilferage (figs. 2 and 3).[7] In 1910 Qing officials reportedly contemplated tearing down the city walls

Fig. 3. A Beijing alleyway (*hutong*). Narrow, twisting side streets were left unpaved. This commercial *hutong* boasts a long line of businesses, including a hat shop and a jewelry store. Note the old-style signboards and intricately carved facades. Courtesy of the Library of Congress.

and laying streetcar track in their place.[8] Considering that at that time Beijing's walls still symbolized, concealed, and protected imperial authority and the person of the emperor, the notion was a radical one. Although the city walls, as the expression of cosmological canon, still had a potent ally in the sheer inertia of these ordered ranges of earth and brick, modern-minded Chinese began to imagine their removal.

By the birth of the Republic in 1912, a rusty, potholed grid of wire, pipe, and macadam mimicked, if not threatened, the ancient geometry of the city's walls and gates. New government bureaus, universities, factories, and foreign legations functioned as modern enclaves in the midst of preindustrial and culturally traditional Beijing. The streets themselves, with their complement of new devices and social roles, including telephone communications, rickshaw and (eventually) automobile travel, and formal policing of public behavior, systematically projected modern ideas and invention throughout the city. As Marshall Berman has observed, the modern avenue, of which Hausmann's Parisian boulevards and Petersburg's Nevsky Prospect are outstanding examples, is a "distinctively modern environment," which "served as a focus for newly accumulated material and human forces: macadam and asphalt, gaslight and electric light, the railroad, electric trolleys and automobiles, movies and mass transportation."[9] When the European city was exported whole or in part to the Third World, modern avenues of the kind constructed in early-twentieth-century Beijing formed both the skeletal structure and the nervous system of a new urban organism.[10]

In some cities, like Shanghai, modern enclaves and infrastructure transformed urban life. The city itself became an enclave in the midst of a preindustrial hinterland. In most other cities, especially those like Beijing, located inland from China's maritime fringe, the changes were less decisive. But the attendant emergence even in smaller numbers of new buildings housing factories, universities, and modern government, and of new people, like proletarians, capitalists, and a cadre of politicians and assorted professionals, represented a significant alteration in the pattern of urban life. Anarchists throwing bombs, students making speeches, and entrepreneurs floating joint-stock companies could not fail to make an impression even if a uniformly politicized citizenry or a forest of smokestacks did not yet exist to underscore their long-term significance.

Imperial Beijing, with its cosmologically dictated ceremonial and administrative architecture, congested commercial districts, and flat expanses of courtyard residences, easily absorbed the initial transformative threat posed by a few modern buildings and machines and a thin layer of pavement. But the fragility, even the absurdity, of ventures advertising themselves in the form of malfunctioning, sometimes dangerous machinery, hectoring policemen, and shouting rickshaw men could not disguise the insistent way in which new technologies and practices pressed up against the lives of Beijing residents and subtly altered the speed, scale, and direction of city life. Once the empire's unwobbling pivot encased in massive walls, Beijing began a long and halting re-

Fig. 4. Fashionably dressed men and women enjoying a sled ride. For centuries simple sleds like this one had been available for hire on the "palace lakes" north of the Imperial City. The laborer pulling the sled wore special shoes equipped with iron hooks that gripped the ice. Once the sled picked up speed, the puller hopped on to coast along with his passengers. (H. Y. Lowe, *The Adventures of Wu: The Life Cycle of a Peking Man*, vol. 2 [Princeton: Princeton University Press, 1983], pp. 132–133.) UPI/Bettmann Newsphotos.

emergence as the armature of modern state power wrapped in telephone and telegraph wire and powered by mass nationalism instead of a mandate from heaven.

By the 1920s this redirecting of city life was well advanced. A streetcar system operated, along with scores of modern factories, dozens of newspapers, a racetrack, cinemas, an airfield, and several railway stations. Political parties, a chamber of commerce, labor unions, patriotic societies, literary clubs, and professional societies of lawyers, bankers, and newspaper reporters claimed tens of thousands of members. But despite the inspired imaginings of late-Qing planners, streetcar track, while it ran through and within the square and rectangular template formed by the Inner and the Outer City, did not replace the city walls. Nor did labor unions and professional associations push aside craft and merchant guilds. They competed and cooperated with each other in an increasingly complex blending of organizational and leadership styles and strategies.

Some cities are like palimpsests. The imperfectly erased past is visible even though only the imprint of the present can be clearly deciphered. By contrast, Beijing in the 1920s, as a human and physical entity, clearly preserved the past, accommodated the present, and nurtured the basic elements of several possible futures. Few cities in China in the 1920s looked so traditional and Chinese and at the same time harbored the essentials of modern and Western urban life. In fact, the city's physical ambiguities provide a metaphor for the uneven and incomplete social transformations of the Republican period. With everything added by way of new technologies and social practices and little taken away through the uniform application of factory system, modern administration, or thoroughgoing social revolution, Beijing cultivated incongruities and forced accommodation between old and new forms of production and social action (fig. 4).

Beijing and Beiping:
Taking the Measure of a Capital in Decline

West of the Forbidden City and within the walls of the Imperial City lie three artificial lakes or seas (*hai*): Bei (north), Zhong (middle), and Nan (south). The two southern lakes, or "Zhongnanhai," are surrounded by palaces and pavilions, which form the southwestern corner of the Imperial City.[11] The main entrance to the Zhongnanhai complex is Xinhua Gate, which faces south on Changan Avenue, running east and west. During the Ming and Qing dynasties, emperors and the court used Zhongnanhai as a retreat from the more austere setting of the Forbidden City. Following the 1911 Revolution and beginning with President Yuan Shikai, most Republican heads of state used Zhongnanhai as residence and office complex.[12] Since 1949 top officials of the People's Republic have lived and worked in the same, palatial setting.

While the 1911 Revolution left imperial Beijing physically intact, dethronement of the emperor jarred political authority loose from the symbolic design of the city's walls and palaces. After 1911 real and putative power resided transiently in Zhongnanhai, in the cabinet offices at Iron Lion Lane in the East City (the eastern districts of the Inner City), in the parliament building in the West City just north of the wall separating the Inner and the Outer City, or in the imperialist bastion of the Legation Quarter. The Forbidden City was given over to parks and museums and, until he was expelled in 1924, the residence of the deposed Manchu monarch. This spatial decentering of political Beijing presaged the wobbling, errant course of the Republic and the degrading of Republican institutions located variously in reconverted palaces and mansions, like Zhongnanhai, and Western-style buildings, like parliament.

Zhongnanhai, which served as headquarters for the Republic's first head of state, also housed its last resident in Beijing: Marshal Zhang Zuolin. As military dictator based in Beijing from December 1926 to June 1928, Zhang presided over the demise of the Beijing Republic (prior to its rebirth in Nanjing under the Nationalists).[13] Continuing a slide toward insolvency begun early in the decade and accelerated by Zhang's military adventures, impoverished officials contrived to sell brick from the city walls and ancient trees from imperial temple grounds to pay government salaries.[14] Even by comparison with previous masters of the Beijing regime, Zhang Zuolin's commitment to republican virtue was feeble. He marked his tenure in office with sacrifices to Confucius and other gestures hinting at imperial ambitions.[15] Admittedly, he never went the full route followed by Yuan Shikai, who in 1915 and 1916 tried to make himself emperor. Perhaps Zhang understood that declaring himself monarch would have only substituted "a parody of the empire" for "the parody of a republic."[16]

By spring 1928 Zhang Zuolin's forces were in retreat from the allied armies of the Northern Expedition led by Chiang Kai-shek. The militarist prepared to leave Zhongnanhai and Beijing and return to his base in the northeast. Just after midnight on June 3, 1928, a twenty-car motorcade carrying Zhang sped out of Xinhua Gate, heading for Beijing's East Station and a special armored train bound for Mukden (Shenyang).[17] Shortly before dawn the next day, on the outskirts of Mukden, a bomb planted by the Japanese army blew up the car Zhang Zuolin was riding in and mortally wounded the warlord.[18]

For the next week, in a pattern followed in the 1920s on previous occasions of flight and conquest, a consortium of prominent ex-officials, merchants, and bankers governed the city through a Peace Preservation Association (*zhian weichi hui*). The body maintained order with the help of Zhang Zuolin's garrison commander, Bao Yulin, who remained behind Zhang's retreating forces with a contingent of soldiers. The consortium also orchestrated an orderly transfer of power from Zhang's troops to the Nationalists. On the morning of June 8, raggedly dressed advance elements of General Yan Xishan's peasant army entered Beijing through the southern gates of the Outer City.[19] Meanwhile, by prearrangement, General Bao and his troops, looking impressive after months of urban garrison duty, took leave of the city from Chaoyang Gate on the eastern side of the Inner City. Xiong Xiling, a former premier, a Beijing entrepreneur and philanthropist, representing the Peace Preservation Association, gave a speech praising Bao's performance as garrison commander. The Beijing chamber of commerce presented Bao with honorific gifts and provisions for his men. A group photograph was taken to commemorate the event.

As in the past when the capital changed hands, Beijing became the site in June and July for meetings among the victors. Chiang Kai-shek and the militarists who supported the Nationalist drive to the north arrived in Beijing aboard armored trains to consult each other and pay respects to Nationalist-movement founder Sun Yat-sen, whose remains had been temporarily interred in the

Temple of Azure Clouds in the hills west of the city at the time of his death in 1925. But this time the meetings did not have, as they had in the past, the goal of reconstituting a national government in Beijing. The Nationalists had chosen Nanjing as their capital and renamed Beijing ("northern capital") Beiping ("northern peace").[20]

In moving the capital to Nanjing, the Nationalists were following the wishes of Sun Yat-sen, whose death from cancer had come during a fruitless attempt to negotiate unification of north and south. The choice of Nanjing also made strategic sense in that a southern capital removed the regime's center from proximity to the Japanese threat in the northeast. Nanjing was located in the midst of China's economic heartland and closer to the southern cradle of the Nationalist revolution in Guangdong.

However, the Nationalists were also motivated by their strong dislike of Beijing. Nationalists partly blamed the city and its inhabitants for the failure of the Republic and expressed concern lest their own movement become contaminated by contact with the old capital.[21] Even in speeches appealing to city residents to support the Nationalist cause, Nationalist leaders could not refrain from condemning the mix of Manchu, militarist, and Communist influences thought to be concealed in Beijing. On June 30, 1928, at a rally held in Central Park (soon to be renamed Sun Yat-sen Park) just west of Tianan Gate, city residents listened patiently in the rain as a military official from Hunan, named Li Pinxian, praised Beijing's fame as a cultural center as he attacked its more recent history. Beijing, he declared, "has been occupied by warlords as well as by the poisonous vestiges of monarchy to the point that customs and habits have become deeply corrupted."[22] Worse still, Communists had taken advantage of the fact that Beijing was "rife with corruption" to promote a cause that appeared attractive by comparison. Li concluded his speech by testifying that on his way out to visit Sun Yat-sen's tomb in the Western Hills he saw a man wearing a Manchu-style queue and that many people could be seen wearing Qing-era summer hats. These, he said, were "obstacles to carrying out the revolution" and "ought to be eradicated."

Beijing residents, through the press and local organizations like the chamber of commerce and the hotel guild, mounted a vigorous defense of the city's reputation and her fitness to be the capital.

Beijing, they pointed out, was "grand and imposing."[23] What other city in the country could boast such a magnificent array of palaces and museums? Nanjing might be at the center of the eighteen-province heartland of the country, but China also included Xinjiang and Mongolia. Reestablishing the capital at Beijing would send a signal to Russian and Japanese imperialists that greater China and its northern borders would be defended. As if to prove the depth of Beijing residents' nationalist feelings, the Beijing chamber of commerce sent an open telegraphic message to the nation, announcing a drive to raise funds to erect a bronze statue of Sun Yat-sen in Beijing and plans to host a national festival in his memory.[24]

The Nationalists charged guilt by association. Beijing people posed as innocent bystanders. One petition sent to Chiang Kai-shek and his colleagues slyly pointed out that although talk of "Beijing corruption" was certainly "fashionable," since the Nationalists had arrived in Beijing they too had established numerous bureaus and official organs. Official statements sounded much like past declarations. Following the Nationalists' own logic, would not these actions likewise be a form of corruption?[25]

Needless to say, the Nationalists were irritated by the Beijing residents' attempts to be accommodating in a fashion tailored to their own interests and regarded them as a confirmation of their prejudices against the city. When Chiang Kai-shek arrived in Beijing on the morning of July 3 he greeted the crowd of local notables and organizations, which had been waiting all night at the train station for his arrival, with a wave of a hat, a brief word of thanks (*xiexie, haohao*), and a refusal to have his photograph taken.[26] He and his entourage left almost immediately for the Western Hills to pay their respects to Sun's body. Afterwards, as he left the Temple of Azure Clouds, a reporter asked him about "the question of the national capital" and Chiang replied, "In Nanjing, of course." One year later, when Chiang returned to the city in an unsuccessful attempt to forestall a revolt by two of his erstwhile northern militarist allies, several hundred merchants marched on the hotel he was staying at and demanded the return of the capital.[27] Chiang termed the request "ridiculous" on the grounds that the whole matter was purely an "affair of state."[28] To residents of the "old capital," long accustomed to viewing national affairs as a local industry, loss of paramount administrative status and the rebukes delivered by Chiang and his fellow Nationalists constituted grievous blows to both livelihood and city pride.

As the decade progressed fewer and fewer political authorities outside the capital had paid any attention to the government within the walls, except as a target for attack. While some ministries and bureaus continued to function, the regime faced mounting difficulties in paying its employees even a bit of what they were owed.[29] Staffed by unpaid and demoralized officials, government offices became derelict places.[30] Even so, a palpable administrative and political aura clung to the city. As long as there was a chance that an effective national government might be reestablished in the city, tens of thousands of political aspirants and hangers-on hovered about in a cloud of connections, factional intrigue, and patronage.[31]

As the national government faded and finally disappeared in the 1920s, leaving only archives and museums as markers of the high tide of early Republican administration, Beijing retained a "heavy official atmosphere."[32] The city exuded what others more prosaically termed a "bureaucratic odor."[33] Beijing's hotels, inns, provincial hostels, restaurants, theaters, teahouses, parks, and bathhouses continued to provide a congenial setting for the practice of politics. The city's newspapers mirrored political goings-on with varying degrees of accuracy and distortion. Much of the economy had direct or indirect ties to government and politics, ranging from the service sector, which housed, fed, transported, and amused officials and politicians to less likely beneficiaries, like the bicycle trade, which equipped the messengers stationed outside government offices and private mansions.[34]

Beijing society naturally oriented itself toward power—the city's principal product and resource for over five hundred years. The early Republic encouraged the continuation of this orientation in a form that made Beijing people appear servile and spoiled to outsiders. "Generally speaking, Beiping society is utterly feeble and decrepit. . . . When Guangdong people are at the end of their rope, they face the danger directly. Shandong people leave hearth and home to struggle on elsewhere. But Beiping people make a point of acting like the bereaved heirs of the Qing empire."[35] In a mocking way, the author of this passage, who knew Beijing well in the 1920s as a practising social researcher, suggests that the removal of the capital in 1928 and the city's loss of status had been anticipated by the personal and collective loss experienced by Qing bannermen, who were in a literal sense "bereaved heirs" of the old regime.

The banners, identified by the color and pattern of their battle flags, were the original fighting units of the Manchus. After their seventeenth-century conquest of China, bannermen and their dependents were settled in and around the capital and throughout the empire in strategically placed communities.[36] In the 1920s, bannermen and their families, who included Chinese and Mongolians but who were predominantly Manchu, still constituted one-third of the city's population of approximately one million.[37] They were popularly regarded as having lost their martial spirit and retained an unwarranted sense of entitlement. In outward appearance, customs, and habits bannermen differed little from the average Chinese resident of the city. Given their more than 250 years of residence, Manchu bannermen had become quintessential Beijing people (Beijing *ren*). Bannermen were entitled to receive stipends and rations in accord with their status. But these monies and benefits had diminished considerably by the eve of the 1911 Revolution.[38] As stipend payments became irregular and anti-Manchu sentiment mounted, bannermen were satirized and ridiculed as lazy wards of the state and as absurdly devoted to defending their declining status.[39]

After the 1911 Revolution, the Republican government continued to pay banner stipends and rations, although by the early 1920s these payments were in arrears, like most government obligations.[40] As their financial situation became ever more precarious, Manchus began to take whatever work they could find. Thousands became policemen and soldiers. Tens of thousands pulled rickshaws. Others found jobs as peddlers, servants, prostitutes, actors, and storytellers.[41] In this regard it is difficult to tell what observers found more disconcerting: the Manchus' alleged indolence or their unseemly willingness to fill low-status occupations, many of which required considerable enterprise and hard work.

The decline of Beijing Manchus became synonymous with the

decadence of the imperial regime. As the Republican state experienced a comparable, accelerated decline, stereotypical representations of Manchus as a "feudal" residue seemed germane to an accounting of Beijing's essential character. As a friendly southern observer remarked in his assessment of post-1928 Beiping, the old capital was "placid, passive, easygoing, conservative, venerable, leisurely, and feudal."[42] The city's style of life resonated with the softening or corrupting of government in the 1920s, not because the old capital was corrupt in the ordinary sense of the word (*fuhua*), but because, like most capitals, it made its living and derived its meaning by following the lead of officialdom.

In addition to sharing and supporting a politics of decline, which placed a premium on hanging on at all costs to whatever scrap of power remained within reach, Manchus and the decadent Republic had a common preoccupation with the care and feeding of politically derived status. If by the mid-1920s Beijing no longer fulfilled its traditional role as a setting for the large-scale production and use of political power, the city continued to cater to displays of status and rank. Beijing people were willing players in this game because many of their livelihoods depended on the spending habits of political operators of all stripes and, it appears, because they found the manipulation and use of status and power aesthetically pleasing. As inveterate theatergoers and avid fans of Beijing opera, city residents of all classes could appreciate clever twists of plot, subtle gestures, and calculated bravado exhibited by ministers and warlords, as well as by ordinary folk caught up in the many situations where official Beijing intruded into the broader arena of urban life.

A seriocomic example of how complex this game could be occurred on an April morning in 1924 on an avenue outside Xuanwu Gate in the Outer City. A heavily laden, mule-drawn night-soil cart driven recklessly down the center pavement of the street was stopped by a policeman on watch. The policeman chided the driver for abusing the mule and for illegally driving the cart on the paved center section of the road. The newspaper account of the incident reported that the carter replied angrily, "with eyes flashing," "What business is it of yours?"[43] The two men drew a crowd and argued for nearly an hour. When the policeman finally told the driver he must accompany him to the station, the man "laughed coldly" and said, "Let me tell you something. This night-soil cart [and the excrement within] is from the presidential palace [at Zhongnanhai]. You wouldn't dare take me to the station." The policeman would not be bullied, and he was not entirely persuaded that the driver was who he said he was. Members of the crowd offered to mediate, but to no avail. The newspaper account concluded by noting that "by then there was no choice but to go to the station. Whether or not he was really from the Presidential Mansion we were unable to determine." The claim to be in possession of sewage from the mansion of President Cao Kun, who had shamelessly bribed legislators to obtain his office the year before, undoubtedly had less potency than one made when Zhongnanhai was occupied by someone as powerful as the Republic's first president, Yuan Shikai. But even in decline, official Beijing still affected the calculations of those who fell within its diminishing circle of influence.

Beijing was famous in the 1920s not only for its venal politicians, rapacious warlords, job-hunting officials, and idealistic students, but also for its courteous but insistent policemen, rancorous mule drivers and night-soil carriers, polite but status-conscious shopkeepers, officious streetcar conductors, and artful pickpockets. An admiring observer suggested that Beijing people placed "in a difficult situation are able to fight." But they are also more likely to retain their composure because their sense of "human relations" (*renqing*) is so acute.[44] A combination of confidence and wariness natural to those who lived at or near the center of the Chinese political world made Beijing people circumspect in the way they sized up situations. As the case of the policeman and the night-soil carter suggests, city residents displayed both persistence and prudence in charting a course through the uncertainties associated with status, power, and things redolent of a bureaucratic odor.

Local Politics in a Centerless Polity

If Beijing is measured against the course of its decline and fall as China's capital, one can surely make a case for its essential decadence. The city's monumental structures, which once projected immense power and authority, by the 1920s graphically recorded the progress of decay. A journalist who visited Zhang Zuolin in Zhongnanhai in 1928 observed that the palace complex was in poor repair. "The paint and lacquer is peeling off in large chunks and broken panes of glass, instead of having been replaced, are found mended with glue and paper."[45] A European traveler who toured the Forbidden City found that "ideas of physical decay and death...haunted one at every turn....The Palace itself was dying; grass grew thick on its eaves; and even its official custodians had begun to sell its treasures. Other monuments were going the same way."[46] Late-Qing and early-Republican reforms failed to reverse this trend even though they left as legacies the partial modernization of city life.

As old Beijing crumbled new Beijing rusted, suggesting not so much a bright structure of modern technique competing with peeling paint and lacquer as two forms of decay. Decay at the center in the form of run-down palaces, electric power outages, and militarized civilian institutions offered a visual and social impression of city life likely to provoke critical, even despairing, comments by cosmopolitan Westerners, who associated decadence with the "Orient," and by censorious Nationalists, who saw Republican corruption superimposed on Manchu complacency. If these judgments were true, then the only chance remaining for Beijing, and by extension for the rest of Republican China, was to submit to moral and social renovation at the hands of self-proclaimed revolutionaries like the Nationalists or their Communist rivals.

However, beyond the compass of Zhongnanhai, the Forbidden City, and the foreign legations lay a Beijing more complex and vital than the romantic meditations of foreigners or the polemical attacks of political radicals might suggest. The city had one of the finest police forces in Asia, staffed in the main by supposedly indolent Manchu bannermen. While Beijing newspapers and news services were often creatures of warlords and politicians, the size and output of journalistic enterprise in the city had few rivals in the country. The city's university system although buffeted by financial problems and political repression, employed some of China's best minds and produced some of the decade's most famous political activists. And against the stillness of Beijing as home to museum, archive, and decomposing bureaucracy, rose the bustle of the marketplace, which sounded "a cacophany, a pandemonium, that has no counterpart in Europe, even in the nois-iest southern marketplace."[47] From this commercial, craft, and service-industry base local bodies, such as guilds, a chamber of commerce, and labor unions, spun out strategies and policies de-signed to promote their particular interests and ideologies. Along-side the "bureaucratic banquets" and fin de siècle entertainments of Beijing's official circles (*guanjie*) flourished a lively, politically sophisticated, associational life belonging to and shared by mer-chant (*shang*), laboring (*gong*), and student (*xue*) circles (*jie*). Political instability and uncertainty stimulated a myriad of adjust-ments, responses, and initiatives on the part of an increasingly politically conscious urban citizenry. Local politics could not fill the political and cultural vacuum created by the collapse of the Republic. But the free surfaces and empty spaces left by devalued and departed government institutions were quickly covered by the graffiti of social movements and occupied by the local authors of new political rituals and factional intrigues.

The "grand and imposing" setting offered by Beijing heightened the dramatic effect of the Republic's political demise. But the prob-lem of a putative political "center" turning out to be empty, ab-sent, or immobilized and unable to enforce its will or values was not unique to Beijing. The empty, unformed, or deformed center is a defining characteristic of the Republican era. Warlordism sig-nified a haphazard decentralization of authority down to regional and provincial power holders, many of whom aspired to recogni-tion as national leaders on the basis of their supposed representa-tion of the "people." Under these conditions the notion of central authority had little practical meaning. As they made their way from a world centered on the emperor as "Caesar-Pope" to a pol-ity based on an ill-defined popular will, politically conscious Chinese suffered a profound "cultural crisis."[48]

Powerful local organizations, such as the police, the chamber of commerce, and when circumstances allowed their unfettered emer-gence, student and labor federations, were positioned atten-tively, and somewhat nervously, just shy of where a political center might have been and sometimes threatened to be. Center stage in Beijing, as in other Chinese cities, was occupied in turn by massed demonstrators, convocations of national or local elites, the entou-rage of an itinerant militarist, imaginary self-government schemes, and scaffolding for the planned construction of new institutions. While governmental institutions trembled and fell, local elites and the organizations they captained strove to cushion the impact of invading armies and collapsing regimes. By mid-decade, local elites, as the 1928 episode involving Zhang Zuolin's withdrawal from Beijing suggests, had refined the management of dangerous and impecunious visitors to an art. If Chinese statecraft had long concerned itself with the management of disruptive social forces, city elites had crafted a set of strategies capable of buffering the arrival and departure of disruptive political contenders. Deputations of merchants and retired officials, alerted by suburban shopkeepers or police posts, met invading troops in the suburbs, ushered their generals into the city, negotiated extortionate demands for tribute, and saw them to the train station when the balance of power on the north China plain shifted again.

Governmentless or government-poor cities are not necessarily anarchic if, as was true in the Chinese case, civic traditions include substantial quasi-governmental functions in the hands of local elites.[49] Encampment around empty or underpowered governmental institutions engendered a kind of pluralism. Secular trends that placed considerable power in the hands of merchant and gentry managers had been formalized in the last decade of the Qing by the officially sponsored creation of a system of self-regulating professional associations (*fatuan*), such as chambers of commerce, lawyers' guilds, and bankers' associations. In the 1920s these institutional encampments, or "city trenches," to borrow Ira Katznelson's term to describe the "fortified" nature of an urban social order, worked to contain instability.[50] Organizations originally designed to be manned by co-opted elites as barriers against unruly markets and movements ironically functioned to check the advance of dangerous regimes and protect the interests of elites and their constituents.

For local elites, politics then became a two-front war against official and outside economic interests, intruding from above, and rank-and-file constituents, exerting pressure from below. An organization like the chamber of commerce could function both as the first line of defense against official exactions and interference and as the last line of defense against turmoil in the market or workplace. For city people without elite status, politics meant either accepting the logic of elite representation and protection or finding a means of breaking through these defenses. A principal current in Beijing politics in the 1920s involved attempts by unrepresented or underrepresented strata, such as students, workers, women, and peasants, to join or challenge the charmed circle of *fatuan* and win a modicum of power for themselves.

City residents experienced politics as a path that began within their immediate world of shop, school, or neighborhood and spiraled up through guilds, unions, associations, federations, and chambers. Beyond organizations operating at the citywide level lay the uncertainties, dangers, and opportunities of regional, national, and international politics. Political contenders in these larger arenas, such as warlords, the Nationalists, and the Communists, who hoped to mobilize or neutralize the political energies of city residents of necessity followed the same paths or surveyed and laid out new ones of comparable dimensions. Mastering the art of city politics in this context required both a talent for bold strokes and dramatic gestures capable of suggesting the promise of a new, unified political order when none in fact existed and the ability to patch together a base of support from the diversity of interests and loyalties natural to a city of the size and complexity of Beijing. Mapping out the full extent and significance of these strategies requires leaving the royal road of national political struggles for the parallel and adjoining avenues and alleyways of local politics.

Two

The Rickshaw:
Machine for a Mixed-up Age

Perspectives on city life and politics which emerge from an examination of monumental and official Beijing suggest a well-organized deathwatch around a ruined republic and a falling away from past greatness.[1] Political decadence at the center provoked a compensatory community activism representing new forces rising amidst decay and decline. While the novelty and idealism generally associated with these ventures contrasted with the seemingly moribund and corrupt nature of the Republic in decline, contemporary observers were divided over whether these newer forces represented a means of revitalizing Chinese society or merely another form of decay.

Rickshaw pulling was a prime example of the unexpected courses cut through local communities by technologically induced change. A modern device equipped with inflatable tires and ball bearings, the rickshaw achieved great popularity as a means of transportation and employment and, simultaneously, notoriety as a sign of social dislocation.

The importance attached to rickshaws and rickshaw men by writers and pundits was based both on the singular nature of the vehicle and on the large numbers of rickshaws present in Chinese cities. Rickshaw pulling was a public spectacle in Beijing in the 1920s. Sixty thousand men took as many as a half million fares a day in a city of slightly more than one million people.[2] Sociologist Li Jinghan estimated that one out of six males in the city between the ages of sixteen and fifty was a puller. Rickshaw men and their dependents made up almost 20 percent of Beijing's population.[3]

By the early twenties the rickshaw was the "most numerous, or at least the most conspicuous thing" in the city.[4] In busy intersections "a thousand telephones seemed to be ringing" from signal bells in the floor of rickshaws, used with abandon by passengers to warn off other vehicles.[5] The crush of pullers waiting for fares outside the entrances to train stations, public parks, and theaters led to hard words and fights among laborers and passengers and the policemen who tried to keep order. A visitor to the city concluded that the "hoarse voices and gargling oaths of quarrelsome rickshaw men" were essential to any rendition of a Beijing street scene.[6]

Rickshaws and rickshaw men were included in realistic portraits of the Republican-era city or more imaginative attempts to interpret signs of change and turmoil posted along the route taken by urban development. So many writers and poets featured rickshaw men as central characters that a minor genre of "rickshaw works" emerged.[7] Romantics, like the poet Xu Zhimo, and realists, like the revolutionary Zhou Enlai, found the rickshaw man to be a useful literary device in the discussion of themes ranging from life's mysteries to the nature of capitalism.[8] Social scientists like Li Jinghan practiced their craft on rickshaw men as intriguing and convenient objects of study. Rickshaw men were, as another researcher put it, the "most numerous and accessible" workers in the city.[9] Rickshaw men also appeared as stock characters in newspaper vignettes about the trials and tribulations of urban life. Newspapers carried frequent accounts of tragic and comic incidents involving rickshaw pullers who stole from their passengers or were swindled themselves; who had once been princes, generals, or high officials; who fought well or badly in street brawls; or who killed themselves in despair. The rickshaw seemed to carry with it a natural air of melodrama that poets, professors, and editorialists found irresistible.

No one understood the central place of the rickshaw in Republican cityscapes and in the popular imagination better than Beijing novelist Lao She. Lao She, a Manchu whose father was killed in 1900 during the Boxer disorders, wrote moral fables of Republican decay and disorder from an accumulated store of detailed, camera-like observations.[10] He once confided that the "moment I think of Beiping, several hundred feet of pictures of the 'Old Capital' immediately unroll in my mind like a film."[11] Rickshaw pullers appear within the descriptive and narrative frame of Lao She's short stories and novellas as residents of courtyard tenements, as family servants, and as insurgent proletarians.[12] He also made a rickshaw puller the protagonist and title character of *Camel Xiangzi* (Luotou Xiangzi), his great novel of Republican Beijing.

The idea for *Camel Xiangzi* came to Lao She, who was sojourning in the Shandong port city of Qingdao at the time, as he spoke with a visiting friend from Beijing. The friend related two true anecdotes about Beijing rickshaw men typical of the human-interest stories journalists and their readers were so fond of. In one, a puller had three times purchased and three times been forced to sell his rickshaw. The other concerned a rickshaw man who had been kidnapped by soldiers and then had escaped with several purloined camels. Lao She interjected that "quite possibly one could write a whole novel based on that."[13] He later used the two tales as the germ of the story and character of "Camel" Xiangzi. "The cast of characters and the plot line were not hard to think up with Xiangzi and rickshaw pulling at the center of things. All I had to do was to have everyone develop a connection to rickshaws so as to tie them to Xiangzi, like goats tethered to a willow tree in the midst of a grassy field."[14] In the course of the novel Xiangzi pursues his elusive goal of independent rickshaw ownership through a dozen adventures, including being kidnapped by soldiers, a shakedown by a secret police agent, being tricked into a loveless marriage, helplessness in the face of disease, and final degeneration into a paid police informant and claquer in political demonstrations.

In deciding to "place rickshaw pulling at the center of things," Lao She necessarily rejected other possibilities in the tableau of figures representative of Republican urban society: rebellious students, iconoclastic intellectuals, ambitious politicians, ruthless militarists, petty bureaucrats, and profit-minded entrepreneurs. These latter individuals and images appear in the novel tied to Xiangzi in such a way as to force the reader to evaluate the dynamism and decay of the times in terms of their effect on the travail of an ordinary person. Lao She set the action of the work outside the palaces, ministries, mansions, and universities of the old capital and in the midst of the city's markets, teahouses, alleyways, and courtyard tenements where Beijing's ordinary folk lived and worked. Lao She imagined the forces impinging on rickshaw men —both societal forces, like the urban transportation market, and natural ones, like dust storms and the winter cold—and then mapped out the rest of the city from a rickshaw man's perspective. "Thinking about it in this way, a simple story was transformed into a vast society."[15]

The collective biography of Beijing rickshaw men, like the fictional story of Xiangzi, presents a street-level perspective on Republican history measured from the periphery to the center. Rickshaw men lived in poor circumstances in Beijing's capillary-like systems of narrow, twisting alleyways. Every day, in search of fares, they were drawn out along city avenues toward the ministries, schools, parks, guildhalls, and opera houses that served as focal points of Beijing politics, commerce, and culture. Rickshaw pullers were joined through their work to the basic rhythms of city life expressed in collective activities ranging from marketing and theatergoing to political protests and panics. Like traditional servants, they had access to the household and social life of the moneyed, propertied, and official classes. Like modern taxi drivers, they picked up and dispensed news and rumor. Like the poor everywhere, rickshaw men were sensitive to even small changes in the cost of living. Of course, a rickshaw puller would not have a merchant's knowledge of market conditions, an official's grasp of political hierarchy, a militarist's sense of tactics and ability to track movable wealth, a journalist's knowledge of current events, or a student's sense of national mission and proprietary right to the political spotlight. But rickshaw men were well placed to be perpetual witnesses and occasional actors as history was made in their presence and in their midst.

The Rickshaw as a Modern Invention

Invented in Japan in the late 1860s, possibly as an aid to the crippled and the convalescent, the early rickshaw resembled a sedan chair awkwardly mounted on an axle and oversized wheels.[16]

Refinements, such as the use of springs, ball bearings, and rubber tires, soon produced a lighter, more efficient machine, which spread rapidly in the late nineteenth and early twentieth centuries to China, Korea, Southeast Asia, and India. This simple technology joined small amounts of capital, large pools of unskilled labor, and robust consumer demand for personal transportation so successfully that the rickshaw became a characteristic feature of Asian cityscapes. The addition of a bicycle mechanism in the 1940s contrived a final, more enduring mutation: the pedicab, or trishaw.

The first rickshaws, marketed from Japan and privately owned, appeared on Beijing streets in 1886 and immediately stirred controversy.[17] Mule carters, angered at the competition, "threw the horrid foreign things, which degraded men to the level of animals" into a canal.[18] At that time, mule litters and carts, horses, sedan chairs, and wheelbarrows provided the only other means of personal transport in the city. Beijing streets were dirty and unpaved. Country carts, equipped with narrow wheels to traverse the road-poor hinterland, carved deep ruts wherever they went. The ruts filled with water and at times made Beijing's broad avenues and tangle of *hutong* impassable. Inner Asian dust and sand storms periodically spilled their contents onto the city. "No wind and three feet of dust; a rain storm and streets of mud," complained a local proverb.

In 1900, a few months before Boxer armies seized the city, rickshaws reappeared in significant numbers.[19] Rickshaw garages opened and rented out vehicles to laborers, who in turn solicited on the street. With one man in front pulling, and another in back pushing, the rickshaw overcame poor road conditions to win a small clientele of merchants, officials, and foreigners. A Japanese visitor noted that the number of rickshaws and pullers increased rapidly in the spring and summer of 1900 in tandem with the risings of peasants outside the city.[20] He even wondered whether the Boxers had used rickshaw pulling as a cover to infiltrate the city's laboring classes. It must have seemed logical to pair the two new and unusual happenings, sprouting up simultaneously in the countryside and the city. Perhaps, as later happened in the teens and twenties, rural disturbances swelled the ranks of city people looking for the kind of unskilled and temporary work the rickshaw offered. No doubt some of the new rickshaw men had Boxer sympathies. But when the insurgents invaded Beijing in the summer of 1900, in their campaign against foreigners and foreign things, they destroyed the newly imported vehicles.

The rickshaw trade resumed business once foreign troops cleared Beijing of fighters and, in cooperation with the Chinese government, restored order. In the next several years, two developments enhanced the ability of the rickshaw to compete for new passengers. First, designers and craftsmen built a better rickshaw. The 1900 model was rough-riding and noisy. The body and the wheel rims were made of iron, and the shafts held by the rickshaw man were short and mounted high in such a way as to make pulling difficult. Rickshaws made a terrible clanking noise, bounced passengers around in their seats, and easily got stuck in the mud. Even people who were not xenophobes or habitual mule-cart or sedan-chair users found rickshaw travel uncomfortable. Women especially found being pushed and pulled around in the new vehicle unseemly. By mid-decade a lighter frame and rubber tires, at first solid and later pneumatic, eased the lot of both passenger and puller and lessened the need for a second laborer to push from behind.[21]

The rickshaw business also benefited from the creation of European-style paved avenues. Replacing dirt or cobbles with pavement was a prerequisite for the successful introduction of the rickshaw in cities as diverse as the riverine port of Changsha, the lakeside tourist center of Hangzhou, the seaport of Fuzhou, and the hilly provincial capital of Chengdu.[22] In Beijing, where post-Boxer reformers paved the center sections of major city avenues and left unpaved the cart tracks along the sides and most alleyways, rickshaws took advantage of the parallel road systems to speed along the macadam with other light or broad-tired vehicles (like bicycles or automobiles) while still being able to work their way along unimproved streets.

When rickshaw men became caught in traffic congestion around city gates or in shopping districts like the area outside Qian Gate, they still experienced the wrath of jealous competitors. A government official who first came to Beijing in 1909 recalled seeing mule-cart drivers strike rickshaw men from above and hurl insults, such as "Why don't you drive carts? You prefer to drag them. You would be like animals or beasts of burden although you could easily be men."[23] But by the teens the rickshaw had overtaken the mule cart in popularity. In 1915 there were approximately twenty thousand rickshaw men in Beijing. By the mid-twenties their numbers had tripled.[24]

However incongruous the image might seem to contemporary eyes or in retrospect, the rickshaw succeeded in winning a place in China's urban economy as one of a cluster of newly imported technologies. Shortly after the turn of the century, Qing modernizer and reformer Zhang Zhidong ordered part of the Hankou city wall torn down and a modern road built in its place.[25] To stimulate economic activity, Zhang added one hundred rickshaws available for hire at officially posted rates. Rickshaws racing along the pavement, electric lights piercing the preindustrial darkness, a new marketplace, and the new premises of the Nanyang Brothers Tobacco Company, one of China's premier capitalist enterprises, were all components of Zhang Zhidong's modernization scheme for Hankou. Rickshaws arrived and multiplied in Beijing as a result of private entrepreneurship rather than formal or governmental planning. But the effect was the same. The rickshaw modernized urban transportation and speeded up the movement of people around the city in a manner comparable to the way in which telegraph wire hastened intercity communication, and factories accelerated production.

Passengers

Not everyone, however, had the pace of his life quickened from a walk to a run. Transportation was not a daily concern for the majority of Beijing residents, who typically lived where they worked, in a shop, factory, attached dormitory, or nearby courtyard tenement. Studies of household budgets indicated that almost half the families in Beijing spent little or nothing on personal transportation.[26]

On the one hand, for many people, including factory workers, shop clerks, and craftsmen, Beijing was, and remained until the bicycle took over the city streets in the 1950s, a "walking city."[27] On the other hand, anyone who sought to use or experience Beijing as a complete ensemble of resources and opportunities could not easily remain a pedestrian. Republican Beijing did not have one, compact center of political, economic, and cultural life. The area within the walls of the Inner and the Outer City covered more than twenty square miles, with government offices, schools, stores, restaurants, and parks scattered throughout. The Forbidden City center of prerevolutionary Beijing had been surrounded by satellite hubs of commercial, artistic, and residential life. By the 1920s the subordinate centers, which in most cases were miles apart from each other, had become preeminent: the university center northeast of the Forbidden City, the Legation Quarter, Inner City ministries and bureaus, and Outer City business and entertainment zones. In the past, officials, gentry members, and wealthy merchants had used mule- and horse-drawn carriages to make formal calls and circuits of the city.[28] The rickshaw provided a less elaborate means of transport for persons whose occupations or leisure pursuits required regular travel around Beijing: aspirants for administrative office, journalists, students, politicians, businessmen, tourists, and anyone who lived in hostels for visiting provincials in the Outer City and who worked or studied in Inner City governmental, financial, or educational institutions.

Given the nature of the rickshaw and the social background of the puller's clientele, economic utility inevitably became intertwined with status considerations and conspicuous consumption. The rickshaw puller saved the passenger the trouble of walking and hastened his or her movement from place to place. Just as important, rickshaw travel allowed a status-conscious individual to arrive or depart in a dignified manner, unsullied by street dirt or mud. Even after the center sections of avenues had been paved, negotiating the unpaved side-lanes and alleyways meant risking dust or mud. During Beijing's wet summers travel by foot was like "walking in a dish of photographer's paste."[29] As newspaper columnist Xi Ying observed, "Men who wear long gowns may not walk. It's like an unwritten law in Beijing."[30] Of course, some men in long gowns could not afford rickshaw travel, a galling circumstance in a context where the practice was encouraged as a matter of practicality and decorum. A poor student from Shanxi, who arrived in Beijing in 1923, later recalled that "at the time Beijing had no public buses or streetcars. The rich rode in rickshaws. We walked."[31]

Here the memoirist is engaging in hyperbole. Beijing's middle

classes, not the rich, were the main users of rickshaws. The rickshaw was the second rung on a status hierarchy of modes of transportation climbing in ascending order from buses and streetcars to
public rickshaws, from public to private rickshaws, to the archaic
splendor of a mule- or horse-drawn carriage, and finally from carriage to automobile. Successive acquisition of these emblems of
status demonstrated, according to Xi Ying, that you had "made
it" or "struck it rich." Wryly noting that he had somehow managed to avoid buying a rickshaw even after several years in Beijing,
Xi Ying remarked that the private rickshaw "really is the passport
of the petite bourgeoisie." People tended to think, "If you don't
even have a private rickshaw, what on earth are you?"

The tremendous expansion of the Beijing rickshaw trade in the
teens and twenties came about because of the suitability of the
vehicle to the city's flat terrain and the transportation needs of Beijing's professional and mercantile classes. But rickshaw travel also
represented a form of conspicuous consumption linked to social
status. The city's official, moneyed, and propertied classes, aug-
mented by new professions and vocations, could choose from a
variety of rickshaws, ranging from ordinary to elaborate and from
public to private as an expression of rank and privilege. Rickshaw
technology was a Qing import. As a conventional means of transportation, it became a Republican institution.

Pullers

Plotted against income and numbers, the class distribution of Beijing's population in the 1920s resembled a child's inverted top.
According to a 1926 police census, wealthy households made up
only 5 percent of the city's total.[32] From this tapered summit,
occupied by rich merchants, bankers, and high officials, the
population sloped and bulged downward through a substantial
"middle class" (22 percent) and a huge "lower class" (47 percent).
Tucked in beneath the lower class lay a minority of "very poor" (9
percent) and a more sizable knob of "extremely poor" (17 percent) households.

Rickshaw passengers were drawn mainly from the city's middle
class of shopkeepers, teachers, and minor officials. Most rickshaw
pullers were situated in the lower reaches of the working class,

beneath skilled craftsmen, modern utility workers, and some shop clerks, and just above common laborers. Rickshaw men earned between ten and twelve dollars a month, an income comparable to that of policemen, unskilled craftsmen, servants, and most shop clerks.[33] Hard work and few or no dependents kept the average rickshaw man from sharing the fate of "beggars, those who eat at soup kitchens, and all the rest of the poor who do not have enough to eat and wear."[34] If most rickshaw passengers were well-off but not rich, most rickshaw men were poor but not impoverished.

A sizable minority (nearly one-quarter) of Beijing rickshaw men were former peasants.[35] Lao She's Xiangzi is a farmer drawn to the city and his new trade by the lure of urban opportunity. "The city gave him everything. Even starving he would prefer it to the village. . . . Even if you begged in the city you could get meat or fish soup. In the village all one could hope for was cornmeal."[36] Because of the great disparity in urban and rural incomes, even a "lower class" occupation like rickshaw pulling might satisfy a peasant's ambition for a better livelihood.

The relatively high standard of living achieved by the working poor astonished one landlord family, driven to the city as refugees from rural banditry in 1930. The landlord rented space for his family in a courtyard compound shared by households headed by a rickshaw man, a servant, and a water carrier. The rural refugees at first regarded their neighbors with disdain. "We looked down upon them: the rickshaw man toiling like an ox or horse, a servant who carried around chamber pots, and a water peddler."[37] But the landlord family finally came to marvel that their accustomed standard of living was lower than that of their working-class neighbors. The landlord's wife observed with some consternation that "the Liu family, our rich neighbors back in the village, own over 1,000 *mou* [10 hectares] but they only eat steamed bread [*mantou*] made from wheat flour once, at year's end. They [the rickshaw man, servant, and water carrier and their families] haven't an acre of land and yet they eat wheat-flour *mantou* the year through. My goodness!" After deducting the rent paid to the rickshaw-garage owner and the cost of meals taken while pulling, their neighbor, the rickshaw man, took home fifteen dollars a month to his wife and two children. In addition to wheaten bread, the family daily enjoyed vegetables fried in oil or prepared with vinegar or sesame oil, and pickled vegetables as a condiment. The landlord complained that while in the countryside there was no shortage of vegetables, they all had to be pickled. Cooking oil was scarce, and preserved vegetables were made with too little salt and so had a sour taste. The rickshaw man's family ate meat two or three times a month, and the children were given a few coppers a day to buy fruit and snacks. At fifteen dollars a month, the puller's family was edging up from a condition sociologist Li Jinghan termed "making the best of a bad situation" into the "comfortable living" available to those who made between fifteen and twenty dollars.[38] At that income level the majority of Beijing's lower classes, comprising fully half the city's workers and laboring poor and including the upper strata of rickshaw men, enjoyed moderately decent food, clothing, and housing and perhaps even extra cash for opera tickets or other forms of entertainment.

The percentage of Beijing rickshaw men of peasant background increased in the winter when thousands entered the city in order to supplement their farming income. Each summer thousands of rickshaw pullers left the city to work as farm laborers during the peak agricultural season.[39] On balance, the proportion of rural migrants in the trade was less than in other cities with large numbers of pullers. Most of Shanghai's seventy thousand rickshaw men came from rural areas north of the Yangzi River.[40] Of thirty thousand rickshaw pullers in the Wuhan cities in the 1920s, most were rural migrants.[41] They came without their families and lived in squatter huts on the edge of town. Both Shanghai and Wuhan had numerous factories and mills to absorb the urban poor and unemployed. Beijing had a much smaller modern utility and industrial sector and a large pool of men out of work or with jobs that paid less than rickshaw pulling. As a result, when peasant outsiders like Xiangzi walked into Beijing looking for work and chose the rickshaw trade, they joined not a uniform class of uprooted peasants but rather a mixed congerie of men from urban, suburban, and rural backgrounds. A low level of industrialization meant that city residents and rural migrants competed for positions in the rickshaw trade.[42]

Bannermen formed the largest block of men of urban background in the rickshaw trade. As late as the 1920s, banner status still counted as employment, and fully one out of four pullers surveyed in 1924 gave membership in the banners as their previous occupation. The Manchu presence in Beijing and banner stipends, together with other Court and government expenditures, had favored commercial, craft, and service-industry development.[43] This market had attracted merchants and laborers from throughout north China and the empire who established trades and founded guilds based on native-place ties. Many occupations in Beijing were made up exclusively of men from particular provinces or counties. It was taken for granted that most night-soil carriers came from Shandong, tailors from Ningbo, and sugar-cake makers from Nanjing.[44] Once the Manchus lost their politically enforced status and connections, they found the preindustrial economy, originally designed to serve them, resistant to their participation. As their banner stipends and rations dwindled, Manchus took whatever work they could find, including rickshaw pulling.

The decline in Manchu fortunes accounts in part for the urban character of Beijing rickshaw pullers. But there were other reasons why city residents became pullers. As Lao She recorded, many rickshaw men were "fired policemen and school servants, peddlers who had eaten up their capital, or unemployed craftsmen who had reached the point where they had nothing left to sell and nothing more to pawn."[45] In his survey of rickshaw men, Li Jinghan compiled a list of former vocations that included "cobbler, carpenter, policeman, cook, embroiderer, gardener, fisherman, musician, soap maker, typesetter, student, jade worker, silversmith, tailor, copyist, actor, newspaper boy, weaver, shop proprietor, rug weaver, distiller, miner, launderer, workman in a government mint, domestic servant, soldier, office boy."[46] Occasionally women disguised themselves as men and pulled rickshaws.[47]

The urban economy, organized around guilds and more prosperous shops and enterprises, included peripheral constellations of less stable ventures. A large turnover in shop openings and closings existed as a normal feature of economic life.[48] Marginal sums of capital and small labor forces of clerks and craftsmen continually dissolved and recombined. According to a government study, each year over one thousand Beijing workers became rickshaw pullers because they had lost their old jobs.[49] In addition, apprenticeship, which was the key institution in recruitment to guild work, did not always lead to permanent employment. In some trades, such as the carpet industry, owners and managers commonly recruited large numbers of apprentices from the countryside, employed them for three years at little more than room and board, and then discharged them at the point at which they would have been eligible for regular-worker status.[50] Many former apprentices went to work as rickshaw men.[51]

Notwithstanding a presumed preference for a stable career within guild-regulated commerce and industry, it was not unusual for workers to piece together livelihoods out of seasonal or casual labor. For example, Beijing residents who could afford it shaded themselves from the summer sun by having woven-mat awnings erected in front of shops and over open courtyards.[52] Over two hundred firms in Beijing engaged in this business, and aside from firm managers and a few apprentices, all the labor was casual. Workers congregated at particular teahouses in various parts of the city and were hired as needed by go-betweens. In late summer and fall thousands worked at rolling coal dust and dirt into small balls used during the winter heating season. In the winter casual laborers cut, pulled, and stored ice from Beijing's artificial lakes for summer use in restaurants, fruit stores, the buffet cars on trains, and as a luxury good in private homes.[53] The men who pulled the blocks of ice from lake to underground cellars were recruited from "among the beggars, the aged, and the unemployed." Even trades organized into strong guilds, as in the construction industry, made use of casual labor in the peak seasons of spring and summer. Drawing on the fluid labor market that existed alongside the more rigid structure of native-place requirements and guild membership, rickshaw pulling formed what social researcher Tao Menghe termed a "big labor reservoir" for the "unskilled, the semiskilled, and even the skilled that sometimes finds itself out of work."[54]

If rickshaw pulling provided a channel for upward and lateral mobility among immigrants and the urban poor, the job also functioned as an occupational life raft for downwardly mobile urban residents. As Beijing's status as administrative center declined, bankrupt bureaucracies stopped paying officials and clerks their full salaries. Some bureaus and government-supported schools collapsed completely, releasing their staffs onto the local economy in search of a livelihood. Primary-school teachers, government clerks, and even Qing-era generals could be found pulling rickshaws to supplement their income or simply to survive once all other funds or prospects had been exhausted.[55] One Beijing essayist, writing about the "rickshaw question," reminded his readers that Beijing rickshaw pullers "are not all the men of humble origin some people imagine them to be—all illiterate and from the countryside. Some are politicians from the early Republic, Qing-era degree-holders, or young heirs to the banners who have lost their means of livelihood."[56] While these déclassé elements did not typify the average rickshaw man, who was most likely a former peasant, low-ranking bannerman, or craftsman, they underlined the social diversity and unsettledness of the pullers as a class.

Reports of Manchu princes, former officials, "sons from good families," or college professors pulling rickshaws dwelt on the melancholy symbolism of such a fall from grace.[57] Journalist Xi Ying wrote of the consternation that greeted his decision to leave the provinces for the capital. A relative advised him not to go, but if he went, not to become a scholar. "I read in the newspaper that some teachers in Beijing are so poor they pull rickshaws at night. In a faraway place, if you don't have money, it's no joke. And besides, people like us aren't strong enough to pull a rickshaw."[58]

Rickshaw men disturbed intellectuals partly because their vocation seemed backward and inhumane. But rickshaw men also served as rough reminders of how precarious claims to rank and status could be in the Republican era. A teacher who also wrote a popular column for a Beijing newspaper recalled chiding an acquaintance for not appreciating the kinship that existed between different social classes, based on common uncertainties.

My friend, a teacher, having been subjected to indignities by a rickshaw man cursed him as a "dumb animal." I told him, "You should not curse him like that. His skill as a rickshaw puller is a formidable one. You must know that if we could not teach, we would wish to be dumb animals, and yet we wouldn't have the strength to pull a rickshaw. When you are born into a mixed-up age of change and uncertainty, who knows where one might rise or fall to in the future? I have an old friend who was chief of staff for a certain lieutenant general. He is now telling fortunes for a living."[59]

Even if they did not see their own descent into rickshaw pulling as likely, intellectuals might be drawn into the controversy surrounding the rickshaw, in part because, as members of the middle class, they could afford to ride in the vehicle. As they traveled to and from work, social gatherings, and political meetings, they found themselves staring at the back of a sweating worker. Writing in 1919, a few weeks after the May Fourth Incident, a contributor to the journal *New China* pointed out the moral contradictions involved when a person subscribing to modern values hired a rickshaw: "A rickshaw puller is a human being the same as we. . . . We talk about democracy and humanism, about everyone being treated equally and having an equal opportunity. How can we then sit in a rickshaw with the puller working like an ox or a horse in the rain and the mud?! Urging him to risk his life running. . . faster. . . faster. . . faster."[60]

A writer for a reformist Beijing daily admitted in a column entitled "Change Your Topic" that he had become obsessed by automobiles and rickshaws as symbols of the problems troubling Beijing society. He was alarmed by the injuries and mayhem caused by autos and by the moral and social dilemmas posed by the rickshaw. He could not get them out of his head.

When we think about the state of Beijing society, automobiles and rickshaws immediately spring to mind. When criticizing Beijing society, it's easy to be dragged into discussing them. But when I write those columns, some people say to me, "Can't you change your topic?" Then I try to change, but the hooting of car horns and the panting of rickshaw men always seem to be right in front of me.[61]

Two days later, true to his admission, he wrote another editorial piece, entitled "The Right to Struggle," in which he made street altercations involving rickshaw men symbolic of China's political disorders. Chinese, the columnist suggested, resemble rickshaw pullers who constantly quarrel with each other while competing for fares and who react extravagantly and angrily to the slightest affront. The result is civil war and bitter internecine conflict. But when faced with police or soldiers, rickshaw men "dare not do a thing," just as Chinese remain passive in the face of imperialist aggression.[62] Another commentator, making a more literal connection, described the anger he felt each time he saw a foreigner "sitting in a rickshaw with a Chinese as his slave" (fig. 5).[63]

Fig. 5. Rickshaw men and passengers pose after a nonstop run of eleven miles from the city to the Summer Palace. The pullers are wearing typical laborer's garb: trousers, shirt, and cloth shoes. Their rickshaws are first-rate machines of the kind required for the foreign tourist trade. Courtesy of the Library of Congress.

The success of the rickshaw as a mode of transportation and as a means of signaling status led directly to the vehicle's prominence in contemporary political and literary rhetoric. For a modern invention, the rickshaw had some peculiar effects. In a sense, the rickshaw represented technological progress, since pulling one was easier than bearing a sedan chair. Over short distances the rickshaw was faster than some kinds of traditional wheeled vehicles, such as the heavy, slow-moving mule cart common to north China. But at the same time, instead of simply substituting machine for animal or human power, the rickshaw also intensified the need for the most strenuous physical exertion. A walking puller saved steps for his passenger. A running puller saved time. The market duly rewarded the swiftest and strongest and created the spectacle of poor men straining to pull a largely middle-class clientele. Not only did the rickshaw become a popular method of conveyance in cities like Beijing, Shanghai, and Hankou; the sight of one human being pulling another also became a symbol of backwardness and exploitation.

Critics of industrialization in the West, like J. L. and Barbara Hammond, depicted "human animals" being dragged by "machine animals" in the process of molding individuals to the discipline of factory production. Rickshaw pulling accomplished an unsettling reversal of this relationship by having the puller, a "human horse," drag his machine and exploiter behind him. In China, the sordidness of the image, recognized by mule carters and intellectuals alike, was heightened by formal Confucian stress on humane treatment and the stigma attached to beastlike behavior. Reformers writing in journals during the May Fourth period condemned rickshaw pulling as a "kind of unproductive labor and meaningless way to live," which, while associated with the appearance of other, less ambiguously modern devices like automobiles and trains, constituted an "abnormal development."[64] The rickshaw was deemed "irrefutable proof of the backwardness of China's material civilization."

Trapped by circumstances and their style of life into doing something they found morally distasteful, a few intellectuals felt compelled to try to bridge the gulf between passenger and puller. In a discussion of new sociological findings on living and working conditions among Beijing rickshaw men, Xi Ying characterized as failures his own efforts at communications across class and linguistic boundaries.

I do not understand statistics . . . so I've never thought of rickshaw men as material to be gathered for social research. However, I have often wished to chat with them and ask them their views on many matters. But my Mandarin is pretty awful. There is a wall between us. If I do happen to ask a question, I have to explain again and again what I mean in order to make myself understood even a little. This makes me discouraged and I fall silent. Sometimes they take my silence as a form of rebuke. (And in their lives rebukes are a common enough occurrence). I can sense their embarrassment. And that makes me even more discouraged and silent. As a result, although I've known hundreds of rickshaw men, I really haven't seen into their hearts. That they do have hearts I have no doubt.[65]

The physical proximity of the intellectual in the city and the puller on the streets, and the symbolism suggested by the image of a long-gowned or Western-clad rider perched behind and above a working-class puller, encouraged the use of the rickshaw as a marker for the class and cultural fault-lines running through Chinese society. By depicting rickshaw men as figures driven by larger social forces and trapped with passengers in a social conundrum devised by a not always rational or reasonable process of modernization, writers could use the lives of rickshaw men to illustrate and explain how these forces and processes worked. This illustrative and diagnostic function helps explain the point and potency of countless true and fictional stories that appeared in Republican-era books, magazines, journals, and newspapers.

Conventionally, the rickshaw man was portrayed as a guileless Everyman or a corrupted innocent. In the course of the 1920s, Beijing rickshaw men, like numerous other groups previously excluded from public and political life, acquired considerable guile and a modicum of political consciousness. As rickshaw men were brought to the center of public attention as figures emblematic of Republican-era social problems, they sought, sometimes with the help of intellectuals less reticent than Xi Ying, the will and political compass to make the journey themselves. By placing rickshaw men and the rickshaw question at the center of things, a point of entry opens up to the disorder and turbulence of Republican China.

Three

Rickshaw Men:
Careers of the Laboring Poor

Contemporary writers dramatized the life of the rickshaw man in order to underline what was wrong with Republican society. The rickshaw represented poverty and social dislocation, qualities best conveyed by depicting as a victim the man who pulled it. However, this image reflected only part of the reality of being a puller. To stereotype rickshaw men as paupers or beasts of burden ignored the flair for the dramatic they exhibited in the public performance of their job. In time, these "social dramas" produced a politics of the street, which in turn prepared rickshaw men to participate in mass politics, the common destination of both intellectuals and workers in the 1920s.

Earning a Living on the Street

In his checkered career as a rickshaw man, Lao She's Xiangzi pulled a rented rickshaw for public hire, briefly enjoyed the status of owner-operator, and temporarily served as a private puller for individual families. A small minority of pullers in Beijing were retained by individual households, and about 3 percent of them realized Xiangzi's dream of owning a vehicle.[1] For most pullers, income was determined by the value of fares minus the rent taken by the garage. In his search for the requisite number of fares to pay the owner and support himself and his dependents, the typical rickshaw man spent on average nine to twelve hours out on the streets and was actually involved in pulling passengers about half

Fig. 6. A young woman and the carefully wrapped carcass of a pig (plus a fistful of sausages) suggest the outer limits of a rickshaw's load capacity. Used in this way, the rickshaw provided servant, shopping cart, and personal conveyance rolled into one. UPI/Bettmann Newsphotos.

that time.[2] Success at soliciting fares required some understanding of the layout of the city and skills as a peddler of rickshaw travel as a minor luxury. But the basic demands made by the trade were physical.

The hard part of rickshaw pulling had less to do with the weight of the load than with the premium passengers placed on speed. A well-balanced rickshaw could easily offset a plump or package-laden fare (fig. 6). Pulling heavier consignments of produce or goods was commonplace then, as now, in China. The hard part was having to run while pulling. Running, hands on the poles at one's sides, keeping one's balance, not running into anyone or anything, and not tripping took strength, stamina, and a certain amount of skill. The first day or two of pulling might well incapacitate a man. Lao She depicts Xiangzi's initiation to the trade as leaving him bedridden for two days with his ankles "swelled up like gourds."[3] Communist organizer Wu Guang, assigned to infiltrate the ranks of Beijing rickshaw men in the thirties, described in his memoirs the back pain and leg cramps that afflicted pullers. He also recalled, "When I began pulling a rickshaw, I was not in good shape. My arms especially were weak. As a result I grasped the rickshaw poles unsteadily, which in turn led to considerable shaking and swaying back and forth. I really worried about being upended and throwing my passenger on the ground."[4] If a puller did not trip or fall down as a result of poor road conditions or his own ineptitude, he risked other dangers, ranging from stampeding livestock to collision with another vehicle on streets crowded with everything from cars to camels.[5]

Very young and old rickshaw pullers were particularly vulnerable to physical ailments associated with the occupation. Several thousand rickshaw "men" were under seventeen years of age. Although the practice was illegal, children as young as ten or eleven could be seen pulling adult passengers. A reporter found the pitiful case of three children, aged sixteen, fourteen, and eleven, pulling one rickshaw as a means of supporting their sick mother and grandmother.[6] Passengers were also sometimes shocked to discover that the puller they had hired was in his seventies.[7] In one case, a professor, to his acute embarrassment, accepted the call of a rickshaw man behind him by naming a destination and a fare, only to turn to see a seventy-one-year-old man waiting to pull him.[8] Researchers expressed concern about the dust that rickshaw men breathed in, chills brought on by standing outdoors in sweat-soaked clothes, and general exposure to the elements.[9] In a series of articles on health problems in Beijing, the *North China Daily* asserted that rickshaw pulling led to an early death. "Besides the many who have died suddenly from strokes and heart attacks, the slow worsening of internal injuries also takes its toll. It is becoming increasingly evident that a rickshaw man reaching old age is a rarity."[10]

Beijing newspapers regularly carried reports of rickshaw men dying in the course of their labors or being found dead sprawled on the ground or sitting in their rickshaws. Rickshaw men suffered attacks while running, which left them sick and helpless from exhaustion, complicated in some cases by opium addiction.[11] Some of these deaths and injuries were attributed by the police to the practice of *feipao* ("flying run"), in which pullers ran at top speed for extra money or to maximize the number of fares taken in a day.[12] The police tried to ban the practice of *feipao*, but the economics of rickshaw pulling in Beijing made restrictions on speed and unreasonable exertion difficult to enforce. The number of rickshaw pullers in the city more than doubled from the mid-teens to the mid-twenties while Beijing's population barely increased. A fierce buyer's market resulted in which a growing army of rickshaw men competed for a ridership tied to Beijing's gradual increase in population and its relatively stable number of middle- and upper-income residents and sojourners. The disadvantageous position of rickshaw men in the marketplace for transportation was reflected in the actual decline in the conventional, average rate per hour charged by pullers from twenty-five cents in 1911 to ten cents in 1926.[13] Faced with these pressures, Beijing rickshaw men ran noticeably faster than their counterparts in other Asian cities, like Tokyo.[14]

The physical nature of the work, and the fact that rickshaw travel represented a kind of conspicuous consumption, made the most accomplished rickshaw men into figures resembling athletes. Sleek, almost dandified in appearance, they wore tailored jackets and trousers, knew a smattering of foreign phrases for the tourist trade, and specialized in making a few, fast trips a day.[15] Young men sometimes raced each other for sheer sport and in defiance of traffic regulations.[16] They flirted with young women by pulling them for free. And the swiftest rickshaw men acquired a certain fame and nicknames like "Ili Horse" (Ili in Xinjiang being famous for fast steeds) and "Locomotive."[17] At the peak of his powers and before he begins his moral and physical decline, Xiangzi is vain about the strength and grace of his stride and contemptuous of fellow pullers who stumble or who attempt to disguise physical weakness with a theatrically vigorous but slower running style.[18]

Dressed in rags, other pullers struggled along one step from beggary because advanced age, extreme youth, or illness impaired their performance. As Lao She explained, "Their rickshaws are broken down and their gait is slow. They mostly walk rather than run and demand little money from their passengers. They also work in the melon, fruit, and vegetable markets pulling produce.

The pay is bad but they don't need to run fast there."[19] Pullers who could no longer compete for human passengers found work taking live pigs to market, "trussed up in filthy rickshas, slightly too human to be regarded comfortably."[20]

The average rickshaw man lived within reach of a moderately comfortable living and yet close to dire poverty. Everything depended on the quantity and quality of fares brought in each day and the number of mouths he had to feed. Small reverses could devastate a puller and his family. Social researcher Qu Zhisheng found rickshaw-puller households so poor that the family slept without bedding on dirt floors in rooms emptied of possessions except for a pile of pawnshop tickets.[21]

Bad judgment or bad luck could bring disaster. One winter evening in 1928, a policeman on patrol was passing Ice House Lane near the canal surrounding the Imperial City. Looking down the darkened alley, the patrolman saw a young rickshaw man about to hang himself with his waistband. Confronted by the policeman, the youth, named Yao Yingrui, broke down and wept. Yao lived in an area just north of the Drum Tower with his mother and three younger brothers. One of his brothers was severely retarded, and the other two were still children. The family was six months behind in their rent and so poor that Yingrui had to wear his mother's only pair of trousers to work in the bitter cold. Yao Yingrui had done well enough earlier in the day to buy himself a bit of food and put aside cash to take back to his family. But someone had stolen the money from the rickshaw's trunk when he had stopped to use a public latrine near the train station outside Qian Gate. He only discovered the loss sometime later. Without even the money to pay the rickshaw rent and too ashamed to return to his family, he decided to kill himself. The policeman sent Yao home and promised that the police department would give his family assistance if his story proved true.[22]

A longtime Beijing resident described the sickening poverty Yao Yingrui was so desperate to avoid or escape.

Small children in the lanes are sickly and stunted. Their little arms and legs are like sticks. They lack a single spark of childlike gaiety. On their faces and bodies most have ulcerous sores and scars left by sores. Many exhibit oversized heads, blindness, crooked mouths, missing noses, and other signs of being maimed or crippled.[23]

Impoverished families, including rickshaw-puller households, sometimes sold their children to survive.[24] Others flocked to makeshift soup kitchens, where police sometimes used clubs to beat back "thousands of ragged, shivering men, women and children who are more than hungry."[25] In the winter, as many as five hundred individuals died each month from cold and hunger.[26] In the summer the monthly figure dropped to eighty or ninety. Since the police paid for the coffins of indigents, they kept accurate count.

Beyond the day-to-day task of avoiding a sudden descent into dire poverty, rickshaw men faced the long-term prospect of increasing economic insecurity. Guild work at least held out the possibility of advancement from apprenticeship to skilled worker or labor boss and, finally, master.[27] Rickshaw pulling as a career described an arc, which began to fall and finally to plummet once age sapped one's strength. Pullers like Xiangzi aspired to own their own garages or to accumulate enough capital to become peddlers or petty shopkeepers (fig. 7). But researchers who studied rickshaw men found that only a few were able to save even a portion of their earnings.[28] Perhaps 5 percent of pullers saved enough to set themselves up in another trade.[29] If a puller could not amass enough capital through earnings or loans to open a small business, or raise sons to support him when his rickshaw days were done, he would slip into the even more uncertain life of seasonal and casual labor. Pullers from the countryside could return, like other sojourners, to their villages in middle or old age. But most pullers were city people and of necessity fashioned strategies for advancement and survival from the city world they knew.

Courtyard Slums

Courtyard residence and shop (garage in the case of the rickshaw puller) were the two basic kinds of housing available to Beijing workers. About three-fifths of the city's rickshaw men lived, like Yao Yingrui, with their families in courtyard tenements (*da zayuan*) or other poor-quality housing.[30] Most of the rest of them roomed, usually by themselves, in rickshaw garage dormitories.

Allowing for the absence of modern plumbing and heating facilities, the courtyard compound, walled off from street noise

Fig. 7. Peddling provided an alternate career for workers who managed to amass a small amount of capital. The Beijing police estimated that over 25,000 individuals, selling everything from melons to coffins, earned their living on the street. Between fares, rickshaw men often ate at little food stands like this one. Courtesy of the Library of Congress.

and outside observation and composed of rooms surrounding and centering on an open courtyard, was pleasant enough. Beijing's most beautiful mansions were formed from a series of interconnecting courtyard dwellings. The courtyard compound could charm residents and visitors with its subtle blend of closure to the outside world and openness to peddlers, friends, gossip, and sunlight.[31] Even a tough social critic like Tao Menghe conceded that "Peking houses have a dignity of their own, which can hardly be found in any other city in this land."[32]

But the dwelling was also vulnerable to overcrowding. In tenement courtyards, rooms designed to function as elements of a larger household were rented out to individuals or to whole families.[33] Lao She has Xiangzi give a grim assessment of living conditions in these overcrowded "horizontal" tenements.

Unlikely as it might seem, Xiangzi thought of getting married right away. . . . But how could he raise a family on a rickshaw puller's pay? He knew the plight of the pullers who lived in the courtyard tenements. The man pulled a rickshaw. The woman did mending. The children scrounged for bits of coal. In the summer they chewed on melon rinds from garbage piles. In the winter the whole family was driven to soup kitchens.[34]

In other writings, Lao She suggested that bitter competition for space and income poisoned life in the courtyard slums, creating an atmosphere of misdirected anger and despair. The narrator of his story "Liu's Courtyard" observes that "you have to be careful walking through the yard if you do not want to step on someone, and there are bound to be words if you do. Everyone carries a belly full of grudges with him and all welcome an opportunity for a quarrel."[35]

Pockets of poverty were scattered throughout the city with concentrations of poor people, including rickshaw men, adjacent to the city walls and outside city gates.[36] But with the exception of the Bridge of Heaven district in the Outer City, these concentrations of poor people did not develop into slums or recognizable working-class districts. The primary class division in residence was not between rich and poor neighborhoods but among courtyards within neighborhoods. At the start of the decade, sociologist Sidney Gamble noted that "Peking has no real slums, but in almost any district rich and poor can be found living close together."[37] By the end of the decade, segregation by class was more noticeable.

It is indeed true that Peking has not developed its slums, nor has it presented such glaring contrasts of wealthy and poor districts as most modern cities, yet there is the unmistakeable sign that Peking, too, is tending to conform to the pattern of the modern city. People of the poorer classes are gradually driven to the outskirts of the city, back streets around busy districts, or sections where dilapidated houses abound.[38]

Reflecting this incipient separation, each day and night, shifts of rickshaw pullers drifted in from the poorer, peripheral areas of the Inner and the Outer City toward the city center in search of fares. These daily migrations suggested a newly emerging correlation of class to urban space. But rickshaw men did not appear on the streets of Beijing as the collective visitation of working-class communities or spatially discrete slums. Instead, they offered evidence of a poverty that could be traced in veins and pockets throughout the entire city.

Owners and Renters

To become a passenger, a person hailed a rickshaw on the street or arranged to have one at his or her disposal. To become a puller, a man went to one of hundreds of rickshaw garages in the city and arranged to rent a vehicle. By paying a bit extra one could stay in a dormitory attached to the garage.[39] The rental transaction itself usually required an introduction from someone the garage owner knew or a document called a "shop guarantee" (*pubao*). A rickshaw represented an investment of up to one hundred dollars, and garage owners were keen to establish some hold on the puller to discourage theft or damage. If the rickshaw was stolen, for example, the individual or shop supplying the guarantee would be liable for compensation.

Guarantees of this sort facilitated all kinds of transactions, including loans and apprenticeship contracts. *Pubao* were ranked according to the wealth of the individual or business making the surety. Rickshaw garages could not make too great a demand for guarantees, because of the poverty of their clientele and because garages themselves conventionally were given a low financial ranking. For example, in 1921 when two brothers applied to a government-sponsored "Poor People's Loan Agency" for capital to start a business peddling sweet potatos, they were told they needed a *pubao*. But when the brothers brought back a shop guarantee from the rickshaw garage their deceased father had rented from and where they lived with an older brother who was a puller, agency officials told them that they would need a more impressive chop than that. "Shop guarantees from shops selling paper funeral wares [to be burned for the dead], rickshaw garages, retail coal shops, iron-working shops, secondhand clothing stores, and the like are not at all acceptable."[40]

Often, personal connections (*guanxi*) were sufficient to persuade an owner to rent out a rickshaw. The experiences of Communist labor organizer Wu Guang provide an illustration.[41] When the Communist underground instructed Wu in the early 1930s to become a rickshaw puller as a first step toward organizing a union, Wu began to lead a double life. He resided in a small inn in the West City and registered with the local police precinct station as a Beijing University student. But during the day, instead of attending class, he pulled a rickshaw. Wu's need to disguise his identity meant that obtaining a *pubao* was impossible. Anticipating the problem, Wu had befriended a veteran puller who introduced him to a garage owner. The owner "had complete faith in the old rickshaw man" and agreed to rent to Wu without asking for a *pubao*.

The relationship between garage owner and puller, though often casual relative to higher orders of transactions, followed prevailing economic conventions. Bonds of mutual dependence and guarantee might be more tentative and tenuous than at the centers of urban economic activity, where the web of such relationships was more densely arranged and carefully policed. But owners still strove to extend this web of contracts and commitments over the men who disappeared each day with the garage's capital in tow.

Like most economic units in Beijing, rickshaw garages were small in scale, averaging less than thirty rickshaws to rent out. Like the owners or managers of other small businesses, garage owners often cultivated patron-client ties with the men who rented from them. Unlike those in other cities, Beijing owners and pullers dealt with each other directly, without middlemen or brokers.[42]

Owners drew on a standard repertoire of shop paternalism to attract and keep pullers. The cultivation of patron-client ties offset to a degree the uncertainty and insecurity that plagued the lives of rickshaw pullers. And defaults on rental fees and thefts of rickshaws happened often enough to make maintaining a regular corps of pullers attractive to an owner.[43]

In *Camel Xiangzi*, Master Liu, the owner of "Human Harmony Garage," where Xiangzi often went to rent a rickshaw, displays the combination of benevolence and menace associated with the role of patron. In his youth Liu had been a gambler, street thug, kidnapper, and loan shark. After spending time in prison for these offenses, he settled down as a rickshaw garage owner. "Originally having led the life of a ruffian, Liu knew how to deal with poor people. He knew when to tighten the screws and when to let up."[44] In presiding over a large garage renting out sixty rickshaws, Liu charged a bit more for rent because he kept only top-quality vehicles in stock. But he let pullers sleep in the garage dormitory at no extra charge and allowed pullers more rent-free days at holiday time than other owners. If a puller did not settle his accounts, Liu threw him out "like a broken bottle." But if you were sick or in trouble, "without a second's hesitation he would go through hell and high water to help you out."

An owner like Liu might be benevolent and despotic by turns. Or he might use his power over his pullers in a consistently ruthless way. The Zhang brothers from Haidian, a suburban town northwest of Beijing, were notorious for their "unusually fierce" dispositions.[45] At their "Zhang Garage" they regularly beat and cursed the pullers who rented from them. Zhang Qingyuan (no relation), a thirty-nine-year-old puller, had been faithfully paying his rent of twenty coppers a day for over a month when he suddenly hurt his foot. He lived at home and managed to pull his rickshaw there but was unable to return to the garage. Assuming that Zhang Qingyuan had stolen the rickshaw, the Zhangs sought out his introducer, who in turn went to the puller's home and found out about his injury. When Zhang Qingyuan finally returned to the garage, the brothers demanded back rent from him. When Zhang Qingyuan pointed out that he had no money and would have to pull in order to pay them back, the enraged Zhangs beat the worker so terribly he eventually died.

Smallness of scale may have made the owner and pullers seem like a family. Columnist Xi Ying recounted the sounds of laughter and music that often came from a garage near where he lived.[46] Even so, patron-client ties usually develop to the fullest extent where market forces are weak and choice on the part of superior and subordinate is strictly limited. In the twenties, just as market forces guided transactions between puller and passenger, puller and owner bargained over rental terms. Variable rates charged by owners, as well as differences based on location and type of vehicle offered, provided strong incentives for pullers to shop around. Garages experienced a 60 percent turnover rate in pullers, owing in part to the prevalence of market forces over patron-client ties.[47] Rickshaw pullers gained a measure of security by placing themselves in the grip of owners like Master Liu. But in doing so they lost the chance to pick and choose among the packages of economic incentives available in the marketplace.

Street-Level Perspectives on Power and Status

The working lives of most Beijing residents were hidden from public view. Courtyard walls, shop facades, and factory gates concealed economic activity from casual scrutiny. Managers, masters, and labor bosses formed a buffer or barrier between the workers they supervised and the outside world. Apprentices who worked nearly every day of the year, twelve hours a day, rarely went outside shop or factory. On the other hand, in a preindustrial city a large number of economic functions are performed in public. Things are sold, services are provided, and goods are carried, loaded, and unloaded in the open. Shops and other businesses tend to spill out into the street with stalls, tables, tools, and workers encroaching on streets and alleyways. Rickshaw men of necessity faced the public every day in search of fares. In the course of their work, rickshaw pullers, like policemen, water carriers, streetcar conductors, and others who plied the streets and crowds as part of their job, experienced urban life as an intense, tactical struggle for space and recognition.

Because most people in Beijing could not afford to ride rickshaws regularly, a puller's passenger was usually someone of a higher status than he. The one exception to this rule was the soldier who was willing to pay for the luxury or to use force to obtain a free ride. Since the passenger customarily bargained with the puller over the fare, there was always room for a misunderstanding. When the misunderstanding was colored by class differences or if one of the parties was armed, the transaction could take an ugly turn. The rickshaw man had to rely on his wits or fists to keep from being cheated or abused. On the other hand, when the advantage was in his favor, a rickshaw man might cheat or intimidate his passenger.

The gulf in social status between puller and passenger was clearly reflected in differences in dress. Passengers wore long gowns or Western clothes if they were men. Pullers wore trousers and a short coat, the uniform of the working class. In the winter a rickshaw man might add a long coat or robe (see figure 6). The contrast is vividly illustrated in Wu Guang's memoir of his double life as student and rickshaw puller. Wu would leave his lodgings each morning dressed as a student in a long gown and then surreptitiously change his costume as he dodged and darted among lanes and alleyways on his way to the rickshaw garage. "First I took off my long, unlined blue gown and threw it over my shoulders. Then I twisted the gown and wrapped it around my waist, concealing it beneath my shirt. Then I took out cloth bands to tie up the bottoms of my trouser legs. Finally I took a towel out and wrapped it around my head. The transformation of a student into a rickshaw man was complete!"[48]

Transactions between puller and passenger began in the street or other public place, usually with several pullers bidding for the privilege of transporting a passenger to a certain point. Athletic pullers with first-class rickshaws were able, as Lao She noted, to "maintain their dignity" during the bargaining.[49] The majority of pullers needed to advertise and negotiate their services with the vocal intensity of the hawkers and vendors they shared the street with.

Not infrequently, the puller or the passenger tried to change the agreed-upon price once they reached the passenger's destination. A puller might decide that the energy he had just expended justified a higher fare. A passenger might find fault with the rickshaw man's performance. One winter day in 1928, a rickshaw man named Zheng Jinyang was hired by a shop specializing in sheep intestines to transport a bag of salt. He was directed to pull the salt and an employee of the shop named Mr. Ji to an address given to him as Moon River Temple, the closest landmark to the shop. But when they arrived at the temple, Ji decided he wanted the salt delivered to the shop itself. Then he told Zheng to carry the bag inside. Zheng complied but afterwards demanded extra pay for what he considered extra work. Perhaps because they measured distances step by step, rickshaw men could be stubborn about going any farther than absolutely necessary. Ji refused, and the two men began first to quarrel and then to scuffle. Two clerks ran out of the shop to help Ji, and together the three shop employees beat up Zheng and knocked over his rickshaw, cracking the trunk. Zheng picked himself up and hurried to the nearest police station to file a complaint. The police agreed to charge the three men.[50]

The incident illustrates some of the problems faced by rickshaw men working alone and on the street in a city of powerful collective attachments. During the initial bargaining, the fare could be decided by mutual agreement. But once a resident had reached his or her destination, the puller faced an adversary who had yet to pay and who could call on reinforcements from inside shop, residence, or university or government compound.

Rickshaw men could also use their wiles and superior knowledge of the city to take advantage of passengers. For example, during a summer rainstorm a puller with a brothel attendant as passenger decided to raise the fare in mid-journey. When the man protested that he did not have that much money with him, the rickshaw man stopped in the middle of a muddy street and refused to pull the passenger to dry ground until he paid up. Intervention by a policeman cost the puller two days in jail for "wicked behavior."[51] In February 1925 the police arrested a rickshaw man named Li Luer for trying to cheat and then beating a passenger.[52] The passenger, Du Qiucheng, hailed Li and his rickshaw just west of the Forbidden City near the bridge separating Beihai and Zhonghai. Li could tell at a glance that Du was fresh from the countryside. The old man still had a Manchu-style queue fifteen years after the 1911 Revolution and wore a short blue padded jacket and a white felt cap. According to the newspaper account of the incident, from the moment the rickshaw man saw Du Qiucheng, he had "larceny in his heart." The universal story of naive rustic victimized by street-wise city dweller seemed about to unfold. Du wanted to travel to the North New Bridge area in the northeastern part of the Inner City. The two men negotiated a fare of eighteen coppers. Li then proceeded to Earthly Peace Bridge just north of the Forbidden City and only about halfway to the agreed-upon destination. Since "North New Bridge" is legendary rather than real, Li must have thought he was playing a rather clever trick on Du when he told him to get out on the span of the Earthly Peace Bridge. But Du Qiucheng was not so easily fooled and began to argue that this was not North New Bridge. Li then hit Du and knocked him to the ground.

As a result of incidents like these, rickshaw men earned the reputation of being cunning and untrustworthy. One sign of the low regard pullers were held in by the general public was the fact that good deeds done by rickshaw men were judged to be especially newsworthy. One rickshaw man was lauded for persuading a despondent passenger he had pulled to a river bank not to jump in and drown himself.[53] Rickshaw men who returned money left in their vehicles and refused proffered rewards were praised as "worthy of respect."[54] Policemen at one precinct station gave one dollar to a raggedly dressed puller who sought their help in returning a bundle of clothes to an old woman who had forgotten it in his rickshaw.[55] On the whole, the police and the public viewed rickshaw men as capable of misbehavior or criminal activity if given the opportunity. The *Metropolitan Police Gazette* prefaced an account of a puller who stole from a passenger with the observation that "some rickshaw men are good. Some are bad. Although there are those who are honest and reliable, many are crafty and cunning. If you're not careful a rickshaw man will take advantage of any opportunity to make off with your belongings."[56]

Because of their freer, more disorderly life, rickshaw men could escape some of the customary controls that dictated life in shops and factories. They might even profit from the confusion and disorder of the streets and the crowds. On the other hand, they themselves could be beaten, swindled, or intimidated. Passengers sometimes hailed rickshaws, used their services, and then slipped away without paying. On a winter day in 1925, a forty-year-old rickshaw man, who had been a carpenter until he was forced to take up pulling, agreed to take a passenger around the city all day for one dollar. Toward the late afternoon and after miles of pulling through practically every district of the city, the passenger left the puller and went into a busy shopping area. He left a "painting" in the rickshaw to reassure the puller that he would return. When the man failed to come back, the puller examined the parcel which turned out to be a rolled up newspaper. In despair over loss of the fare, the rickshaw man went home and tried to kill himself by drinking poisonous brine left over from beancurdmaking.[57] Dishonesty was a problem for passenger and puller alike in an urban culture in which the norm for agreements required go-betweens, guarantors, or at least knowledge of whom you were dealing with. Pulling a rickshaw through an urban "world of strangers" left plenty of room for deceit and bad faith on both sides.

Rickshaw Pullers and the Police

In the absence of strict regulation of the rates charged rickshaw passengers, escalation from vigorous bargaining to misunderstandings, hard words, blows, and injuries was a common occurrence.[58] When victimized by passengers, rickshaw men could appeal to the police for help. Policemen arrested and jailed passengers who beat pullers for not running fast enough to suit them.[59] They mediated disputes with passengers.[60] Rickshaw men sometimes sought out a policeman or the local precinct station to register complaints or initiate law suits.[61] When a young puller named Zhang Chun bumped into a seventy-year-old rickshaw man named Lu Yu, the two men quarreled and then fought until Zhang struck old Lu hard in the face. A peacemaker in the crowd that gathered to watch stopped the fight. But when Lu reached home he found that his face had swollen up and his beard whiskers had begun to fall out. Enraged, he chased down Zhang and hauled him off to a police station to level charges against him.[62]

But despite police willingness to come to the aid of pullers in trouble, the conventional wisdom in Beijing was that rickshaw men hated policemen and that policemen in turn despised pullers.

Wu Guang refers in his memoir to the "constant beatings and scoldings" that rickshaw men received from the police. "Whenever a passenger and a rickshaw man got into a fight, policemen were invariably partial toward the passenger and rebuked the rickshaw man. . . . As a result of years of abuse, rickshaw pullers hated street policemen. They believed that street policemen were their most immediate enemies."[63] A newspaper editorialist agreed that "if a rickshaw man by mistake trespasses into a forbidden area, the policeman on watch will grace him with a shout and a blow on the head."[64] A Beijing folk song listed the policeman as one of the puller's chief tormentors.[65]

Puller and policeman were bound to each other in a relationship that was adversarial and cooperative by turns. The development of Beijing's modern-style, bureaucratically organized police force paralleled the growth of the rickshaw trade. The former grew in a deliberate, planned way, the latter in a disorderly response to market forces. Both took the newly paved avenues of the city and suburbs as their territory, and both recruited members from the ranks of the laboring poor. As Lao She pointed out, the occupations of policeman and rickshaw puller were the "two tracks laid out for the poor of the big cities."[66] If you were illiterate and had no craft, you became a puller. If you could "recognize a few characters and had a bit of culture," you could apply to join the police force.

As early as 1913 the police department issued detailed regulations concerning the behavior and appearance of pullers on the street.[67] No one, in the first place, was supposed to pull a rickshaw if he were under eighteen or over fifty, physically infirm, afflicted by "infectious diseases or bad habits," long-haired, hatless in intense heat or severe cold, or naked or barefooted. Pullers were ordered not to run fast along crowded thoroughfares or at corners. At night they were forbidden to run without a lamp-equipped vehicle. Pullers were supposed to park and solicit only at designated spots and not in the roadway or at intersections.[68]

The police codes were designed to protect pullers, passengers, and the flow of traffic. But by restricting the rickshaw puller to designated areas and attempting to keep rickshaws away from the entrances to parks, theaters, and other public places, where the most lucrative fares were to be found, the police placed themselves at odds with the income strategies of the pullers. A struggle ensued which was no less intense for being based on the prosaic issue of parking regulations.

Common class background and professional training likely created some feelings of empathy or responsibility on the part of the policeman for the rickshaw man. But the policeman also followed the dictates of law and custom which sought to regulate, reform, and demean rickshaw pullers. The policeman had a stake in confirming that his was the higher "track" and that a marginal difference in cultural and educational background placed social as well as official distance between his role and that of the puller. A newspaper reporter told of coming across two pullers chatting at the side of the road. The one had recognized the other as a policeman moonlighting as a puller. He had a big family and his pay was in arrears. The full-time rickshaw man could not help teasing the policeman-puller: "I never thought that those of you who specialize in beating rickshaw men also pulled rickshaws. Where has the prestige that comes from beating us gone to?" The policeman replied: "Don't laugh. Circumstances forced this on me, but don't imagine that I've lost my power to manage rickshaw men. Tomorrow I'll put my uniform back on and beat you as usual."[69]

Some rickshaw men, toughened and educated by their experiences on the street, contested police authority as a matter of course. Toward the end of *Camel Xiangzi*, Lao She's protagonist becomes this kind of roughneck for whom a few days in jail for defying the police holds no terrors.[70] The police knew these men as "rickshaw hooligans" (*chepi*). Pullers who ran afoul of the law, like a man named Zhang Shude, won this epithet.[71] "Young and possessed of a fierce temper," Zhang specialized in carrying prostitutes on their calls in the "Eight Lanes" brothel district. Late one summer afternoon, he was speeding along when the wheel of his rickshaw ran over the foot of Policeman Xu Lianzhong, who was standing watch in the roadway. Xu ran and caught up to Zhang and ordered him to stop. Zhang put down the handles of his vehicle, walked over to Xu, and without further ado lifted the hapless policeman up by the collar with an insolent, "What am I going to do with you then?" Fortunately for Xu, a police sergeant saw the difficulty he was in and ran up and arrested Zhang. Zhang Shude was taken to the local station and given the maximum administrative sentence of fifteen days in jail.

Men Without Power

Short of behaving like a ruffian or counting on the benevolence of policemen, an individual puller in distress could look for the serendipitous appearance of someone else willing to stand up for him. One puller, who found himself in a seemingly hopeless situation only to be rescued by the sudden appearance of a benefactor, wrote a letter of thanks to a Beijing newspaper.[72] He had been injured and his rickshaw damaged in a collision with an automobile. Noting that "I am a man without power," the rickshaw man explained that the driver of the auto would have simply driven off had not an official from the Ministry of Agriculture and Commerce stopped to help. The official called over a policeman and made sure that the rickshaw man received compensation.

Scattered throughout the city in courtyard tenements and garage dormitories, forced to compete against one another for fares, and absorbed in tactics designed to use or blunt the force of official and private power, rickshaw men could easily find themselves "without power." Powerlessness seemed inextricably bound to the role rickshaw men played in Beijing society. Rickshaw men were conceded their petty crimes and swindles almost as a kind of compensation for the abuse they were continuously subjected to.

In a city of walls, screens, and practiced concealment, the rickshaw man's visibility meant that he had little chance of shielding himself from threats posed by rivals and adversaries. Even though rickshaw men as an occupational group were not at the absolute bottom of urban society, it was easy to conflate their readily apparent social and political vulnerability with socioeconomic status. Wu Guang wrote that the city's rickshaw men "lived at the bottom of society. Their political position was the most 'lowly' (*beijian*)."[73]

An individual rickshaw man might use deception or force to offset the lowly niche he found himself in. Or he might confound the stereotypical view of his position and capacities. In response to incessant police regulation, some pullers became quite knowledgeable about the law and their formal rights. One spring day in 1921, on Dazhalan Street in the busy commercial area outside Qian Gate, a rickshaw man accidentally ran into and slightly injured a pedestrian. The injured man responded angrily by grabbing the puller's hat. The policeman who intervened in the incident allowed the pedestrian to leave (with the hat) and took the rickshaw man into custody. At the district police office, the rickshaw puller confessed to having bumped into the other man but insisted that his action was unintentional. On the other hand, what could be said for someone who would steal another man's hat? That, he declared, was an "offense of misappropriation." The puller demanded to be allowed to make a formal complaint. Taken aback by the puller's clever use of legal terminology, the investigating officers were, for a moment, left speechless.[74]

The predominantly urban background of Beijing pullers encouraged this kind of street-wise glibness. In addition, many pullers were at least marginally literate. Huang Gongdu's survey of one hundred rickshaw men found that sixty-one knew at least a few characters. Two could compose a letter, and two had elements of a classical education.[75] Other responses to his questionnaire suggested that the pullers had been exposed to a variety of written and oral literary and cultural forms, including tabloid newspapers, Beijing opera, storytelling, and political slogans and speeches.[76] Journalist Xi Ying, referring to Beijing rickshaw men, observed:

Many of them are completely literate. Aside from a minority who prefer to spend their free time on the job gambling or gossiping, reading a tabloid is their most common activity. They can often be seen on streets or lanes, parked with their rickshaws on the side of the road, casually, even elegantly seated in their vehicles, passing time with a newspaper.[77]

Xi Ying mused that "this really confirms Beijing's reputation as a 'cultural city.'"

Rickshaw men frequented the opera and other kinds of theatrical performances, drinking establishments, brothels, and teahouses.[78] In the course of these entertainments, pullers acquired a basic familiarity with urban culture. Some pullers, by dint of their service to Beijing's middle and upper classes, had regular exposure to Beijing's feasting and banqueting circuit. If a rickshaw man's client or "master" was invited to a banquet, the host customarily gave the puller money for a meal, which he would eat in the company of the other guests' rickshaw men. Since Beijing's restaurant and entertainment districts contained a range of high-, medium-, and low-priced restaurants, teahouses, and brothels, rickshaw men of this category could expect to enjoy a sequence of less elaborate but still pleasurable diversions paralleling the social life of their employers. Some rickshaw men kept in readiness in the trunk a set of clothing suitable for party-going, and reformers expressed alarm about the decadent pursuits of these, mainly privately retained, rickshaw men.[79] Occasionally, the parallel pursuit of pleasure by servant and master might intersect. In *Camel Xiangzi,* Xiangzi contracts venereal disease from the young mistress of the official who employed him for a time as his private rickshaw puller.

Pullers with higher status had a sense of their own, superior position which they expressed through habits of dress, cuisine, and behavior in public. During their working day, these, mainly young, rickshaw men congregated in teahouses to refresh themselves. They could afford to spend money on simple pleasures, like a cup of good tea in pleasant surroundings in the company of men of similar standing. While struggling to save money toward the purchase of a new rickshaw, Xiangzi hovers on the edges of these small communities, anxious that he not squander his savings.

In teahouses rickshaw men of his rank, out of breath after a *feipao*, liked to have a good, ten-cent cup of tea with two lumps of sugar in order to cool off and recuperate. When Xiangzi had run until he was dripping with sweat and his chest was burning, he really felt like doing the same. But for him, this was a bad habit and wasteful. When he really needed tea to quench his thirst he would gulp down a one-cent cup made from tea-sweepings.[80]

As Lao She suggests, unlike Xiangzi, the average puller was willing to surrender a penny or two for a comradely cup of tea. And even though rickshaw men operated largely as individual entrepreneurs, they did on occasion act together. A rickshaw man on a long-distance journey could call to another puller to take over for him if he was exhausted, in effect selling what remained of his fare.[81] Xi Ying noted that among the "many unwritten rules" subscribed to by pullers was the correct way to cut in front of a slower puller without insulting him or triggering a race to prove who was stronger.[82] Rickshaw men transporting a group of clients would often slow down to the pace set by the weakest puller.[83] And rickshaw men like Xiangzi who were too ruthless in their

Fig. 8. An officially designated rickshaw stand bustles with activity as pullers prepare to depart with passengers. The embroidered cushions visible in empty vehicles advertise the comfortable ride available to the rickshaw's clientele. Policemen sometimes dispersed illegally parked rickshaws by grabbing cushions and tossing them down the street. From Heinz v. Perckhammer, *Peking* (Berlin: Albertus-Verlag, 1928).

quest for fares faced ostracism by their fellows. On the other hand, judging by the frequency of quarrels among pullers over prospective passengers, the same buyer's market that forced pullers to run fast tended to undermine these customary practices. Cutthroat competition and a tentative sense of communal feeling and interest coexisted uneasily in the society of rickshaw men.

When they were not pulling, rickshaw men waited at roadside rickshaw stands designated by the police or other places where potential passengers congregated (fig. 8). Lao She notes that rickshaw pullers could be classified according to where they plied their trade.[84] For example, those who lived outside Xizhi Gate, at the northwestern corner of the Inner City, specialized in long journeys to Haidian (the home of Yanjing and Qinghua Universities) and the Summer Palace. Others concentrated their efforts in the Eight Lanes district or the Legation Quarter. Pullers who worked in the foreign-controlled legation area were formally licensed and informally attached to specific embassies. In the mid-twenties when the Soviet Legation attempted to dispense with the services of the rickshaw men camped outside their compound, the laborers' protests forced the Soviets to back down.[85] Outside of the Legation Quarter, groups of rickshaw men attempted with mixed success to assert control over particularly lucrative spots for soliciting. To enforce territoriality, rickshaw men had to repel fellow pullers who coveted the same choice locations and defy or elude the police who viewed the practice as illegal.[86]

Although market forces split rickshaw men into competing individuals and warring groups, a puller in distress might summon help from his fellows. Wu Yinxiu, a member of the Blue Banners and sole support of his aged mother and younger siblings, became a rickshaw man when his pay as a military policeman went into arrears. One day in August 1923, a soldier and an army cook hired Wu and another puller to take them to the train station. Arriving too late to catch their train, the two military men ordered the pullers to take them back to their barracks. On the way, Wu, who was by now exhausted, tripped on a stone and spilled the soldier to the ground. The soldier, aided by the cook, turned on Wu and began to beat him. Rickshaw men in the area tried to mediate, but the soldier cursed them for interfering. The pullers then surrounded the soldier in a threatening way and chased after him until he escaped by leaping into a moat.[87]

Rickshaw men who had won a measure of status within the trade seem to have been especially aggressive when challenged. A month before Wu Yinxiu had his run-in with the two military men, ten rickshaw men from the Eight Lanes district decided to relax in a teahouse near where they worked pulling prostitutes. The teahouse was in the Bridge of Heaven district and adjoined a public park frequented by revelers and guests of Beijing brothels. Dressed in brightly colored clothes, the men sat down and ordered cups of good-quality tea all around. After they had paid, the manager told their waiter his establishment did not serve rickshaw men even if they had the money to pay. He instructed his employees to throw them out. The pullers took offense, leapt up, and prepared to fight. A public security official who happened to be in the teahouse mediated the dispute and narrowly prevented a brawl.[88]

Collective Action: Premonitions and Precedents

With a well-earned reputation for individual combativeness and the basics, however tenuous, of group solidarity, rickshaw men regularly demonstrated that they could overcome an equally well documented reputation for powerlessness and vulnerability. As pullers became legion in the teens and early twenties, officials and commentators wondered aloud whether rickshaw men might someday rebel against their condition. The guilt that intellectuals felt while patronizing rickshaw men was tinged with presentiments of a time when pullers would no longer accept their lowly position.

Xi Ying reported hearing a fifty- or sixty-year-old puller tell a companion that "a person who pulls a rickshaw has a puller's fate. The gentleman who is a passenger has that fate. . . . I once rode in a rickshaw and felt like a bloody fool!"[89] But the columnist doubted that that was the way most pullers felt about things. He imagined that envy or anger was more representative of their feelings than fatalism. Writing in the aftermath of the 1919 May Fourth Movement, a Beijing intellectual opined that the city's pullers would not bear their "wretchedness" much longer.[90] Citing disturbances among pullers in Shanghai, he speculated that an "unimaginable crisis" might result. "Foreign countries have had their bread revolutions. Whether or not in the future China will have a *wowotou* [the steamed bread basic to the diet of the urban poor] revolution I dare not predict."

Compared with pullers in other Asian cities, Beijing rickshaw men were slow to act and organize. Rickshaw men carried out the first strikes in Japanese and Korean labor history.[91] In Chinese cities like Shanghai and Guangzhou rickshaw men formed what labor historian Jean Chesneaux terms a "turbulent army" willing and able to strike and protest.[92]

In Beijing low rents probably dampened tensions between owners and pullers.[93] The small, shoplike scale of ownership at the garage level personalized conflict without providing the basis for a more regimented militancy. As Wu Guang noted later, smallness of scale inhibited broad-gauged organizing efforts.[94] The enormous numbers of pullers and their scattered deployment throughout the city also made citywide organization or action a daunting task. The ubiquitous nature of pullers, which fueled the imaginations of outside observers, masked significant obstacles to mobilization.

Under these circumstances rickshaw men might have relied on traditional merchant-guild representation to defend their interests. Even workers without their own craft guilds could place themselves under the protection of owner-dominated bodies. Unfortunately, garage owners themselves had trouble acting in concert, and when they did combine they proved less than reliable as patrons. In 1913 owners organized a "Metropolitan Rickshaw Federation," but it soon disbanded for lack of interest.[95] In 1924 garage owners joined with rickshaw builders, mule-cart operators, and bicycle-shop proprietors in a successful attempt to form a guild and block a police plan to collect the city's "vehicle tax" in silver rather than debased copper coin.[96] The police department finally backed down when rickshaw men joined the opposition. According to a newspaper report, "Tens of thousands of rickshaw pullers heard about [the tax policy] and rose up in a mass" to oppose it.[97] Since the tax directly affected only a minority of pullers who were owner-operators, rickshaw men must have realized that the de facto tax increase would be passed on to them in the form of higher rents or rents calculated in silver.[98] Unrest among rickshaw pullers continued for a month before the police capitulated.[99]

Scarcely had owners and pullers won this common victory than garage owners demanded a rent hike or a switchover from copper to silver as the medium of payment. In April, Chen Shiho, the owner of a thirty-vehicle garage in the West City, decided to raise the rent he charged and called on other owners to do the same.[100] When the pullers in his garage heard about the planned increase, they met with Chen in an attempt to dissuade him. But the mediation session quickly dissolved into an angry confrontation. It was reported that Chen's proposal did not attract wide support among his fellows. Three months later, another group of owners tried to force rickshaw men to pay their rent in silver coin or its equivalent.[101] Acting in response to unspecified protests from rickshaw men, the police vetoed the plan.

The value of the owners' guild to rickshaw men was limited,

partly because the body was weak (only 10 percent of Beijing's some nine hundred garages belonged) and partly because owners sought to use what strength they had to wring concessions from the pullers.[102] The paternalism and benevolence of some owners did not become general guild practice, and most owners were unable to extend whatever control they had over pullers in the garage to cover their behavior in the street. Rickshaw men had access to and familiarity with certain features of guild organization, but they did not live under a guild regimen. As a result, rickshaw pullers were freer and more independent than many workers. But they were also deprived of the leverage and access to the higher realms of city politics which merchant and craft guilds accorded trades as diverse as water carriers, carpenters, bricklayers, blind storytellers, night-soil carriers, and other shop clerks, craftsmen, and service workers.

Even though pullers tended to be poorly organized and represented, they could always find an audience to listen to their grievances. Their workplace was the public thoroughfare. Compared with the isolation of the courtyard, the customary restraint of guild procedure, and the paternalism and discipline of the shop, factory, and work gang, the street was a freer and less predictable environment. Rickshaw men were given countless opportunities to maintain or drop conventional masks of passivity, random criminality, and helplessness while fellow residents looked on with interest and apprehension.

Longtime Beijing resident George Kates observed that "for an informal open court, the inevitable 'cloud of witnesses' is ever ready in China to pronounce judgment."[103] People on the street and in other public places were "always free to look and never abashed at using their privilege; free to comment on what was happening on the public stage." Rickshaw pullers could easily translate personal troubles into grievances within the public realm of the "informal open court." As Lao She wrote, "Among rickshaw men, individual grievances and difficulties are matters of public gossip. At intersections and in small tea shops, rickshaw pullers describe and quarrel about their own affairs and then these affairs become the property of everyone. They travel from place to place like a popular song."[104]

Rickshaw men faced serious obstacles to effective political action. But physical distance from each other, from fellow Beijing residents, and from the agents of public and private power were not among them. Rickshaw men were a crowd within a crowd in the midst of daytime commerce, the nightly restaurant and theater trade, and political calls to arms. Any change in weather, prices, public security, or political temperature affected them immediately. Their social and political vulnerably made them especially sensitive to changes in the way the urban community was managed and in the ways people participated in politics. The building blocks for a larger, more militant politics already existed in their casual habits of insolence and defiance and in periodic episodes of street-level comradery. All that was needed was for these elements of consciousness and organization to be assembled.

Four

Policemen as Mediators and Street-Level Bureaucrats

Rickshaw men experienced manifold pressures in their workaday lives. They felt the weight of market competition, patriarchal authority, social discrimination, and public opinion. In their position it was hard to avoid being underbid by a colleague, scolded by a garage owner, tricked or berated by a passenger, or patronized by well-intentioned reformers. But it was hardest of all to elude the eye of the policeman. Policemen, recruited to the task of keeping order as pioneer agents of the modern Chinese state, faced in rickshaw men a moving target resistant to social control.

When Huang Gongdu asked his one hundred rickshaw-puller respondents in 1929, "What is the national government?" the replies included "the officialdom," "the Three People's Principles," "don't know," "Chiang Kai-shek," "Sun Yat-sen," "the rich," "the generals," "Nanjing," "a government that takes care of the people," and "not Zhang Zuolin."[1] The term conjured up a collection of bureaucrats, a set of ideals, a living, dead, or deposed leader, soldiers, a popular administration, paternalistic regime, a place, a class, or a program. Perhaps out of an ironical appreciation of the coercive face of state power in Republican China, perhaps out of ignorance, one rickshaw man answered, "the public security bureau" (*gongan ju,* or police).

In Beijing the government of the street and the courtyard slum was the police force. Whether he spoke from ignorance or insight, the lone rickshaw man in Huang Gongdu's survey who identified the national government with the police force hit upon a key aspect of being a rickshaw puller and a member of the city's laboring poor. Political modernization in twentieth-century China meant a more intrusive, regulatory, and tutelary state presence. Rickshaw men felt the weight of evolving administrative practices destined to confront every citizen with the reality of a policed society, if not a police state.[2] In the process, policemen and rickshaw men emerged as unlikely collaborators in the development of a new civic tradition of close contact between ordinary people and official power. It was no accident that from a particular angle the national government looked like the police, and the local police resembled a government.

Late-Qing Police Reforms

Before 1900 several government organizations shared responsibility for keeping order in Beijing.[3] A gendarmerie of ten thousand men stationed inside the walls patrolled the city and guarded the gates.[4] Banner forces helped keep order in the Inner City, and a special censorate and district magistrates ruled on civil and criminal cases.[5] Imperial Beijing within the city walls was divided into five districts, each presided over by a censor.[6] The city was also split on a north-south axis between Daxing and Wanping counties, which in turn were administered as part of a twenty-county prefectural unit centering on the capital. Imperial practice, as a general principle, denied cities, including the capital, political status as integral units and encouraged overlapping jurisdictions. What these complex arrangements lacked by way of systematic control of urban society, they partly made up through a penchant for administrative overlap and redundancy. As Alison Dray-Novey has observed, Beijing's ethnic mix of Manchu and Han Chinese residents encouraged such redundancy. Banner-staffed gendarmerie units maintained order in predominantly Manchu Inner City districts while district censors "dealt mainly with the non-banner Chinese world."[7] In addition, small-scale, neighborhood-based organizations called *shuihui* ("water societies," or fire brigades) played a role in policing the city. Financed and directed by local degree-holders and merchants, these societies caught thieves and turned them over to the authorities, worked to prevent crime, and dispensed relief to the poor.[8]

The disorders associated with the Boxer uprising in 1900, in combination with the general reform program initiated throughout the empire after 1902 and known as the New Policies (*xinzheng*), provided the impetus for the creation of a modern, city-wide police force in Beijing.[9] The siege of the foreign legations in the summer of 1900 and the lifting of the siege by an allied expeditionary force in August caused much destruction and death.[10] A few days after the occupation of the city, Beijing was divided into districts under control of the foreign armies.[11] Of the eight nations that contributed forces for the assault on Beijing, six still occupied sections of the city in the spring of 1901: the United States, Britain, France, Germany, Italy, and Japan. Several of the six recruited Chinese as policemen for their districts.

The commander of the Japanese police district was a self-taught China expert named Kawashima Naniwa who had close ties to the Japanese military.[12] Kawashima typified the generation of ex-samurai adventurers who went to China to make their fortunes. In April 1901 he founded the Beijing Police Academy and began training Chinese recruits in modern police methods.[13] Kawashima, with the backing of the Japanese military, took good advantage of the opportunity created by the occupation to demonstrate the attractiveness of the Japanese model of police reform. Whereas other occupiers simply recruited poor people off the street, the Japanese made a concerted effort to train and properly equip the police under their control. The faculty of Kawashima's police academy was drawn from Japanese military and civilian officials who were knowledgeable about police affairs and who could speak Chinese.

Prince Su, a Manchu nobleman, was Kawashima's most important patron and connection to the Qing government.[14] After the Boxer Protocols were signed in September 1901 and foreign armies relinquished control of all but the Legation Quarter, Prince Su was charged with maintaining order and repairing damage done to the city during the siege.[15] Kawashima persuaded Prince Su, by then an enthusiastic supporter of police reform, to extend the Japanese-style police system throughout the city. Kawashima and his handpicked faculty remained in charge of the police academy and were given official rank in the Qing government.

Police modernization quickly spread from Beijing to other cities, and even rural areas in north China. This diffusion of modern police methods was partly due to Kawashima's aggressive sales-manship. When Yuan Shikai became governor of Zhili province in November 1901, Kawashima approached Yuan with his blueprint for police reform and found him receptive.[16] Summoned to Bao-ding, the provincial capital, Kawashima spent ten days working with Yuan's subordinates on plans for a police school and a police bureau there. Beginning in 1902 Yuan and his lieutenants estab-lished police forces in Baoding and Tianjin and later at the county level in Zhili.[17] As part of the New Policies, which represented the Qing dynasty's last great effort to save itself through a comprehen-sive package of military, political, economic, and educational re-forms, police reform drew strength from a general willingness among officials to experiment with foreign models of the kind Kawashima was promoting.

Meanwhile, the Beijing Police Academy continued to produce both officers and patrolmen in courses of three to nine months. Graduates were placed directly in police forces in Beijing and in other cities. In 1902, with Kawashima's help, Prince Su dispatched another Manchu, Yu Lang, to Japan for a firsthand look at the Japanese model of police organization.[18] Yu Lang stayed three months in Japan and when he returned was made a police super-intendant in Beijing. Soon after, a stream of students followed the path laid down by Kawashima, Prince Su, and Yu Lang and en-rolled in Japanese police schools. When they returned to Beijing, these students, together with the graduates of the Beijing Police Academy, staffed the growing number of precinct stations in the city.

Expansion was slow. The new system was established first in the Inner City in 1902 and was extended to the Outer City three years later.[19] The old gendarmerie force, in decline since mid-century, naturally opposed police modernization as a threat to its position.[20] But by courting conservative officials and recruiting members of the gendarmerie into the new force, the reformers blunted the opposition. Kawashima Naniwa hired several officials from gendarmerie headquarters to teach Qing law at his school and paid them generously.

The Japanese model followed in Beijing had been originally borrowed from Europe by Meiji reformers attracted to the French and Prussian emphasis on a centralized, bureaucratic command system and to British reliance on community-based patrols and surveillance.[21] Lao She, in his novella portraying the life of a Beijing policeman, burlesques the police academy by having his narrator-protagonist ridicule his instructors as aged opium-smokers or young devotees of everything foreign.[22] To the young police recruit, lectures on Japanese police procedure and French legal codes may have seemed, as they do to Lao She's hero, irrelevant and un-Chinese. But it was the forced synthesis of theory and practice, foreign and Chinese ideas, and new and left-over personnel which made the training program and the new police workable and politically acceptable.

Prevailing social conditions provided reformers with a ready pool of applicants. The disordered nature of administrative life during the post-Boxer decade and uncertain prospects for career advancement convinced men with examination degrees to apply for police work.[23] Ordinary policemen were recruited largely from the ranks of bannermen. The Boxer disorders and the flight of the Court from Beijing had interrupted the payment of banner rations, and many young members of the hereditary warrior class were driven to police work by poverty.[24] Familiarity with strategies of social control, originally acquired through work as gendarmes, undoubtedly helped many banner recruits accept the new role of policeman. Ironically, but conveniently for Qing reformers, the disorders which the new police system was designed to deal with also pried loose from the existing bureaucracies, sinecures, and social structures the human material needed for the kind of institution-building Prince Su and Kawashima Naniwa had in mind.

A political crisis in 1905 gave new urgency to the police reforms. On August 26 a revolutionary threw a bomb at a party of government dignitaries at the Beijing train station. The officials escaped harm when the bomb went off prematurely. But the audacity of the attack alarmed the government. For a time, officials dared travel in the city only in the company of bodyguards.[25] Meanwhile, the wholesale dismissal of government employees for reasons of economy, and the end of the examination system in 1905, filled Beijing with discontented scholars and civil servants.[26] In an atmosphere of discontent, charged by the shock of the bombing attack, the central government showed a new interest in police reform. A central Police Ministry was established with Yuan Shikai's close aide Xu Shichang at its head. One thousand uniformed policemen from Tianjin were transferred to Beijing.[27]

Xu Shichang had no special expertise in police matters. But he recognized that in the past policemen had languished in lowly, even despised positions. Xu insisted that the policemen be paid regular wages and be treated on a par with other civil servants. He also emphasized the importance of strict discipline and the maintenance of high morale. This was the same formula British Home Secretary Robert Peel had used in the early nineteenth century to develop his "new police," or "Bobbies." Peel, like the Beijing police reformers, combined a pay scale comparable to that of an artisan with intensive discipline to mold a force attractive to status-conscious members of the laboring poor.[28] With Xu's support and Yu Lang's commitment to police professionalism, the police were kept within the civilian administration, paid decent wages, and accorded respect as officials.[29] Records from 1907 show the intensity of the consolidation program.[30] During the year, with 3,887 officers and men in the Inner City command, 1,980 fines were levied for internal offenses, 473 reprimands were issued, and 318 policemen were dismissed from the force. Offenses included falling asleep on duty, negligence, failures in reporting, failure to assemble quickly in time of fire or some other emergency, missing curfew at police dormitories, and drunkenness or opium intoxication. During the same period, 7,898 merit citations and monetary awards were handed out for "routine diligence," "extraordinary diligence," and injury or death in the line of duty. This made for an average of three rebuffs or awards per man for the year. As Peel's earlier exercise in police reform had demonstrated, this kind of obsessive concern for discipline was an important factor in building morale in an initially hostile public environment.[31]

One measure of the expanding power of the Beijing police in the last decade of the Qing was conflict in 1907 between the new police force and local magistrates.[32] The new police force had been given the power not only to make arrests but also to render judgments on minor civil and criminal cases.[33] The police could collect fines and impose short jail sentences. Officials who resented the intrusion of the police into their former jurisdictions wrote memorials complaining of the avarice and incompetence of the police.

Xu Shichang, in an extended reply to the charges, produced statistics that showed that crime had been dramatically reduced under the new system.

Not everyone was pleased with the expanding administrative presence represented by the modern police. Commenting upon the ingrained prejudices policemen faced, a Republican-era police officer noted that police in China were popularly thought of as "a body of vagrants contributing nothing to the welfare of the people." The word for police (*jingcha*) "was invariably associated with wild animals and poisonous snakes, deeply abhorred and avoided by the public."[34] As low-level functionaries, policemen invited comparison with the much despised *yamen* (government office) clerks and runners of imperial times, who routinely abused the power invested in them by magistrates and who were treated as outcasts on a par with actors, prostitutes, and beggars.[35]

In creating a modern Beijing police force after 1900, Qing officials, with the help of Japanese advisers, had broken with the *yamen*-runner past and laid the groundwork for an enduring local institution. The Beijing police, along with a large percentage of its original complement of officers and men, survived the 1911 Revolution, the early Republic, the failure of constitutionalism, warlordism, and the Northern Expedition. By the teens and twenties Beijing had earned the distinction of being "one of the best-policed cities in the world."[36] This reputation was based not on arrest records or skill at crime detection but on the "semipaternal way" in which police would "look after the city, settling little disputes that arise over collisions on the street, giving advice here and there." In addition to mediating disputes, controlling traffic, and fighting crime, the police also regulated all manner of economic, cultural, and political activities. The imperial gendarmerie had also taken order-keeping to include a range of tasks beyond the narrower mandate of crime prevention.[37] In displacing the gendarmerie, the Beijing police seem to have absorbed their predecessor's taste for a broad-gauged approach to the maintenance of order. Policemen enforced hygiene standards in the food businesss, made sure that public toilets were cleaned regularly, gave licensing exams to medical practitioners, regulated the storage in temples of coffins awaiting shipment back to the deceased's hometown or village, and tried to prevent the indiscriminate dumping of toxic or

contaminated waste.[38] Policemen censored public entertainments
and political expression. They supervised a variety of institutions
designed to administer to and control the city's poorest residents,
including soup kitchens, schools, reform schools, and workhouses.
After close study, the premier Western student of Beijing society
during the Republican period, Sidney Gamble, concluded that the
police were "responsible for most of the [governmental] work
done in the city and touch almost every side of the life of the
people."[39]

Recruitment and Deployment

By 1911, after a decade of development, the Beijing police department had acquired a fixed organizational structure with a headquarters and district and precinct offices throughout the city. By
the late teens, the force approached its earlier goal of 10,000 men
in uniform, or about 12 policemen for every 1,000 residents. This
ratio was extraordinarily high when compared with European
capitals like London, Paris, and Berlin, which employed only 2 or
3 per 1,000.[40]

Three or 4 percent of the force worked in the headquarters
office just inside Qian Gate, supervising special departments
directly attached to it and the district offices. The chief of police in
Beijing was a political appointee. In the late Qing and the early
Republic, the top official in the department often had police or law
credentials. In the course of the teens and twenties, the police chief
came to be selected from among the staff officers of whichever
militarist happened to control the city and environs. However,
most middle- and higher-level officers continued to be career policemen.[41] One-quarter of the police force staffed the special units.
These included a large paramilitary force, a police band, firemen,
mechanics, detectives, and the staffs of the police academy, poor-
houses, and jails. Over 70 percent of the force was assigned to
district- and precinct-level posts. At these levels, pay differentials
among officers, sergeants, and ordinary policemen were rather
small. In 1920 officers were paid $22 a month, sergeants, $11 to
$15, and patrolmen, $7 to $9.[42] This meant that the bulk of the
force lived at or just above the poverty line.

The original, and probably continuing, bias toward the selection of déclassé bannermen meant that in the 1920s upwards of three-quarters of the force had banner status.[43] Casting down on their luck, Manchus as policemen had fitted well with the Meiji-restoration atmosphere of the original Qing reforms. Most of Japan's first policemen were ex-samurai. The late-Qing banner-man certainly paled beside his fiercer samurai counterpart. But Beijing bannermen did have a residue of martial spirit, and they, like the samurai, were available for recruitment into novel ventures. Perhaps more important, bannermen had lived all their lives in Beijing and knew the city and its neighborhoods exceedingly well, as a good policeman must. Police status also helped arrest, or at least cushion, the social decline of the Manchus. The wages were poor, but by way of compensation, policemen received specialized training, a uniform, and the rank of civil servant. In status-conscious Beijing society these were significant concessions. The police recruit in Lao She's *My Life* admits that before he chose the job he had thought of being a policeman in terms of "pounding the macadam," joining the "stinking foot patrol," or becoming a "Grand Secretary for Avoiding Trouble."[44] But he did not want to be a rickshaw man. With a wife and two children and a temperament that was "cultured" rather than "savage," he thought that soldiering was too risky. He notes, not without irony, that considering that "neither my maternal uncle nor my elder sister's husband was a high official," a position as a policeman, being "neither high nor low" was not a bad bet. And one got to wear in the bargain a "brass-buttoned uniform" (fig. 9).[45]

The pattern of deployment of these poor and lower-middle-class individuals placed large numbers of officers and patrolmen in the neighborhoods and on the streets.[46] Photographs of Beijing street scenes from the early twenties show the systematic way in which policemen were stationed at their posts (figs. 10 and 11).[47]

Police Rhetoric and Practice

The deployment of Beijing policemen in the streets and neighborhoods of the city in proximity to the average resident represented a redrawing of the boundary line between state and society. But having arrived in his new, forward position, what was the policeman to do or say? He could enforce laws and regulations, levy fines,

Fig. 9. The genial expressions of these officers and men belie the stern image cultivated by the police department. Recruitment from the old banner units, a modicum of professional training, and the common task of order-keeping evidently promoted a sense of comradery. Courtesy of the Library of Congress.

and send miscreants to jail. Each district office had a lockup for short jail terms, and Beijing had a number of old as well as "model" prisons. But the success of the Beijing police was not based on a capacity to function as a conduit, drawing deviants and troublemakers into an ever expanding prison system. Rather, as many observers attested, the Beijing policeman's effectiveness depended on the way he used his authority to make convincing arguments on behalf of social order and civil peace.

The lectures given at the police academy contain a theory of police work, as well as specific examples of how these general principles related to conditions in Beijing. Presented during the formation and initial expansion of the police system, the lectures represented a commentary on reforms in progress.[48] They stressed

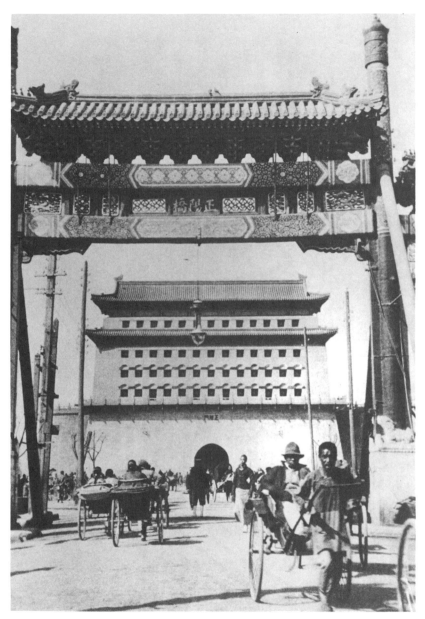

Fig. 10. The sturdy, broad-backed figure of a policeman parts the flow of traffic heading to and from Qian Gate. The gate is framed by a ceremonial arch from which an electric lamp is suspended. The arch marked the entrance to the commercial district outside Qian Gate. From Heinz v. Perckhammer, *Peking* (Berlin: Albertus-Verlag, 1928).

Fig. 11. A view looking south from Qian Gate over the roofs of Outer City shops and temples. Qian Gate, the ceremonial arch, and distant Yongding Gate (the middle of three gates along the south wall of the Outer City) line up perfectly with each other and suggest a subtle counterpoint of imperial plan to the jumble of buildings, streets, and lanes characteristic of merchant Beijing. At least six uniformed policemen are visible. One is standing at ease in front of a line of traffic signs and lanterns dividing the roadway. Two others are similarly posted in the middle of the street. Another is walking toward a colleague who is staring down a side street. The sixth stands on a sidewalk, craning his neck in the same direction. From Heinz v. Perckhammer, *Peking* (Berlin: Albertus-Verlag, 1928).

above all the anticipation and prevention of crime and disorder. From their posts and while out on patrol policemen were supposed to nip problems in the bud. "For example, Zhang kills Li. The injury has happened. Can one *then* protect Li and prevent Zhang from killing? Gentlemen! That is too late to protect anyone."[49] The emphasis was not on the use or threat of organized violence but on careful observation and information gathering, interpretation of law and custom, and timely intervention. The lecture drives home this point, quoting a line from the classics: "According to the sayings of the ancients, 'Although there are laws to govern by, I am afraid for the country if there are no men to do the governing.'"[50] The policeman was enjoined to govern not only by law but by virtue.

In accordance with his official status, the policeman was supposed to be serious in the midst of the freewheeling, often raucous atmosphere of Beijing streets and markets. "If you make jokes, you cannot govern the common people," observed the lecturer.[51] The policeman was supposed to have all the conventional virtues of prudence, frugality, and uprightness of character. The job of policeman also required the sensibilities of a Confucian scholar.

What sort of person is a policeman? He is a man of learning. A learned man is diligent night and day in accordance with his official responsibilities. A policeman is also sharp of eye and ear and quick-witted. When he comes across something, he can take one look and decide whether it is important or insignificant, trivial or weighty.

For example, if there were a group of people discussing how they were going to rob someone's house, evil intent is readily apparent. You must apprehend them and get to the bottom of the matter. . . . It is not a case where a few sentences of admonition are enough.

But suppose two people are walking down the street and because they are not careful one bumps the other and they start fighting. In this kind of situation do you immediately arrest them and send them to the station? No. . . . You can just admonish them not to fight.[52]

Clearly, the kind of learning required to make these distinctions has more to do with common sense than with scholarship. But the fact that practical problems are posed as tests of one's erudition reflects the general concern that policemen identify with the role of the learned official. Policemen were to act as modern day *junzi* (Confucian "gentlemen") and carry with them an air of moral authority.[53]

In a memoir of Beijing in the 1920s the scholar Yoshikawa Jojiro recalled an encounter with just such an individual.[54] An acquaintance of Yoshikawa's, who was visiting from Japan, was waiting one day for a streetcar at Dongsi Arch, a major intersection just east of the Imperial City. On impulse he went into a curio shop to browse until the streetcar arrived. While in the shop he accidentally broke a porcelain vase. The shop owner demanded compensation considerably in excess of what the pot was worth. The Japanese knew only a little Chinese and so he telephoned Yoshikawa and another friend for help. But when they arrived they too were unable to persuade the shop owner to lower his price. Finally someone suggested taking the matter to the police. Both parties agreed and they hired rickshaws to take them and the broken shards to the nearest police station.

The district headquarters was located in an old, courtyard-style mansion. The offices faced in on trees and a flower garden. The four men went into a waiting room. Presently a policeman appeared, puffing on a cigarette, and asked what they wanted. When they explained what the dispute was about, they were taken into an "investigation room." In the room, sitting behind a wooden podium, was an officer with short-cropped hair and clad in a Sun Yat-sen style of uniform. The officer was eloquent. He began by stating that "the task of the police is 'to mediate disputes.' In other words, our task is to resolve disputes, not entrap people in crime." Yoshikawa recognized the phrase "to mediate disputes" from *The Historical Records (Shiji)*. The officer went on to counsel both sides. "The ornament is, of course, worth a certain dollar value. The amount the curio dealer is asking is improper. But it was you who erred in breaking it. Shouldn't you pay a little above the market price to compensate the dealer for his hurt feelings?" The officer named an amount and asked both the Japanese and the merchant to "please accept" it. Both sides agreed and the dispute was settled. Writing years later, Yoshikawa recalled: "I was greatly moved by the incident. To this day I feel it. I remember the man in charge saying that his duty was 'to resolve disputes.' What moved me was not so much the quotation from the classics. It was the idea that the responsibility of the police was not to create bad feelings but to bring tranquility."

The imagery is certainly striking: chain-smoking cadre ensconced in an old mansion, dressed in modern uniform, weighing the facts of the case in a moral rather than a strictly legal manner, and quoting from the *Shiji*. The civility and skill he displayed may have been a function of the relatively trivial nature of the problem confronting him or a consequence of the foreign and upper-class status of the plaintiffs. But the incident also reflected the Beijing police force's commitment to a distinctive brand of public service, which stressed mediation and the artful maintenance of social peace.

Of course, the role of the policeman was defined not only by indoctrinated norms but also by specific rules and regulations. One set from the early Republic draws a harsh picture of life and discipline for ordinary members of the force.[55] The stress on a serious demeanor and attention to duty is similar to that of the academy lectures. But the tone is very different. Some of the rules appear to have been taken from a military manual. The policeman's uniform must be in order: no caps at angles, no underwear showing, and no collars or buttons left undone. Other rules have a more eclectic flavor. Policemen are ordered not to play with their weapons, curse, joke, or join in festive occasions while on duty. Nor is one allowed to sing opera, a favorite Beijing pastime, while at his post. The regulations represent another aspect of the policeman's role; he was the object of attempts by the larger organization to make him conform to rigid and easily evaluated standards of behavior. And yet both the academy lectures and the regulations display a common concern that the policeman be punctilious and respectable.

Although a public impression of uprightness was attractive in theory and practically suited to appeal to the moral sensibilities of Beijing residents, striking this posture also made policemen liable to mockery and intimidation. One spring evening in 1924 a policeman discovered two privately employed rickshaw men parked and blocking traffic outside a fancy restaurant. Inside, the rickshaw pullers' employer was entertaining friends at a banquet. When the policeman asked the laborers to move, they at first ignored him and then, referring sarcastically to his authoritative tone, said, "You don't imagine, do you, that just because you are 'wearing a tiger skin,' you will be able to take us to the Second District Station?" The policeman replied, "You needn't waste words on me. Public matters are properly handled by public officials (*guanshi guanban*). I have the legal authority of the police. If you don't follow orders, I will take you to the station." At that point the rickshaw men began cursing him. The policeman by way of reply grabbed the two men and pulled them into the restaurant. There he explained to the employer and his guests the "barbarous" way the pullers had behaved. The rickshaw men expected their employer to protect them; instead, after listening to the policeman, he replied, "My rickshaw pullers haven't got an ounce of good in them. They are wicked things. Please take them to the police station and fine them." [56]

As a practical matter and so as to maintain harmony, the policeman sought an accommodation with those he policed and overlooked petty offenses. This softness might easily earn the ire of legalistic superiors, whereas remedial toughness risked provoking citizen defense of customary practice. When in June 1921 a precinct sergeant named Chen was ordered by his district commander, Zhou, to investigate reports of illegal gambling in a railroad yard outside Xuanwu Gate, Chen contrived to find nothing amiss. Suspicious, Zhou sent Zhao Wenyuan, a plainclothes detective, to make a further investigation, and Zhao discovered a man named Wang Gan and four other workers gambling. He succeeded in arresting the five but was then set upon by a crowd of their co-workers. Zhao and a uniformed policeman who came to the detective's aid were beaten and had their arrest cords and whistles stolen. Wang Gan, the organizer of the gambling session, was so enraged at the interruption that he marched over to the local precinct station brandishing a shovel. While he cursed and threatened, the lone policeman in the station at the time remained inside and gently tried to persuade Wang to go away. Wang's indignant reaction suggests that he may have had an understanding, perhaps cemented by a small bribe, that the police would look the other way when he and his mates gambled. [57]

The status of policemen combined conflicting expectations as to what the policeman's role should be. Poverty, indoctrinated ideals, the instrumental demands of the organization, and popular views of police work all conditioned this social role. Like other government bodies in the 1920s, the police experienced protracted financial crises, which left the pay of officers and men in arrears for months. Cases of policemen caught stealing to feed their families or committing suicide in despair over their poverty testify to the kinds of pressures they fell under. [58] As a newspaper essayist noted, policemen seemed to be beset by troubles and pressures from all sides: "Generally speaking, being a policeman is bad. . . . [They] suffer indignities from above and are reviled from below. Being in between contending parties is a difficult situation to be in."[59] But then "being in between contending parties," forming a buffer between government and people, between rich and poor, and between quarreling groups and individuals, was one of the policeman's central tasks. Many policemen performed this task well. Others cracked under the pressure or gave in to the *yamen*-runner syndrome.

Precinct stations, which gathered basic information about neighborhoods, especially household registry data, and supervised the daily routine of postings and patrols, were the key units for holding policemen in position to play this buffering role. Lao She drew an evocative portrait of the role and attitudes of a good precinct sergeant in a cluster of residential compounds:

Sergeant Pai [Bai] was over forty years old. He was clean-shaven and looked energetic. He was very talkative. When he came to the houses of the families—when they fought or quarreled—he was able at the same time to scold them and pacify them. He could thus melt the big problems down to small ones and melt the small ones away. . . . He knew very well that his duties were heavy and great. If there are no police, there is no order, and although he was only sergeant of police for the Little Sheep Fold district, he felt that the whole of Peiping, more or less, belonged to him.[60]

The ideals expressed in the police academy lectures, and the pattern of the force's deployment, which placed policemen close to city people and their problems, encouraged individuals like Sergeant Bai to take an activist and paternalistic stance and resist the demoralization brought on by poverty and regimentation. Although men like Sergeant Bai may have taken an occasional bribe, petty corruption would not have necessarily diminished or negated their mastery of "human relations" (*renqing*) and their ability to mediate conflicts and dampen disorder. As long as policemen continued to venture outside district and precinct offices to take up their posts in fine weather and foul, minor deviations caused by conflicting official and community norms need not have undermined the order-keeping potential of the force. In fact, the success of the Beijing street policeman hinged on his ability to seek an accommodation between these cross-pressures.

Police Violence and Moral Theater

Given the degree of discretion intrinsic to the role of mediator or buffer, a policeman might abuse his power. Police brutality was a particular feature, as we have seen, of the relationship between policemen and rickshaw pullers. An extreme example took place one afternoon in February 1925 when a policeman accosted a rickshaw man who had just dropped off a fare.[61] The policeman shouted, "Get the fuck out of here fast. Don't you know you are blocking traffic?" The puller, who was still trying to catch his breath, replied angrily, "Let me tell you something. You don't scare me. I've done police work myself. I was a policeman for three years. I know the regulations. I parked my rickshaw on the proper side of the road. How is that blocking traffic?" The quarrel between the two became heated and a crowd gathered to watch. But, as the newspaper account of the incident lamented, the bystanders "looked on without even lifting a finger." Finally, in anger, the rickshaw man turned to grope in his rickshaw for a club he kept there. As he did, the policeman drew and raised his sword. When the rickshaw man whirled around, club in hand, the policeman struck the puller on the temple with his blade. The rickshaw man fell bleeding to the ground and died almost instantly. Horrified by what they had witnessed, the crowd turned and fled, with people crying out that a policeman had killed someone. A nearby patrolman and his sergeant heard the commotion and hurried to the scene, where they arrested the policeman. The local prosecutor's office was notified and it dispatched a special investigator. The police could not immediately identify the dead man. But the department announced that it would supply a coffin and pay the cost of the puller's funeral.

A rough sort of justice, or injustice, sometimes prevailed on Beijing streets. Policemen with clubs or swords at their waists faced rickshaw men who kept clubs in the trunks of their vehicles, groups of laborers willing to fight as gangs if provoked, students who fought for the right to present their views in public, the occasional common criminal armed with gun or knife, and most threatening of all, bands of armed soldiers accompanying sojourning militarists. On the other hand, the streets and public spaces of Beijing could also provide a congenial environment for confrontations in which policemen, willingly or not, played a central, mediating role. The success of the police depended, in part, on their ability to incorporate elements of moral showmanship into the actions they took. In Erving Goffman's terms, the policeman was called upon to devote considerable energy to "dramatizing" the role he played so as to "manage the impressions" he made on both miscreant and audience.[62] Since spectators and the accused were bound to have a strong sense of how a policeman as mediator or *junzi* manqué ought to behave, the patrolman filled a role "socialized" or "idealized" by public expectations.[63] Policemen who misbehaved, stood mute, or said the wrong things risked becoming the villain in these set-piece social dramas.

Thomas Metzger has described the traditional elite officialdom as staffed by both bad officials and "budding sages."[64] External incentives and disincentives restrained and punished the former, while government, as a field for moral action, provided opportunities for the latter. Police reformers in Beijing used the myth of government as a moral project, and policemen as *junzi*, to establish a police presence in the city with a minimum reliance on coercion and a maximum appeal to residents for active cooperation in maintaining social peace. A policeman completing a training course of only a few months could hardly replicate a lifetime of self-cultivation by a scholar-official. On the other hand, even in dilute form, the Confucianist mentality, with its inclination to scold, meddle, and mediate, inspired effective police work.

Paternalism, Patriarchy, and the Boundaries of Policed Society

At a minimum, policemen held the line against obvious threats to public order in the form of fights and open criminal activity. Ideally, they were also alert to opportunities to root out deviance and sustain a moral order. Policemen were taught to distinguish between people who were "patriotic, filial, and honest" and those who were "villainous and prone to robbery and licentious behavior."[65] If you suspected someone, you were to "watch his actions, listen to conversation on the street, note what people in his house are doing and what sort of friends and visitors he has." Telltale signs of suspicious activity on the street included people who concealed their faces, were not wearing shoes, who seemed to have something hidden in their clothing, or who traveled at night without a lantern.[66]

Policemen listened for the sound of fights and brawls.[67] They sniffed about residential compounds to ferret out opium use.[68] Policemen apprehended traffickers in untaxed liquor after being tipped off by the odor of a concealed shipment.[69] They uncovered fraud by street vendors who sold camel meat as beef.[70] Policemen functioned like sensors tuned to detect moral and social dissonance. Acute attention to the sensory experience of street and *hutong*, marketplace and courtyard life was part of a Beijing resident's ingrained sensibility. Since the typical policeman was a bannerman and thus the product of generations of family residence in Beijing, the police department enclosed a prodigious supply of these qualities, which could be drawn on in its surveillance and management of city life.

The police academy lectures stressed that attention to detail, and a policeman's ability to pick up cues from people's behavior, could sometimes be a matter of life and death.

If you see a woman running with hair all disheveled, her behavior is suspect. She might try to kill herself by hanging or by jumping in a river or down a well. Normal women comb and wash their hair and dress up. So if a woman is seen [behaving aberrantly], this is a sure sign that she is worried and angry. This is all very surprising. She wants to die. Why would this be?

It is some kind of madness. She has felt the anger of her in-laws. She and her husband had a fight. Or her husband is not successful enough. He does not understand her anxiousness and helplessness. Or she has somehow lost face. His family has been too strict with her and there has been a row. That sort of thing.

This kind of situation is fraught with danger. It is a job for the police. If attention is not paid, it might become a matter of life and death. There [recently] was a suicide attempt in the Imperial City. One evening in the bright moonlight inside Xian Gate, a woman was seen on the street scratching her head, [behaving] anxiously, and walking fast. Someone asked her what she was doing. She replied in a wild manner that someone was chasing her. Then she went off to Yuhe Bridge and drowned herself. *If there had been a policeman there*, that woman would not have drowned.[71]

In 1928 the *Metropolitan Police Gazette*, the official organ of the police department, reported with pride a case in which an alert policeman had jumped into a canal to save a woman who was trying to commit suicide.[72] When the police learned that her actions had been precipitated by an argument with her husband, the police summoned him to the station. The officer in charge lectured the couple and admonished them to be content with their lot and avoid future domestic quarrels. The case was a model of correct procedure and evidence of the value of both the police department's extensive presence in the city and its tutelary role. The police had been in the right place at the right time, had drawn the proper moral lesson, and by its own account, had restored harmony in the home.

Unfortunately, not every police intervention in family-related disorder ended so happily. We know that the practice of "arrest avoidance" in the case of domestic conflict and violence can perpetuate rather than resolve such strife.[73] A case in point transpired one autumn afternoon in 1920 outside the gate of a mansion near the center of the Inner City.[74] An altercation between a man and a woman attracted a crowd. The woman was weeping and had apparently been beaten. She directed a stream of accusations toward the man, who was her husband. She said he had no job and depended solely on her for income. She worked as a servant for the family residing in the mansion. Now the husband wanted money from her and had beaten her when she refused. She declared to her husband, and to the crowd, "I have never spoken angrily to you. But you still do not understand me. At night you go out eating, drinking, gambling, and whoring. You never even glance at your children. They are at home, cold and hungry. How can I give you money if you squander it?" The woman lost her voice momentarily from crying so much. Many of the spectators were weeping as well. But the husband, according to the press account of the incident, "laughed in a cold and frightening way." He told his wife that if she did not give him the money she would have to leave her job and return home with him. As the crowd grew larger, a policeman came forward and intervened.

The woman laid her case before the policeman. Repeating her grievances against her husband, she implored the policeman to "take responsibility and make a decision." The policeman responded by severely criticizing the husband for his behavior and ordering him to return home without his wife. Nearly all the elements of moral theater, the public dramatization of social norms and values, were present: eloquent plaintiff, a sympathetic crowd of "jurors," and a stern, censorious policeman. Unfortunately, the husband refused to play the role of chastened wrongdoer. He replied angrily to the policeman, "What do you know about my family affairs? Please stop bothering about matters that do not concern you. This is not the responsibility of the police." A more willful policeman might have pursued the issue, but in the face of the husband's obstinacy the patrolman allowed the matter to drop.

But the woman would not let things rest. She went on her own to the local precinct station to try to file a complaint. The officer in charge was unsympathetic. He told her that "this place does not handle that sort of thing. If you want a lawsuit, you must go to the *yamen*." He ordered the woman to leave. But she began to weep and said, "What *do* you handle then, if you don't handle this? My husband will beat me to death." The policeman replied, "When he beats you to death, then we'll deal with it."

Intervention in the dispute and attempted mediation by the police allowed the woman to plead her case and resulted in public criticism of her husband. But the police would go no further in helping her resolve the conflict or even take action to protect her from further beatings. Policemen were in fact instructed to stay out of family disputes unless "one of them picks up a knife" or otherwise created a life-threatening situation.[75] Normally, "if family members quarrel and come to blows, you must allow it to happen. It is of no concern to anyone else and has nothing to do with the police." The police academy lectures do not say how a policeman is supposed to know when domestic violence is about to turn lethal. If he was like Sergeant Bai, he bent or broke this rule and took a more activist stance in defusing family conflict. If he was like the precinct officer approached by the abused wife, he used the rule to justify his complacency. The Beijing police force was not designed to manage or police family affairs, even though placement of policemen on streets and in lanes and neighborhoods within hearing distance of households and with a general mandate to keep order made such a de facto extension of police control inevitable.

Paternalistic police practices reinforced patriarchal authority. In the absence of some other bone of contention, policemen, husbands, fathers, and fictive family heads, such as shop owners and guild masters, were natural allies in the maintenance of social order. When women fled the authority of their husbands, or apprentices the authority of their masters, policemen sought to block their escape. Shop owners could notify the police about escaped apprentices, and precinct stations would be alerted to be on the lookout for them.[76] Oftentimes, apprentices, who were forcibly returned by the police, had fled because they had been abused by their employers. In these cases, the police department used the opportunity to chide the master for maltreating the apprentice. In the process the police force advertised simultaneously its benevolence and its support for the prevailing social order.[77]

Police respect for the boundaries that surrounded family and shop angered liberal reformers, who would have preferred a more activist and interventionist role for the police in defending the rights and interests of the weak. One essayist condemned what he saw as a double standard applied in the policed and unpoliced realms of urban life.

If I hit someone, you pay attention. If I beat an apprentice, you do not. You are a policeman. You must allow shop owners to discipline and educate apprentices. . . . If I beat an apprentice on the street, that counts as a crime against your police code. Without exception, you will deal with me as an offender. But if in a shop I beat an apprentice, as the saying goes, "Households have a rod for punishing children and servants. Shops have shop rules." You have your police code. I have my shop regulations.[78]

The police patrolled the public realm (*gong*) between official (*guan*) and private (*si*) affairs. *Gong* was the zone within which officials and nongovernmental elites had traditionally shared responsibility for maintaining social peace. As government organs like the police became more intrusive, the relationship between official and nongovernmental actors within the public realm, on the one hand, and between public and private affairs, on the other, became ambiguous. Households and shops had their own regimes for "disciplining and educating" members and inmates. But this control function might also be handled in a relatively public fashion through the mediation of a local notable or a guild and thus invite official scrutiny or participation. The internal politics of self-policed institutions periodically produced "disorder," which spilled over into the realm of direct police control either because a crime was committed or because the disorder took place in public rather than within shop or compound walls.

The policeman's task was not to reform these private or public institutions but to control the deviance they generated. But by building up strength within the public realm and along the border between *gong* and *si*, the Beijing police found itself in the same position a reformist organization would have occupied. Beijing policemen were within a few steps of policing family and workplace. Closing the distance depended on personal inclination and the ability of individuals, such as battered wives and abused apprentices, to persuade policemen to intervene. The moralizing style of the police made bad behavior by husbands and employers subject to occasional scrutiny and censure. Nonconforming wives and apprentices felt the combined weight of police and private power.

Complicating the issue of the proper boundaries governing police work was the traditional involvement of private associations like *shuihui* in policing urban society in China. If Beijing's modern policemen threatened to tumble into household and workplace as they patrolled the streets and adjacent public places, Beijing's moneyed and propertied classes habitually adopted a forward defense of their interests by deploying guards, watchmen, and militia. Within the large districts blocked out by the broad avenues that crisscrossed the capital, the city's warrens of alleyways and the walled-courtyard and compound style of architecture contributed to the ease with which residents might defend themselves. In some neighborhoods, streets were closed off at night by locked pallisades. Keys to the gates were kept at local precinct stations as well as by residents.[79] In times of trouble a shop owner could station a couple of armed employees outside his establishment. Or a street of merchants could pool their resources to build barricades of wood or barbed wire or hire a few local martial-arts experts for extra protection.[80] Typically, these merchant militia (*shangtuan*) cooperated actively with the police. But in a sense they were also rivals. In one case, a merchant militia began issuing its members

uniforms closely resembling those of the police, and the department demanded that they be changed.[81]

Beijing Police Rhetoric and Ideology in Comparative Perspective

Allan Silver has written that "some modern nations have been
police states; all, however, are policed societies."[82] The change
from an "unpoliced" to a "policed" society took place in western
Europe and North America in the late eighteenth and the nineteenth century. In the West, the formation of a bureaucratic police
emerged in reaction to what Silver terms "cultures of riotous
protest." In Paris, London, and other great urban centers in the
eighteenth and nineteenth centuries, popular views and interests
were expressed through the medium of riot and insurrection.
The new police put distance between the propertied classes and
the political and criminal violence of the "dangerous classes."

Modern police forces were effective not only because of their
superior organization but also because of their appeal to a new
moral consensus that defined virtually all urban residents as
citizens and worthy of protection. The extension of police control
over everyday life coincided with the extension of core values into
the social periphery and subcultures of the city. European police
reformers stressed the importance of obtaining the "moral assent"
of city people if the new policing methods were to work.[83] A
purely organizational approach or one relying on simple coercion
would have been too expensive and provocative to sustain. And
so, "even the earliest policemen were elaborately instructed in the
demeanor and behavior required to evoke, establish and sustain
that assent." Peel's policemen were ordered to be "civil and attentive to all persons, of every rank and class" and counseled that
"there is no qualification more indispensable to a Police Officer
than a perfect command of temper."[84]

Beijing and other late-Qing and early-Republican cities produced riots and all manner of collective political action. But it cannot be said that these riots, strikes, and demonstrations amounted
to a "culture of riotous protest." In the West, police reformers
began by working with categories like "dangerous classes," which
reflected deep cultural and social separation, and ended by de-

scribing crime and urban violence as "deviance." Chinese police
reformers began by assuming that consensus was natural and
possible even in the turbulent context of city life and that deviance
was present as an inevitable undercurrent. The Chinese borrowed
organizational tables and the concept of police professionalism.
They did not have to borrow bourgeois notions of consensus and
deviance, the ideology and rhetoric that underlay a modern,
bureaucratically policed society. The Chinese had their functional
equivalent in Confucian precepts on moral display and the suppression of the heterodox.

Beijing policemen were supposed to be both acutely sensitive to
any hint of deviance and supremely confident in the depth of
popular attachment to moral and social order. A policeman was
properly offended by discordant sounds thrown out from the
tumult of street and marketplace. The police academy lecturer
reported, somewhat priggishly, that during a long walk through
Beijing, "Every step I took on road and lane filled my ears with
crude jests, defiant talk, atrocious speech, lewd words, and bad
language. . . . Even women and girls use these expressions."[85] In
keeping with the moral display attached to his position, the policeman was supposed to admonish people not to talk that way, and
to set a good example himself.

Still, some of the most important displays of moral consensus in
the Chinese city, such as festivals and rituals associated with family life, tended to use the noise and disorder of street and marketplace to enhance their appeal and meaning. The bureaucratic
policeman was imagined to need special instructions not to interfere with this kind of legitimate disorder. The police decreed that
there "shall be no loud singing of songs and operatic arias," which
disturb people's sleep. People sing and celebrate to express their
feelings and emotions. There is nothing wrong with that. But "if at
night you hear people singing opera or other songs without good
reason, or making a big racket, or striking gongs or drums and
blowing horns, or setting off firecrackers," you can order them to
stop. If they ignore the order, arrest them. The only exceptions are
during festival time (lunar new year and dragon-boat and mid-
autumn festivals) and the emperor's birthday, or "if a family has a
festive occasion or a funeral, or a baby is one month old, or a

member of a household takes a wife, or is betrothed, or receives companions to lodge for the night." In these cases it is perfectly all right to "celebrate by singing opera and other songs, setting off firecrackers, and blowing and drumming."[86] In other words, enforce the law except when it conflicts with or is overridden by customary practice. In fact, the singing, blowing, and drumming fireworks of Beijing's unpoliced realms of social action seem about to overwhelm the rather stiff and serious moral display of the bureaucratic and Confucian policeman. Administration and regulation is tempered by confidence in nongovernmental and nonbureaucratic forms of social control and in an underlying moral consensus, which extended, in the words of the academy lectures, from "the princes and nobles and greater and lesser officials down to the common people."[87]

In nineteenth-century Europe, in a context of riotous protest, police control and bureaucratic control in general were extended over daily life. "Street-level bureaucrats" broadened and deepened the base of state power.[88] No change that profound could go unchallenged. Regions, language groups, classes, and cultures rebelled against the degree of uniformity insisted upon in a bureaucratized, policed society. Typically, these rebels were either crushed or, paradoxically, made to fight battles to shape core values and control bureaucracy rather than reject outright the advance of modern organizations and ideas like the police. In early-twentieth-century Beijing, the extension of police control over everyday life was closely followed by a rejection of established values by radical nationalists, feminists, language reformers, labor unionists, and young people in general. In part this challenge was generated by the politics of unpoliced or weakly policed institutions, like the family, the shop, the factory, and the school. In part the challenge was a product of policing actions themselves. But even when Beijing residents resisted police regulation, the ability of a bureaucratic police force to influence the terms and locus of conflict—between state and citizen in proximity to residence and workplace—signaled a qualitative advance by the state into civil society. And while the prevailing orthodoxy was attacked, the categories of consensus and deviance, which are central to a policed society, found few traditional or modern challengers.

Repression and Mediation

"Special Police Laws for the Preservation of Order," promulgated in 1914, made virtually all forms of spontaneous political expression illegal.[89] According to these laws, one could not make a speech in a public place, hold a meeting concerning public affairs, or even put up a public notice without government permission. These laws were continually broken in the decade and a half to follow. New rituals, coalescing into a calendar of protest, threatened to overwhelm the bureaucratically policed sphere or realm. The pyrotechnics of the May Fourth era, including marching, haranguing, and pamphleteering instead of (or perhaps in addition to) singing, blowing, and drumming, set a pattern based on the breakdown of social controls and an appeal to a new moral consensus.

The police enforced laws and regulations vigorously enough to earn the enmity of a widening band of individuals and groups committed to freer expression. Chafing under the restrictions imposed by the 1914 laws, a Beijing publicist complained in 1925 that the

freedoms of speech, assembly, and association are entirely subject to the everyday control of the police. This is particularly the case in Beijing where in all these areas the policeman is the judge of whether something is legal or not. The police themselves can administer various kinds of punishments. As a result, encountering a policeman in the city of Beijing who "strictly upholds the law" is like being in a hell crawling with demons.[90]

This rhetorical flourish owes a debt to the equation of *yamen* and hell in the popular imagination. But in bureaucratically policed Beijing, the demons have swarmed out of the confines of official compounds and static garrison posts to make the entire city an inhospitable place for political activists.

Policemen likewise experienced intense pressure from politically conscious Beijing residents. New institutions like schools and factories produced whole classes of people who resisted police efforts to control or contain their collective energies. This conflict between "the police and the people" was most clearly evident in student politics.[91] During the movement phases of student politics police tried literally to contain student activists by surrounding the numerous school compounds scattered throughout Beijing. Students, sometimes armed with bamboo staves and sticks, would try to break out of police encirclements in order to reach political gathering places like Tianan Gate.

Political activists resented and resisted police-imposed limits on their activities. At the same time, reformers and revolutionaries saw other purposes to which police power could be put and accepted as a matter of course the basic notion of a policed society. Communist party founder Li Dazhao, for example, in a 1919 reformist tract on the need to improve conditions of city life in Beijing, called on the police to "better regulate" night-soil carriers, improve traffic control, and get beggars off the streets and into appropriate institutions.[92]

Communal and corporate resistance to intervention and regulation periodically challenged the force's bureaucratic coverage of the city and its moral pretensions. On the other hand, the internal politics of groups and institutions sometimes cracked the facade of solidarity presented to the outside world. On these occasions, one faction or another might invite the police into their common domain to settle a dispute. Even an individual policeman could be drawn into group conflict in such a way as to make intervention decisive to the side he favored.

One summer day in 1924 a woman named Zhang Lianshi and twenty other female workers blocked the gate to the compound of the canning factory where they worked.[93] The women denounced in strong terms to passersby the two labor bosses who had recruited them to work in the factory. Before long, a crowd of one or two hundred onlookers had gathered, and Sergeant Xu Liansheng arrived from a nearby precinct station to investigate. Speaking to Sergeant Xu and the crowd, Zhang Lianshi accused the two male labor bosses of sexual harassment, failure to provide separate toilet facilities in the compound for women, and forcing workers to labor overtime without compensation. During the course of Zhang's accusations, the women became so angry that Sergeant Xu was only narrowly able to dissuade the workers from taking immediate vengeance against the men. The policeman summoned the two bosses to the gate, where they admitted they were at fault and pleaded with Xu to devise a way of resolving the dispute. Sergeant Xu then went into the compound and made inquiries into the women's complaints. Finding support for their charges, Xu publicly denounced the bosses as "really bad" characters and asked the women whether they would accept mediation. The women refused and unanimously decided to go on strike and take the labor bosses to court. Sergeant Xu accompanied them to the district station to begin the proceedings. The workers' action, premeditated or not, succeeded in creating a disturbance sufficient to draw a crowd and, in turn, attract the attention of a policeman. In the resulting public discussion, with the policeman acting as mediator and street-corner magistrate, the women gained important leverage over their adversaries.[94]

The police force's field of control was centered in Beijing's streets and public places. Police were sometimes directed or drawn across the boundaries separating public and private realms in pursuit of order-keeping duties. Increasingly in the Republican city, the proliferation of groups and organizations resistant to social control based on interlocking networks of patriarchal elites made scrupulous observance of this boundary line difficult to justify in terms of practical police work. Professional association (*fatuan*) status allowed a limited number of officially chartered organizations like chambers of commerce to redraw the line around themselves to accommodate a mix of self-regulation and government control. But formally and informally, voluntarily and involuntarily, a much larger segment of urban society opened itself up to policing.

Groups could and did attempt to reverse this trend by closing themselves off again, especially when the intrusiveness and high cost of bureaucratic policing became apparent. High status and political connections might also shield one from police power. And the armed men who fought for control of Beijing were often able to defy police authority. Even Beijing's style of architecture, with its walled residences and compounds, conspired to screen out and wall off household and corporate life from outside scrutiny. Some classes, such as street workers who could only claim an absent master, and poor people who shared courtyard dwellings and lived in semipublic settings unprotected by gatekeepers, were more heavily policed than others. Nonetheless, bureaucratically deployed and supervised Beijing policemen could only be deflected and held off by a counterforce directed against this new vector of state power. In this manner, the coercive and regulatory apparatus of the state edged imperceptibly closer to the average citizen even as state power at the national and regional levels lapsed into decay and disorder. Conflict within compound walls, as well as extramural politics on the part of politically conscious groups, opened up new lines of communication, authority, and influence between state and civil society.

Paying the Price of Bureaucratic Expansion

Philip Kuhn accounts for the poor quality of the late-imperial "sub-county control apparatus," or the services rendered by *yamen* clerks and runners, by arguing that "they could be effectively disciplined neither by bureaucratic accountability (since they did not have regular bureaucratic status) nor by intimate or regular relationship to the natural units of local society. Hence they formed in effect a local interest group oriented solely toward its own enrichment."[95] Qing reformers attempted to solve this problem in Beijing by giving policemen bureaucratic status as officials. As long as policemen were paid regularly and the citywide network of district and precinct offices remained intact, the potential for avarice and dereliction of duty was curtailed.

This radical expansion of local officialdom was a bold and expensive stroke. The budget of the Beijing police department was on a par with a regular national ministry in the 1920s (between 165,000 and 200,000 yuan a month). Insolvency on the part of the national government shifted the burden of paying for the police onto the city itself. At first, budgetary shortfalls were met by contributions from bodies like the chamber of commerce and the bankers association. These organizations relied on the whole city's being orderly and appreciated the value of a policed society. Unpaid policemen, like unpaid soldiers, could themselves constitute a threat to local order by striking or rioting. On one occasion in the 1920s, Beijing policemen demonstrated for back pay and, on another, went on a one-day strike.[96] More troubling to the average resident or shopkeeper were the effects of months without pay on police morale. At one point in 1923 the police were rumored to be ready to strike and "without the strength to arrest" anyone.[97]

Financial exigiency meant months without regular pay for police. Food rations, constituting a bit less than half of a patrolman's monthly pay, could continue to be distributed only by drawing on funds for other police-sponsored activities, such as soup kitchens.[98] Loss of revenues at the headquarters level forced decentralization of finances to the district level, where local officers had to seek contributions from moneyed and propertied individuals and groups within their jurisdictions. As an economy move, in 1924 police headquarters issued a directive ordering districts to resolve petty cases on their own and report their disposition to the center.[99]

After several unsuccessful attempts (in 1915, 1921, and 1924) to institute a municipal tax to pay police expenses, Zhang Zuolin's regime put a house tax into effect in 1927. By then there was little opposition. Perhaps the harshness of Zhang's rule discouraged dissent. But that cannot be the whole explanation, because Zhang's attempt to impose a "luxury tax" for his own use in 1927 and 1928 met with bitter and partially successful opposition from the merchant community.[100] At first the house tax, which was on renters rather than on owners of houses and shops, produced only a small percentage of the revenue needed. And so in March 1928 the rates were raised and more tax categories were added. With the new rates, and an apparent reduction in passive resistance, the amount collected jumped to $115,000 a month.[101] With the house-tax receipts, $25,000 from a livestock-slaughtering tax, and revenue from miscellaneous taxes on theatergoing, prostitution, vehicle registration, and tobacco and other goods and services, the police department became practically self-sufficient. This final, if grudging, willingness to pay taxes to support the police signified wider acceptance of bureaucratic police control among the general public.

The survival of the Beijing police force as an institution closely resembling the one designed by its founders was due to more than the simple extension of bureaucratic organization to a realm once occupied by *yamen* runners. Beijing also established an intimate and regular relationship with the natural units of local society: neighborhoods, residential compounds, shops, and the street. This close contact was a product both of professional indoctrination and of community demands and expectations concerning public leadership. Confucian rhetoric and values turned out to be practically suited to modern police work. Emphasis on moral display and cultivation reinforced the self-esteem and professionalism of the déclassé Manchus who made up the bulk of the force. The stress on discussion and mediation rather than on simple coercion made it easier for the police to achieve rapport with the neighborhoods and groups they administered. Residents contributed moral and material support in return for predictable intervention by the police in their affairs in line with prevailing community standards.

In the urban community, policemen faced competing forms of activism, as well as simple acceptance and outright resistance. By the late nineteenth century, as the history of the *shuihui* suggests, the realm of public affairs was already a rich medium for the evolution of local varieties of public leadership.[102] The twentieth-century expansion of political participation left the public realm crowded with new leaders and constituencies. An important current in this intensification of community politics was a "self-image of public responsibility—a sense of service or 'cadredom'—which characterizes local leadership in Chinese culture."[103] This quality of cadredom was pursued aggressively by the Beijing police and formed a connecting bridge between traditional ideas about good government and contemporary demands for new, more comprehensive public services. Beijing policemen followed the dictates of a public-service ideology. At the same time they imitated the public posturing and role aggrandizement of other community activists.

Five

Jeweler, Banker, and Restaurateur: Power Struggles in the Beijing Chamber of Commerce

As order-keepers, policemen worked the streets and adjacent public and private spaces with enough diligence to create a "policed society" within the larger urban world of Beijing. Their success in this endeavor owed a great deal to direct and tacit alliances with others who had a stake in the maintenance of order. Residents, with varying degrees of enthusiasm, accepted police authority and mediation and paid a "police tax." This did not mean, however, that a near-consensus on the need for an orderly city automatically produced common agreement on what rules and standards should apply in areas like political expression, family conflict, or labor unrest.

In defining the real dimensions of public order, the police shared the roles of arbiter and enforcer with other organized groups in Beijing society. The traditional practice of ceding considerable power in managing local affairs to nongovernmental elites and groups like merchants and guilds and the modern idea of assigning the task of self-regulation to officially chartered organizations like chambers of commerce encouraged the idea of shared responsibility for public order. While the police sought to administer the city, organizations representing merchants, lawyers, bankers, students, workers, and other groups attempted to police their own ranks and influence the behavior of other groups, including the police. In this politically complex, pluralistic process, the Beijing chamber of commerce played a critical role in handling a range of issues related to public order, from welfare policy to city planning.

Both the police and the chamber of commerce sprang from the same New Policy reforms, and both represented a reordering of official and public affairs. The police extended the official realm well into the public life of the city and to the edge of private institutions. Through participation in the chamber of commerce, private and corporate interests found a formal place on the margin of official power. The New Policies not only generated local institutions that survived the 1911 Revolution and shaped the urban order of the 1920s; they also set in play rival interests and competing principles of governance. Conflict and cooperation between individual policemen and shopkeepers over issues like the treatment of apprentices coincided with conflict and cooperation between police chiefs and chamber of commerce presidents at the citywide level.

Administration and representation need not be mutually exclusive. The policeman as street-corner magistrate might represent the interests of an individual or a group. Chamber of commerce officials, as we shall see, sometimes sought to enforce their policies against the opposition of members. In a more general way, administration and representation might be bridged through the medium of an elected city council or a mayor. In Beijing in the 1920s the absence of an elected municipal government enhanced the importance of corporate representation. The chamber of commerce and similar organizations, ranging from bankers associations to student federations, could claim to speak for otherwise unrepresented members and the larger public. The quest for power and influence in city life could be served by winning control of nongovernmental, citywide offices like the chamber presidency. As a result, chamber of commerce politics, and kindred struggles within other professional associations (*fatuan*), federations, and unions, came to embody city politics in the same way that the police department appeared to many as an avatar of city government.

The Origins of the Beijing Chamber

The Beijing chamber was organized in 1907, five years after a Qing reformer and industrialist pioneered the idea in Shanghai and at a time when over 150 cities and towns in China were accomplishing the same feat of imitation.[1] The Qing government evidently hoped that an empirewide network of chambers of commerce would both encourage economic elites to identify their interests with those of the state and provide a means of exerting greater control over economic affairs.[2] Chambers of commerce appeared to be cost-effective instruments for extending administrative reach. Merchants would regulate themselves and support regime initiatives in areas like economic development and order-keeping while the government provided guidance and an aura of legitimacy. As Susan Mann has recently suggested, this attempt to give power and take control at the same time is "somewhat puzzling" unless one keeps in mind the long tradition in China of merchant self-regulation and civic activism.[3] As William Rowe has demonstrated in his study of the great commercial center of Hankou in the nineteenth century, wealth, social connections, civic consciousness, and guild organization could give merchants de facto control over the management of city affairs even as imperial officials retained formal hegemony.[4] Chambers of commerce in theory formalized this power while reinforcing merchant dependence on the bureaucracy for legitimacy and guidance.

Most chambers did begin by acting as if they were "part of the machinery of government."[5] But in modernizing cities like Shanghai merchants and businessmen soon used the new organization to advance their own interests. In smaller, inland cities, chambers were slower to free themselves from official control.[6] As Marie-Claire Bergère notes, "In the conduct of daily affairs businessmen went out of their way to obtain the goodwill of officials so essential to the success of their enterprises."[7]

Beijing merchants, too, were inclined toward accommodation with, even subservience to, official power. As economic elites in an inland, administrative city, they were on a slower track toward class consciousness and political independence than their counterparts in Shanghai, Guangzhou, and Hankou. Reflecting the merchant community's deference toward official and gentry leadership, the Beijing chamber had degree-holders and expectant officials as its founding officers.[8] In an early drive to raise funds for construction of a new chamber building, several modern-style banks, including the Bank of Communications and the Imperial Bank of China, and the newly formed, officially backed Beijing

Waterworks joined the silk, cloth, shoe, pastry, and other established guilds in making substantial contributions.[9]

Within a year of the chamber's founding, members had agreed to construct a thirty-two-room headquarters building designed to house a central meeting hall as well as smaller side rooms for guild meetings.[10] The undertaking was justified on the grounds that temporary residence in a hostel or guild deprived the organization of a firm claim to public (as distinct from official or private) support and a stately presence consistent with the chamber's status.[11] The new chamber building was located in the Outer City at the intersection of the main avenue leading south from Qian Gate and east-west–running Xizhushi Street in the heart of the Beijing business district. (See figure 11 for a view of the business district outside Qian Gate.) The location contrasted with the trend by modern banks and utilities to open offices clustered near government buildings inside Qian Gate, in the Legation Quarter, or in the eastern district of the Inner City. The chamber's intended function as a bridge between government and business, and its apparent role as mediator between modern and traditional enterprises, had not lifted it out of the city's traditional merchant core.

The formalization and professionalization of local leadership groups through the granting of *fatuan* status left local elites in an uncertain position. They were dependent on the government for their formal authority and were subject to bureaucratic supervision.[12] And yet as the Qing weakened and local elites joined preexisting bodies, like guilds, to citywide or province-wide organizations, like chambers of commerce, these bonds of dependence were loosened or severed. In the 1911 Revolution, chambers of commerce in Hankou and Shanghai actively supported the revolutionaries.[13] Elsewhere chambers mediated between rebel forces and the Qing government.[14] And in most cases local chambers of commerce were actively involved in shaping the immediate postrevolutionary order.[15]

In Beijing the 1911 Revolution brought accommodation rather than conflict between officials and merchants. One of the Qing regime's last acts, as the Wuchang rebellion spread from city to city in October, was to loan Beijing merchants, through the offices of the chamber, 1,150,000 taels to quiet the city's panicky money and commodity markets.[16] The Ministry of Interior called the chamber leadership in to outline the steps necessary to restore order, and the Ministry of Finance disbursed the money. While many of its sister organizations were expending energy and funds to topple the regime, the Beijing chamber was earning dividends on its political connections to the collapsing political center.

The merchant classes in cities as diverse as Beijing and Shanghai reacted to the political opportunities and dangers created by the Qing-Republican transition in very different ways. But in all cases, whether they acted as insurgent, mediator, or licensed agent of the state, chambers of commerce displayed the pivotal importance of *fatuan* as representatives of urban elites in general and the merchant class in particular. What chambers and other *fatuan* could not do was dictate terms to old or new power-holders. In the months and years immediately following the 1911 Revolution, the promise of extensive local elite influence in the new regime faded as businessmen and politicians quarreled over money matters, and merchants found it difficult to extend their power beyond the local level. Even the brief Nanjing regime, which was bankrolled by Shanghai business interests, excluded businessmen from high office.[17] Its successor in Beijing under Yuan Shikai was further hardened against pressures by *fatuan* struggling to behave as interest groups. In Beijing, merchants suffered the rudest possible reminder that in politics, as Thomas Hobbes observed, clubs are trump. In 1912, in an apparently calculated move associated with Yuan's campaign for the presidency, troops rioted and looted the city's business center.

The Rise and Fall of An Disheng

Through the mid-teens the Beijing chamber of commerce maintained a passive, dependent relationship with political authority. The rapid succession of Yuan Shikai and his regime to power left only the smallest window for the assertion of merchant interests. In 1915 when Yuan attempted to make himself emperor, the president of the Beijing chamber played the role of courtier in the royalist cause.[18]

Three years later the Beijing chamber appeared to abandon its subservient posture. Under the leadership of a jeweler named An Disheng, the chamber challenged the regime on grounds of both foreign and domestic policy. Merchants participated in the student-led May Fourth Movement and resisted government financial policies, which were playing havoc with local money

Fig. 12. Jeweler An Disheng (left) wears government orders of merit that represent decades of public service under both empire and republic. His open expression bespeaks his straightforward, principled approach to politics. Banker Zhou Zuomin (right) was An's nemesis in chamber politics. A generation younger that An and a man whose fortunes rose as the financial structure of Republican politics became more complex, Zhou favored subtlety and indirection in his political dealings. From *Who's Who in China* (Shanghai: The China Weekly Review, 1931).

markets. In the course of strengthening the chamber as a citywide organization, An Disheng not only broke with the past policy of appeasing government officials. He also brought to the surface latent tensions within the chamber between those who favored citywide association and representation for economic elites and those who felt threatened by this mobilization process.

In 1918, the year he first won election to the chamber presidency, An Disheng was fifty years old (fig. 12). Born in Xianghe county, south of Beijing, An received a classical education, passed the official examinations, and in 1902 was appointed to a position in the prestigious Hanlin Academy.[19] Two years later the Qing government designated him an "expectant magistrate" in Shuntian prefecture, the twenty-county area surrounding and including Beijing. After the 1911 Revolution he held a number of elective and appointive offices. He was a member of an advisory committee on municipal affairs, and in August 1918, while president of the Beijing chamber, he was elected to the prefectural assembly. In 1934, seven years after An had left Beijing to return to his home area, he was chosen magistrate of Xianghe.

An Disheng was one of the founding members of the Beijing chamber of commerce and the director of a commercial exhibition hall. By associating himself with New Policy reforms, An made the transition to the Republican period with status and position intact. In this regard, An was not unlike other individuals who attached themselves to late-Qing modernization projects, ranging from the chamber and police force to national-level ministries and armies. Under An's leadership the jewelry guild grew in size throughout the teens and twenties even as other segments of the precious-metals sector, like gold shops, declined in number and importance.[20] An enameling process invented by An Disheng aided in the production of luxury goods attractive to both foreign markets and the new Republican elite.

Led by An Disheng, the chamber put pressure on the government and two financial institutions with strong ties to the government —the Banks of China and of Communications—to take action to control the issue of paper notes in the local money market. Several Beijing banks had been licensed by the government to issue paper money. In 1916 the Banks of China and of Communications unilaterally stopped redeeming their notes in silver. In the resulting financial panic, farmers, leery of being paid in unstable currency stopped bringing food into the city.[21] In 1918 the Beijing chamber petitioned the government to redeem the notes with government bonds and make a public bonfire of the depreciated paper outside Tianan Gate.[22] The government refused and the notes continued to depreciate. By December 1919 the value of the notes had fallen below 50 percent. The government blamed speculators. The chamber of commerce blamed bank officials. At a special meeting of the chamber, merchants passed resolutions threatening to file suit against the top officials of each of the two banks unless they took steps to redeem the notes.[23]

Simultaneously, An Disheng led the chamber in an attack on the government's supine role at the Versailles Peace Conference. The day after the May Fourth student protests began, An Disheng convened a special meeting of the chamber to discuss the foreign policy crisis and send a circular telegram to other chambers, calling for a common patriotic front.[24] When the chamber met two weeks later to consider a boycott against Japanese goods, An spoke in favor of economic sanctions and fines against those who violated the ban.[25] In a proposal obviously colored by his own experiences in facing Japanese and foreign competition in the cloisonné trade, An proposed that a society to promote national products be established in Beijing. Merchants like An Disheng who were modern in their political outlook and commercially sensitive to foreign competition anticipated and then responded with alacrity to the nationalistic rhetoric of the May Fourth Movement. Merchant-gentry elites like An who had once followed the lead of the Qing and Republican governments as a matter of prudence and status affinity now saw in regime policy betrayal of the nationalist agenda they had originally adopted at the encouragement of official Beijing.

Only 17 percent of Beijing's over 25,000 commercial establishments belonged to the chamber as individual members or through guild affiliation.[26] Although the body grew in size and inclusiveness in the 1920s, it always remained a minority within the larger merchant community. Since the chamber represented a merchant constituency larger than its actual membership, a chamber leader like An Disheng faced multiple audiences for his policies, spreading out in concentric circles from a core of guildsmen and business professionals to a much larger number of small traders and shopkeepers (figs. 13 and 14). Each member trade, guild, or enterprise sent from one to eight delegates to chamber meetings. Certain categories like banks and companies were allowed to exceed these customary parameters. Only these several hundred representatives were allowed to vote for directors and hold office. Only directors elected the president and vice-president. Elections were supposed to take place every two years. However, because of resignations and scandals, a total of ten elections were held from 1920 through 1929.[27]

Guild or group membership in the chamber did not guarantee

Fig. 13. A small grain and vegetable store. The store front is designed to be shuttered at night and open to extend shop activity out into the street during the day. Laborers are unloading beans outside while colleagues work in the dark, windowless interior. Shops like this one typically bought goods from specialized brokers and in turn sold small stocks to street vendors and to the general public. As a result, a given trade in vegetables, grain, pork, or other commodity might include several levels of wholesale and retail exchange, each with its own formal or informal organization. Courtesy of the Library of Congress.

representation on the board of directors. Even groups with large delegations could not be sure, even by block voting, that one of their number would get on the board. The cutoff point for election as a director varied, but it was never less than forty votes. In 1918 modern bankers had thirty representatives, but not one banker was elected a director. To be elected, representatives had to appeal for support beyond their own group or guild. And to be reelected again and again one needed a special kind of prominence or popularity.

An Disheng easily won reelection as chamber president in February 1920 and allowed deputations of chamber directors to

Fig. 14. This peanut and candy vendor, having bought his goods at an early morning, open-air market near one of the city's gates, sold from street to street and lane to lane. Depending on size of operation, street vendors and peddlers played the role of petty trader or self-employed worker. Unlikely to be represented directly through guild or chamber of commerce, such individuals still needed to be attentive to issues basic to the merchant community, such as taxes, public order, and currency fluctuations. Courtesy of the Library of Congress.

persuade him to accept a second term.[28] He appeared to be riding the crest of popular support in the chamber for his handling of the bank crisis and the May Fourth Movement. President An had also modernized the chamber's staff organization, repaired the headquarters building, opened a commercial library, offered evening classes for members, carried out price surveys, and used the media to promote issues of concern to merchants.[29] An's record as civic leader and urban manager and his performance as merchant politician seemed unassailable.

Yet less than one month after his triumphant reelection, An Disheng suffered the public humiliation of arrest and imprisonment on charges of misappropriation of chamber funds. On March 6, police investigators accused An, his vice-president Yin Haiyang, and the chamber's thirty-year-old accountant of embezzling a portion of the money collected to repay the 1911 silver loan. Yin, who was leader of the wholesale coal-dealers guild, faced the additional charge of opium possession.[30] An Disheng quickly discovered, if he did not know already, that his activism had earned him enemies. A long list of organizations, groups, and individuals had mobilized against his leadership to precipitate his arrest, cause his ouster as president, and profit from his misfortune.

An Disheng's criticism of the government's foreign and economic policies marked him as an opponent of the Anfu-clique-dominated government.[31] As the Republic entered the first phase of warlord politics, competing factions of militarists, bureaucrats, and politicians, like the Anfu clique, scrambled for the power that Yuan Shikai had amassed before his death. In 1919 the government had unsuccessfully tried to unseat the president of the Tianjin chamber because he had been active in leading his city's merchants in the May Fourth Movement.[32] By An's own account he had challenged "Anfu's entrenched and swelling power" during his first term and had suffered the consequences when his "simple and upright temperament"compelled him to speak out against the "traitorous cliques" that had betrayed the nation.[33]

An's campaign against speculators and bank officials threatened banking interests, which profited from the government's disorderly fiscal and monetary policies. After An and Yin were deposed, their positions were filled by bankers. President Yuan Baosan was an old-style banker who owned a gold and silver shop.[34] While some old-style bankers may have looked favorably on An's attempts to stabilize the local money market, others surely were involved in speculation. Vice-President Zhou Zuomin was a member of the Communications clique which controlled the Bank of Communications.[35] He was also a protégé of Cao Rulin, one of the principal popular villains in the May Fourth Movement.[36] Yuan and Zhou were reputed to be "the most powerful figures in the Beijing money market."[37] Because of Zhou's connections to national-level politics and the Banks of Communications and of China, a local journalist concluded that the leadership change meant that whereas the An and Yin administration had been "purely merchant" in character and "without the slightest bureaucratic odor," the chamber now had come "under bureaucratic direction."[38] Bankers and officials had frustrated An Disheng's attempt to chart an independent course for merchants in a city "clotted with government and crowded with bureaucrats."

The police who arrested An and Yin were part of this hovering assembly of bureaucrats. The department was also party to the controversy surrounding the 1911 silver fund. Repayment of the Qing loan had been deferred by the Republican government because of the devastation wrought by the troop riots in 1912.[39] Beijing merchants had returned part of the money in 1915, and in 1919 they had come under renewed pressure from the government to complete repayment.[40] The police had won approval from the Finance Ministry to use the fund to establish a charitable factory for poor people. Specifically, the predominantly Manchu force planned to use the project to help impoverished bannermen.[41] Building new factories for the city's poor would have also added to the police department's growing network of welfare institutions and services. In addition, An Disheng alleged that Police Chief Wu Bingxiang had a grudge against him because of An's May Fourth activism and Wu's membership in the Anfu clique.[42]

While the government, the police, and the bankers were predisposed to act against An and his associates, the timing of the arrests was linked to guild denunciations of An's policies and the personal animosity of a key chamber director. Evidence made public at An Disheng's trial showed that he had used money collected to repay the 1911 loan to finance routine chamber expenses and his special projects.[43] Although a court eventually found An and the others innocent of charges of having personally profited from this creative accounting practice, monies earmarked for retirement of the chamber debt had in a sense been misappropriated. It is small wonder that the police arrested An, Yin, and their accountant on the spot when they discovered that a portion of the funds they coveted had been temporarily reallocated. The police already suspected that something was amiss because guilds belonging to the chamber had earlier written to the authorities complaining of wrongdoing.[44] Following a pattern pioneered in the May Fourth affair when press leaks had been used to criticize the regime's negotiating position in Paris, the guild charges had also been passed to the newspapers.[45]

Police representatives had been invited by director Gao Delong to visit chamber offices on the day the arrests took place.[46] Gao had been serving as director and "settling accounts officer," the officer in charge of insuring that debts and obligations owed by and to the chamber were paid at the three major yearly festivals in accordance with customary business practice. Prior to his reelection, An had ruled that, based on chamber of commerce regulations banning officers and directors from serving more than two consecutive terms (article 24), Gao would have to step down. This rule was sometimes waived, and An Disheng's legalistic and formalistic stance, which was consistent with his character and approach to public affairs, apparently infuriated Gao.[47] Perhaps Gao felt that President An should have been at least as scrupulous in his approach to bookkeeping. Gao Delong devised a trap for An. He informed the police, who had been given permission by the Ministry of Finance to take possession of the 1911 fund, that the money was ready to be picked up, even though that obviously was not the case. As a result, the police arrived at chamber headquarters on March 6 primed with suspicions planted by rumor and guild complaints, as well as with expectations raised by Gao and the Finance Ministry. They were unlikely to be put off by An's protestations of innocence.

After the arrests, An's supporters, especially fellow jewelers and merchants from his home county of Xianghe, tried in secret meetings to organize member guilds of the chamber to go on strike in protest.[48] But An's friends were rebuffed by the guildsmen. They complained that An had behaved dictatorially as president by monopolizing chamber affairs and that the arrests had nothing to do with the interests of the merchant community as a whole. Even merchants who were not chamber members but who had a bone to pick with An joined the attack. Three weeks after the arrests, seventy of the city's brothel managers petitioned the police, accusing An of embezzling $4,000 in contributions from the brothels, intended to pay for road repairs in the "flower market" quarter and collected by the chamber for that purpose.[49]

An Disheng's considerable power and influence, which had radiated out from the president's office toward the government,

the police, and other *fatuan*, and into the chamber and the larger
merchant community, suddenly collapsed as lines of influence
became lines of attack and his adversaries drove him back to
the narrow base of home guild and home county. An had helped
redesign the chamber as a more efficient vehicle for antiregime
nationalism and the articulation of merchant interests. This brave
attempt impressed his fellow chamber members and earned him
praise from the liberal press. But his activism must have also made
his more cautious colleagues nervous. They identified dependence
mixed with a measure of self-regulation and autonomy as the key
to maintaining order and profits. Once An Disheng came under
attack, pride in his accomplishments yielded to trepidation in the
face of Anfu power and to irritation at the costs and dangers
associated with An's activist policies and energetic style of leadership.

In the summer of 1920, as An Disheng and his two fellow defen-
dants languished in jail, the Anfu clique was defeated in the brief
Anfu-Zhili war. The change of regime meant that An's case would
be heard in a context sympathetic to his contention that he was the
victim of a politically inspired frame-up. By August, An, Yin, and
the accountant had been tried and acquitted of the charges of
misappropriation.[50] As one journalist noted, "judicial circles were
no longer restrained by power considerations."[51] The former vice-
president, Yin Haiyang, was fined eighty dollars for opium-related
offenses. The local press, emboldened by the altered political
climate, portrayed An's arrest as the product of scheming bureaucrats and militarists.[52]

Following his acquittal, An Disheng began campaigning for his
return to office and the removal of bankers Yuan Baosan and
Zhou Zuomin. He sent a circular telegram to assemblies, associations, and chambers throughout the country, proclaiming his
innocence.[53] An Disheng pictured himself as a reformer who had
suffered as a direct result of his attempts to break with the corrupt
and politically subservient practices of the past. He argued that
ever since chambers of commerce had been created by the Qing,
merchants had followed the lead of the government without ever
looking at things from the standpoint of "group autonomy" (*tuanti zidong*).[54] This state of political dependence had changed in recent years "as knowledge progressed." But "minority elements" in

the chamber, in alliance with "traitorous cliques" in the government, had sought to undo the enlightened and independent policies championed by An. "What does the law have to say? What does public opinion have to say?" he concluded.

An and his supporters generated enough pressure to cause Yuan and Zhou to submit their resignations in February 1921.[55] But the chamber directors, who within the past year had with near unanimity elected An and Yin, deposed An and Yin, and elected Yuan and Zhou, could not come to a consensus on whether to accept the resignations. And so An's initial attempt to win back the presidency failed. As Yuan and Zhou must have known, resigning was one of the most effective ways to defend their positions. The act simultaneously raised the specter of a leaderless, and potentially disorderly, merchant community and a return to An's confrontational policies.

While Yuan and Zhou had sought to ignore or circumvent chamber rules and procedures, they had not been insensitive to guild prerogatives and interests. When two directors resigned for health reasons, Yuan and Zhou had encouraged the guilds the two men came from to pick replacements.[56] This ad hoc procedure violated the rule that directors were elected from delegates to the chamber as a whole rather than selected to represent individual guilds. Having come to power as a result of individual guild opposition to An Disheng's chamber-wide and community-wide style of leadership, the bankers appeared willing to accept a system of representation that guaranteed each guild a director. Critics of Yuan and Zhou charged that this concession to guild autonomy masked a weakening of the chamber board of directors as a decision-making body. Yuan and Zhou were accused of attempting to establish an eight-man executive committee to administer chamber affairs.[57] Instead of a strong leader accountable to a large and politically attentive directorate responsive in turn to a mass constituency, the chamber would operate at its center more like a modern business grafted onto an old-style guild federation. A small board controlled by managing officers would handle the interests of an alliance of guilds formed in the traditional manner. This fusion of modern administrative practice and a traditional style of representation promised a depoliticized, conservative chamber receptive to administrative pressure.

The new system had not been instituted formally in 1920, because the guilds and the bankers could not agree on how many seats on the board would be allocated to banking interests. The original proposal, which emerged during the interregnum between the arrest of An and Yin and the election of Yuan and Zhou, would have given each guild and modern factory or company one director, and the twenty modern banks six altogether.[58] The bankers demanded a directorship for each bank. The proposal for reordering the chamber finally collapsed, even though, in the months following, Yuan and Zhou behaved as if a compromise based on the principle of one seat per guild or enterprise were still possible.

A Banker's Chamber

Little is known about Yuan Baosan from available sources. After his 1920–1922 term as president, he no longer played an active role in chamber politics. But Zhou Zuomin remained a force in north China and Beijing political and economic circles throughout the decade. Zhou and An Disheng made interesting adversaries. Both were transitional figures: An between the Qing social order and the reformism and corruption of the early Republic, and Zhou between the banks and bureaucracies of the Qing-Republican transition and the militarism and one-party hegemony of the warlord and Nanjing periods.

Zhou Zuomin (see figure 12) was born in Jiangxu province in 1882 and educated, in part, in Japan.[59] He began his banking career in the last years of the Qing and rose to prominence in national financial circles in the mid-teens. In 1916 he joined the Bank of Communications and the next year was made manager of the Beijing-based Jincheng (Kincheng) Banking Corporation. Jincheng was one of the "four northern banks" consortium. Like its three partners, Jincheng held heavy investments in north China cities but was dominated by financiers from the Shanghai area.[60] The Jincheng Bank was prominent in local Beijing affairs. For example, Jincheng helped finance the local grain trade and made loans to the police department when it was in financial difficulties. Although Zhou did not hold public office in the 1920s, his membership in the Communications clique placed him near the center of national political intrigue. In 1921, while vice-president of the chamber, Zhou was reported to have been offered a high post in the Ministry of Finance, which he turned down.[61]

Even after An Disheng's attack on their legitimacy had been thwarted early in 1921, Yuan and Zhou faced continued opposition to their handling of chamber policy. In the spring of 1921 they agreed to a new tax on shops to benefit police coffers and then had a difficult time persuading members to accept it. When the chamber met to discuss the issue in April, "unexpectedly, all the old shops opposed the tax; and only with the greatest difficulty was the vice-president [Zhou] able to bring about an understanding."[62] Later in the year the chamber was faced with another monetary crisis involving the Banks of China and of Communications. At the height of the panic in mid-November 1921, over ten thousand depositors and note holders assembled outside the two banks and demanded their money.[63] But this time, under the leadership of bankers, the chamber reacted quite differently than it had under An Disheng. Instead of confrontation between the chamber and the government and banks over note depreciation, there was cooperation.[64] The chamber attempted to persuade the government to return some of the money it had withdrawn from the banks, withdrawals that had precipitated the panic. But the chamber also put pressure on its members to accept the bank notes.[65] The police threatened severe sanctions against merchants who refused to comply. Twelve merchants who refused to accept the notes were arrested and were paraded through the streets with notices of their "crime" stuck to their backs.[66] By late November the bank crisis had been brought under control by elite-level negotiations, transfer of funds to the banks, and a certain amount of coercion. There were "still some people, mostly money changers and street hawkers, who are agitating against the banks, but the authorities are dealing with them."[67] In alliance with the city's financial elite and the police, Yuan and Zhou extended their power from the center of chamber decision-making through the membership, into the larger merchant community, and finally to the hawkers and peddlers who worked its periphery.

As the next scheduled election in 1922 approached, An Disheng had reason to be hopeful of winning the presidency and defeating his enemies. The resolution of currency and taxation issues in

1921 in favor of the banks and the government, together with An Disheng's well-publicized, melodramatic exoneration in 1920, placed him in a favorable position. He could present himself as champion of merchant interests, patriot untainted by association with appeasers, and man of integrity victimized by the incumbent leadership's disregard for legality and democratic procedure. On the other hand, his experiences in 1920 revealed significant opposition within the chamber to the style and substance of his leadership. The chamber could be brought to the brink of activism and some distance beyond, but not without risk of defections and fractional opposition. Therefore, An devised a strategy based largely on mobilizing public opinion and support outside the chamber.

Early in 1921, as his attempt to regain the presidency was foundering, An published a proposal for municipal reform. From his position as a former member of the prefectural assembly dissolved by Yuan Shikai, An attacked the existing Municipal Office in Beijing as corrupt and inefficient.[68] He noted that since 1914 the "temporary" management of municipal government by officials had become permanent. His remedy was a municipal assembly, and he called for monthly meetings of gentry and merchants to discuss how this idea might be implemented. In the following months, in response to indications that the government might be prepared to allow municipal reform along democratic lines, dozens of citizen and self-government groups were organized.[69]

An Disheng became identified with a "self-government preparatory association" composed largely of former assembly members like himself.[70] In January 1922, when it appeared that there would be a delay in calling a chamber election, An chose a public meeting of several self-government groups to denounce the chamber's failure to fix a date for the electoral contest he hoped to win.[71] He also appealed to the self-government movement for support. He asserted that chambers of commerce and self-government were "closely related." And from his standpoint they were. Both could be imagined as vehicles for democratic reform and national revitalization. The jeweler's guild also sent an open letter to the chamber, calling the delay a "shame on merchant circles."[72]

The delay appears to have been caused by another attempt to change the chamber's electoral rules to give guilds and trades automatic seats on the board of directors.[73] While An Disheng sought to enlist public opinion on his side in open meetings of groups favoring wider use of elections in and out of government, elements within the chamber proposed a return to the status of a glorified guild federation. Elections would be limited to selecting the president and the vice-president from among a board picked by the guilds and individual enterprises. Since election of the top officers was usually guided by an informal consensus, this reduction of the role of elections in the life of the chamber would mean the virtual end of public competition for office. Corporate representation would deprive democratic forms of any meaning. In response, the jewelers-guild letter pointedly referred to article 18 of chamber rules, which stipulated that "directors are elected by members, and the president and vice-president are then elected by the directors." Relying on the weight of law and public opinion, An Disheng and his supporters were able to block direct corporate representation. An Disheng succeeded in ensuring that the uncertainty intrinsic to democratic competition would be retained. He was rewarded with a nasty surprise.

Sun Xueshi and the Realm of Social Intercourse

When the election was finally scheduled for February 10, to be held under the old rules, An Disheng was confident of winning. On the eve of the election a Beijing newspaper reported that "the one who has the greatest hope of being elected is An Disheng. His movement is heating up and has reached its peak."[74] In the initial round of voting for directors, An's confidence seemed borne out. He garnered the largest number of votes by one over restaurateur Sun Xueshi and forty more than Zhou Zuomin.[75] An proved that he still had considerable popularity among the broad membership of the chamber and perhaps sympathy in his drive to restore his honor and reclaim the presidency. But in the second round, An fell to third place behind Sun, who won, and Zhou, who came in second. An Disheng was then elected vice-president as a kind of consolation, but he resigned in anger.[76]

The victor, Sun Xueshi, was the owner of a chain of roast-duck restaurants and pastry shops. His power was based on the restaurant guild and his Shandong native-place ties. He was also known to be an adept practitioner of network politics. His restaurants were located in the midst of the Eight Lanes brothel district outside Qian Gate in the heart of the commercial quarter. Many of Sun's customers were members of the "brothel aristocracy," the group that had attacked An Disheng in 1920.

Mr. Sun relied on this fact to make the acquaintance of wealthy men. Because of Sun's extensive personal ties to them, the owners of "pleasure houses" in the "flower markets" chose Sun "chairman of the board of the flower market" area. On account of the people he is intimate with, Sun has special powers there and he is a clever fellow in the realm of social intercourse. In the course of this election he took advantage of his hold on that realm.[77]

In 1920 Beijing brothel managers had denounced An Disheng as an embezzler. In 1922 they had their own candidate. Even though brothels did not belong to the chamber, they were central to the merchant community. Merchants and politicians congregated there to conduct business in a neutral, informal atmosphere. Both restaurants and brothels were important social institutions for the predominantly male and sojourning population outside Qian Gate. While An Disheng had been mobilizing support in and out of the chamber on the basis of past prestige and identification with progressive causes, Sun had relied on his prominence as social impressario and his command of informal networks. As one reporter sardonically observed:

With regard to this election, An Disheng had anticipated a great and vigorous movement. Everyone reckoned Mr. An would be elected. Mr. An himself believed he had victory within his grasp. But, unexpectedly, the outcome was defeat. Even worse, the presidency was snatched away by Mr. Sun, who belongs to a low-class trade. One can imagine how depressing this was for Mr. An. Although Mr. An's background is as a jeweler, that trade is higher in status than the restaurant business. Intellectually speaking, An is imbued with the new thinking as opposed to being familiar with the banqueting and feasting business and the use of flattery.[78]

The reporter concluded, "Alas, Sun is without much foundation in the science and study of commerce."

The defeat of An and Zhou and the rise of Sun neatly summarize some of the forces that shaped group politics in Beijing in the

1920s. Both An and Zhou had attempted to pull the merchant community toward the center—An in order to represent merchants within a self-government institution, Zhou in order to administer merchants on behalf of central bureaucratic and financial interests. But the center, which An Disheng imagined as a power base and a destination for merchant and municipal politics, was doomed by the rise of militarism and the decline of constitutional forms. The chamber of commerce still abided by its charter. But what higher-level political entity could say the same? The national institutions and interests Zhou and the bankers were allied with were either atrophying or being militarized. Both sought to pull the chamber as a web of group interests and affiliations toward a higher level of integration: toward the assertion of merchant power in An's case and acceptance of bureaucratic domination in Zhou's. Both courses promised to be costly and dangerous, and it is not surprising that they excited opposition within a body that was as much a coalition of groups as it was an organization that could be led like a party or administered like a bureaucracy. By staking a claim to a place for the chamber at the center of an imaginary assembly or a collapsing bureaucracy, as actor or as pawn, An and Zhou stretched to the breaking point the chamber's capacity to lead and follow.

Sun Xueshi appears to have had a finer sense of the tensile strength of the relationships that bound the merchant community together. This kind of understanding was more likely to be arrived at over tea or a meal than through the study of the science of commerce. Sun was not "imbued with the new thinking." But he was receptive, as any good politician would be, to how political practices of the sort An Disheng pioneered could be used. Soon after his election in 1922 he indicated an interest in joining self-government associations as the representative of the merchant community.[79] As chamber president he wielded an expanded authority that was part of the legacy left by An Disheng's activism and Zhou Zuomin's opportunism.

One Year of Unopposed Leadership

Sun Xueshi was reelected president of the chamber in 1924 despite intense controversy surrounding a protracted dispute with the new

Beijing streetcar company. (See chapter 6.) In 1926 Sun was succeeded by wine merchant Gao Jinzhao, who had been his vice-
president from 1924 to 1926. But when Gao was arrested a few
months later on fraud charges, Sun was pressed to take office again
on a temporary basis.[80] In December 1926 Zhou Zuomin was
elected president but declined to take office. In a new election
held in March 1927, the chamber chose as president Wang Wendian, the north China representative for Nanyang Brothers Tobacco Company. Wang's tenure in office was brief. After less than
one year, he voluntarily resigned to lead a study tour abroad and
was replaced by the irrepressible Sun Xueshi.

Wang Wendian's abbreviated term was notable for his display
of political and business acumen. In his inaugural speech, Wang
promised to make the chamber more democratic and more broadly representative of the city's merchant circles.[81] He declared his
intention of extending chamber membership to previously excluded businesses like bathhouses and theaters. In one year chamber membership did expand in dramatic fashion from 4,699 to
7,361 by adding new trades and guilds.[82] Shortly after Wang's
election, Nanyang Brothers prodded 110 cigarette shops into
forming a guild and joining the chamber of commerce.[83] Wang
also used his position as chamber president to ban tobacco products marketed by Nanyang's arch rival, British American Tobacco,
from Beijing's Central Park. In July 1927 the park's board of
directors declared the ban and announced that both Wang and his
vice-president had been invited to join the board. For its part,
the chamber of commerce agreed to finance a new athletic area in
the park.[84] A key component in Wang's formula for success undoubtedly was his brief tenure in office and his voluntary departure before opposition had time to form. Like An Disheng, Zhou
Zuomin, and Sun, Wang used the chamber as an instrument of
power. Unlike the others, Wang did not wait around to face the
consequences.

The chamber of commerce had been originally designed by
officials for use by merchants who had demonstrated their basic
loyalty to and dependence on the state. This posture of dependence lasted longer in Beijing than in other large Chinese cities,
partly because of the state's overweening presence and partly because dependence was profitable. By the 1920s the state's control

over the chamber, and other *fatuan*, could not be taken for granted. The chamber could be used by democratic reformers like An, bureaucratic capitalists like Zhou, political bosses like Sun, and modern businessmen like Wang. On the other hand, instrumental use of the chamber had to be preceded and accompanied by appeals to moral and ideological sentiments as well as to constituent interests. Otherwise, leaders could be toppled or humiliated by politically aggressive and conditionally deferential followers.

Six

Profits and People's Livelihood: The Politics of Streetcar Development

The chamber of commerce prospered partly by imitating and enclosing traditional institutions like guilds and partly by commanding new loyalties and resources in the name of novel principles like nationalism and democracy. Modern surfaces barely concealed older social practices. The technical and organizational requirements of other ventures, like streetcar development, dictated radically new social roles and methods of operation. Placing something as massive and intrusive as a streetcar system in what was still by and large a preindustrial city was bound to provoke powerful reactions. The straight-line regularity of the streetcar and the uniform behavior demanded of employees and passengers could not help but collide with rival vehicles and established interests and values.

Local Reaction to Technological Change

The Chinese streetcar was a product of the country's maritime fringe, bright with the promise of dramatic technological change and redolent of the style of treaty-port Westernization.[1] The basic technical and material needs of the electric streetcar were the same throughout the world.[2] Streetcars required room for track and a reinforced roadbed and a power supply running through overhead lines or the track itself. But people and institutions in different social settings may respond differently to new technologies. A uniform technology like the electric streetcar, suddenly and extensively applied on a global scale, can provide a kind of yardstick for measuring differences across cultures and regions. For example, historian John McKay found little resemblance between North American and European reactions to streetcar modernization.[3] In the United States, entrepreneurs had free rein to build and operate streetcar systems on the basis of profitability and without consideration for wider community interests. Municipal governments were weak, officials could be bribed, and there was little initial popular or elite opposition to the streetcar. By contrast, European city councils worried that streetcar track, poles, and lines would deface squares and avenues. Governments demanded that extensive safety precautions be taken to prevent accidents, that the streetcar system itself revert to municipal ownership after a specified number of years, and that fares be kept low. In Europe, streetcar developers "had to work within the framework of strict public regulation of urban transportation."[4]

Beijing offered streetcar developers a restrictive rather than an open environment. Although money, aesthetics, safety, and municipal autonomy entered into the controversies surrounding the streetcar, the key issues centered on welfare and public order. The motivations of the principals involved in the conflict were complex. But the most powerful argument made against the streetcar was not based on a perceived contradiction between efficiency and progress, on the one hand, and the city's cultural or municipal integrity, on the other. The real sticking points had to do with an unsentimental appreciation of the social consequences of depriving large numbers of Beijing residents—namely, rickshaw men— of their jobs, a deep attachment to traditional notions of social and economic rights and obligations, and a jealous regard by citywide organizations like the police and the chamber of commerce for their prerogatives in local affairs. In the initial planning and financing of the Beijing streetcar system, profits and progress, as well as visions of the public good and private enrichment, were closely intertwined. Subsequent political battles unraveled these public and private goods as different groups and classes in the city reacted to opportunities and threats created by a new technology.

The Founding of the Beijing Streetcar Company

Just before the fall of the Qing, high-level officials in Beijing had broached the idea of a streetcar system for the city.[5] With streetcars running in Shanghai and nearby Tianjin and elements of a modern urban infrastructure already in place in Beijing, adding electric streetcars to other utilities, like running water, electric lights, and telephone service, must have seemed a logical step. Qing reformers spun out plans for technological and political modernization as if the two kinds of change branched out from the same root.

The 1911 Revolution gave China a new constitution and passed the initiative on Beijing streetcar development to a Republican regime. But the logic of simultaneous political and economic change, which encouraged Qing officials to confound constitutions and streetcars into a single formula, assumed a concentration of power and resources which the early Republic did not have. Ambitious plans for completing modernization of the capital were quickly overshadowed by elemental struggles for political survival. The rights to economic development became marketable concessions used to finance short-term government expenses.

In 1913 Yuan Shikai's government gave the Beijing streetcar project to the Sino-French Banque Industrielle de Chine (BIC) as one of a package of commercial and industrial concessions designed to sweeten investor interest in the bank. In return, the BIC loaned money to Yuan Shikai's regime to pay pressing political and administrative expenses.[6] In addition to the right to build a streetcar system in Beijing, the French, through the BIC, were invited to reorganize the Chinese-owned waterworks and electric light and power company, repair and expand the city's Ming-vintage sewers, pave roads, and build museums, public gardens, and government buildings.[7] The French viewed the concessions as an opportunity to stamp the Chinese capital with their own cultural and architectural imprint.[8]

The BIC quickly expanded to over twenty branches in China, Europe, and America. The bank's popularity in China stemmed from its close relationship to the government, high interest rates on accounts, and large dividends paid to shareholders. However, the BIC did very little building in China and none at all in Beijing. Beijing did not begin to resemble an eastern Paris or a northern Hanoi. Instead, the bank succumbed to the heady financial atmosphere of the early Republic in which a cash-hungry government initiated round after round of borrowing and rescheduling of debts. Speculation in government bonds and high-interest loans promised higher profits than capital investment in projects like a Beijing streetcar system.

The BIC held the rights to streetcar development in Beijing and did nothing. But the idea of the streetcar as a radical, lucrative technology continued to exert a hold on the imaginations of Chinese investors and reformers. In 1919, Li Dazhao, director of the Beijing University library and future founder of the Chinese Communist party, published a manifesto entitled "The New Life Beijing Residents Ought to Demand."[9] Li complained that Beijing was "boring, dessicated, dirty, dilatory, inconvenient, uneconomical, unhealthy and devoid of amusement." As remedies, Li proposed twenty reforms, including the construction of libraries, hospitals, rescue centers for prostitutes, schools and factories for the poor, orphanages, and old-age homes. He also saw in the streetcar solutions to a number of vexing urban problems. "Build a municipally managed streetcar system at once. This will enable us ordinary residents to avoid wasting time en route to where we are going, eating filthy street dust, consorting with oxen and horses, and dodging the wheels of automobiles."[10]

Li Dazhao imagined that a streetcar system would speed newspaper delivery, relieve traffic congestion, and make a more rational city plan possible. He wanted to ban factories from residential areas and create separate zones for cultural, industrial, governmental, and residential use. Li realized that such a division of residence and workplace presupposed an efficient means of transport. He also assumed that the streetcar would drive the rickshaw out of business. Like most intellectuals, Li felt that eradication of the rickshaw would be a good thing. In the meantime, Li wanted to provide rickshaw pullers with raincoats and hats and gauze masks to keep out the street dust, encourage rickshaw men to wear clean clothes, and open small restaurants and rest houses for them.

According to Li Dazhao, heightened regulation and institutionalized care of indigents, expanded public services, and deployment of novel technologies like the streetcar would make Beijing a cleaner, less disorderly, and more convenient place to live. Most of the reforms championed by Li Dazhao required increased government expenditures at a time when fiscal crisis had begun to threaten most government agencies. Only the streetcar seemed to promise both profits and a positive transformation of city life.

In the fall of 1920, a group of Chinese investors, attracted by the profit-making potential of the new technology, approached the BIC and the government with a plan to revive the streetcar project by reducing the role of the bank to financial intermediary instead of principal investor. The government and the bank approved an arrangement whereby $4 million in capital would be raised, half in "government shares" (*guangu*) and half in "merchant (private) shares" (*shanggu*). The merchant shares would be offered to the general public, and the government shares would be raised as a BIC loan to the Republic.[11] The willingness of the BIC to surrender a portion of its monopoly rights sprang from the bank's own financial troubles. Unbeknownst to most of its East Asian shareholders and customers, the BIC teetered on the edge of bankruptcy in 1920.[12]

The 1920 agreement led to the creation of an office in Beijing authorized to arrange the sale of stock in a "Beijing Streetcar Company." When the stock, restricted to Chinese buyers, went on sale in May 1921 in Beijing and Shanghai at $100 a share, within a few hours investors ordered $8 million worth, or four times the amount solicited.[13] To the chagrin of local investors in Beijing, most of the shares went to prominent bankers and bureaucrats.[14] Half of the one hundred largest investors were "directly or indirectly linked to officialdom."[15] Another 30 or 40 percent were wealthy financiers, and 20 percent were "ordinary citizens" from Beijing and elsewhere. Local enthusiasm for the stock issue did not translate into local ownership. The shares were sold on a national market through banks accustomed to servicing the needs of an elite clientele, and the resulting ownership structure of the company reflected national and regional, rather than local, interests.

Formal inauguration of the company in June 1921 stimulated the first local protests against the project. The press reported a "great agitation" among rickshaw pullers and garage owners, who believed they would be driven out of business by the streetcar.[16] Citizen groups protested the circumstances under which the stock was sold and the fact that most of the shares had been bought up by interests foreign to Beijing.[17] Merchants at Gold Fish Lane in the Inner City, upon hearing that a section of track would be laid through their neighborhood, voiced fears that their shops and homes would be torn down.[18] But for the moment, as the company materialized from the calculations of Chinese and foreign investors, the biggest threat to the project came from Paris. On June 30, the same day shareholders met in Beijing to organize the streetcar company, the BIC headquarters office in Paris finally closed.[19] Two days later the BIC branch in Beijing followed suit.

The BIC's bankruptcy left in doubt the government half of the financing of the streetcar company. The company's Chinese shareholders advocated direct financing by their own government and exclusion of the French.[20] But the weakened financial condition of the Republic militated against that option. Another solution would have been to throw bidding open to the public for the remaining shares. A local self-government group seized on this possibility and proposed that the utility be "locally and publicly managed."[21] The group demanded that the Beijing streetcar company, which in their view had been "mortgaged to a foreign country," "yield to public opinion" and be "returned to the people of the city."

As the French struggled, successfully as it turned out, to retain their influence in the streetcar project, Beijing bankers consolidated their hold on the utility.[22] According to Liu Yifeng, an officer of the company in the twenties and thirties, Zhou Zuomin's Jincheng Bank and the Salt Industrial Bank were the utility's two most powerful financial backers.[23] These crosscurrents of financial and political, as well as foreign and domestic, power resulted in a management structure closely attuned to the balance of forces that gave birth to and sustained the company. The government and private-shareholder sides each selected five directors for the company's board. Each was also allowed to pick a business director to supervise day-to-day operations. For their part, the French retained proprietary rights to a number of top administrative and engineering posts for French nationals and middle-level positions for former Chinese employees of the French-owned streetcar company in Shanghai.[24] Since government officials assigned to manage the company did not, as a rule, spend much time on the job, responsibility for running the company tended to slip into the hands of the private directors and particularly into the grasp of representatives of the Jincheng Bank and the Salt Industrial Bank. According to Liu Yifeng, Yuan Dian, who was a major shareholder in both banks and who sat on the streetcar company board along with Zhou Zuomin, outmaneuvered his fellow directors to become the de facto manager of the company, with the nickname "Emperor."[25]

The company founders consciously designed the enterprise to fit smoothly into the international, national, regional, and local contexts from which it would draw its financing, technology, official authorization, and passengers. In addition to accommodating the French, the government, and financiers, the company carefully selected the former premier and local notable Wang Shizhen as the company's first chairman of the board and a veteran district police chief named Deng Yuan as director of the company's business office.[26] Deng in turn brought many former police officers along with him as functionaries in the middle and lower levels of the company. With Wang "above" and Deng "below," the company hoped to defuse potential opposition to its operations and policies.[27]

The Politics of People's Livelihood

Scarcely had the company placed its relationship to French interests in order and begun construction when the Beijing chamber of commerce, under the leadership of Sun Xueshi, attacked the project. Sun, who had just defeated Jincheng Bank manager and streetcar company director Zhou Zuomin for the presidency of the chamber in 1922, raised the specter of Beijing's army of rickshaw men thrown out of work by the streetcar. Sympathy for the plight of the rickshaw men in Beijing merchant circles hinged in part on the antagonism some local businessmen felt toward the bureaucrats and bankers who financed and managed the streetcar company. The Banks of China and of Communications panics and the An Disheng affair were still fresh in everyone's mind. Although there is no evidence that Sun Xueshi shared An Disheng's dislike of bankers, Sun's defeat of Zhou made the chamber available for independent initiatives critical of higher-level elites. Sun had his own power base in the merchant community outside Qian Gate and was not constrained by connections to the government, financial interests, or bureaucratic capitalism.

Sun Xueshi, like many Outer City merchants, was a leader of a *shuihui*, the archetypical neighborhood defense organization specializing in fighting fires and crime and, in a self-interested way, in caring for the poor.[28] For *shuihui* leaders and members the issues of welfare and social order were closely linked. The streetcar threatened to alter dramatically the city's employment structure and create disorder in the neighborhoods. As construction proceeded in 1922 and 1923 alarms were raised about streetcar company lines strung too close to electric lines, piles of construction materials and rubble obstructing roads, the destruction or removal of ceremonial arches deemed too low for the passage of streetcars, and the need to move or tear down private walls and shop fronts to accommodate track, poles, and lines.[29] The higher reaches of Beijing society, including capitalists like Zhou Zuomin, politicians like Wang Shizhen, and prominent intellectuals like Li Dazhao, may have supported streetcar development. But elites with city-wide and neighborhood perspectives, who did not stand to profit directly from the project, saw the issue in light of the traditional notion of "people's livelihood" (*minsheng*).

Traditional ideas can make a positive contribution to reform and modernization projects. Confucian rhetoric and values were practically suited to modern police work. The traditional gentry style of civic activism formed an important component of An Disheng's career as a nationalist and a reformer. Other elements of the Confucian tradition stood in more ambiguous relationship to modernization. Traditionally, official and popular opinion attached greater weight to the value of people's livelihood than to economic growth. Orthodox Confucianism "conceived of economic welfare not in terms of economic growth but in terms of subsistence, of satisfaction of the basic needs of the masses."[30]

By the turn of the century a consensus had been reached among national political forces and leaders on the need to change this orientation and promote rapid growth. But throughout most of China the material conditions that nurtured statecraft views on the importance of maintaining *minsheng* did not change. The Chinese economy, including Beijing's, was still basically preindustrial. Under favorable conditions the economy developed slowly. Dramatic economic change was typically negative rather than positive, the result of famine, flood, or war rather than of technological breakthrough or a massive infusion of labor or capital. *Minsheng* was not designed to thwart gradual economic expansion. The concept was meant as a means of mobilizing the resources of the state and the community to defend established markets, trade patterns, and jobs in time of crisis. The government anticipated and remedied popular unrest by being sensitive to the issue of livelihood. Groups and classes in society used the idea and related rhetoric to rally local communities and demand relief from the government.[31] In Beijing in the 1920s the term *minsheng* was commonly used to refer to that part of the established social order which supported the material well-being of townspeople.[32]

Sun Xueshi and the chamber of commerce demanded that the streetcar company build a factory for unemployed rickshaw men by way of compensation for the damage done to their trade.[33] Sun was no Luddite, and his position, while resonant with the concept of "moral economy," did not reject economic modernization as evil or unnatural.[34] He simply wanted the streetcar company to pay the cost of the disruptions it promised to inflict. In fact, faith in the power of progress and technology meant that Sun and other Beijing residents assumed that the streetcar's profit-making potential placed this kind of largess well within its means.

Proposals like Sun's for factories for the poor reflected a general sentiment running through public opinion that philanthropic projects of this sort were necessary correctives to unregulated growth. In 1919 the police had prosecuted An Disheng in an effort to obtain the funds to open a factory for poor bannermen. Liberal commentators touted "charitable factories" that provided food and housing, but no wages, to inmates as a "model for Chinese industrialists."[35] Joint public and private factories for the poor were conceived of as part of a "plan for [enhancing] people's livelihood" (*minsheng jihua*).[36] The charitable activities of guilds and *shuihui* and established uses and abuses of the apprenticeship system provided ample precedents and models for institutions that mixed charity, social control, and profits. Such factories might employ several hundred persons in handicraft and light industrial jobs.[37] Other poor-factories were simply abandoned temples or other buildings taken over for the winter months by the police and supplied with food, coal, attendants, and rudimentary materials for handicraft production. With its joint official and private nature and industrial veneer the poor-factory resembled a caricature of grander projects like the Beijing streetcar system, with the latter expected to perform the role of host to the former. In 1923 in the course of negotiations between the chamber and the company, sponsored by the police, the streetcar company agreed to contribute $60,000 to open a poor-factory.[38] Soon after, the company gave $20,000 of the agreed amount, to be held in trust by the police department.[39]

The chamber, however, was not satisfied with promises and partial payments. In November 1923, as the company finished laying track everywhere but in the Outer City, the chamber went back on the attack with renewed vigor. The merchant organization complained that, in addition to the threat to the livelihood of rickshaw pullers, streets in the Outer City were too narrow to accommodate streetcars.[40] By December all work on the streetcar had halted, and the press reported that "those in the know" gave credit to Sun Xueshi.[41] Sun had ordered all shops and commercial establishments in the city to stop paying shop taxes and license fees to the police.[42] The police department, which was the recipient of revenues regularly collected by the chamber in the form of the shop tax, was thereby deprived of income at a time when the force was experiencing extraordinary financial difficulties. The chamber's strategy of indirect pressure was effective and succeeded in turning the company's police connections against it. Deng Yuan's policy of recruiting policemen into the company had created tensions and jealousies between those offered the opportunity to earn significantly higher wages and those who found themselves excluded from the patronage.[43] In short order the streetcar company felt the weight of police pressure, and by late January 1924, company officials proposed a factory employing seven or eight thousand men.[44] The company also offered to hire rickshaw men who were "clever and strong enough" to be streetcar workers.

Sun Xueshi's victory was immediately clouded by criticism of his tactics and approach. One self-government association questioned whether, once the streetcar company had come to terms on a contribution to the chamber for the poor-factory, the chamber would pay any further attention to the streetcar issue.[45] The citizens' groups felt that the key issue was the company's general disregard for the public rather than the particular problem of the rickshaw men's livelihood. More serious for Sun Xueshi, his opposition to the streetcar company became an issue in the February 1924 chamber election. The chamber included a large contingent of bankers and factory owners predisposed to oppose Sun's attempt to impose a de facto tax on industrial development. As the An Disheng scandal showed, the chamber also harbored significant numbers of merchants who balked at the costs and dangers involved in aggressive citywide leadership. As a result, many chamber members opposed Sun's stand.[46] Sun then forced the hand of his critics by calling together chamber directors a month before the election and declaring his intention to resign the presidency in order to "protect his reputation."[47] Faithful to the conventions involved in protest resignations of this sort, groups of notables implored Sun to remain in office until the end of his term. Sun relented and then mounted a campaign of restaurant meetings designed to ensure his reelection.[48]

This combination of tactical retreat in the pose of injured party and aggressive advance through the "realm of social intercourse" and the practice of "banqueting and feasting" enabled Sun to keep the presidency. Under his leadership the chamber had succeeded in asserting its quasi-governmental role as regulator of the economy and representative of *shimin* (townspeople) and *shangmin* (merchant community) opinion. The interlocking nature of citywide organizations redounded to Sun's favor as pressures exerted by the chamber forced the streetcar company to agree to the rickshaw-puller compensation scheme.

As leader of the chamber, Sun Xueshi spoke as representative of the vehicle guild and, indirectly, of the mass of rickshaw pullers. Since rickshaw men in the brothel district, where Sun's restaurants were located, were among the most vocal and status conscious of Beijing's younger and better-paid pullers, their concerns about the streetcars must have been audible in the form of grumbling and personal appeals. During negotiations with the streetcar company, Sun appeared before a mass meeting of pullers to discuss the factory idea with them.[49] Either as a result of pressure from the pullers or because the summer agreement with the company began to break down, Sun supported a final attempt to block the opening of the streetcar system.

On December 16, 1924, the day before the streetcars were scheduled to begin running, the company received a phone call from Police Chief Li Dasan.[50] Chief Li had just been appointed to his position in the aftermath of General Feng Yuxiang's October coup d'état, which installed Duan Qirui's provisional government in power. Li warned the company that the next day several thousand Beijing rickshaw men planned to throw themselves onto the streetcar tracks. Alarmed, company officials dispatched company directors Zhou Zuomin and Yue Qianzai, of the Jincheng Bank and the Salt Industrial Bank respectively, to the cabinet offices on Iron Lion Lane in the East City to ask the Duan Qirui government to intervene. The cabinet secretary, Liang Hongzhi, in turn sought out Police Chief Li to find out more about the source of the threat. Li said he had learned about the planned protest from the chamber president, Sun. Liang then passed the information along to Duan Qirui, who, as it happened, had already lent his prestige to the inauguration of streetcar service in Beijing. The streetcar company's characteristic attention to political detail and its connections with the powerful paid off in this case. Chief Executive Duan delegated his son Hongye to handle the problem.

Duan Hongye had already achieved a measure of public notoriety as one of China's "Four Young Lords" (*si da shaoye*), akin to sons of other prominent politicians, like warlord Zhang Zuolin's son Zhang Xueliang and Sun Yat-sen's son Sun Fo. Duan met with Police Chief Li Dasan and immediately offended the older man with his brashness. In response Li told young Duan that when thousands of rickshaw men lay down on the tracks the next day, "as police superintendant I cannot take responsibility." Duan banged on the table and retorted that the streetcar opening had been approved by the cabinet and that Li would indeed be held responsible for any incident. At that point Zhou Zuomin and Yue Qianzai, who were also present, offered to continue discussing the matter with Chief Li. As Li, Zhou, and Qian left the cabinet offices Li told the two bankers that negotiating with Sun Xueshi was the key to resolving the dispute.

Zhou and Yue returned to the company's offices nearby and entrusted ex-policeman Deng Yuan with the task of bearding President Sun in his Qianmen wai (the merchant district outside Qian Gate) den. Within the next few hours, Deng three times tried to see Sun and three times was turned away on some pretext. Deng angrily complained to his colleagues that when he was a district commander one phone call had been enough to summon someone like Sun to come and see *him*. When Deng finally managed to arrange a meeting with Sun, the restaurateur told him that thousands of rickshaw men had already assembled in the Bridge of Heaven district just south of chamber headquarters. Deng informed Sun that the streetcar company had the highest political backing, from Duan Qirui himself, and that Police Chief Li had been told that he would be held responsible for any incident. "Tomorrow, if, when the cars start running, there is an incident, Chief Li is going to come and grab you." Gauging the tenor of Deng's words and strident tone, Sun Xueshi said that he would go and discuss the matter with the police chief. Later in the day, Sun phoned Deng to let him know that his talks with Li had been successful and "possibly there would be no trouble."

The next day, as Sun had promised, the company was able to hold its inaugural festivities without incident. A visitor compared the excitement to a "mammoth circus parade" with crowds lining the streets to catch a glimpse of cars gaily decorated with red, green, and yellow cloth banners and paper flowers.[51] Officials made speeches and the company provided tea and cakes for the spectators. The public was invited to sample streetcar travel at reduced rates, and the crowds were so vast that the police had a hard time keeping order.[52]

Sun's militancy as spokesman or apologist for the angry crowd of rickshaw men evaporated in the face of political threats emanating from Iron Lion Lane. According to the recollections of streetcar company official Liu Yifeng, Deng Yuan was so dispirited by the affair and by subsequent troubles experienced by the company that he resigned his position.[53] Rickshaw men, brought to the brink of what streetcar officials feared would be a "monstrous disturbance," watched the streetcars clatter down the track without protest. Worse still for the pullers, the money allocated for their relief remained unspent. Or rather, the police spent the $30,000 they held in trust on police salaries, which were in arrears.[54] A vacant lot donated by the chamber of commerce remained empty, with a sign reading "Rickshaw Puller Factory" the only visible evidence of the project.[55] For all the negotiations, mediation, threats, phone calls, and personal confrontations, rickshaw men remained uncompensated and aggrieved. The elaborate dance of local, regional, and national elites had lent legitimacy to the puller's right to a livelihood without producing concrete remedies.

Streetcar Beijing

Although the streetcar company was spared the spectacle of thousands of rickshaw men blocking the newly laid track with their bodies, the streetcar generated its own brand of mayhem. On the first day of business a policeman on watch was struck by a streetcar and sustained internal injuries.[56] Police officials rushed to the scene, and the press speculated that the company would compensate the patrolman. In succeeding days a child was nearly killed climbing onto a streetcar, and in reaction to a spate of such accidents, the police imposed new restrictions on company operations. Speed limits were lowered, special care by conductors and motormen for the very young and the old was mandated, and procedures for dealing with accidents were outlined in which motormen would be taken immediately to the nearest police station for questioning.[57] Perhaps still smarting from the pressure placed on the department to resolve the dispute with the chamber and the pullers in favor of the company, the police made it clear that motormen who broke traffic regulations would be punished.

Policemen could be observed taking a protective stance toward fellow pedestrians frightened or injured by the streetcars. One puller crossing a streetcar track panicked when he saw a car coming, abandoned his rickshaw, and fled. The streetcar smashed into the rickshaw and kept on going. A policeman on duty took down the number of the car and shepherded the distraught puller to the district police station, where the officers phoned the company on behalf of the rickshaw man. "Not wanting to make trouble with a poor rickshaw man," the company agreed to pay to repair the rickshaw.[58] In another incident a peddler selling steamed buns was knocked down by a streetcar speeding along the line that ran through the Outer City business district. The snowy white buns spilled out into the roadway and turned black as they rolled in the dirt. Fortunately, the peddler was not badly hurt, although he had been knocked ten feet through the air; he wept as he picked himself up in a dignified manner. The motorman would not admit to any error. "Didn't you hear the bell? Why on earth didn't you jump out of the way?" But the policeman on the scene and the crowd of bystanders took the peddler's side and criticized the motorman.[59] Beijing residents were also reported to be upset with the mixing of sexes and the prevalence of pickpockets on the streetcars.[60]

Nonetheless, in the bitter cold of a Beijing winter, passengers squeezed into the twenty-eight cars the company had in operation.[61] Rickshaw garages reported a dramatic decline in the numbers of vehicles rented out as rickshaw men calculated that not enough fares were to be had to justify the rent they were charged.[62] In the next six months the number of rickshaws licensed by the police for public soliciting dropped by one-third.[63] Garage owners stopped buying new rickshaws, and a number of garages went out of business.[64] The press reported scenes of shivering rickshaw men waiting with empty vehicles as crowded streetcars sped by.[65] The first weeks of the streetcars' operations in Beijing seemed to confirm the hopes of reformers and investors and the fears of rickshaw men and their sympathizers.

The chamber of commerce continued to apply pressure on the streetcar company to proceed with the plan for the poor-factory. But mediators were unable to overcome mutual hostility between the chamber and the company.[66] Duan Qirui, whose intervention had helped deflect last-ditch opposition to the company's opening, was reported to be angry because the utility had not followed through on its promise to compensate rickshaw men.[67] The company had maneuvered Duan into defending its interests, and now the chief executive was left in the awkward position of agreeing with the company's critics that the streetcars' "seizure" of public thoroughfares threatened local order.

However, the blow delivered to the rickshaw trade proved not to be fatal. Streetcars were unable to overtake the rickshaw business in total fares or revenues.[68] The loss of sixty thousand fares precipitated a sharp reversal for the rickshaw trade. But the 30 percent drop in rickshaws for hire on the streets in early 1926 represented an overreaction to a 15 percent real inroad into the pullers' market. Within four years the ten thousand rickshaws taken out of circulation in 1925 had been relicensed or replaced.[69] And while the rickshaw trade recovered, the streetcar was unable to acquire many more passengers after riding the crest of the first wave of enthusiasm for the new technology in 1925. Even with an increase in the number of streetcars in operation to seventy in 1926, eighty in 1929, and ninety-six in 1935, the number of passengers using the utility remained about the same.[70]

While the durability of the rickshaw as a mode of transportation surprised many contemporary observers, the streetcar's inability to clear the market of its principal competitor is understandable in retrospect. The "streetcar revolution" in Europe and America and some East Asian cities like Tokyo and Shanghai took place when streetcar companies were able to press their low-fares advantage to create a whole new market for mass transport, usually by replacing horse-drawn trolleys or other animal-powered vehicles, but also by luring passengers from the working class.[71] In Beijing the streetcar could not lower its fares enough to place regular use of the system within the budgets of most city residents.[72] Access via streetcar travel to higher-paying factory jobs might have made new expenditures on transportation attractive or essential. But, unlike Shanghai, no such industrial zone existed in Beijing. Since most people lived at or near their place of employment, working-class use of streetcar travel remained a luxury. As a result, the streetcar and the rickshaw competed for the same class of riders: middle- and upper-income residents and visitors.

Since the average streetcar ride cost half as much as hiring a rickshaw, and since not even the most athletic puller could run as fast as an electric streetcar over any distance, the streetcar had a strong competitive edge.[73] On the other hand, the rickshaw had an advantage in availability, access to narrow streets and lanes off the main avenues, and portal-to-portal service. Nor could a status-conscious resident of Beijing afford to put aside considerations of comfort and prestige. Streetcars were faster and cheaper, but they were also crowded and frequented by pickpockets and rowdy, at times violent, soldiers. The streetcar company tried to make the cars safer and more comfortable by forbidding eating or smoking, drunken or armed passengers, and livestock.[74] Solutions like reserving special cars for women and for soldiers may have eased the situation.[75] But the slower, more expensive rickshaw continued to provide comfortable, reliable, and dignified service, which compared favorably with its more modern rival.

Unable to monopolize public transportation in its first months and years of operations, the streetcar company found itself penalized by the capital- and technology-intensive factors that were supposed to be the key to generating big profits, and by its politically complicated management structure. The company lost money eight years out of ten from 1926 to 1935.[76] By 1927 the firm was nearly four million yuan in debt.[77] The company lost control of its financial affairs to the point that creditor banks sent representatives daily to the company to take a share of the ticket receipts. According to Liu Yifeng, who by his own account struggled to reform the company's operations, the higher echelons were overstaffed—partly as a result of the politically inspired redundancies built into the firm—and salaries were inflated on a scale commensurate with a government ministry.[78] The streetcar's static share of the city's transportation market proved to be a narrow foundation for this outsized, politically and financially tangled management structure.

Beijing society's taste for political privilege and status also undermined something as basic to the health of the enterprise as the ability to collect fares. The users of modern public utilities in Beijing were notorious for their reluctance to pay bills. Telephone, running water, and electricity customers who had status or influence commonly used these connections to avoid having to pay what they owed.[79] Likewise, officials, policemen, soldiers, and anyone else with a claim to status or power might insist on riding streetcars free and then, when challenged, argue or fight with company employees.[80] Since the police and law court officials were among the groups who expected to ride without charge, seeking legal redress did not guarantee the company a sympathetic hearing. Soldiers were particularly resistant to the idea of paying for the privilege of riding a streetcar, and forcing soldiers to pay could easily result in violence. Within the first weeks of the streetcar operations, an altercation between a conductor and a man in uniform led to a brawl in which soldiers wrecked a streetcar and the whole system temporarily shut down.[81]

In the 1920s, when the writer Walter Benjamin visited revolutionary Moscow, he saw in streetcar travel a metaphor for social and political transformation.

Travel by streetcar in Moscow is above all a tactical experience. Here the newcomer learns perhaps most quickly of all to adapt himself to the curious tempo of this city and to the rhythm of its peasant population. And the complete interpenetration of technological and primitive modes of life, this world-historical experiment in the new Russia, is illustrated in miniature by a streetcar ride.[82]

Benjamin was struck by the rough but good-humored comradery of Moscow streetcar passengers kept in necessary order by fur-wrapped conductresses. Ex-peasant urbanites accepted the uniformity demanded by the machine-synchronized ballet of queuing up, buying tickets, and finding a seat or a handhold. Equalitarian sentiments buffered the inevitable pushing and shoving, which took place "without a sound and with great cordiality."

Streetcar travel in Beijing demanded a comparable degree of regimentation in a population capable of both studied politeness and a prickly defense of rank and status. Equalitarian feelings were not unknown in Beijing. Emergent social movements, ranging from nationalism to unionism, depended on a certain amount of comradery. But travel in French-made streetcars by passengers selected by the ticket price from the city's status-conscious middle classes was unlikely to excite the sensation of citizenship or moral equality. Adding the band-of-brothers mentality of rule-breaking soldiers to the social mix heightened tensions and sharpened the tactical dimension of streetcar travel.

Streetcar conductors and motormen were assigned the task of educating Beijing residents to the routine of mass transportation. By most accounts, they carried out their responsibilities with a kind of missionary zeal. "Beijing conductors are very honest, simple, and upright. They have a sense of responsibility. When we boarded a streetcar, we could see them hurrying back and forth, busily selling tickets and yelling 'Tickets! Tickets!'—striking terror into passengers who tried to avoid paying and acting self-important."[83] Passengers found their brusque efficiency irritating. In mid-February a conductor forced a passenger who had just purchased a ticket to get off an overcrowded car and told him to wait for the next streetcar. The man, who appeared to be a middle-aged merchant, angrily pulled the conductor down onto the street, threatening a lawsuit and denouncing the conductor's "rude behavior." The policeman who hurried over to mediate urged the indignant passenger to hire a rickshaw instead.[84] In another episode a hapless passenger who missed his stop because he could not push his way out through the crowded car found himself accused by the conductor of fare cheating.[85]

On at least two occasions in the early months of streetcar operation, disputes between passengers and streetcar employees escalated into collective violence. In March, when two Beijing police-school students in uniform were slow in paying for their tickets, the conductor cursed them out and pushed them off the car. Residents in the area, a poorer neighborhood in the northwestern section of the Inner City, had come to resent the streetcars on account of a spate of injuries caused by the vehicle, and the fares, which were too expensive for most people to pay. When the townspeople saw the conductor manhandle the two cadets they reacted by crowding around the streetcars and tossing stones and bricks to break the windows. The conductor and motormen fled, and the crowd only dispersed when a squad of policemen appeared.[86]

A second incident proved to be more serious. On an unseasonably warm spring afternoon in April the whole streetcar system experienced a power outage. Passengers immediately demanded their ticket money back. But the conductors refused, and all along the line arguments broke out. In one instance, fifty passengers, crowded onto two cars in the midday sun, watched in disbelief as the conductors and motorman left their posts to find a cool spot to wait for power to return to the lines. The passengers, who by that time had been stuck in the streetcars for an hour, began stamping their feet and cursing. "In one voice," they demanded their money back and, when they saw the frightened streetcar workers flee, surged out of the cars and toward a streetcar company ticket booth on the other side of the road. The crowd smashed all the windows in the kiosk and ransacked the interior. Altercations con-

Fig. 15. A streetcar passes east of the outer tower of Qian Gate. The massive twin-towered structure was remodeled in the teens to allow traffic to flow on either side and through openings in the wall separating the Inner and Outer Cities. The northern edge of the merchant quarter is visible behind the streetcar. Although the avenue is not congested, the presence of handcart, donkey, rickshaw, mule-cart, and pedestrian traffic suggests potential dangers of and impediments to streetcar travel. Courtesy of the Library of Congress.

tinued throughout the system until late afternoon when the power was finally switched on again.[87]

Despite these attacks and a raft of more minor misunderstandings, the streetcar soon became a fixture in Beijing's public life (fig. 15). Advertisements picturing streetcar travel began to appear in newspapers, including one for patent medicine in which two men were shown seated in a car and chatting happily.[88] A newspaper columnist wrote a lengthy essay on the types of people one encountered in the second-class section.[89] He identified Beijing's new breed of regular commuters as passengers who "grope for their coppers as soon as they board" and who sit or stand in silence. He joked that passengers who received polite responses to their enquiries from conductors must be friends or relatives of the normally officious workers and that men who chose to sit next to people on near-empty cars were probably pickpockets. The columnist noted with relish that on streetcars you could "meet people from various parts of society who wouldn't be easy to meet elsewhere," including fashionably dressed young women who spoke English, amiable types who warned conductors when investigators for the company were about to board, and passengers with the disgusting habit of spitting wherever and whenever they liked.

In time, widespread use of the streetcar and general acceptance of industrial routine tended to transform the vehicle into a relatively benign part of everyday life, a true utility.[90] But in Beijing in the 1920s most people experienced the streetcar less as passengers than as spectators. From the vantage point of the street, as pedestrians or slung up a bit higher in a rickshaw, the streetcar appeared noisy and dangerous. In the teens the rickshaw had speeded up the pace of Beijing as a "walking city." In the mid-twenties the streetcar further accelerated the movement of people around Beijing, to the distress of rivals like rickshaw pullers and, often, to the annoyance of the general public. In the 1920s the streetcar was never able to establish a clear identity as a necessary convenience for enough people to overcome its other images as victimizer of rickshaw men, an appropriate target of taxes and welfare tariffs, a dangerous foreign contraption, and a talisman of modernity of dubious value.

Seven

Bosses, Guilds, and Work Gangs: Labor Politics and the Sprouts of Unionism

Proletarian Politics in a Preindustrial City

In January 1925, a month after streetcars began running in Beijing, drivers and conductors went out on strike to protest harassment by fare-cheating soldiers.[1] Officious streetcar men and poorly disciplined soldiers seemed naturally to provoke each other. The resulting arguments, fights, wrecked cars, and spontaneous strikes by workmen became regular occurrences along Beijing avenues and were insistent reminders of the disruptions caused by warlordism. These streetcar incidents also put on public display the somewhat rarer (for Beijing) spectacle of modern labor militancy. The product of an elite-centered politics largely restricted to financiers, officials, political hangers-on, and civic leaders, the streetcar venture had pulled out of the hat of financial speculation and political intrigue a body of uniformed, technically proficient workers quick to organize, protest, and strike. As labor historian Jurgen Kuczynski argues, the modern working class is "the creation of the machine—to be exact, of the mechanical tool. No machines would mean no working class."[2] The streetcar, as a characteristic artifact and tool of the machine age—noisy, dangerous, and efficient in stamping out new habits and outlooks on workers and consumers alike—could not help but stimulate proletarian impulses.

And yet, in Beijing in the 1920s, as in much of urban China, the politics of most workers was not, strictly speaking, working-class politics any more than merchant politics was, in the main, bourgeois. The "horizontal" solidarities associated with class weakly competed with "vertical" loyalties and affiliations associated with the authority of patrons, brokers, and bosses and the factions, trades, and work gangs they commanded. A case in point was the hesitation and passivity shown by rickshaw men in the winter of 1924–25 as their livelihoods seemed about to be snatched from them and as their tie to erstwhile patron Sun Xueshi came undone.

The factory system and the scale of organization associated with modern capitalism is capable of ordering elites and masses into regimented ranks and warring parties. But capitalism had gained only a narrow bridgehead in Beijing. No more than several thousand of Beijing's hundreds of thousands of laborers worked in mechanized factories or enterprises. Up until 1945, handicrafts accounted for 80 percent of Beijing manufacture.[3] The weight of Beijing society still rested on the underpinnings supplied by a craft, commercial, and traditional service economy. Workers who carved, cut, pulled, carried, painted, pickled, peddled, and served by hand and foot dominated the workaday world (fig. 16).

In this machine-poor, predominantly preindustrial environment, streetcar men and kindred utility workers, railway men, and modern factory employees were exceptional people with influence beyond their numbers and with numbers that limited their capacity to determine the overall shape of worker politics. These limits were of immediate concern in the 1920s to radical politicians intent on organizing a labor movement among Beijing workers. Their quest for connections to a "working class" was tinged by ambivalence toward ordinary laborers who lacked factory or modern industrial credentials.

The search for a proletarian base for radical politics commenced in 1919 on the eve of the May Fourth Movement when Li Dazhao and his followers at Beijing University organized a "mass-education speaking corps" directed at workers.[4] The project met with scant success because of class and cultural differences between students and workers.[5] Given the small number of factory workers in Beijing, Deng Zhongxia, a Beijing University student and future Communist party member, decided to organize rickshaw men.[6] Deng began by hailing a rickshaw man on the street. But

Fig. 16. The preindustrial nature of much of Beijing's economy was readily apparent to the casual observer as workers like this man passed on the street with loads of all sizes and kinds. To one spared having to labor with his hands, "so much of the routine of daily living was made of simple muscular labor that it gave a curious and quite archaic beauty to the life of the city" (George Kates, *The Years That Were Fat* [Cambridge: MIT Press, 1967], p. 99). However, the simple use of manual labor created numerous social complications when labor bosses tried to manage teams of workers and when guilds, the chamber of commerce, and the police tried to regulate competition among individuals and groups. From Heinz v. Perckhammer, *Peking* (Berlin: Albertus-Verlag, 1928).

the puller soon deserted the young student and his earnest talk for a more likely fare. Deng finally persuaded a few pullers he met at a teahouse to assemble at a rickshaw stand near Tianan Gate to discuss ways of lowering rickshaw rents. The rickshaw men pulled their vehicles into a square and began their deliberations within the relative privacy of a wall of parked rickshaws. They refused to respond to the inquiries of the first policemen on the scene, who complained that the pullers were blocking the street, but were unable to ignore a larger contingent of policemen who arrived to break up the gathering. Deng Zhongxia could only "helplessly" return to his dormitory. After his miscued encounter with Beijing rickshaw men, Deng turned his attention to printers on the assumption that their higher "cultural level" would make them more receptive to unionism. But his tentative contacts were broken off when supervising labor bosses used their power to intimidate workers sympathetic to Deng's overtures.

Deng Zhongxia's flexibility and inventiveness foreshadowed his later success as one of the party's most effective labor organizers. As Peng Pai and Mao Zedong eventually demonstrated in the case of the Chinese peasantry, adapting Marxism to Chinese conditions required adding elasticity to European concepts and categories. But in the early 1920s would-be organizers had difficulty seeing the broader urban world of work as a springboard for revolutionary politics. Even when they made the perceptual leap executed by Deng, practical methods for organizing workers proved elusive.

By the end of 1920, frustrated by the scattered, seemingly inaccessible nature of workers in Beijing and by the prevalence of a "guild ideology," Deng Zhongxia and his comrades took the radical step of leaving Beijing, not for the industrial city of Shanghai or the countryside, but for the small railway town of Changxindian located ten miles south of the city.[7] The workers of Changxindian had already advertised their political availability. In the early months of May Fourth protests and rallies, five hundred Changxindian railway men had joined patriotic societies and given support to the Beijing student movement.[8] They even managed to organize a union on their own, which, however, was soon forced to disband.[9] Deng and his fellow students founded a school for workers and managed to neutralize the power of the labor bosses who stood between them and the railway men.[10] A firsthand account of a May Day rally at Changxindian in 1921 bears witness to their success in persuading many of the three to four thousand workers to embrace the ideals and rhetoric of the labor movement and radical politics.[11] Still wary of competitors for the loyalty of the workers, rally speakers enjoined those assembled "not to love the labor bosses who stifled" them. In the procession that followed the May Day meeting, participants carried banners reading "Eight-Hour Work Day," "Bureaucrats Are Public Servants—Workers Are Gods," and "Our Enemies Are Those Who Eat But Do Not Work." For leftists who despaired of building a revolution from rickshaw pullers, tea pourers, and craftsmen, Changxindian was a beacon of modern working-class politics. Nonetheless, not even the earnest radicalism of Changxindian railway men measured up to the expectations of their intellectual mentors. A report later written by Beijing Communists noted that when evening classes were first organized for Changxindian railway men in 1920, "the workers there were even more backward than the Shanghai proletariat."[12] Imagining themselves rightly as China's intellectual avant-garde, Beijing's young radicals looked in vain for a comparably advanced working-class culture.

Beijing itself, as Deng Zhongxia had discovered, with its efficient police force and a succession of governments hostile to mass movements, did not offer easy passage from academe and the world of politicians and publicists to the factory floor. While May Day was being celebrated in 1921 in Changxindian in scenes suffused with working-class militancy, May Day in Beijing consisted of meetings confined to the campus of Beijing University and the surreptitious distribution of leaflets.[13] The leaflets promised future May Days when workers would be allowed to "erect arches, let off fireworks, and hang up lanterns."[14] Alluding to Beijing's role as a status factory for the country's elite, radical publicists observed that "those who have secured an official position know how to celebrate their own acquisition of rank and wealth" but have no interest in a "day of remembrance for us poor people." The leaflet concluded that "Beijing is a prison." Communists who operated in Beijing in the 1920s complained that the political situation was "extremely reactionary" to the point that "it was impossible to carry out concrete work."[15]

Hemmed in by official repression, guild competition, and Marxian orthodoxy, radical labor politics tended to follow along horizontal and vertical lines of least resistance to create a precariously balanced network of official patrons, cadres, and working-class constituents. For example, Communist leader Li Dazhao struck a bargain with the northern warlord Wu Peifu, who made a public show of progressive views, to allow six Communist party members to work as undercover inspectors on the Beijing-Hankou rail line. Wu, as secret patron of the Communists, received help in rooting out the influence of political rivals in the railroad organization in return for protection of fledgling union branches.[16] By joining high-level political connections to militant communities of railway men through the mediating device of Leninist party organization, the Communists set the stage for a successful strike in August 1922 along the entire Beijing-Hankou line.[17] Wiring together political assets in this fashion was an inspired improvisation, which momentarily amplified Communist and railway-worker influence. But the move also meant dependence on warlord support and isolation from an urban mass base. When Changxindian workers led Beijing-Hankou railwaymen in another massive strike in February 1923, Wu Peifu chose to crush the movement.

Radical labor organizers had proven at Changxindian that the natural militancy of Chinese labor under capitalism could be given specific political content and appended to party organization. But assembling these working-class communities into citywide or nationwide movements was more difficult. Successful examples of union organizing were scattered. In some cases, like Changxindian and the Anyuan mines in Hunan, work sites were located outside population centers, so that workers were isolated from both potential allies and converts. In addition, even modest organizational gains threatened to bring the heel of warlord reaction down on workers.

Guilds and Worker Interests

Organizers who failed to win workers away from the authority of labor bosses and guilds blamed Beijing's "feudal" mentality and the presence of a "guild ideology" among workers. Considering Li Dazhao's vertical alliance with Wu Peifu and the clique- and faction-ridden nature of the city's intellectual community, criticism of workers for showing an affinity for patron-client ties rings a bit hollow. The rule of thumb for political action in Beijing, where ties to persons of influence and with brothers and sisters under the skin were both valued, was mobilization in all directions to include patrons and followers, as well as friends, fellow provincials, and comrades. In this sense "elite" and "mass" politics shared a common preoccupation with husbanding and deploying the protective and predatory powers held by patrons and bosses. Scholars like Jean Chesneaux have tended to dismiss the survival of guilds in Republican China as a traditional residue typical of workers who clung to the past. And yet Chesneaux's classic account of Chinese labor in the 1920s contains numerous examples of guilds and guildsmen participating in strikes and protests, both of an economic and of a broader political nature, which belie his assertion that workers "could no longer rely on the protection formerly given them by their guilds."[18] More recent studies, like Gail Hershatter's history of Tianjin labor, show that the continued vitality of guilds had more to do with their practical political value than with cultural inertia. Guilds "survived because they were experts at giving and receiving patronage, and patronage was the coin of the realm in pre-Liberation Tianjin."[19] In Beijing and elsewhere guilds were entrenched in good part because they were so effective in representing worker interests. Contemporary observers sought to explain the relative weakness of the modern union movement in Beijing for much of the decade by noting the timely way in which the city's craft guilds responded to increases in the cost of living.[20]

The responsiveness of guilds was tested at mid-decade when the accumulated effects of several years of price inflation and copper currency depreciation threatened the standard of living of Beijing workers. The year 1924 alone saw a 23.5 percent rise in the cost of living and a 40 percent plunge in the value of copper currency.[21] Since wages had been customarily calculated in copper cash, these two economic developments put immense pressure on the city's laboring classes. In response, workers struggled to raise their wages and to shift from copper to silver as the basis for setting wage rates.

Some guilds, like those representing painters, carpenters, sawyers, and bricklayers or masons in the building trades, were extremely attentive to livelihood issues. The carpenters guild had increased wages six times in the six years prior to 1924.[22] The guild included craftsmen who built houses and also those who embellished buildings with ornamental wood carving. Both those men who owned or managed carpenter shops and those who worked in the shops were eligible for membership. These shops or work gangs were hired for specific jobs by lumber or construction yards. Lumberyards had their own merchant guild, affiliated with the chamber of commerce. The yards, which numbered more than four hundred by the end of the decade, employed over twenty thousand carpenters, masons, painters, and ordinary laborers in one of the city's largest trades.[23]

The carpenters guild, composed of six district branches, held two citywide meetings a year.[24] In a meeting during the third lunar month wages and other issues related to compensation were discussed. Feelings often ran high when wage rates were discussed, and it was not uncommon for brawls to break out. The second meeting during the fifth lunar month focused on ritual and religious expressions of solidarity. These procedures suggest the degree to which traditional labor organizations could accommodate conflict and debate within organizations marked by strong patriarchal and elitist tendencies. Leaders elected by the membership invariably were the oldest and most respected craftsmen.[25] On the other hand, the leadership structure was relatively spacious, with 120 positions to be filled. Labor bosses often initiated policy and led workers in their struggles against owners.[26] But other guild members necessarily approved, or rejected, their policies.[27]

Under the inflationary pressures of mid-decade, the normal arrangements for handling conflict showed signs of strain. In 1923 carpenters and bricklayers could not wait for the first scheduled meeting and began agitating for increases directly after the lunar new year.[28] Some bricklayers had already put down their tools. At the first meetings of carpenters and masons in 1924, conflict broke out between skilled and unskilled workers over proposed increases in wage rates for the latter.[29] Labor bosses, who took a percentage of the wages of both categories of workers, had accepted an earlier proposal stipulating a significantly higher percentage of increase for skilled workers. While labor bosses and skilled workers monopolized positions of power in the trade and the guild, unskilled workers and apprentices could influence guild policy simply by displaying their dissatisfaction at general meetings. The bias toward achieving a consensus in guild meetings strengthened the hand of low-status groups willing to disrupt the proceedings with their demands.

Once guilds agreed on a new wage structure, they needed to force owners and managers to accept the change and prevent anyone else from working for less. In the spring of 1925 carpenters and masons presented demands to lumberyard owners, but the owners failed to respond. The guilds then printed up leaflets, which were distributed in yards throughout the city, declaring that unless the owners agreed to the new wage rate the workers would strike. A five-day strike finally forced compliance.[30] Painters made their demands for wage increases at the same time, using the same tactic of declaring a fait accompli in printed circulars. The owners, reportedly "reeling" from the strike by carpenters and bricklayers, agreed to negotiate.[31]

At mid-decade guilds and workers who pursued guildlike strategies were generally successful in adjusting wages and means of payment to relieve economic pressures. Construction workers, incense-shop employees, cobblers, used-clothes-store clerks, weavers, papermakers, coal-shop workers, carpet makers, tea pourers and waiters, pork-shop clerks, kiln laborers, farm laborers, bakers, tailors, embroiderers, water carriers, and butchers grumbled, petitioned, demanded, threatened, and struck to win the concessions that would allow incomes to keep pace with prices (see fig. 17). Even Buddhist priests and monks organized briefly on a citywide scale to negotiate with temple abbots and head priests increases in the fees paid for chants and scripture readings.[32] After agreement was reached, a circular with the new rates was distributed to temples throughout Beijing.

Feuds, Fights, and Factions

As befit their hierarchical nature, guilds and less formal boss-worker arrangements conspired to subordinate the interests of labor bosses to owners, of workers to bosses, and of apprentices to higher-status workers. On the other hand, the rhetoric and practice of a paternalism that stressed mutual obligations allowed subaltern ranks to question and resist the arbitrary exercise of author-

Fig. 17. Striking textile workers, joined by bystanders (nonworkers are identifiable by their long gowns and fedora and straw hats), assemble outside their factory. The small, upside-down sign in the foreground reads "maintain order," an indication of a common worker concern for policing their own ranks. Dated 1925, the photograph probably records a strike in March at the Linji weaving factory located just inside Chaoyang Gate in the East City. Linji's two to three hundred workers organized in a nearby teahouse and later demanded pay increases, shorter hours, Sundays off, and the firing of an unpopular factory official. (*Yishi bao,* 4 March 1925.) UPI/Bettmann Newsphotos.

ity. The band-of-brothers mentality latent in work groups lent force to these minor acts of rebellion.

Reflecting the clientelistic tenor of these lines of command and representation, guild politics often centered on leadership struggles among rival factions based on personal followings, territory, and subethnic identity. For example, the blind-storytellers guild was divided into Inner and Outer City factions. The guild's five hundred members experienced economic difficulties in the 1920s as urban entertainment tastes changed, placing the guild officers under pressure to reform and modernize the storyteller's repertoire. When the guild met in late 1923 to elect new officers, the

Outer City storytellers nominated their leader, incumbent president Zhang Zizhen, for reelection. Inner City members objected that Zhang had already served three terms and proposed vice-president Hu Junsheng, who hailed from their part of the city, for the top position. The Outer City storytellers were loathe to give up control of the guild and the Inner City group accused their rivals of monopolizing guild affairs. The resulting debate between the two sides took the form of a "verbal war" bordering on real violence. Finally, a middle faction restored order and mediated a compromise. Zhang and Hu would switch positions.[33]

The continued vitality of craft guilds represented recognition among workers that citywide organization along traditional lines was worthwhile. But not all trades successfully passed the threshold dividing informal coordination of neighborhood and enterprise interests from formal organization and unified leadership. In some cases owner or police repression frustrated worker attempts to organize citywide guilds. When six thousand workers supplying soles to shoe stores attempted to register as a commercial guild in 1920, the police refused on the grounds that makers of shoe soles, despite the fact that they sold goods to the shops, were craftsmen. Eventually, the workers organized secretly and timed their strike in 1925 to take advantage of a spate of new government orders for military boots contracted for by the shops.[34] In other cases, obstacles to citywide organization were largely internal. The old-style ink trade included two hundred skilled and three hundred unskilled workers at sites in and around Beijing. Even though workers were able to meet in 1925 at a southern-suburb temple to discuss a wage increase, the workers explained that they were still without a guild "because human nature is not uniform and grouping together is difficult to do."[35]

Workers who once had and then lost guild representation found formal solidarity difficult to reclaim. The water trade, which supplied city residents with potable water through networks of merchant-owned wells and carriers employed by the merchants, had a formal guild structure in the nineteenth century (fig. 18). But when the modern waterworks was built in 1909, the threat of competition and the weight of official backing for the modern utility led to the breakup of the guild into informal district bodies divided among Shandong, Baoding, and Beijing natives.[36] The ex-

Fig. 18. After loading his wheelbarrow, a carrier delivered fresh well water to customers along an established route. Like night-soil carriers, water carriers strove to defend their particular turf against traditional and modern competitors and against would-be regulators like the police. Courtesy of the Library of Congress.

pected domination of the city's water supply by the waterworks did not come to pass, however, and only a small, but steadily growing minority of households, businesses, and bureaus had running water piped in. Early in the 1920s an attempt had been made to reorganize the guild but the police blocked it.[37] In 1924 a Baoding well owner named Zhu Beidong initiated negotiations with the numerically dominant Shandong group to establish a guild.[38] The merchant guild of well owners would have managed, and indirectly represented, the carriers. Beijing owners and carriers, who were fewest in number of the three ethnic groupings, heard about Zhu's plan and became convinced that he was bent on winning monopoly control, which would "pinch [them] off at the throat." When representatives of the Shandong and Baoding

groups met at an East City teahouse to work out terms of an agreement, forty Beijing water carriers suddenly materialized and
denounced the meeting as a plot against them. Strong words led to
blows, and an hour-long brawl erupted. Police arriving on the
scene attempted to mediate the dispute, to no avail, and the com-
batants were taken off to the station.

A citywide guild, finally established within the next year, meant
a stronger protective cloak for the trade and probable subordination of the weaker Beijing faction.[39] Strong pressures based on
political opportunities for leaders and better benefits for the rank
and file pushed trades to organize formally and extend their
territorial coverage. But costs in terms of financial exactions, loss
of autonomy for constituent units, and political defeat of leaders
made redundant through merger encouraged defections and
opposition. When grain-milling workers in the city's suburbs
attempted to organize a guild in early 1925, the effort was frustrated by intragroup conflict between a "strong faction," based in
the eastern and southern suburbs, and a "weak faction," representing the northern and western suburbs.[40] In the past the two
groups had met twice a year to discuss wage rates but had not been
able to agree on common leaders and a common organization.
Mediation between the two sides failed. When the stronger faction
attempted to impose its will, the numerically weaker body of mill-
ers, like the Beijing faction of water carriers and well owners,
decided to use every means at its disposal, including violence, to
abort the creation of a guild likely to institutionalize the dominant
position of their rivals.

This contentious process resembled state building in miniature.
When one considers that fully developed guilds performed a range
of quasi-governmental functions, the resemblance becomes less an
analogy than a description of the development of extensive local
commitment to the management, control, and representation of
city residents. Even when workers and residents resisted incorporation into citywide bodies and uneven or abortive development
resulted, the terms of the struggle forced those involved to be conscious of power as it was constituted beyond the confines of neighborhood and workplace.

Internal dissension did not prevent guilds from fighting within
the larger arena of city politics for communal and collective rights

and interests. Merchants and workers in Beijing's night-soil trade, who collected excrement from households and public latrines and composted the substance outside the city walls for sale to farmers as fertilizer, were famous for their solidarity and militancy. Their leaders were known in Beijing, in an ironic bow to the warlords (*junfa*), as *fenfa* ("night-soil lords"). They shared this style of appellation with "water lords" (*shuifa*), who were similarly combative.[41] When the police attempted to enforce sanitary regulations on the night-soil business, or when the waterworks tried to install running water, *fenfa* and *shuifa* threw up an "impenetrable military wall," and from behind this they engaged in passive refusal to pick up waste, in the case of the night-soil carriers, and guerrilla campaigns of machine-breaking, in the case of the water carriers.

One might have imagined that a "wall" of guild or guildlike solidarity implied an orderly, consensually based internal politics. But as factionalism in the water trade suggested, and as internecine conflict in the night-soil guild confirmed, conflict and cohesion were two sides of the same corporate coin. Further complicating the picture, this vertically organized factionalism, which sometimes united owners and workers in common cause against rivals, could coincide with class conflict within the trade. A few weeks after the ethnically and territorially based clash among Shandong, Baoding, and Beijing natives in the water trade, water carriers from various parts of the city met in an East City teahouse to discuss the need to raise wages in response to a decision by well owners to raise prices. The carriers threatened a strike, and well owners agreed to a mediated settlement.[42]

Unlike the water trade, the night-soil business was represented by a formally constituted guild. The owners of drying yards dominated leadership of the guild, and carriers were informally attached to the body through their ties with the yard owners. When the guild was not defending its communal interests it was wracked by internal disputes. In August 1925 the police ordered yard owners and carriers to move drying yards to less-populated areas to protect the public health.[43] The carriers responded by striking for three days until the uncollected waste became so offensive that a public outcry forced the police to rescind the order. However, within the trade itself factionalism was endemic. From

1918 to 1925 the presidency of the guild changed hands eleven times.[44] Guild meetings were characterized by the watchful presence of an intensely critical crowd of laborers who were deeply suspicious of guild leaders and ready and willing to demand the resignation of any officer who offended it.

In July 1924 the guild vice-president, Niu Changli, proposed to member yards that from then on each carrier would be assessed monthly dues of forty coppers to underwrite guild expenses and as a means of expanding the range of social services provided members.[45] Niu had the support of a few other yard owners and the carriers who supplied them with night soil. But most other carriers bitterly opposed Niu's plan. They cited their own poverty and suggested that the only possible reason for amassing such a sum was that Niu intended to embezzle the money. Guild president and yard owner Tang Zhishun, no doubt aware of the fate of previous officers, took note of the carriers' objections and indicated his own opposition to the scheme. Later, as Niu and Tang met to discuss their differences, they were surprised by a crowd of fifty carriers who declared their intention of giving Niu a beating on account of his "inhumane" conduct. Tang shielded his vice-president from the workers, and Niu was forced to flee. Instead of feeling gratitude toward Tang, Niu went immediately to the police to denounce president Tang for inciting the carriers to riot.

The carriers then met together and decided to go on strike if Niu Changli did not resign.[46] This represented a victory for the moderates. A more radical group of workers wanted to find Niu and carry out the beating they had earlier been prevented from delivering. In response, a general guild meeting was called to mediate the disputes between Tang and Niu and between Niu and the carriers. The workers, however, proved intransigent. They would settle for nothing less than Niu's ouster. Meanwhile, Niu's younger brothers and sons had gathered together carriers from Niu's drying yard outside the meeting place, armed with clubs and night-soil ladles.[47] They shouted that they would fight to the death to prevent Niu's overthrow. The anti-Niu laborers heard the shouts and, with their "bellies full of resentment with no way to let it out," and yielding to their supposedly "fierce" Shandong temperaments, rushed out to fight the Niu forces. Mediators tried to separate the two sides but were wounded in the attempt. President Tang reacted by announcing that he would resign rather than take responsibility for further disorder. The guild directors rallied to support Tang and to demand that Niu be removed from office. A director named Gan criticized Niu for "all kinds of evil behavior" and made the necessary motions, which were passed. When Niu heard about his expulsion he went to Gan's home and stabbed him to death.[48]

The level of violence reached in the night-soil guild was unusual; but the phenomenon of escalating factional conflict was not. During the same summer of 1924, three other guilds underwent similar internal struggles. The ten-year-old, eight-hundred-member cobblers guild split into two factions over the question of whether to reorganize as a "federation" (*lianhe hui*). The incumbent president, Ding Guangshun, led the "Ding party," supported by leather-shoe makers in the western and northern sections of the city and challenged by the "Liu party," backed by cobblers in the eastern and southern neighborhoods. Liu accused Ding of embezzlement and of taking advantage of his faction's numerical superiority to monopolize guild affairs. Liu's followers planned to use force to topple Ding if their court suit failed to dislodge him.[49] The used-clothes guild, numbering 750 workers within the city walls, also split over the question of whether to modernize its guild organization. The incumbent leadership invited the police to intervene in its affairs and arrest the challengers as troublemakers.[50] A majority of papermaking guild workers held a mass meeting to oppose a minority proposal to amend guild rules.[51] They appealed to both the chamber of commerce and the police for help in derailing the reform faction.

Internal conflict opened up trades and occupational groups to outside intervention as one faction or another sought leverage against its adversaries. A common front of opposition or accommodation vis-à-vis outsiders like the police or competitors often masked a delicate intramural political balance that could easily be pitched from consensus to conflict when money, power, or status threatened to flow in new directions.

As the frequency of territorially based factionalism within guilds and trades suggests, districts of the city, neighborhoods, or even a few streets or lanes could provide a basic frame of reference for worker organization. In Beijing, guilds, or trades without a formal guild organization, were divided into *kouzi* (small groups associated with the "intersection" or "opening" of streets or lanes). For example, the city's seven or eight hundred noodle-and-dumpling-shop workers lacked a guild but maintained a network of *kouzi*, which could send representatives to an ad hoc citywide meeting to discuss wage demands.[52] Coffin makers supported a citywide guild, which was in turn divided into four "big" *kouzi* located in the North, South, East, and West Cities.[53] While citywide organization might lie beyond the reach of the average worker, sublocal bodies like *kouzi* operated both as arenas for the conduct of basic-level politics and as bridges to competition and cooperation at higher levels.

The course of conflicts at the shop and neighborhood level frequently turned on personalities. Some owners were willing to negotiate worker demands. Others took an extremely hard line. Cloisonné workers in one shop requested a meal of meat dumplings (*jiaozi*) at festival time, and the owner responded by suggesting meatless, and cheaper, steamed buns (*mantou*). After discussing the matter among themselves the workers went out on their own to dinner and the opera. The owner, "fearing that the workers would join together and oppose him," reimbursed the men for their banquet and opera tickets.[54]

Once a conflict had been joined, much depended on the moderation, or lack thereof, exhibited by the owner or manager. After a four-day sit-down strike at a mat-weaving factory, the firm's assistant manager made the mistake of locking in the workers. They responded in Luddite fashion by destroying sixteen machines, using knives to cut phone and electrical lines, and ruining stockpiles of raw materials. When the assistant manager unlocked the door, the workers grabbed and beat him.[55] In another case, workers in an iron shop came to resent the owner on account of his stinginess, and a group of newly recruited apprentices debated among themselves whether to quit or go on strike. The owner got wind of the dissension and tried to persuade some of the veteran workers to accept the idea of firing the new recruits. But in a small shop where laborers and bosses lived and worked practically on top of each other plots and conspiracies were difficult to conceal. An apprentice overheard the owner's entreaties and said in a loud voice, "We shall go on strike tomorrow!" In a rage the owner clubbed the apprentice to the ground and was about to throw him out the shop door when a policeman arrived.[56]

Workers might act to expel managers who threatened their interests or provoked their anger. A government-affiliated carpet factory in the East City near Dongsi Arch was managed by an official named Xie who was well liked by his employees. But the assistant manager, Hu Jinfang, was roundly hated for his abusive treatment of the apprentices who made up the bulk of workers in the carpet trade.[57] He punished the slightest mistake with a beating. Graver offenses resulted in workers being tied up and thrown into a dark room or left exposed to the elements.[58] Hu managed the factory like a private fiefdom, checked only by Xie's benevolence. News that Xie had been promoted out of the factory and that Hu would replace him galvanized workers, appalled at the prospect of falling under Hu's exclusive control. The factory's six master craftsmen (*gongshi*) called a meeting of apprentices in the company's reception room to discuss a strategy for ridding themselves of Hu. But Hu's personal servant overheard the discussions and reported back to his boss. When Hu angrily confronted the workers, relations between Hu and the workers had already become so poisoned that his outburst caused the crowd of laborers to surge forward to attack him. He barely escaped out the back door. The workers told police sent to investigate the altercation that Hu Jinfang was guilty of corruption and embezzlement. In a bill of particulars issued later, the carpet workers alleged that Hu had skimmed off enough funds to open his own factory, appropriated company furniture for his personal use, and systematically cheated workers out of better food and fuel by substituting coarser grains and lower grades of coal than were customary and pocketing the difference.

Driven out of the factory by a crowd of indignant workers, Hu Jinfang returned a week later with ten of his personal followers.[59] He summoned masters and apprentices to his office and announced that the factory would close because of a lack of funds. One of the masters spoke up and told Hu that he owed them back wages and that once the local courts had ruled on compensation, all the workers planned to resign. Hu refused to acknowledge the debt and gave the workers fifteen minutes to clear out of the factory. Hu's riposte enraged the workers, who broke through the circle of retainers surrounding Hu, caught him as he ran out the back door, and beat him until he was covered with mud and blood. After this humiliation, Hu resigned. In a final act of revenge Hu lured several of the masters to his house on the pretext of handing over money to them and had them tied up, beaten, and thrown out into the street. When the carpet-factory workers heard what had happened they considered attacking Hu Jinfang in his house. But the masters prevailed on them to seek legal redress instead.[60]

Other owners and managers cultivated the loyalty of employees to the point where they were able to mobilize workers to support them and defend their personal or the shop's interests. Wang Xiaogui, nicknamed "Barking Dog" and owner of a large night-soil drying yard outside the southern wall of the Outer City, was such an individual. One summer day in 1924, when Wang tried to buy some meat at a pork shop just inside the wall near picturesque Taoranting Lake, he got in a terrible argument with a shop clerk. The shop was notorious in the area for its rude treatment of patrons, and Wang and the clerk nearly came to blows before people from nearby stores rushed in to mediate. Wang left the shop and returned to his yard, where he rallied sixty night-soil carriers armed with ladles and buckets of excrement. They marched to the pork shop and dumped shit over everything. Under the circumstances, "mediators dared not come in," and the shop owner ordered his clerks to counterattack. Thirty policemen had to be dispatched from the nearest district station to stop the brawl.[61] In a similar incident, the owner of a vegetable farm outside Xizhi Gate mobilized twenty of his field hands, armed with carrying poles, to exact revenge on a group of soldiers who had beaten him on the way to market.[62]

Labor bosses or master craftsmen, who stood between owners and managers, on the one hand, and workers, on the other, often were at the focal point of small group or enterprise conflicts. Because labor bosses were responsible for paying their charges and taking a cut themselves, bosses were subject to intense worker scrutiny. At a military-uniform and tent factory outside the northern wall of the Outer City, four female labor bosses, who supervised seventy or eighty poor women, cheated the workers when they changed the "big" money they received from management into "small" money to distribute in wages.[63] When the women discovered what was happening, they confronted the bosses and demanded a "settling of accounts." The labor bosses not only refused to hand over the back pay, but also accused the workers of fomenting disorder. Angered, the women threw the bosses to the ground and began beating them. This drew the attention of company officials, who came over to mediate. When the manager discovered the reasons for the altercation he had the four bosses arrested.

Defeated in the workplace, the labor bosses and their allies plotted revenge. The bosses' husbands met at a neighborhood teahouse to figure out a plan to free their wives and intimidate the workers. The men used a contact in the government to secure the freedom of the four bosses and then recruited local ruffians to prepare a surprise attack on the women as they left the factory in the evening. As the factory let out at 6 P.M., supporters of the bosses and their kin, led by the four, greeted the women with a hail of rocks. But instead of being intimidated, the women "closed in a swarm" and grabbed the ringleaders, pummeling them and pulling their hair. The attackers, bloodied and disorganized, were driven off.

Because the role played by labor bosses was so critical in the day-to-day management of work and in mediating between the work group and owners and others in positions of authority, laborers naturally sought, if possible, to influence the behavior of bosses and remove those whom they found objectionable. In early 1920, half the seventy workers in a French-owned iron factory went on strike because they did not like the new labor boss put in charge of them.[64] In the spring of 1925 eighty workers at a papermaking factory staged a strike to protest "savage" treatment of apprentices and servants by two master craftsmen. The thirty-two apprentices at the factory, none older than sixteen years, had been kept isolated from their families, who had been barred from the compound on orders of the two bosses. During the struggle the other masters at the plant sided with the workers and made representations to the managers on their behalf. The dispute was resolved when the master was fired.[65] When the labor boss of a mat-weaving factory refused to entertain worker requests for higher wages, the indignant laborers added his dismissal to their demands.[66]

When bosses sided with management, workers and apprentices were deprived of their most readily available source of effective leadership. When bosses acted as brokers and representatives, they played a role congenial to worker interests. This more complex portrait of the labor boss and guildsman contradicts Chesneaux's assertion that such individuals exercised "absolute power."[67] We need not share his puzzlement over the fact that "strangely enough the constant resentment felt by workers toward foremen. . .did not exclude a certain sense of loyalty." Absolutist pretensions come naturally to bosses and patrons even when this status depends on tenuous connections to higher-ups and on the wavering loyalty of one's followers.

The Sprouts of Unionism

Craft guilds acted aggressively to adjust wages to maintain living standards. Workers could also seek broader improvements in working conditions. In 1925 workers in shops specializing in aromatic and vegetable oils asked for longer vacations at festival times, two days off each month, protection against arbitrary firings, and larger year-end bonuses in addition to an increase in wages.[68] Guilds customarily, though not in all cases, provided support for medical treatment and, in the event of death, a coffin and shipment back to one's native place. In 1925 pig butchers at Beijing slaughterhouses, who were mostly from Shandong and worried about the threat of illness or death far from home, added these concerns to their demand for higher wages.[69] In this expanded form, guild-based worker politics shaded over into the kind of reforms associated with labor union activity.

Aside from the price and currency pressures that stimulated worker politics at mid-decade, laborers in Beijing worked under conditions that could easily be converted into a list of union grievances. Carpet-factory workers labored from 7 A.M. to midnight seven days a week for four dollars a month, or slightly less than what the average rickshaw man made, taking into account the two or three meals a day provided by shops.[70] The factories themselves were badly heated in the winter, poorly ventilated, and dirty.[71] Children as young as eight or nine worked as apprentices. Two-thirds of the Danhua Match Company's one thousand workers were children aged nine to sixteen, who worked sixteen or seventeen hours a day under "hellish" conditions in buildings thick with yellow phosphorus fumes and slept in broken-down shacks that served as dormitories.[72] The larger mechanized and handicraft factories used guild-style apprenticeship to hold down labor costs without being able to offer mobility or job security to the youngsters recruited. In large and small, traditional and modern enterprises apprentices were subject to corporal punishment and mistreatment.[73] The police cited abusive treatment by owners or labor bosses as a prime factor causing apprentices to flee shops and factories.[74] In one murder case, the wife of a leatherworker was accused of beating a fourteen-year-old apprentice to death.[75]

Cognizant of general economic pressures and particular injustices, Beijing workers in the traditional trades were capable of playing a complex, multileveled political game. While guilds and guildlike bodies may have limited the nature and comprehensiveness of worker demands and grievances, the nested hierarchy of shops, work gangs, *kouzi*, district or big *kouzi*, and citywide organizations offered a framework for expressing and discussing grievances within occupational groups.

Feuds and intensely personal conflicts were common because basic-level economic units like shops and work gangs adopted a self-consciously family-like style of operations organized around patriarchal leaders and subleaders. It was not uncommon for solidarity in these small groups to be based on real kin, friendship, or native-place ties. Workers, labor bosses, managers, and owners had good reason to take conflict personally. The frequency of strikes and unrest over personal issues like unpopular labor bosses also reflected the general sensitivity that Beijing people displayed in matters touching on status and rank. Turn-of-the-century strikes in France show a comparable emphasis on "personal issues," attributable in part, according to Peter Stearns, to a French cultural preoccupation with "personal, individual dignity."[76] In China the dignity of the group and the position of individuals within the social hierarchy of the group played a similar role in stimulating and escalating factional and communal strife. In the compacted, totalistic world of the work group, challenging the authority of a master or a labor boss was a "revolutionary" act and was treated as such by leaders and followers alike. Violence and personal humiliation served to unmask and neutralize bosses targeted by workers for replacement. Insurgent laborers in turn became the object of a kind of "counterrevolutionary" terror by desperate bosses.

When these smaller units passed authority up to larger federations and associations or became the targets of the mobilizing ambitions of those higher up in the hierarchy, a transfer or a widening of allegiance took place. The groups involved were acutely conscious of the costs and benefits represented by these transactions, especially if the rise of a new level of organization was associated with increased power for a particular leader, faction, or subethnic community. Within the boundaries of trades and occupations, workers were likely to have reached a modicum of political and class consciousness simply by dint of experiencing the power struggles woven into the fabric of shop life and trade politics. At the very least, the "consciousness of status" characteristic of guild and corporate life provided the basis for the outbreak of a kind of positional warfare waged within and among shops, work groups, and *kouzi.*[77]

Initially, workers who were organized in guilds or who operated within guild-influenced trades were better prepared to defend their interests than were workers in modern factories and enterprises. Although guild workers sometimes acted or organized in secret, they would have been unlikely to resort to anonymous demands of the kind issued by postal employees during an abortive labor action in 1922.[78] Anonymity is a prudent strategy when "forms of collective defense are weak."[79] Complex, tightly organized work groups composed of labor bosses, workers, and apprentices, who might well also be friends or relatives and share the same hometown, had an almost reflexive capacity for collective defense, which could be turned to more outward-looking strategies. Workers in modern industry, initially less well organized, formed larger, more obvious targets for labor organizers. But factory workers could also be more vulnerable to repression. In the aftermath of the streetcar workers' brief strike in January 1925 to protest attacks by soldiers, the company made a list of strike leaders, secretly trained new employees, and then fired twenty-nine conductors when replacements were available.[80]

In 1924, as radicals began to take a new look at the political potential of Beijing workers, they faced laborers in the old trades, who were already organized along traditional lines, and workers in the modern sector, who displayed both receptivity to union overtures and a tendency to replicate the success of guild strategies and methods. Beijing printers, with their close connection to government and the highly politicized newspaper industry, were among the first Beijing workers to establish ties with radical politicians and labor organizers. Li Dazhao and fellow Communists supported printers in a three-day strike in late 1924.[81] Despite contacts between the printers and radical politicians, printers continued to follow the tried and true guild pattern of teahouse meetings to discuss grievances and strategy, selection of representatives to confront owners, and strikes to break the resistance of management.[82]

Elsewhere in China where labor organizers were able to make inroads into traditional guilds, as was the case in Changsha in the early 1920s, mobilization often proceeded with great rapidity because workers "were already organized."[83] In her study of Tianjin, Gail Hershatter explains the relative "quiescence" of ironworkers and machine makers in one district of the city, in part, by noting the area's weakly articulated guild tradition.[84] In Beijing, labor organizers were finally spurred on to organize workers in the preindustrial economy after witnessing what guildsmen could achieve. Non-Communist Nationalist labor activists, recruited in Beijing universities, began to organize city workers in 1925 partly as a means of countering Communist influence in local politics.[85] Observing that the Communists' own base was largely confined to the city's modern factory sector, the Nationalists looked to the city's vast preindustrial economy for support. The night-soil-carriers strike in the summer of 1925 was decisive in demonstrating to them the modern political potential of traditional labor.[86] By 1926 these organizers, several of whom would reemerge in 1928 as leaders of a new Nationalist union movement, had discarded student dress and were eating and living with the workers they were trying to mobilize. They recorded some successes among newspaper deliverers, water and night-soil carriers, postal workers, and rickshaw men.

In 1928 and 1929 the natural responsiveness of the modern sector to union organizing, and the established openness of much of preindustrial Beijing to new opportunities for workers to advance their interests and resolve internal conflicts, laid the foundation for a powerful union movement. But if guilds could function like labor unions in representing worker interests, unions could operate like guilds and reproduce an intensely personal, faction-prone internal politics, which gave enormous patriarchal or "feudal" authority to leaders while exposing them to "family" rifts, succession crises, and rebellions in the ranks. Within the Beijing labor movement, proletarian politics and its attachment to reformist and revolutionary currents became entangled with the factionalism and personalism of guild and guildlike politics to create a political tiger, which leaders and followers found difficult to ride and dangerous to dismount from.

Eight

Citizens in a New Public Sphere: Widening Circles of Political Participation

If Beijing was grudging in its production of a modern working class, the city was more generous in cultivating residents who considered themselves modern citizens. Beijing was the fountainhead of a focused and militant nationalism flowing out of the 1919 May Fourth Movement and the city's modern universities and colleges. By mid-decade and the outbreak of the May Thirtieth Movement, nationalist rallies drew hundreds of thousands of demonstrators.

Despite Beijing's long association with imperial power and politics, city residents themselves had no special rights or responsibilities related to public discussion or debate. As Frederick Mote has observed, the Chinese city had nothing analogous to institutions like the *polis* or commune to give autonomy to civic traditions, no concept of citizen to legitimize individual or group initiatives in the realm of public affairs, and few civic monuments to rally around.[1] On the other hand, the preindustrial Chinese city supported a rich variety of public activities, including marketing, theatergoing, worshipping, and teahouse and restaurant socializing. Examination, merchant, and craft guilds sustained a tradition of debate and discussion within their halls and chambers among their separate constituencies of scholars, traders, and craftsmen. At moments of community crisis, official and merchant centers of power were capable of spinning out citywide consortiums of elites to exert a measure of control over urban affairs.[2] What was missing was the legal rationale for municipal government and an ideological justification for expanding the compass of politically active individuals beyond scholar-officials, examination candidates, and guild leaders. Once these ideological and legal underpinnings were in place, public spaces ranging from temple grounds and brothels to public parks and theaters became available to house city politics. Old conventions guiding public behavior, like meeting in teahouses to mediate or conspire, combined with new ideologies and organizations, like unionism and political clubs and parties, to underpin a radical expansion of political participation.[3]

This new political arena or public sphere was a synthesis of old and new practices and attitudes. The high value traditionally placed on the public realm (*gong*) of gentry and merchant leadership reinforced the modern notion of public opinion as a vastly expanded sphere of discussion and debate.[4] In Europe this public sphere emerged between the state and civil society as a zone where voluntary associations formed and the state was defended and criticized.[5] Initially suspended precariously between the modern absolutist state and traditional estates, this sphere was remade and expanded by an insurgent bourgeoisie. In China the dependence of gentry and merchant opinion on official power (*guan*) was loosened during the late Qing and then broken under the Republic. Urban elites never gathered the strength and the will to support a fully autonomous public sphere. But the trembling of the state in the 1920s, the weak legitimacy of private interests (*si*), and the positive moral and political evaluation of *gong* as a zone of discussion and concern encouraged newspaper editors, new and old civic leaders, and ordinary citizens to improvise tactics and strategies for expressing political views in public.[6] Thus constituted, city politics took on a life and a logic of its own as opportunities to engage in political discussion and action expanded.[7]

As a basic precondition for political interaction, social communication in Beijing had intensified by 1920. Many public and private offices in the city were connected by telephone. Fifty to a hundred newspapers were published, ranging from major papers covering national and local politics to "mosquito" papers oriented toward social news and entertainment.[8] Popular dailies reached circulations of ten thousand copies.[9] Limited-circulation magazines could easily obtain credit from printers to publish their views

Fig. 19. Young women stroll in Central Park (Sun Yat-sen Park after 1928) past cafe tables. Originally the site of the imperial Altar of Earth and Harvests, the park was opened to the public in 1914. An entrance fee discouraged use of the park by the city's poorer residents. Patrons drank tea, dined, bought souvenirs, listened to band music, or simply promenaded. On occasion, political meetings were held in the park. Courtesy of the Library of Congress.

and ideas on a shoestring.[10] Other, more informal yet public, forums of political discussion included Beijing's Central Park, where journalists, officials, and politicians gathered in the evening to exchange gossip and political intelligence (fig. 19).[11] The city's numerous bathhouses, thousands of restaurants, and hundreds of brothels provided congenial environments for political and social machinations. After the 1911 Revolution, new-style bath "gardens" had opened, equipped with modern furnaces, electricity, and telephones. "As the vanity of townspeople deepened, the influence of the bathhouse industry grew by leaps and bounds," and bathhouses became "centers of social intercourse" for city elites.[12] The restaurant trade also flourished under the early Republic. The practice of holding banquets at fine restaurants, already well established under the Qing, "spread like wildfire" with the addition of politicians and military men to their clientele.[13] An official in the Ministry of Interior, discussing the custom of belonging to informal "eating associations" (*jucan hui*), claimed that the practice had begun with parliamentary politicians and had spread to the universities and professions and beyond.

Taking advantage of such informal meetings, employers discuss among themselves the best way of securing from their workers the maximum efficiency with the minimum pay, while employees will devote their conversation to shorter hours and better wages. Small groups of railway and postmen are seen dining in street corner restaurants on weekends. When debate on the merits or demerits of a boss becomes too hot they may end . . . with a free-for-all fight.[14]

Less public, but completely respectable were meetings held in the city's "flower world."[15] Brothels provided meeting places for merchants, politicians, male students, and, in lower-class houses, male workers. For example, it was reported that key decisions guiding the development of the May Fourth Movement were made in a Beijing brothel in 1919.[16]

Guildhalls (*huiguan*) for fellow provincials and the locality clubs (*tongxiang hui*) they housed were also put to new, more overtly political purposes. Four hundred of these hostels had been established in Imperial Beijing to serve the needs of visiting officials and examination candidates, as well as, to a lesser degree, sojourning merchants.[17] (Merchants also had their own guilds specifically devoted to commerce, like An Disheng's jewelers' guild.) In 1921 a newspaper editorialist noted that while *tongxiang hui* had always had a "relationship with politics," they were now being used openly as "political weapons."[18]

Under these favorable conditions, citizens groups met to protest poor electrical and water service, oppose taxes, deal with food shortages brought on by warfare, promote self-government, and protest outrages by soldiers. Disgruntled consumers of public utilities publicized their complaints in the press and agitated for nonpayment of bills.[19] A "Manchu Advancement Society" formed to press for aid to destitute fellow ethnics.[20] Clerks and minor officials in government bureaus and ministries united in "salary-demanding associations" to attempt to pry months of back wages from precariously financed governments. Women established a political association and a birth control society.[21] The visit of eugenicist Margaret Sanger to Beijing in 1922 demonstrated how attentive many Beijing residents were to public affairs and how this level of interest, combined with the intensity of social communications in the city, could contribute to the founding of voluntary associations.[22] Sanger gave a lecture at Beijing University with famed philosopher Hu Shi as her interpreter. Copies of her pamphlet "Family Limitation" were passed out to the audience in the crowded hall. By the following morning the tract had been translated into Chinese. By that afternoon five thousand mimeographed copies were in public circulation. Six months after Sanger's visit a Beijing Birth Control Society was established by fifty women influenced by her lecture and the debate it generated.

Public awareness of issues, and the pervasiveness of small and informal gatherings of like-minded persons with shared interests, were basic facts of political life in Beijing. However, the political permissibility of organizing small groups into large ones, and informal congeries into unions, societies, and associations, was subject to a host of qualifications, restrictions, and rules. The sphere of public discussion and politics was bounded by convention and by law and was at times heavily policed. Professional associations (*fatuan*), like the chamber of commerce and bankers association, and high-status individuals and groups, like gentry and well-connected politicians, had the de jure or de facto right to hold meetings and to petition the government. "Police laws" required official permission for any political meeting held outside the realm of *fatuan* activity and banned outright political action by women, workers, and students.

Confrontations between police and city residents over the right to meet and assemble were settled in a variety of ways, depending on the prevailing political climate and a shifting calculus of numbers and moral authority. In November 1921 police prevented five thousand Beijing and Zhili province gentry from holding a meeting in a Beijing guildhall.[23] The police objected to the size of the assembly, and so the *tongxiang hui* was forced to reconvene two months later under a representational system, which brought four hundred people together. In the fall of 1923, when a crowd of city residents tried to meet outside Tianan Gate, the police hired bands of street entertainers and musicians to drown out the political speech-making.[24] In other cases the police were less successful in regulating and restricting public life. In the summer of 1924 a prominent politician and his audience faced down armed police who had come to disband a local self-government rally.[25] During a teahouse meeting of three hundred apprentice printers held the following spring outside normal guild procedures, police sent to investigate were driven away by cursing, knife-wielding workers.[26]

During the twenties Beijing was the site of social movements, such as feminism, mass nationalism, and unionism, which gave new political meaning to public spaces like the area outside Tianan Gate. In the 1920s Tiananmen "square" was not yet a square in the formal architectural sense. The local press referred to the spot as the "empty space outside Tianan Gate."[27] Filling this space periodically with townspeople (*shimin*) and citizens (*gongmin*) projected an evocative, albeit fleeting, image of municipal and national solidarity. Since many other "public" settings, like temples, guildhalls, teahouses, and parks, were either restricted to private or corporate memberships, charged fees, or required purchases of food or drink, spaces opened up to all by the pressure of social movements were critical to the generation of a truly "mass" politics. No less important was the fact that movements like mass nationalism and unionism thrust national and citywide politics into school compounds, shops, factories, temples, and offices. Citywide institutions like chambers of commerce and police forces lent new structure to the widening debate over national and local issues. But social movements that flowed through and around institutions also performed this function. As a result, Beijing residents were faced with an unprecedented range of choices as to when, how, and where to take political action.

Assemblies of Citizens

The Qing government granted legal or professional associations the formal right to discuss matters related to specific areas of competence and responsibility. Merchants, for example, were permitted, according to their chamber of commerce charters, to deliberate on the state of the market. But the Qing and Republican regimes were finally unable to limit debate to carefully circum-scribed areas or to prevent new associations from forming. For example, in 1919, on the eve of the May Fourth Movement, a Beijing "Foreign Affairs Association" (*waijiao xiehui*), composed of representatives of journalists, merchants, members of parlia-ment, and students, actively lobbied the government to stiffen its spine on the question of Shandong concessions.[28] A high-level aide to President Xu Shichang received the group and listened to its demands. Elites who might have once depended on official sanc-tion or informal contacts to coordinate their activities simply declared their formal existence. Only the state could license pro-fessional associations. But these legally constituted bodies were capable of endowing interest groups like the Foreign Affairs Association with a quasi-legal aura.[29] While a reef of societies and associations steadily emerged from the interlocking activities of *fatuan*, mass movements sent waves of public indignation against the state and through urban society. Within and against these structures and movements the role of city resident as citizen took concrete form.

The May Fourth Movement both stimulated the public activi-ties of organizations like the chamber of commerce and drew ordinary residents to demonstrations as spectators and partici-pants. The movement was based in the politics of student com-munities and university enclaves. Student marches, speeches, and arrests dominated the weeks of protest in Beijing. But student lead-ers also found journalists, merchants, and provincial clubs recep-tive to overtures appealing for support and solidarity.

At the first protest meeting on May 4, 1919, outside Tianan Gate, according to press reports, "many townspeople" joined the three thousand students who had marched there from their univer-sities and colleges.[30] The townspeople would have been recogniz-able because of the contrastingly uniform dress and youth of the students and the school-by-school order they had fallen into.[31] The crowd assembled on the marble bridges beneath the gate and listened to speeches by student leaders and the entreaties of police chief Wu Bingxiang, who noted that "the weather is very warm. I beg you gentlemen to return home at once and rest."[32] Instead, the crowd marched south between the long walls that still enclosed the approach to Tianan Gate, and then swung east to confront guards

Fig. 20. Tianan Gate and the twin marble pillars that stand before it are visible in the distance beyond the smaller Zhonghua Gate. The western border of the Legation Quarter is on the right. The space beneath Tianan Gate, where crowds of demonstrators assembled, was boxed in by low walls and dotted with trees. In addition to providing a dramatic physical setting at the center of the city, the site was convenient for deploying columns of protesters against government offices and the entrances to the Legation Quarter. From Heinz v. Perckhammer, *Peking* (Berlin: Albertus-Verlag, 1928).

and police who blocked entry to the Legation Quarter. (See figure 20 for a view of the area in question.) Many Beijing residents wept openly at the sight of the marching, shouting youths.[33] The order of the march was later broken when the students reached Minister Cao Rulin's house in the East City. Youths and police clashed in a violent episode in which Cao's house was burned and another high official was beaten. The symbolic and real violence of the movement, including banners and petitions written in blood, the baton charges of the police, and assaults on the persons and property of men of status and position, served to underline the radical nature of the remonstrance.

As student protests mounted, the Foreign Affairs Association planned a rally in Central Park for May 7, the fourth anniversary of the hated "Twenty-One Demands" imposed on the Republic by the Japanese in a "final ultimatum" on that date in 1915. On the morning of the seventh, as one or two thousand citizens converged on the entrance to Central Park, they found over two thousand police, gendarmes, cavalry, and soldiers deployed along Changan Avenue to block access to the park.[34] A hundred protesters tried to reassemble outside Tianan Gate, but by one thirty in the afternoon more troops arrived to block off streets running into the center of the city. Journalists estimated that ten to twenty thousand people were prevented from reaching Tianan Gate that afternoon. Association leaders finally retired to guildhalls to regroup.

While access to the streets, squares, temples, and parks of the city were contested by students and townspeople, police and troops, crowds of citizens could rely on the social and organizational base provided by their control of school compounds and guildhalls as sanctuaries and staging areas. The government often succeeded in bottling up or otherwise obstructing the movement of protesters, but lacked the will or the means to attack the institutions that generated elite and popular support for protest. A tradition of corporate self-regulation gave citizens platforms from which to speak and act and defended positions from which to fight and sally forth. In the absence of strong guarantees of individual rights, a powerful sense of group prerogatives and territoriality provided citizens with a measure of protection against state repression.

City residents could hardly fail to be impressed by the heroic style of protest and remonstrance patented by Beijing students in May 1919 (fig. 21). Newspaper reports of encounters between student activists and townspeople in Beijing suggest an intensity of feeling that helps explain how and why the May Fourth pattern of protest and patriotic expression rose again and again in the 1920s. In the weeks following the May Fourth Incident, student lecture brigades appeared throughout the city to press their case against the government. When students spoke merchants and workers in the crowd demonstrated their appreciation by sending pots of tea up to the speakers.[35] In one case, as lecturers declaimed in a vacant lot next to the New World entertainment arcade, a used-clothing dealer was so moved by what he heard that he spontaneously committed himself to the organization of an anti-Japanese boycott in

Fig. 21. The message affixed in patches to this student's gown reads, in part, "Eradicate unequal treaties and, without flinching, forge ahead to the bitter end." The presence in the same city of officials eager to placate foreign interests and of students opposed to any compromise on questions of national sovereignty helped insure the continuation of the May Fourth tradition of protest. UPI/Bettmann Newsphotos.

his guild. Near the chamber of commerce headquarters, six or seven hundred listeners responded enthusiastically to the patriotic sentiments expressed by the students. An old man in the audience wept uncontrollably.[36] When challenged by the police to disperse, the students, backed by the crowds, launched into polemics, which intimidated policemen or won them over. "If one took off this uniform, who wouldn't sympathize with your opinions," one policeman admitted. "Are you a Chinese or a foreigner?" the students insisted.

For its part the government occasionally declared its intention to completely "eradicate the 'sprouts of disorder' (*luanmeng*)" represented by the student movement. The police claimed that the Beijing Student Federation was not a *fatuan* and therefore had no legitimate public status.[37] But despite a tendency, evident throughout the decade, to become absorbed in intramural conflicts, students preserved and promoted the May Fourth style of politics with its radical moral tone and clear commitment to political action in public settings.[38] Increasingly, citizens outside the university appropriated this modernized version of the traditional practice of remonstrance. The notion of the moral equality of all "commoners" or citizens, though ambiguously felt and practiced by students who were acutely conscious of their special status, was appropriated by Beijing residents along with the tactical lessons of student politics. A year and a half after the May Fourth Incident, a Beijing rickshaw man who had been cursed out in public by a well-dressed student declared, "Mister, let's not have that sort of thing. We are both Chinese. How can you curse me like that? Even though I pull a rickshaw, I'm still as much a human being as you, a gentleman. In school, don't they teach you about equality? I haven't studied. But that is what I often hear you gentlemen discussing."[39]

Citizen participation, cast away from the summit of state power by politicians and militarists who bribed and bullied members of parliament and fixed elections, came to rest at the local level, in the politics of communities, groups, and the street. For example, representative democracy, which lay dying on the vine of bureaucratism and militarism, survived in symbolic form at the local level through the practice of convening ad hoc "citizens assemblies" (*guomin dahui*). The citizens-assembly idea gained popularity in

the aftermath of the May Fourth Movement as an antidote to corrupt national institutions. Local rallies were to serve as preludes to
an all-China convention of *fatuan* and "citizens groups" (*gongmin
tuanti*).[40] The stated goal was reform of the political system and a
halt to what appeared already by 1920 to be "an epidemic of warlords and selfish politicians."[41] In early 1920, as a continuation of
the May Fourth Movement, citizen groups in cities throughout the
country held public assemblies to discuss the issue of Shandong
concessions.[42] Deprived of legitimate institutions, protesters im-
provised their own.

Beijing residents had planned to hold such a rally on February 6,
but soldiers and policemen successfully banned it. With only one
day's public notice, in order to give the authorities no time to
block it, a mass meeting was called for February 29 on the vacant
lot next to the New World arcade.[43] Twenty groups attended the
meeting, and several "impassioned" speeches by individuals simply identified as "citizens" were heard, including one by a seventy-
year-old matron. As the crowd grew the police moved in to disperse those gathered and to tear down their banners. Fights broke
out between police and citizens. Several student speakers finally
entered the New World complex, where a part of the crowd had
gone to view the rally, and continued their speeches.

The police tended not to interfere in mass meetings when they
were held on university campuses or in guildhalls.[44] But when
citizens attempted to appropriate public space for political use,
they needed a powerful rationale and a collective will to elude or
deflect state repression. The idea of a citizens assembly proved to
be an effective, though not irresistible, device for holding the police
and soldiers at bay long enough to block off a space for the conduct of city politics.

Self-Government

A national citizens assembly was never convened. Future political
developments dictated that paths to citizen involvement in national
politics would more often than not follow the Leninist route of
mass mobilization. But for a time in the 1920s, urban Chinese
imagined that independent local self-government might be fitted to
the new political consciousness evident among city residents.

"Self-government" (*zizhi*) had a variety of meanings in the 1920s. It could refer either to territorial units or to specific institutions and might signify participation either by elites or by broader segments of the public. In Beijing the Ministry of Interior encouraged hopes for the realization of local self-government with the announcement in the early 1920s that the Municipal Office currently staffed by Ministry officials would be democratized and made the basis of a popularly based municipal government.[45] While the plan finally met the same fate as the citizens-assembly idea, city residents took it seriously enough when it was first broached to organize dozens of citizens groups and self-government associations in the hope of capturing the power and revenues the government proposed to surrender.

By 1922 over forty self-government organizations had been established at the prefectural, citywide, and police-district levels in Beijing.[46] Meetings of individual organizations sometimes drew a thousand or more participants. Citywide associations claimed as many as five thousand members.[47] Lively scenes of club politics and factionalism suggested the first halting steps toward the creation of a political machine recognizable to a turn-of-the-century Chicagoan or San Franciscan. The only elements missing were patronage and elections, and these were supposed to be forthcoming. The free-wheeling, even anarchic quality of the movement appalled one editorial writer, who characterized self-government as an unseemly scramble for recognition, position, and wealth.

Those who think the whole movement is a great joke are now too numerous to mention. Some [participants] smash heads and others curse each other in a barbarous fashion to the point where civilized meetings degenerate into savage brawls. . . . People who say that among the Chinese civic mindedness runs shallow and selfishness runs deep can point to this as evidence.[48]

At a district meeting attended by three thousand members of one self-government association, a fight that sent stools flying through the air began when it appeared that one side was trying to stuff the ballot boxes in an election of branch leaders.[49] Critics mocked self-government as an idea that was "certainly elegant and stately" but in practice was really a "movement to hunt for official positions" (*lieguan yundong*).[50] The outrage of observers who protested the transformation of "public concerns" (*gongwu*) into "selfishness" (*sixin*) resembled the indignation of American reformers over the way machine-style politics seemed to subvert the "public interest." As Philip Kuhn has pointed out, modern notions of local self-government in China imagined a "happy blending of public and private interests" and a means by which local elites "might be disciplined in the public interest."[51] The spectacle of unbridled competition among private interests and undisciplined behavior by putative elites was disturbing to both traditional- and modern-minded observers.[52]

In Beijing in the early 1920s each self-government association tended to represent a particular group, stratum, or social type, ranging from "big shots, politicians, businessmen, gangsters, and local bullies" to middle- and primary-school teachers, students, and bannermen.[53] Since shop taxes were a prime component of municipal revenues, merchants led by chamber president Sun Xueshi displayed a proprietary interest in self-government.[54] A well-organized "education faction" recruited middle- and primary-school teachers.[55] Another society based at Beijing University elected Hu Shi to its slate of officers and invited the great liberal to lecture on good government.[56] Some Manchus apparently saw in self-government a means of regaining a bit of their former power and prestige. A newspaper vignette humorously described two bannermen in a teahouse discussing how the banners might exploit their numerical advantage in certain districts of the city to take control of self-government institutions.[57]

Some groups focused on specific urban problems, like street repair, sanitation, or crime. One district *shimin* society made up of shopkeepers, merchants, and gentry met in a local temple to discuss the placing of streetcar track in their neighborhood.[58] An East City club advocated the creation of a modern morgue to lessen the health risks represented by the storage in temples of encoffined dead pending shipment home.[59] Other societies appeared more oriented toward personal or group power than toward public issues. An official in the Municipal Office, as a hedge against the possibility that the reforms might actually materialize, created his own self-government group, composed of one hundred "militarists, bureaucrats, wealthy gentry, and the rich."[60]

Not all self-government associations and the individuals who led them were willing to wait for the government to cede power to a new municipal institution. A university student organized a self-government association in the northwestern part of the Inner City and then a "shimin" school for poor children, run under its auspices. He was arrested when, in the course of a campaign for contributions, he made unauthorized use of the name of the Beijing chief of police.[61] One district organization began supplying services like fire protection to residents and collecting contributions from them in return. The district police immediately objected on the grounds that as "preparatory" bodies, self-government societies could express public opinion but not actually govern or provide services.[62]

Despite the ultimate failure of self-government reforms, the idea of co-opting activists identified with the self-government movement into an establishment dominated by *fatuan* and older gentry and merchant networks had practical appeal as a means of broadening elite consensus. By mid-decade self-government activists occupied a regular place in the pool of local elites drawn to citywide and neighborhood civic groups and meetings. In late 1924 a local branch of the "Gentry-Merchant Federation" convened, with the district police commander as chairman and self-government activists, merchants, educators, members of parliament, and newspaper publishers as participants.[63] As an increasing number of Beijing residents chose politics as a vocation or devoted avocation in the 1920s, old distinctions between officials and gentry and between gentry and merchants remained in force. These boundaries continued to demarcate graded zones of involvement in public affairs and centers of concern and interest associated with established gentry or merchant nuclei. But the decay of governmental institutions and the emergence of new political movements ranging from self-government to communism opened up several new fronts in local politics. "Merchants and gentry" still showed up at civic gatherings. But so did newspaper editors and college professors. As city squares and avenues filled with citizens expressing a newly minted sense of national identity, meetings at teahouses, restaurants, guildhalls, and temples included an expanding range of elites, both established and aspiring, intent on demonstrating a new sense of commitment to civic affairs.

The May Thirtieth Movement

The most spectacular expression of mass participation in China in the twenties was the 1925 May Thirtieth Movement. On May 30, 1925, Shanghai police under the command of British officers shot and killed twelve people who were protesting the prior killing and wounding of workers by Japanese factory managers.[64] Word of the killings, telegraphed from city to city, inspired strikes, boycotts, and demonstrations throughout urban China. Later in June foreigners on Guangzhou's Shameen Island fired on a crowd of protesters, killing fifty-two and sending another shock wave through Chinese cities. The two outrages created the momentum for giant rallies, which far exceeded the May Fourth Movement demonstrations in both size and inclusiveness.

The leading element in the May Thirtieth Movement in Beijing, as in past nationalistic protests and demonstrations, was the student community. Through the addition of numerous private colleges in the early twenties, the number of university students, not to mention their middle-school juniors, had doubled or tripled.[65] As a result, the pool of activists and participants available for a May Fourth Movement style of protest activities increased substantially. The day after the Shanghai killings, students from a dozen universities, colleges, and middle schools met in Central Park with the aim of mobilizing Beijing students to serve as cadres (*ganbu*) for the larger movement.[66] On June 2 twelve hundred representatives of ninety schools met at Beijing University's third campus in the northeastern corner of the Imperial City.[67] Eleven thousand of their classmates struck classes in a show of solidarity.

The degree of unity and leadership demonstrated by students was somewhat surprising given the intensity of factional conflicts within the student community in the weeks preceding the May Thirtieth Incident when the contentious, intramural side of student politics had been much in evidence.[68] Student activism had also been worn down by a steady application of police repression in May. When students had attempted to hold a rally outside Tianan Gate on the May 7 anniversary of Japan's Twenty-One Demands, the police blocked the gathering by using the open area to run fire brigade exercises.[69] The police also posted guards at each school to prevent students from holding meetings and forbade circular telegrams, which in the past had been used to rally support in other cities. The authorities justified their harsh stand against student involvement in public affairs by citing a presidential order issued in 1920, declaring that leadership of the student community was "in the clutches of scoundrels" intent on fomenting "disorder" and that the Beijing Student Federation was an illegal organization.[70] In response, the student union declared that it would not recognize the Duan Qirui government as legal or legitimate.[71] The pro-Nationalist newspaper *Chen Bao*, while opposing a student strike, criticized the government for taking advantage of the current weakness of public opinion and the collapse of constitutional norms to restrict liberties. By simply copying Japanese police codes, and on the pretext of maintaining peace and order, the rights of free speech, assembly, and publication had been suppressed. In an interview, police chief Zhu Shen, who had been educated in Japan, countered that the police laws in question were more liberal than the Qing code.[72] Zhu also remarked that he believed that the student movement was over for the moment.

In the face of the Shanghai killings and the indignation they aroused, Zhu Shen's prediction of student quiescence proved false, and the government's attempt to contain and suppress student politics disintegrated. Police and troops could only stand by and watch the spectacle of mass nationalism unfold. Students marched at will through the streets of the city in June, obstructed only by the heavily armed guards at the gates to the Legation Quarter (fig. 22). On June 3 eight thousand students, including hundreds of young women and children, marched all day around the city in processions stretching out almost a mile.[73] Students began the march in two columns originating at Republican University in the West City and at Beijing University in the East. The columns, drawn up in strict order on the basis of school affiliation, toured the city, with stops at key government offices to register their protests. Students also sent lecture brigades to social gathering places like rickshaw stands and teahouses to mobilize townspeople. Travel and communications in the city were disrupted and the streetcars stopped running. As the two processions worked their way through the city streets residents joined the line of march until by the time the two columns met outside Tianan Gate for a

Fig. 22. Students march north along Wangfu jing Avenue toward the main campus of Beijing University. They are likely returning from a demonstration outside Tianan Gate. Banners calling for boycotts of both Japanese and British goods place the march during the 1925 May Thirtieth Movement. Note pennants, probably announcing the puller's refusal to transport British or Japanese nationals, on one rickshaw. UPI/Bettmann Newsphotos.

"citizens assembly" the crowd numbered fifty thousand "students and *shimin*." With the careful order of the original processions now overwhelmed by the spontaneous participation of passersby and groups and individuals drawn by the flowing crowds to the center of the city, the rally became "slightly disorderly." The crowd shouted "Strike! Strike!" (*bashi bagong*—literally, "Market strike! Labor strike!") until the educator chairing the assembly proposed marching to the chamber of commerce headquarters to demand that all shops in the city be closed.

A crowd of approximately ten thousand, mainly students, broke off from the main body of demonstrators and marched south through Qian Gate to surround the chamber. Since both President Sun Xueshi and Vice-President Gao Baoqing were absent, the students were unable to present their demands. Rain drove most of the crowd back to their schools, leaving student representatives to wait for Sun and Gao. Gao finally arrived at nine in the evening and spent three more hours with the students, negotiating an agreement that called for a chamber discussion of the strike question with student representatives present, the creation of a student-merchant federation, and an immediate boycott of Japanese and British goods. In the next few days the chamber successfully resisted declaring a citywide strike but not without experiencing the pressure of periodic sieges by crowds of demonstrators sent south from Tianan Gate.[74]

The high tide of the May Thirtieth Movement in Beijing came on June 10 when over a hundred thousand people assembled in the rain outside Tianan Gate. A photograph taken of the crowd looking north to the gate shows a central platform occupied by Nationalist politicians, beneath a white banner with "Citizens Assembly" written on it and surrounded by a forest of banners carried by participating organizations.[75] The narrow walls leading south from the gate and the locust trees planted within the corridor squeezed the demonstrators into a space never intended to accommodate public meetings. Its original function had been to frame the approach to the Imperial City's principal gate. In the monumental and symbolic plan of Beijing, open spaces were designed to be empty spaces except when filled by carefully choreographed ritual events. Nationalism transformed the area. Instead of a lesser link in a chain of structures designed to exalt the emperor and awe the visitor, Tianan Gate and the space outside had become a central fixture in the ritual of mass protest. The potency of this public space was reflected in the periodic attempts by the authorities to prevent its use as a political rallying point. In 1919 troops pitched their tents outside Tianan Gate to discourage protesters.[76] In 1926 the authorities tore up stone paving and planted more trees in an apparent effort to reduce the numbers of demonstrators the area could accommodate.[77]

On June 10 demonstrators were organized into contingents of merchants, teachers and workers, students and journalists encircling the politicians occupying the central platform. A total of 157 groups were represented, ranging from *fatuan*, like the chamber of commerce and the journalists association, to provincial clubs, merchant and craft guilds, religious organizations, Marxist study groups, and labor unions. Workers from modern factories and enterprises like electric-light- and waterworks-company employees and printers were present. But so were forty or fifty "dirty-faced, raggedly dressed" rickshaw men under a banner reading "Beijing Rickshaw Pullers Patriotic Group," fifty Beijing University servants and guards, and three hundred peasants from the west suburbs led by Agricultural University students.[78] Observers noted that leaflets and banners distributed and held by the crowd had a uniform content with slight variations on anti-British and anti-Japanese themes. But groups as diverse as representatives from Confucius University and a Beijing temperance society also embellished their messages with quotations from the classics and warnings of the evil of drink.

The chamber of commerce held a *fatuan*'s "limited license" to participate in public affairs. Other groups, like the Beijing Student Federation, carried their own aura of legitimacy but were still liable in ordinary times, when movement politics was not flooding Beijing's public spaces with activists, to restrictions and harassment by the police. Still others, like labor federations and unions, took the opportunity provided by mass rallies to claim a legitimate place in the city's public life. Semiofficial lists of groups and the inclusive, corporatist order of assembly argued for a model of urban politics based on equal representation for each citizen and each functionally defined segment of the population. Understandably, and at a time when their main political apparatus was bottled up in Guangdong, the Nationalist organizers of the rally took the liberty of placing themselves at the center of the human canvas on which they had depicted the polity they were struggling to create. This group-based imagery, composed in pointillist fashion, both reflected and reinforced the movement of groups into politics.

Despite the free flow of people to and from Tianan Gate and other meeting places in June 1925, some constraints on participation were in evidence and were keenly felt by those denied the opportunity to assemble and demonstrate. Printers played a prominent part in the June 10 rally. But employees of the Finance Ministry printing bureau were refused permission to leave work by the bureau head.[79] The press reported that because the printers were "educated workers" they were particularly indignant about missing the chance to express their political views. The workers agitated for several days against the restrictions until they made contact with a group of students who helped them secure the right to join a march on June 15.

Guild workers took advantage of customary procedures for holding meetings and taking collective action to plan their involvement in the movement. Carpenters, bricklayers, and other building-trade workers, who were fresh from struggles to raise their wage rates, met to establish an association to investigate the Shanghai Incident.[80] The assembled craftsmen agreed to contribute to a strike fund for Shanghai workers, to be channeled through the chamber of commerce. Paying student protesters the compliment of imitation, the guilds organized lecture brigades aimed at fellow Beijing workers. A half-day strike was declared for June 24 in memory of those who died in Shanghai, and all members were urged to attend a rally and procession called for June 25.

Interest shown in the May Thirtieth Movement by guildsmen, workers, in modern enterprises, and street workers like rickshaw men culminated in heavy worker participation in the June 25 rally.[81] The organizers of the demonstration selected the date to coincide with the Dragon Boat festival as a means of encouraging involvement by workers who received time off from work only at the major festivals. Rickshaw men, waterworks employees, night-soil carriers, used-clothes-shop clerks, and dozens of other occupational groups were among the one hundred thousand people and one hundred organizations that attended the rally held outside Tianan Gate. The crowd then marched for hours in a great square: east to Dongdan Arch in the East City, south through Chongwen Gate, west through the heart of Beijing's commercial district, north through Xuanwu Gate to Xidan Arch, then back east to Tianan Gate. Under a huge banner reading "Executive Committee of All Circles in Beijing" Nationalist politicians led rank after rank of participating groups and associations, including the Beijing student union, schools, printers, ironworkers, streetcar workers, the chamber of commerce, and rickshaw men.

The May Thirtieth demonstrations differed from past nationalistic movements and protests, not only in terms of scale and variety of participation, but also in the physical space the rallies and processions occupied. May Fourth Movement marches were confined to the university and the official areas of the Inner City. The

May Thirtieth processions covered both the Inner and the Outer City and made a point of passing through commercial and residential areas as well as past government offices and the Legation Quarter. Citywide marches in 1925 symbolized the widening circle of groups and classes involved in politics. In a physical sense the city's political arena was, for the moment, enlarged from the narrower confines of government offices, *fatuan* meeting halls, and university enclaves to include shops, streets, factories, and neighborhoods. In 1919 students circulated among city residents, urging political action through speeches and by example. In 1925 city residents themselves took the initiative to lecture, assemble, march, and remonstrate.

Not all political action in June 1925 was motivated by purely nationalistic sentiments. Some groups saw the freedom of assembly and action fostered by mass nationalism as a unique opportunity to press particular grievances. Nationalistic rhetoric and solidarity became a means for advancing group and class interests.

Just prior to the May Thirtieth Incident, the city's water carriers had intensified their long-standing campaign against the waterworks.[82] In an effort to restrict the slow but steady encroachment of pipe and running water, the carriers had petitioned government ministries, the police, and the chamber of commerce for relief. Throughout May fights between carriers and waterworks employees broke out at company-operated hydrants. Well owners and carriers also faced the unresolved problem of factionalism within the trade among Shandong, Baoding, and Beijing natives.

Initially, members of the water trade responded directly and enthusiastically to the May Thirtieth Movement. In June carriers suspended deliveries to English and Japanese customers and declared a one-day strike on the fifteenth in solidarity with Shanghai workers. One thousand carriers participated in a procession, with the guild's president on hand to deliver a petition to the government authorities.[83] Owners and carriers seemed interested in adding participation in nationalist rallies and marches to their earlier demonstrations of group and communal concerns in much the same way that other guild workers had done.

On June 18 water carriers in the western portion of the Outer City assembled to participate in a scheduled march and, "on the pretext of joining the movement," proceeded first toward the government building designated as the focus of the protest and then suddenly veered off north to attack well houses used by carriers in the northeastern section of the Inner City.[84] While the cause of the attack is obscure, the factional tenor of the incident is clear. One newspaper commented that the attacking carriers had "used student circle (*jie*) power," or rather the freedom to join student-led public demonstrations, to indulge in intramural politics.

A few days later the target of the crowd of water carriers shifted. On June 22 hundreds of carriers from the same Outer City district, armed with flat carrying poles, marched into the Inner City toward the offices of the waterworks company in the East City. As they paraded they reportedly coerced carriers in the northeast, who had been their adversaries days before, into joining the march. Meanwhile, in the West City a minor quarrel between a carrier and a customer over the price of water escalated into a major altercation, drawing hundreds of water carriers to the scene. Then, according to a newspaper account, "all of the West City carriers, all of a sudden (we do not know why), gathered in a great crowd to march on the waterworks."[85] Before the carriers reached the plant, however, someone mediated and turned the procession back. The next day a crowd of six hundred carriers, armed with iron rods and wooden poles, clashed with waterworks company employees laying pipe in the West City. Fourteen workmen were injured, and several arrests were made by police who arrived to contain the riot.[86] A few days later, the police convened a mediation session in a restaurant. The police proposed a compromise giving the waterworks the right to lay pipe to shops and homes that used thirty tubs or more of water per day, and giving water carriers claim to those who used less. The water carriers were reported to be still unsatisfied.

The May Thirtieth Movement gave water carriers the opportunity to extend to the citywide level grievances and conflicts normally confined to neighborhoods and the street or to petitions through the proper channels. This was done with sufficient point and force so that the police had to resort to mediation rather than simple repression in dealing with issues already raised in the petitions of May. As had been the case in the trade's attempt in 1924 to develop a citywide guild, unity could be achieved only through preliminary conflicts in which factional opposition was neutral-

Fig. 23. Worker contingents in an anti-imperialist demonstration held in the aftermath of the May Thirtieth Movement. Banners and pennants held aloft identify participants from foreign-owned automobile companies (probably mechanics or drivers) and Western-style clothing firms. Reflecting the power of mass nationalism (and the instrumental value of patriotic rhetoric in labor-management disputes), workers in foreign companies were more, rather than less, likely to participate in such protests. UPI/Bettmann Newsphotos.

ized or overwhelmed. In the atmosphere prevailing in June 1925, with the police on the defensive and the streets routinely filled with crowds, groups, and crowds of groups, militant carriers saw a window of opportunity for their cause.

The May Thirtieth Movement revealed an impressive capacity for a kind of spontaneous regimentation, which was visible in the line of rank upon rank of marchers and in crowds divided into communities and circles (fig. 23). This order was due in part to the tightly organized nature of group life in Beijing society. As the case of the water carriers suggested, tightness sometimes bespoke inner tensions. But finely articulated leadership and attentive followers also facilitated organized participation in mass events once barriers erected by police and hostile owners, managers, and labor bosses came down.

Professional Politicians and Political Violence

Professional politicians also sought to impose their own brand of order on mass politics. To follow students was to invite leadership that was exemplary rather than narrowly didactic or broadly organizational. Nationalist and Communist political operatives, on the other hand, aimed to become a permanent and guiding presence in the city's organizational life. They formed the most radical wing of the city's emerging elite "cadredom" composed of merchant politicians, old-style gentry, self-government activists, and publicists. The May Fourth Movement left in its wake activists like Li Dazhao and Deng Zhongxia who recruited like-minded intellectuals into study groups, cells, and branches and built bridges to other segments of Beijing society.[87]

As the history of the Beijing labor movement suggests, these insurgent intellectuals did rather poorly in their first attempts to mobilize the Beijing "masses." Dependence on unreliable allies like Wu Peifu and on scattered groups of modern workers like the Changxindian railway men limited and weakened the earliest Communist political ventures. The 1922 united-front policy with the Nationalists, although it was opposed on ideological grounds by some Beijing Communists, placed the party in a better position to take advantage of the associational and mass-movement dimensions of city politics.[88] As worker and citizen groups became more receptive to political action, the problem of penetrating or defeating layers of apolitical or conservative elites became less daunting. On the other hand, greater political consciousness on the part of city residents meant that mobilization took place in a competitive environment, which made it hard simply to impose one's will and ideas on others. Nor had the Communists at this stage broken free of the need to rely on higher-level patrons for protection. Feng Yuxiang's 1924 coup against Wu Peifu gave the Communists a new political ally with genuinely progressive tendencies.[89] But the support of Feng's forces was offset by the adversarial stance taken by the police toward mass politics and the growing hostility of the soldiers of the provisional chief executive, Duan Qirui.[90]

Splits within the Nationalist party in Beijing over the united-front policy further complicated attempts by radical politicians to lead and control local movements and groups. Sun Yat-sen's dramatic arrival in Beijing on the last day of 1924 on a personal mission to heal the breach between north and south attracted enormous local interest and support. Representatives of five hundred organizations greeted Sun at the train station.[91] Three weeks later Sun returned the favor by informing Duan Qirui that he would support a proposed national reconstruction conference only if representatives of public bodies and professional associations (*gongtuan fatuan*), including guilds, unions, student federations, and the like, were allowed to participate.[92] In addition, Sun's presence and the operatic tenor of his illness, his death on March 12, and his massive public funeral added thousands of new members to the Nationalist party. However, at the same time that Sun and his party drew group and popular support to their cause, the Nationalist elite in Beijing began to fracture along left and right and pro- and anti-Communist lines. With the official Nationalist party branch in the city dominated by Communists, dissident party members organized their own "Beijing Nationalist Party Comrades Club."[93] Left- and right-wing politicians bickered publicly in a nasty series of paid newspaper advertisements and, on one occasion, quarreled openly on a May Thirtieth Movement rally platform over who should chair the meeting.[94] In November 1925 prominent anti-Communist Nationalist politicians organized a nationwide challenge to leftists in the party at a meeting in Beijing's Western Hills, where Sun Yat-sen's body was temporarily entombed.[95] This national initiative had a local base in the factional conflicts that raged throughout 1925.

Despite these bitter divisions, the May Thirtieth Movement gave a powerful boost to mass politics and the politicians associated with nationalistic rallies and meetings. Protests continued throughout 1925 and early 1926. The decision by Duan Qirui's government to hold an international tariff conference in October and November 1925 provoked a new series of anti-imperialist demonstrations. Given General Feng Yuxiang's tacit support of the demonstrators, Duan relied on the police and his own contingent of five thousand heavily armed bodyguards to curb the protests. On one occasion, when the police tried to prevent students from leaving the campus of Beijing University to hold a rally outside Tianan Gate, the students broke through the cordon with a hail of rocks and bricks and behind a vanguard of muscular students armed with wooden staves.[96] Later the same students, after successfully assembling at Tianan Gate, dispatched a column to Liulichang Normal University in the Outer City to rescue fellow protesters who had been unable to break through the police barricades. Once freed, the students took revenge against the police by wrecking police kiosks and assaulting several patrolmen as they marched back to the center of the city.

Violence had always been a minor feature of the May Fourth style of protest politics. Bloodshed and attacks on property resulted from police repression and the radical, sometimes reckless response of students to efforts to contain or obstruct them. Recourse to violence was also characteristic of group conflict in the city. The use of fists, clubs, carrying poles, and even swords and knives to settle quarrels among rival bands of workers and employers was common enough. With the joining of the extreme rhetoric of nationalistic sacrifice and ideological struggle to public habits of group violence in the context of the growing militarization of civilian institutions, mass politics reached the edge of a more systematic kind of bloodletting. Many political demonstrations had a festive, consensual air to them and were notable for their overall peaceable nature. But the transformation of governmental centers into armed camps and the addition of armed pickets to protest marches foreshadowed the dreadful events of March 18, 1926, in Beijing and the wave of urban massacres throughout the country which followed in 1927.[97]

Throughout the winter of 1925–26, as war loomed between Feng and Duan's Beijing regime and the forces of Zhang Zuolin, factional struggles among rival political groups and the mass mobilization associated with nationalism proceeded along parallel tracks. For example, on March 12, 1926, more than one hundred thousand people took part in activities commemorating the anniversary of Sun Yat-sen's death.[98] The weather was beautiful, bands played, and a small army of peddlers sold tea and snacks among the crowd. But even in this harmonious atmosphere, left and right factions of the Nationalist party sounded notes of discord by refusing to share the same platform and by holding competing rallies in different parts of the city.

Less than one week later, on March 17, the left and right wings again held separate meetings, this time to protest the "Taku Ultimatum."[99] Citing the Boxer Protocols guaranteeing foreign security interests in north China, the major powers had demanded that Feng Yuxiang's army remove gun emplacements at Tianjin's Taku harbor within forty-eight hours. Since Feng was planning to withdraw from Tianjin anyway in order to tighten his defensive lines against an anticipated attack by Zhang Zuolin, both the general and the government in Beijing readily agreed to the demand. In Beijing, students and Nationalist politicians strenuously objected on principle to the regime's willingness to give in to foreign pressures. The Nationalist right drafted a petition protesting the concession and scheduled a rally for the eighteenth in Central Park. The left met at Beijing University and demanded that the legations of nations signing the ultimatum be expelled from the city. The left, led by the Communists, also called for a rally the next day outside Tianan Gate. Some of the participants in the university meeting later marched to Duan Qirui's headquarters nearby in the cabinet building on Iron Lion Lane. The soldiers guarding the compound refused to admit the protesters, and a fight broke out in which several students were injured.

The March 18 rally outside Tianan Gate began at 10 A.M. with about six thousand people in attendance.[100] Flanking the platform erected for the assembly were banners of many of the eighty or more participating schools and groups. On the platform itself hung the bloody clothes of protesters injured the day before. When a representative of the Duan Qirui government arrived to apologize to the crowd for the beatings, he was jeered. After the rally, part of the crowd, which included Li Dazhao and other prominent Communists, marched to Iron Lion Lane. By the time the procession reached the cabinet offices it had grown to two thousand people. With the crowd at their backs crammed into the narrow alleyway, the leaders of the march confronted the guards in what promised to be a replay of the arguments and altercations of the day before. Suddenly, the guards opened fire at point-blank range, and soldiers with fixed bayonets charged out of concealment into the crowd. A cadre with military experience shouted "Hit the dirt!" but the demonstrators panicked and provided easy targets for Duan's men. In the resulting carnage at least fifty unarmed protesters were killed and two hundred wounded. Most of the dead were students. But workers and merchants were also among the casualties. According to the recollections of Communist party member Yue Tianyu, who was in Iron Lion Lane at the time, cadres who noticed machine-gun muzzles protruding from side windows of the cabinet building pulled Li Dazhao out of the front ranks of the crowd, forced open a side gate, and spirited him away before the shooting began. Yue escaped by jumping over a wall and ducking into a restaurant, where he nervously consumed two bowls of noodles, keeping a lookout for policemen between bites. Li Dazhao and other leading Communists fled to the safety of the Soviet Legation while Nationalists of all stripes sought to escape arrest by the tottering Duan Qirui regime. Within weeks, Duan himself lost power to Zhang Zuolin, a warlord whose record of systematic persecution of political radicals would far surpass Duan's.

The "March Eighteenth incident" was Beijing's worst instance of political violence in the 1920s. The number of casualties was small compared with the thousands killed in Shanghai, Guangzhou, and Wuhan the following year as the united front broke down and Nationalists slaughtered Communists. But events in Beijing were part of a common progression in which urban political violence escalated from beating up demonstrators, policemen, and officials to machine-gunning civilians. Social movements that made government institutions the target of protest became in turn the objects of bloody repression. Politicians who first refused to share the same platforms finally took to killing each other. Urban politics of the kind practiced in Beijing could only bring contenders for power a part of the distance to this killing ground. City politics was intense and sometimes violent. But it was also based on an underlying search for consensus, which encouraged the joining of new groups and elites to hierarchies of guilds and *fatuan* and communities of groups and citizens. This was a politics of addition, not subtraction. The idea of subtracting one's adversaries from the city or from the face of the earth was the brainchild of itinerant militarists and ideologues.

On May 1, 1926, as Zhang Zuolin's forces took control of the city, thirty representatives of one of Beijing's lowliest groups, the rickshaw pullers, met at a Bridge of Heaven teahouse.[101] Rickshaw men, having endured the collective trauma associated with the opening of streetcar service, had surfaced at numerous political rallies in 1925. In the aftermath of the November anti–Duan Qirui protests, six hundred rickshaw men assembled to organize a "Preparatory Committee of the Inner and Outer Cities Rickshaw Pullers Union" and claim the protection of General Feng Yuxiang.[102] Six months later, at their May Day meeting, the rickshaw men decided to postpone organization of a union because of the unsettled military situation. Gauging the prevailing political climate with evident care, the pullers called for the "eradication" of the Communist party and declared that they would not be "taken advantage of and manipulated by factions." A representative named Gao Wang noted that the main purpose of the meeting was to commemorate May Day and that it was regrettable that a larger, citywide celebration had not been possible. For members of the unorganized laboring poor like the rickshaw men, one of the most important features of nationalism and unionism was the opportunity to claim the moral equality owed to citizens and comrades. For workers like the water carriers, who already had a measure of status and protection, the openness of movement politics was significant mainly for the tactical advantage it provided. For rickshaw men, May Days and national days held the potential for a real breakthrough in status and power.

Mass politics in Beijing in the 1920s was modern by dint of its inclusiveness. All citizens were invited to participate so that, as in the novel strategy adopted by popular organizations in late-eighteenth-century Europe, membership would be "unlimited."[103] However, since the principle of radical inclusiveness meant, in practice, the incorporation of groups that in many cases were elitist or exclusive, the "mass" appearance of rallies and demonstrations concealed a structure that conserved a considerable portion of preindustrial and traditional Beijing. Mass politics was not a solvent capable of breaking down barriers based on status, native place, or division of labor so much as it was an opportunity to display these divisions in public.

Mass movements did not reorganize urban society. Popular

demonstrations and assemblies of citizens in the 1920s in Beijing were not an expression of, or a solution to, anomie or rootlessness. They tapped the politics and group consciousness of organizations already in existence. Tens of thousands of Beijing residents in the streets protesting imperialism did not mean that the city was in a state of disorder. On the other hand, the efflorescence of mass and group politics meant that citywide politics was no longer the exclusive preserve of elite mediation and governmental institutions. Citizenship gave townspeople a license to practice politics, which, once issued, could not easily be revoked, even by militarists and ideologues.

Nine

City People Under Siege:
The Impact of Warlordism

During mass events like the May Thirtieth Movement the logic of basic-level city life was suddenly projected onto the larger screen of citywide assemblies and processions as Beijing society opened up to debate, discussion, and public conflict. Massed crowds of townspeople expressed a sea change in political consciousness. Warlord conflict created comparable moments of illumination as the pressures of war and siege caused the urban community to close itself off from collapsing governments and invading armies.[1] A thin line of long-gowned gentlemen emerged to preserve social peace against considerable odds. Their leadership made it possible for residents to limit the burden and contain the dangers represented by armies clashing in the vicinity of the city walls.

As long as imperial or national political institutions in Beijing remained viable, city politics and society remained dependent on the policies, programs, and patronage of civil officials. Even though communities within the city regulated their own affairs to a marked degree, merchants, students, workers, journalists, and others oriented themselves of necessity toward official Beijing in the hope of acquiring concessions, waivers, or subsidies. By the mid-1920s this pattern of dependency shifted radically from "higher levels" within the city walls to armies and generals camped without and headquartered within. Beijing became a prize in the military struggles on the north China plain rather than an arbiter of national policy and politics. A succession of contenders for the power still adhering to ministries and cabinet offices conquered, occupied, and abandoned the city. Changes of regime were signaled to Beijing residents, not by a newspaper report of a new election or factional realignment, but rather by cannon fire, shuttered stores, empty marketplaces, and streets crowded with soldiers and refugees.

Warlords and the armies they led along major rail lines and through strategic passes became principal political actors in national, regional, and local politics. Beijing in the warlord period, like other communities, was subject to the periodic intrusion of armies and warfare. The size of the city, the value of its formal status as capital (until 1928), and the presence of foreign legations capable of threatening militarists with armed intervention and rewarding them with foreign-controlled customs revenues protected Beijing from most of the direct effects of warfare. On the other hand, between 1920 and 1930 six major wars were fought wholly or in part on the north China plain. Each war touched off a government crisis, disrupted communications and food and coal supplies to the city, flooded Beijing and its suburbs with refugees and defeated soldiers, and deprived the city momentarily of formal governmental control.

City Under Siege

In *Camel Xiangzi* Lao She noted how closely attuned Beijing residents were to the threat of war in the Republican period. He wrote: "The almost yearly news and rumors of war resembled the seasonal sprouting of spring wheat. In time, spring wheat and bayonets came to be regarded by northerners as the very symbols of their hopes and fears."[2] For example, in the fall of 1925, in advance of armed conflict between Generals Zhang Zuolin and Feng Yuxiang, rumors of war were sufficient to trigger powerful defensive actions by residents of the city and its immediate environs. Farmers in the suburbs rushed to sell their crops in city markets before soldiers came to confiscate them.[3] Landlords from eighty-seven villages in the surrounding area met to discuss the formation of a militia to guard against the banditry and random looting that accompanied warlord conflict.[4] Other rural dwellers, who lacked faith in these defensive arrangements, began to move into the city for safety.[5] Newspaper hawkers heightened local anxieties by shouting out the latest developments and rumors related to the impending conflict. Depositors made runs on banks associated with the two generals. Fresh rumors emptied markets and places of amusement of customers and patrons. The train station was packed with residents and sojourners fleeing before rail lines were cut off. Commercial life came to a standstill, and even the ubiquitous street peddlers and rickshaw men would of a moment disappear from the streets.[6] And all of this transpired before a shot was fired (figs. 24 and 25).

War had come to occupy a central place in the minds of Beijing residents. This point of sensitivity in the urban mentality can be traced back before the warlord period to the violence of the Boxer uprising and the 1912 troop riots when large sections of the city were burned, looted, and otherwise terrorized by soldiers. Events from the turn of the century through the teens demonstrated to city residents that politically inspired military crises could lead to urban violence. At any given moment there were plenty of armed men within the city walls who, depending on their own decision or the commands of a superior, could turn Beijing within minutes into a battlefield. There was also the possibility, perhaps more real than imagined considering the general level of social control in the city, that troop riots might escalate into wider social disorder. "Street loafers," "beggars," and "hooligans" had joined Yuan Shikai's rioting troops in 1912 and had become scapegoats for the violence, with their "chopped-off heads . . . left in the streets with suitable inscriptions as warnings to would-be imitators."[7] Zhang Xun's abortive attempt to restore the Qing dynasty in 1917 also had something of a social base among former officials and bannermen whose fortunes had suffered as a result of the 1911 Revolution. Supporters of the Manchu monarchy rushed to retrieve the physical insignia and costumes of the Qing from secondhand clothing stores. Theatrical supply houses did a brief but robust business in artificial queues.[8] As the warlordism of the twenties added armies without to the threat of troop riot and social turmoil within, Beijing residents had ample images and experiences to draw on to construct a picture of imminent disaster whenever war appeared on the horizon.

The war between Feng Yuxiang and his "National Army"

Fig. 24. Warlords Zhang Zongchang (center), holding one of his trade-mark cigars, and Sun Chuanfang (right) pose on a Beijing railway plat-form, probably in early 1928 at a meeting called by Zhang Zuolin in the wake of Northern Expedition victories against their forces. Zhang Zong-chang, the so-called "Dog Meat General," was among the most brutal of China's warlords. A Beijing educator asserted that Zhang had "the phy-sique of an elephant, the brain of a pig, and the temperament of a tiger." Sun, who had been Zhang Zuolin's enemy in earlier wars and who had executed one of Zhang Zongchang's subordinates in 1925, dominated lower Yangzi River provinces in the vicinity of Shanghai from 1924 to 1927. The arrival and departure by rail of winning and losing generals signaled to city residents the latest twists and turns of warlord politics. (Howard L. Boorman and Richard C. Howard, eds., *Biographical Dictionary of Republican China* [New York: Columbia University Press, 1971], vol. 1, pp. 122–127; vol. 3, pp. 160–162.) UPI/Bettmann News-photos.

Fig. 25. City residents read posted newspaper reports of the latest news from the front during the first Zhili-Fengtian War in the spring of 1922. The decisive battle in the war was fought only ten miles south of the city at the railway town of Changxindian. The duration, intensity, and proximity of warlord conflicts could have profound effects on the daily life of the city's population. UPI/Bettmann Newsphotos.

(Guominjun) and Zhang Zuolin and his allies lasted from fall 1925 to late summer 1926. In the kind of tortured narrative typical of warlord politics, Feng had betrayed Wu Peifu's Beijing government the year before by switching sides and allying with Zhang. Now Zhang and Feng were again enemies, with Feng defending the capital against Zhang's assault. The war was fought in four phases: a struggle in northern Zhili and southern Manchuria between Zhang's forces and a rebellious former supporter; battles between Zhang's and Feng's armies in December in the vicinity of Tianjin; fighting in Henan in February between the Guominjun and a northward marching, vengeance-seeking Wu Peifu; and finally war in March around Beijing and throughout the late spring and summer at the Nankou Pass north of the city as Feng Yuxiang's armies withdrew in defeat to sanctuary outside the Great Wall. Actual fighting broke out in the vicinity of Beijing only for a brief period in the spring of 1926. But the city was affected by the cycle of mobilization, warfare, and demobilization for more than ten months and in ways that suggest the range of influences visited by warlordism on urban society.

Elite mobilization in Beijing followed the gathering momentum of military mobilization. On November 18, 1925, a "Metropolitan Peace Preservation Association" (*jingshi zhian weichi hui*, hereafter PPA) convened to address the rapid rise of food prices in the city.[9] The association included key members of Beijing's security forces, such as the chief of police, Zhu Shen, and the garrison commander, Lu Zhonglin, as well as influential gentry and merchant personalities, such as the former viceroy and elder statesman Zhao Erxun and the chamber of commerce president, Sun Xueshi.[10] Others invited to participate included individuals who had been active in the self-government movement and local citizens groups.[11] The chamber of commerce and key guilds were well represented, including leaders of the pawnbrokers, silk and foreign-goods shops, and old-style money-shop trades. Pawnbrokering and currency exchange were both politically sensitive trades. The poor in times of personal or general crisis pawned their possessions to sustain themselves. Money shops handled the often volatile exchange between copper and silver and hard and paper currencies. Silk and foreign-goods shops were among the richest enterprises in the city, with much to lose in the event of disorder and much to contribute by way of financial support.

The members of PPA took three actions designed to alleviate local conditions. First, they sent a telegram to Zhang Zuolin's forces asking them to allow more shipments of grain to pass through to Beijing along the rail lines from the northeast and Tianjin. In addition, Lu Zhonglin agreed to find a way to import more millet, the staple of the urban poor, from the region northwest of the city, controlled by his boss, Feng Yuxiang. Third, an effort would be made to increase coal shipments along the Beijing-Hankou line. Urban centers like Beijing were sensitive to the style of warfare practiced by Republican-era militarists because most wars were fought along rail lines, and railroads supplied cities with basic commodities like food and fuel. Since most of the grain and coal consumed in Beijing had to be brought in by train, battles or troop movements along rail lines connecting the city with Hankou, Tianjin, and the northeast had immediate effects on the price and availability of daily necessities.[12] Throughout the fall of 1925, complex negotiations among rival warlords, the PPA, the police, the chamber of commerce, and wholesale and retail coal dealers were necessary to keep the city supplied with coal.[13]

The PPA resembled the merchant and gentry consortiums traditionally assembled in times of community crisis. Both official and merchant Beijing contributed support while local politicians involved in self-government reforms were added to accommodate new sources of civic activism. The program adopted by the PPA, with its focus on maintaining civil peace through attention to the material basis of social order, also represented a line of continuity with past and current social practices. Each year, with the coming of cold weather, local elites in Beijing participated in a "winter defense" (*dongfang*) directed at seasonal unemployment and increases in the cost of living associated with crime and social disorder. The assumption made by local elites was a simple one. If people were cold and hungry enough, they would turn to crime to survive. Indeed, the economic crime rate, measured by prison commitments, doubled in the winter months.[14] Winter defense involved a more intensive policing of the city and its environs and attempts to relieve the sufferings of the poor through the funding of soup kitchens (*zhouchang*). The soup kitchens opened sometime between October and January, depending on the resources available and the severity of the winter. About one-third of the meals served at these kitchens were provided by the police. The rest were donated by merchants and local philanthropic organizations.[15] In late 1925, with food prices rising in the city and war spreading panic and disorder in Beijing's hinterland, elites could reasonably expect a worsening of the "normal" winter social crisis, with more poor people and refugees needing help and more of the kinds of pressure that led to crime and banditry.

In late October it was announced that the police force would be bolstered by two hundred military police armed with swords, and one hundred equipped with revolvers.[16] The police also announced that soup kitchens would be opened soon, and in

November the authorities began distributing wooden tablets to the poor and beggars to be redeemed for gruel when the aid stations began serving.[17] Tragically for city residents who were dying of cold and hunger at a rate of two hundred a month, the soup kitchens did not begin operations until January.[18] By then the police estimated that thirty thousand people were being fed each day from the soup kitchens. Placement of the kitchens outside the walls was customary and reflected both the tendency of the poor and homeless to gather around the gates and a desire by police and local elites to keep them there.

The onset of winter and news of increased fighting heightened local concern for order. Merchants responded to these tensions not only by supporting the activities of the PPA but also by moving money and goods to the Legation Quarter and taking steps to strengthen shop, street, and neighborhood security. Citing a marked "increase in rumors around the marketplaces," merchant houses outside Qian Gate organized a merchant militia (*shang-tuan*).[19] The shopkeepers retained a group of professional boxers from southern Zhili province, who were famed for their prowess, and several expert marksmen to enhance the effectiveness of the volunteer body.

The garrison command, police force, and private and corporate interests cooperated to keep order in the city through a mix of charity and coercion. In the process, conflict broke out between the authorities and the merchant class over a range of issues, including contributions to the war effort and the control of speculation. In January Lu Zhonglin called together the directors of the chamber of commerce and appealed for money.[20] He couched his request in philanthropic terms. The cash was needed, he claimed, to buy land for the burial of Guominjun troops killed in the battle for Tianjin. According to Lu, the merchants of Baoding had already contributed $100,000 and he suggested that the merchants of Beijing should be in a position to make an even more generous gift. One of the chamber directors stood up and complained that the Beijing chamber of commerce had already given the Guominjun $300,000 at the beginning of the war and that depressed business conditions resulting from the conflict made further payments difficult or impossible. All the directors agreed on this point, but Lu remained adamant.

In a normal year the approach of spring and the sprouting of "spring wheat," in Lao She's phrase, signaled an easing of the harsh conditions that necessitated a "winter defense."[21] But in March, under the continuous pressure of the military emergency, poverty and crime linked to poverty continued to climb. The press reported a general feeling of insecurity based on a wave of crimes related to desperate economic circumstances. One reporter noted that "a large number of poor people have been driven to the adventurous trade of robbery and burglary to earn a living. During the last month over one hundred cases of highway robbery have been reported around the metropolitan suburban districts, the majority of the robbers were armed with clubs, knives, or spears, while the things they robbed were only of little value."[22] In mid-March the number of people being fed at soup kitchens had risen to 80,000 per day, and the growing number of war refugees entering the city and its suburbs compounded the problem of feeding the poor.[23] In a retrospective on 1926, a local newspaper estimated that 200,000 to 300,000 refugees, or one-quarter to one-third of the city's normal population, fled to Beijing that spring.[24]

By late March war was no longer a matter of indirect and subtle pressures. Wounded soldiers in automobiles and masses of rickshaws entered Beijing in a constant stream from morning till night.[25] Large numbers of defeated troops roamed outside the city's eastern gates facing the direction of the oncoming armies of Zhang Zuolin and the collapsing forces of Feng Yuxiang. Many food shops outside the gates were forced to close because the soldiers refused to pay for their meals. Others remained open in order to profit from wave after wave of hungry customers.[26] Troops defending the city proper closed the gates in the evening in order to control the flow of soldiers into Beijing. As disorder and crime rose in the eastern suburbs four thousand "merchants and citizens" formed a militia to patrol streets and villages.[27] Rich commercial districts outside Qian Gate deployed militia made up of armed employees.[28] Other shopkeepers moved their valuables into the Legation Quarter, resulting in large profits for banks and other concerns with storage facilities there. The foreign legations made arrangements for evacuation points in different parts of the city in the event that their nationals needed to be brought in to the Legation Quarter.[29] Wedding chairs were reported to be in great demand because parents wanted their daughters under the protection of husbands in case of troop riot.[30] Shops reported that many young apprentices had disappeared, presumably having volunteered for or been impressed into the army, which was taking recruits as young as age fifteen.[31]

In order to deal with the war's threat to the city, consortiums of Beijing gentry and merchant leaders met to fill the gap opened up by the collapse of the regime of Feng Yuxiang and Duan Qirui. On March 22 a small group of former officials met at a palace in the Forbidden City to urge a peace conference to resolve the issues currently being contested on the battlefield.[32] Those present included Wang Shizhen, Zhao Erxun, Hu Weide, and Sun Baoji. Foreign Minister Yan Huijing also participated. Wang was a former premier, bank director, and chairman of the board of directors of the Beijing streetcar company. Zhao, who had participated in the November 1925 meetings of the PPA, had been Zhang Zuolin's patron in Manchuria. Hu, also a former high official, had joined in 1924 to organize the Beijing Gas Company.[33] Sun had been finance minister, premier, an official of Zhili province, investor in a local coal and steel firm, and an organizer, along with Hu, of the Beijing Gas Company. They all qualified as elder statesmen and functioned as a modern surrogate for the old gentry elite on the basis of their government-derived status and wide social connections in and out of officialdom. Ironically, Republican political instability created a ready pool of notables to draw on for occasions like this, with any number of former premiers available to lend their names and energies to the practice of mediation at the citywide level. The four men also shared a financial interest in the Beijing economy and, therefore, connections to local elites as well as national and regional personalities. The group telegraphed its proposal for a peace conference to the anti-Guominjun forces, at the same time emphasizing the need to keep the peace in Beijing. A few days later, on March 27, another group led by the chamber of commerce president, Sun Xueshi, reactivated the PPA and held a new planning session.[34]

In the midst of an increasingly militarized urban and suburban setting, the PPA and the merchant and gentry forces behind it began to form the idea of an independent paramilitary force to keep the peace in Beijing. The exchange of military control of the city between the defeated and the victors was always one of the most delicate, dangerous, and expensive (in terms of tribute payments) moments in the cycle of warlord conflict. A homegrown force seemed to offer a means of bridging or eliding that moment and defending local interests. Chamber director Yang Yijian, who was the owner of an import-export shop and the brother of a general, took over the planning for the proposed force.[35] This rather bold idea never came to fruition. But the idea of a locally controlled force suggested both the increasing confidence of local elites in carving out a formal role for themselves on the citywide level and the need for such a role, given the kind of pressures exerted on local communities by warlordism.

The PPA established its headquarters in the Tianjin Guild in the merchant district outside Qian Gate. By early April the body had divided its work into six departments and had notified the authorities of plans to take over the administration of the police department by electing twenty prominent merchants and gentry to oversee each police district.[36] Six hundred guns were found to equip the self-defense force attached to the PPA. Officials set up reception centers for refugees and petitioned the military to allocate rolling stock to transport food, salt, and coal to the city. The presence of former self-government activists on the PPA, and the declared ambition of the body to take over the administration of the city, suggested an attempt by local elites to use the military crisis to achieve in 1926 what the government had promised and then reneged on earlier in the decade: local self-government.

In an apparent effort to stir panic in the city, planes began limited bombing runs over Beijing. On April 2 a bomb killed an elderly woman.[37] The next day tens of thousands of Beijing residents watched as planes tried to hit the Guominjun headquarters in the Inner City. The bombardment continued for several days, with explosives hitting near Qian Gate and the Temple of Heaven. On one occasion Guominjun planes scrambled to ward off an attack. The PPA protested to Zhang Zuolin, who first denied knowledge of the raids and then advised the people of Beijing to speed the evacuation of Guominjun forces from the city if they wanted an end to the bombardment.[38]

In an attempt to maintain calm while bombs fell, however randomly, on the city, Sun Xueshi invited leading businessmen to tea and asked them not to send valuables to the Legation Quarter, because it was creating the wrong impression among the people Sun and other local elites were trying to reassure.[39] In a reversal of roles, which must have been gratifying to merchant members of the PPA who had been the target of extortionate demands for funds from the government and the military, the PPA asked the government for $40,000 to finance the operations it was undertaking.[40] The government was reported to have agreed to $20,000 as long as the PPA changed its name to something that did not imply police functions. Lu Zhonglin and what was left of the government were no doubt becoming uneasy about the emergence of a "rival sovereignty" within the city walls while they fought a more dangerous claimant outside.

General Lu, faced with the robust growth and popularity of the PPA as a friendly rival to his own authority, finally declared the body dissolved. The police dusted off a tactic long used against the formation of new voluntary associations and ruled that the PPA was not a legal organization even though it was packed with representatives of nearly every *fatuan* in the city.[41] Since the PPA was busy making itself indispensable, and General Lu had one eye on the Nankou Pass, along with the rest of the Guominjun, this "suppression" of the body was not a serious blow. The PPA's strength lay in its base in elite social networks and other organizations like the chamber of commerce rather than its own formal status or legality. It was designed as a "soft" organization, which collapsed to absorb shocks delivered by militarists like Lu Zhonglin while leaving intact the prestige and power of those participating. And so Wang Shizhen, one of the PPA's leading figures, advertised in the Beijing newspapers his withdrawal from the "peace movement" because, he said, the militarists would not pay any attention to him. Even before Lu's ban, the PPA had revised its functions to the narrower one of dealing with the refugee problem and had postponed plans for an independent military force.[42] By this time, however, militia had been organized at the grass-roots level in the city extensively enough that a more decentralized version of Yang Yijian's grander proposal had already been achieved. When militarists pushed, local elites withdrew and defended their interests informally and on a more local level. A structure like the PPA could itself be withdrawn or abandoned and then readily reoccupied at a more propitious moment.

As conditions in the city worsened and Feng Yuxiang's forces prepared to depart, the PPA skillfully reinserted itself into a city-wide leadership role. The police reported finding an average of thirty-five dead bodies each day on the streets as sick and hungry refugees continued to enter the city.[43] Outside the city walls the mortality rate among displaced soldiers and civilians appeared to be much higher.[44] It was becoming apparent that measures associated with the "winter defense," like soup kitchens, would need to be continued or even expanded to cope with the growing refugee population.[45] In a context of deepening social distress, the PPA petitioned the metropolitan prefectural governor to nominate ten PPA members with impressive credentials and reputations as former officials and elder statesmen to take responsibility for governing the city when Lu Zhonglin and the last Guominjun forces left.[46] Lu readily agreed to turn over control of the police to a reshuffled and "legalized" PPA.

In order to establish control over the police force the PPA first needed to find the resources to pay the nine thousand policemen and fifteen hundred gendarmes. The morale of the force and its willingness to obey the PPA were of critical importance now that the plan for a municipal self-defense unit had fallen through. Accordingly, the chamber of commerce, the bankers association, and foreign legations contributed a sum equal to a month's pay to assure police cooperation.[47] Lu Zhonglin and the Guominjun also were paid off. Lu met with the chamber and the bankers and demanded and received two million dollars for "evacuation expenses." The chamber contributed three-quarters of the total, and the rest was made up by the bankers and four months of shop taxes collected in advance.[48] The PPA and the chamber also announced plans to send food and gifts to welcome the invading armies of Zhang Zuolin, Wu Peifu, and Zhang Zongzhang.[49]

The long-expected arrival of the anti-Guominjun forces brought no relief to PPA officials. Instead, the conquering armies brought with them a host of new problems, not the least of which was the vast quantity of unsecured notes the soldiers carried into the city. Zhang Zuolin had relied heavily on the printing press to finance his drive to Beijing.[50] When his troops put these bills, denominated in silver or copper, into circulation, they immediately drove up the value of copper coin.[51] Under these conditions, money-shop owners refused to set fixed rates for the day, as had been the custom each morning, or to abide by official pressure to stabilize the money market. The chamber of commerce called meetings on the issue, but the money traders defended their actions as the only reasonable ones under the circumstances. The chamber and the bankers association drew up regulations to submit to the military, demanding that the generals take steps to secure the notes by depositing cash and securities with the chamber or otherwise demonstrating a willingness to redeem the paper currency.

Meanwhile, the ragged edge of Zhang Zuolin's poorly disciplined forces moved through the city, forcing exchange shops and other establishments to accept the notes at gunpoint.[52] Shop owners hid their copper coins to avoid having to make change with the worthless notes, and a kind of war of wits and nerves broke out between shopkeepers and soldiers. Merchants painted out the names of their shops or put up scaffolding or "closed because of repairs" signs to ward off customers. Exchange shops opened with conspicuously empty shelves where piles of coins once stood.[53] Shoe and clothing stores displayed only small or women's sizes to discourage soldiers from entering. Foreign-goods shops stocked mostly bulky things soldiers would have a difficult time carrying away. Pawnshops delayed opening until noon and then closed early to keep business to a minimum. Clerks dragged out sales for hours to limit transactions.

Refugees and soldiers, as the principal victims and victimizers in this phase of warlord conflict, came to dominate the urban and suburban landscape. Thousands of homeless people wandered through the western suburbs, searching for food and shelter.[54] On a single day in late April, twenty to thirty thousand refugees entered Xizhi Gate at the northwest corner of the Inner City. Pressure on the northern and western suburbs and gates reflected the shift in fighting from east of the city to the northwest where Feng Yuxiang's army was being driven, practically intact, behind defensive positions at Nankou. Refugees continued to stream through the other gates of the city. Most were women and children who had no money for lodging. The refugees brought news and rumors of atrocities, which triggered panics in Beijing. Military officials responded by ordering beheading for a variety of offenses against civilians. Fears were also expressed for the longer-term damage being done to the local economy as a result of military-induced dislocation. The billeting of an estimated 100,000 soldiers in peasant homes in the suburbs was driving rural families into the cities during the planting season.[55] The incoming armies had poor logistics support, and so the troops lived by requisitioning or stealing food and other supplies. Shortly after the troops arrived, suburban food stocks were reported to be exhausted, placing new strains on the city's grain supply.[56] In response, the PPA petitioned the militarists by telegram to send special trains to Beijing with food, salt, and coal.

As the anti-Guominjun forces took control of the city, a struggle began for the choicest administrative posts, providing a picture of Republican and warlord politics at their institutional nadir. The *North China Standard* noted "a double race between the Chihli [Wu Peifu] and Fengtian [Zhang Zuolin] leaders in the seizure of revenue-producing offices in the Metropolis."[57] Office seekers trailed close behind the advance units of the allied armies. Some arrived on the first trains through to Beijing after the siege was lifted.

Government offices that had recently been the scene of turmoil among unpaid employees, political protest, and even occupation by students and disgruntled officials became centers of recruitment to a new, ramshackle political structure. In a number of instances more than one official turned up to claim the same post. Some official buildings were still partly or wholly filled with functionaries who would have to be paid or dismissed. Others stood empty. The parliament building, which had been taken over in part by students looking for dormitory space, became the site of attempts by former legislators to reclaim their old bailiwick. The new Beijing garrison commander refused to allow them in without the approval of both Zhang Zuolin and Wu Peifu.[58] These newly minted or recirculated officials had a level of political credibility approximately equivalent to the bank notes also brought in by the invading forces. While there was no neutral referee or broker available to discount their value, the bankruptcy of their political enterprise was suggested by the fact that the PPA continued to govern the city even as this new wave of political sojourners occupied the administrative shell of the Republic.

Warfare was capable of reducing urban and rural life to a crisis of the most elemental sort. The sight of office seekers struggling over the same position was unseemly. The spectacle of soldiers and civilians struggling for food and shelter, with soldiers winning because they had weapons, or at least better weapons and the skill to use them, was horrifying. The hundreds of thousands of refugees who fled to Beijing with little more than the clothes on their backs testified to the scale of the tragedy. No doubt the militia organized in the countryside to combat crime and banditry held in some areas against undisciplined troops. In some areas troops remained under control. But in general, rural society was much more vulnerable to militarism than were the cities. Rural dwellers voted that judgment with their feet. The limited aerial bombardment inflicted on Beijing by Zhang Zuolin was not deadly enough to diminish the value of the city as a haven from war. The effects of militarism on the countryside were limited only by the discipline and size of the armies involved and the dependence of warlord movements on railways and roads.

Beijing did not entirely escape death and destruction directly or indirectly related to this latest cycle of warlord conflict. In addition to people killed or injured by bombs, refugees and the urban poor fell victim to disease and malnutrition caused or exacerbated by the war despite the efforts of the PPA. Enough people lived on the margin of existence in Beijing that the disruption of economic life caused by closed city gates, rising commodity prices, and confusion in the money market sent them over the edge physically or emotionally. This level of deprivation and desperation caused Lu Zhonglin to post guards at moats and canals during his last weeks in power to prevent suicide attempts.[59] R. H. Tawney described the Chinese peasant as a man standing up to his neck in water so that any wave could drown him. Some members of Beijing's laboring poor shared this precarious position with their rural brethren, although city walls and institutions like the soup kitchens functioned as breakwaters against disorder generated on the battlefield. Urban residents were also subject to political violence associated with militarism. Although the rules of the warlord game allowed losers like Duan Qirui to retire from the field without being killed, others were not so fortunate. One of the victorious army's first acts in Beijing was to shoot Shao Piaoping, the editor of the pro-Guominjun, pro-Nationalist newspaper *Jing-bao*.[60] (Zhang Zongchang, pictured in figure 24, was responsible for this outrage.)

On the other hand, the size and complexity of Beijing placed limits on the use of terror and simple expropriation. The repertoire of strategies that urban residents could use to frustrate the designs of militarists was a good deal larger than that of the typical rural inhabitant. In a city of small-scale enterprises and shop and residential architecture dominated by twisting alleyways and walled compounds, there was plenty of room to be inconspicuous. A character in a Lao She novel set in Beijing reflected on what he had learned from living through the periodic turmoil of warlord politics:

War did not frighten him; peace did not make him unduly happy. . . . He wanted only a measure of quiet and to pass the days without worry for food and clothes. Even if the "scourge of soldiers" should descend or the "rampage of horses," he had plans for meeting them. The most important provision was to keep grain and salt vegetable always in his home, enough for the family to eat for three months. If bullets were flying in the air and soldiers rioted in the streets, he would close the main gate of the compound and place against it a great broken jar filled with stones.[61]

People who did not have enough money and food to sit out the siege behind shuttered windows or gates had little to offer militarists aside from their labor, which warlords often took through press gangs. The militarists lacked the means and knowledge of the urban scene necessary to root out these small, but in composition substantial, caches of food and cash. To pry resources loose from the urban economy they had to work through leaders with access to the shop and guild economy. They had to negotiate with and accept the legitimate role of "gentry and merchants," elder statesmen, miscellaneous civic leaders, and *fatuan* officers as brokers and mediators. While attempts to coerce local elites were not unknown, shooting or jailing the men who were in a position to give you other people's money made no practical sense.

This process of negotiation, compromise, threats, and concessions enclosed the quarrel in late April and May between militarists and local elites over monetary issues. Accepting military notes at face value would have been equivalent to paying tribute or a tax. Chamber president Sun Xueshi and PPA leader Wang Shizhen knew that the militarists had to be paid off if the urban economy, in which they and those they represented had a heavy moral and financial commitment, were to recover. But the chamber and the PPA pressed for conditions. At a special meeting of the chamber, Sun reported that he and the PPA had demanded that the notes be secured with silver transported to Beijing from the warlords' home bases, the right to pay taxes to the new regime in the devalued notes at face value, and prohibitions on the practice of making change for the notes with hard currencies.[62] If these and other, similar regulations generated continuously by the PPA and the chamber had all been subscribed to, Zhang Zuolin and the other militarists would have been forced to make a large net investment in the Beijing economy. That would have undercut the whole point of being a warlord and would have severely restricted Zhang's capacity to mobilize resources. But merchants, bankers, and other elites felt compelled to push as hard as possible because it was inevitable that just as Lu Zhonglin had demanded and received a large sum for peacefully departing from the city, the anti-Guominjun allies would demand tribute for (relatively) peacefully occupying Beijing. Zhang Zuolin and his partners were reported to have demanded a "loan" of two million dollars as the price for driving out Feng Yuxiang and Duan Qirui. Beijing bankers and the chamber responded with a counteroffer of one million.[63]

Gradually, in late April and early May, as the shape of the agreements between the PPA and the militarists became known, more and more shops began to reopen. Slowly, the regular government began to coalesce around those ministries and bureaus able to obtain funds to operate. The foreign ministry was the only ministry able to pay its employees their regular salaries because it had access to customs receipts paid out by the legations.[64] The PPA acted as a negotiating center and clearing house for attempts by officials to obtain the cash they needed to operate. Bankers like Zhou Zuomin loaned the education ministry and the primary and middle schools enough money to pay a portion of the salaries of their employees.[65] The PPA entered into negotiations with Beijing banks to obtain loans to pay the police and garrison forces. The bankers demanded security for their loans, and the PPA complained that interest rates offered were too high. The PPA's success as broker between officials and bankers made the body the target of intense lobbying efforts by government departments throughout May. The organization was "bombarded" by letters from ministries and bureaus, asking for funds or help in obtaining lines of credit.[66]

The PPA was well on its way to being co-opted by militarists who had, in the process, been forced to moderate their wilder and more disruptive tendencies. Former foreign minister under Duan Qirui and a PPA member, Yan Jinghui moved over from the PPA to head a regency cabinet in the new regime. This tendency toward co-optation and politicization had been criticized earlier by some PPA members. As Zhang Zuolin's new regime wobbled to its feet and survived its first financial crisis in the settling of accounts during the June Dragon Boat Festival, the PPA's value as a temporary social base for itinerant generals and politicians and a conditional tie to local society lessened from the point of view of both the regime and local elites. "State" and society met long enough in the zone of mediation and negotiation provided by Beijing elites to cushion the landing of the former onto the latter. Since neither was buying what the other was selling by way of Zhang Zuolin's dictatorial ambitions or the self-government or local self-defense plans of Beijing civic leaders, disengagement was a logical course for both.

Managing Protection Costs

In discussing the "economic meaning of war and protection," historian Frederick Lane wrote that "every economic enterprise needs and pays for protection, protection against the destruction or armed seizure of its capital and the forceful disruption of its labor."[67] In normal times governments monopolize organized violence and determine the rates of protection costs in taxes and bribes. The 1920s in China were anything but normal. Regional militarism acted to blur distinctions among taxes, bribes, tribute, extortion, and plunder.

A good deal of city politics in Beijing revolved around the calculation of protection costs and the assessment of responsibility for the burden of payment. Some groups and institutions were more vulnerable to warlordism than others. Everyone, including residents in thousands of small shops, factories, and residential compounds, was vulnerable to troop riot and looting. But by hiding their cash, shuttering their shops, and relying on neighborhood and street militia, residents could significantly mitigate the effects of war, siege, and urban violence. Persons with a national or regional field of operations had a different set of options. Bankers, politicians, and officials could flee to the foreign quarters in Beijing, Tianjin, or Shanghai. Individuals, groups, and institutions with a citywide frame of reference of necessity took the lead in negotiating and paying protection costs for the city as a whole and then distributing the burden through the networks and organizations they controlled. Testimony to the power and authority of the PPA and *fatuan* like the chamber of commerce and the bankers association is the fact that hundreds of thousands of dollars were collected to pay tribute to militarists in 1925 and 1926 without triggering noticeable dissension among shops, enterprises, and citizens who might have found protection at a cheaper price by relying on their own self-defense strategies. In 1925 and 1926, military crisis produced consensus among city leaders and their constituents. The real and imagined dangers of militarism outweighed whatever reservations contributors had about the fairness of these brokered protection costs. However, given the tendency of vertically organized communities like the merchant class to fracture along factional lines, consensus of this kind needed to be continually reproduced and managed. During the next military crisis in 1928, the issue of protection costs slipped out of the hands of incumbent *fatuan* leaders into those of rivals and insurgent movements.

Except that Zhang Zuolin was inside the walls of Beijing, and his enemies, including Feng Yuxiang, were now marching against *him*, the cycle of military conflict in 1928 followed the by now familiar pattern exemplified by the anti-Guominjun war of 1925 and 1926. War clouds gathered in north China in 1927 in an atmosphere of mobilization and countermobilization. The anti-Zhang forces, led by Chiang Kai-shek and his insurgent Nationalist regime, included warlords Feng, Yan Xishan of Shanxi province, and Bai Zhongxi of Guangxi. The Northern Expedition promised national reunification and revolutionary renewal. But the system of military separatism was still intact.[68] Wars were won through building coalitions among military contenders, and armies continued to rattle north and south, east and west, along China's railway grid.

As Zhang Zuolin made final preparations to leave Beijing in early June 1928 Wang Shizhen announced the formation of another Peace Preservation Association to bridge the interval between Zhang's departure and the arrival of the Northern Expedition.[69] Reflecting the growing importance of the chamber of commerce and the waning of Beijing's administrative position, the 1928 PPA, unlike its predecessor in 1926 (but like the first PPA in the fall of 1925), included the chamber of commerce president, Sun Xueshi, and vice-president, Leng Jiayi, as full members.[70] For the next week, the PPA made an efficient job of governing the city. PPA leaders raised funds to pay the police and troops, ensured the continued operations of public utilities, dampened rumors by holding press conferences and communicating with representatives of various circles in Beijing society, and gracefully went out of business once officials of the Northern Expedition arrived to take over.

The PPA and the chamber authorized shops in Beijing to supply the Northern Expedition armies with food and provisions, with the understanding that the Nationalist regime would take responsibility for reimbursing suppliers.[71] When neither the government in Nanjing or local militarists in control of the city proved willing to make good on their promise, the chamber was able to receive government permission to collect the money in the form of five months of shop taxes. Depending on the size of the establishment, each shop was to contribute between $50 and $300.

Whereas in 1926 the calculation and assessment of protection costs had functioned smoothly in support of the PPA's and the chamber's role as broker, in 1928 the same procedures excited considerable opposition. The collection issue split the chamber of commerce into two hostile camps in the late summer and fall of 1928. Many shopkeepers opposed the contribution, and the hotel-and-inn guild, which had been badly hurt financially by the transfer of the capital to Nanjing, took the lead in attacking the measure in the chamber.[72] With the actual threat of troop riot past, the chamber lost leverage in its moral and practical appeals to contributors. As earlier episodes had demonstrated, chamber leaders were vulnerable to factional and more broadly gauged opposition on issues involving mobilization of resources and concentration of power at the expense of member guilds.

Complicating dissension within the chamber in 1928 was an alliance between opposition forces within the chamber and a Nationalist party mass organization responsible for mobilizing the merchant community. The merchants union (*shangmin xiehui*) was one of five popular organizations under the leadership of the local Nationalist party branch.[73] The union had opened in July as part of the general political mobilization sparked by the arrival of the Northern Expedition and the surfacing of underground Nationalist activists and organizers. At first the merchants union courted the chamber leadership. But then the collection issue provided an opportunity for the union to side with what it construed as the "mass" component of the merchant community. The merchants union argued that the chamber had no legal right to make such assessments and that the contribution was simply another unfair tax.[74] From the chamber leadership's point of view, the food purchased had helped insure that the city and the suburbs were free from marauding soldiers during the transition between Fengtian and Nationalist control. The money now to be collected was, in effect, a "protection cost" to be distributed fairly among all shops.

The struggle over tribute paid to Nationalist forces was caused by the "warlord" behavior of Chiang Kai-shek's formally anti-militarist regime and intensified by radical criticism of the chamber as "feudal" for appearing to condone that behavior. That the attack came from a Nationalist organization indicated the degree to which the state presided over by Chiang was torn by contradictory tendencies. As Joseph Fewsmith has observed, as the Nationalists unified China, often by forming warlord-style coalitions and negotiated transactions with local elites, they violated the "purity" of the movement.[75] Organizations like the merchants unions were only too happy to point out these inconsistencies, to the discomfiture of Nationalist officials and generals obliged to play a political game designed as much by Zhang Zuolin as by Sun Yat-sen. Buffeted by these crosscurrents, the chamber found itself subjected to extortion from above and public criticism from below by the same political movement. The Nationalist party-state was plainly at war with itself. But that was small consolation to chamber leaders Sun Xueshi and Leng Jiayi as they came under bitter personal attack.

Pressured by internal opposition and the campaign launched by the merchants union, the chamber held a rare mass meeting of its membership on November 13, 1928, to give a vote of confidence to Sun and Leng.[76] Assailed for its complicity with warlords by a self-consciously populist body, the chamber leaders organized a forum that emphasized its broad base, democratic procedures, and *fatuan* status. Three thousand members met in Beijing's largest public theater, located outside Qian Gate. The merchants union was represented on the speakers platform by three local Nationalist officials. The Nationalist politicians unwisely ignored Leng's attempt to introduce them formally to the chamber membership, and when one of the three tried to speak, he was met with a chorus of "Down with the Nationalist party" and "We don't want any third party butting into our affairs." The Nationalists stalked out in a rage. When a vote was taken, sixty-eight of seventy-one guilds present voted to collect the shop tax. Three days later the Nationalists mounted a protest march under the banner of the five popular organizations, but only two hundred people participated.[77] Nonetheless, opposition inside and outside of the chamber forced the organization to shift from a policy of coercion to one of persuasion in collecting the tax.[78] Defeated by "feudal" merchants wielding populist weapons of the merchant union's own choice in a duel it had helped provoke, local Nationalist activists became more extreme in their verbal attacks, to the point of calling for the arrest and execution of Sun and Leng.

The reaction of local elites at mid-decade to the intrusion of warlordism into city politics took into account the way in which militarists had radically simplified the Republican state. Liberal constitutional forms had been stripped away or made vestigial. Bristling with threats and weapons, warlord political machines clung to whatever ministries and bureaus still produced revenues or ran the railroads they required for logistics support. They also clung to local elites and the organizations they headed as reliable gatherers of protection money and guarantors of local order.

For all their resemblance to other players on the field of regional militarism, the Nationalists introduced a new element into city politics: state directed and condoned revolution. Prior to 1928 in

Beijing, revolution had bloomed extravagantly and expressively, outside Tianan Gate for a few weeks in 1919 and 1925, or unobtrusively and modestly, in networks and clubs of radical politicians. In 1928 and 1929 network and movement were joined to a citywide organization to produce a body of cadres and allied constituencies who imagined themselves capable of transforming urban society. Rivals to the dominant structure of elite networks and Qing-vintage *fatuan*, they viewed institutions like the chamber of commerce as hopelessly compromised by warlordism and imperialism. The willingness of the PPA and the chamber to pay off militarists and solicit contributions from the foreign legations to purchase the loyalty of police and troops provided prima facie evidence of this complicity. As it turned out, the established urban order in Beijing proved to be more accommodating to their brand of revolutionary militancy than they to it. In a city that operated on the principle that almost anything could be added so long as nothing was subtracted, local revolutionaries who envisioned a Beijing without a Legation Quarter, elder statesmen, and Sun Xueshi were likely to be disappointed.

Ten

Union and Faction: Organized Labor in the Wake of the Northern Expedition

The chamber of commerce's struggle with the merchants union in 1928 over "protection costs" reflected a general intensification of city politics, which followed the arrival of the Northern Expedition. This local political efflorescence was made possible first of all by the more permissive political climate that came with Zhang Zuolin's departure. During Zhang Zuolin's tenure in Beijing political repression had reached unprecedented levels. In addition to the notorious arrest and execution of Li Dazhao and nineteen fellow Communists in 1927, Zhang's agents carried out executions of scores, perhaps hundreds, of other political offenders.[1] Cadres who attempted to carry forward the May Fourth and May Thirtieth styles of political activism risked imprisonment or death.

A new, more liberal political atmosphere emerged in the summer of 1928 despite the illiberal inclinations of the Northern Expedition principals. Deadlock in the winning coalition of militarists Feng Yuxiang and Yan Xishan and their formal overlord, Chiang Kai-shek, prevented anyone from exerting the kind of strict political control over the city which Zhang Zuolin had enjoyed. Supporters of Yan, Feng, and Chiang shared municipal and provincial posts in Beijing and north China. Neither the new Nationalist government in Nanjing nor the northern militarists camped in and near the city could intervene decisively in local affairs for fear of upsetting the balance of regional power. As a result, despite his deep distrust of popular movements and the men and women who led them, Chiang Kai-shek was not in a position to continue Zhang's repressive policies in Beijing.

True, the Nationalist party itself, as the element in the Nationalist regime charged with mass mobilization, was steadily losing power to military and government officials led by Chiang Kai-shek. On a visit to the city in late summer 1928, Chiang warned of "mistaken individuals" in the party who believed that "party power is higher than everyone."[2] Party members were required to "lead the people, do propaganda work, and carry out investigations." In these areas, "party members have duties; [they] have no power." Nonetheless, local party organizers in north China stubbornly refused to surrender the role that gave them power: organizing students, workers, women, peasants, and other groups and classes into politically active unions and federations.

In resisting subordination of the party to Chiang, Nationalist organizers were not attempting to foster a liberal or a pluralistic political system. Their goal was party domination of politics and society. Unfortunately for them, neither the government in Nanjing nor local elites were enthusiastic about this ambitious project. Competing organizations, like *fatuan* and guilds, survived to defend their positions and prerogatives. The Nationalist center proved unable or unwilling to incorporate citizens into a political monolith. The resulting pattern of political mobilization was pluralistic by dint of the party's incomplete conquest of local society and the center's incomplete control over local party branches. Devotees of the one-party state had neither the strength locally to defeat rivals in a contest for the loyalty of urban elites and masses nor the influence nationally to connect themselves and their constituents to a centralizing, unifying state power.

In the immediate aftermath of Zhang Zuolin's departure, Chiang, Yan, and Feng busied themselves with the task of distributing the political spoils remaining in the city after Beijing lost its status as national capital. Chiang's unwillingness to move the Nationalist capital north undoubtedly stemmed in part from a desire to devalue the city's importance to the warlords, who had it within their military grasp, and avoid exposing his regime to the direct influence of these uncertain allies. Beijing, now renamed Beiping, was reclassified a municipality and bequeathed a new governmental structure. A mayor headed an administration composed of eight bureaus, including public security (the police), social affairs, public health, public works, finance, education, public utilities, and land.[3] Most of the city budget (70 percent) was consumed by the public security bureau. As if to reinforce the dominant position of the police in the new government, municipal offices were temporarily housed in the old police headquarters, newly redecorated with Nationalist flags and posters.[4] Public works, employing nearly one thousand men, took over the police force's old task of supervising road maintenance and repair. Social affairs, with eighty-three staff members, mediated labor disputes. These two bureaus, in combination with finance, accounted for most nonpolice expenditures (24 percent of the total), leaving the rest of the municipal bureaucracy understaffed and in a weak financial position.[5]

Cadres

A divided political camp in Beijing and elsewhere in north China forced grudging toleration on the part of higher-level political authorities of new movements, ideologies, and organizations. The principal exception to this general atmosphere of political permissibility was the continued persecution of the few beleaguered Communists left in the underground.[6]

Nationalist party politicians and organizers emerged from hiding to promote a comprehensive plan for the corporate representation of city residents. This political blueprint was based on a vision of a unified populace under Nationalist leadership, glimpsed earlier in mass rallies outside Tianan Gate and attempted in practice in southern cities, like Shanghai and Guangzhou. With Shanxi officials, and to a lesser degree supporters of Feng Yuxiang and Chiang Kai-shek, in control of municipal government, Nationalist party politicians carved out a role for themselves by creating new, "mass" organizations. They chartered labor unions and other popular bodies outside the established social order and beyond Nanjing's immediate political reach.

The local Nationalist party branch went public on June 6, the day the Northern Expedition arrived in the city. Nationalist cadres used a guild for Hunanese located outside Qian Gate for their first headquarters and advertised their presence with posters and a festive display of silk flags.[7] The next day a formal party-branch meeting was held with a ritual reading of Sun Yat-sen's will, five minutes of silence in his memory, bows to a Nationalist flag and a portrait of Sun, and a statement of resolve to guard against Communist activity and maintain order in the city.[8]

Party members had cause to celebrate. Since Zhang Zuolin's victory in north China in 1926, Nationalist cadres had been forced to operate secretly in Beijing, and, while underground, sizable numbers of party workers had been killed or jailed.[9] Harassed by police agents, Nationalist party members had struggled to remain in contact with social forces they aspired to lead and control. In 1926, in the aftermath of the March 18 Incident, non-Communist Nationalist cadres had moved to broaden their base among popular movements.[10] A key figure in this underground political offensive was Ding Weifen, a founding member of Sun Yat-sen's Revolutionary Alliance and a leading figure in the north China branch of the Nationalist party.[11] Ding openly broke with the united-front policy in 1926 by organizing a society intended to combat Communist influence, which later became known as the "Grand Alliance" (*da tongmeng*) faction. In Beijing the core of this group of left-of-center, non-Communist cadres was built around students from Beijing's Zhaoyang University (one of the largest private colleges in the city) who, like Ding, were Shandong natives.[12] Facing stiff competition from the Communists, who had also been expanding their contacts with workers in 1925 and early 1926, non-Communist Nationalists fought for access to night-soil carriers, rickshaw men, water carriers, newspaper deliverers, and printers. "Our knives and swords struck time and again in battle [but we] never retreated," insisted the veterans who survived.[13] Certainly Duan Qirui's attack on the Communists and allied left-wing Nationalists in the spring of 1926 made the competition easier than it might have been. But Nationalists also faced repression once Zhang Zuolin's forces took control of the city. As an indication of the price paid for years of underground activism, one of the party's first objectives after the arrival of the Northern Expedition was to secure the release of members still in prison.[14]

The Nationalist party members who surfaced in June 1928 to begin or continue campaigns to mobilize and organize city resi-

dents were mainly young, university-educated men who had joined
the party in the aftermath of the May Thirtieth Movement.[15]
Many were sojourners, a status common in Beiping trades and
occupations.[16] The rise of the Grand Alliance faction to prominence
within the local party branch was based in part on the Shandong provincial ties of leaders like Li Lesan and Zhang Yinqing,
who came to play a decisive role in mass organizing efforts. Use of
native-place loyalties as a means of developing a core of followers
and extending one's influence was a well-established strategy in
Chinese urban politics. Chamber of commerce presidents Sun
Xueshi and An Disheng had used their Shandong and Hebei (Zhili
province was renamed Hebei in 1928) connections, respectively,
as a base for forays into public life. If anything, the Grand
Alliance's Shandong connection was an asset in Beiping politics,
where many trades, such as water and night-soil carrying, were
dominated by Shandong natives, and where many elites were sojourners from the cities, towns, and villages of the rugged penin-
sular province.

The pool from which leading cadres were drawn was fed by
politicized colleges and universities, increasingly politically conscious laboring classes, and an officialdom buffeted by the forces
of militarism and revolution. A vocation in politics was an especially attractive choice for educated youths, who had few other job
opportunities.[17] A later, hostile Communist account of the Grand
Alliance faction's activities asserts that in 1928 Li Lesan and his
comrades "had neither soldiers nor wealth; they only had Shandong students from Zhaoyang University to serve as their main-
stay. So they used 'mass movements' to consolidate their own
position."[18] The Grand Alliance was also aided by their patron
Ding Weifen's rise to director of the Central Party School in
Nanjing.[19]

Nationalist party members, numbering between two and three
thousand in 1928 and 1929, zealously pursued the task of revolu-
tionizing (*geming hua*) the old capital.[20] Party activists sought to
eradicate what they saw as feudal and reactionary influences visible in city life and culture. The names of streets and lanes judged
to be "feudal" or "meaningless," such as "Pig Head Lane,"
"Ministry of Revenue [under the Qing] Street," and "Hemp
Thread Lane," were changed to "Bamboo Ends Lane," "Public

Security Street," and "Constitution Lane."[21] The party-branch propaganda bureau dispatched agents to photography shops outside Qian Gate to confiscate "counter revolutionary photographs" of warlords and politicians like Zhang Zuolin and Duan Qirui.[22] In an attempt to "modernize" cultural life, the authorities unsuccessfully tried to force city residents to celebrate the new year according to the solar rather than the lunar calendar.[23] On the surface of things at least, as a newspaper columnist pointed out, the city did give off the "aroma" of *geming hua*.[24] Education and politics had been "party-ized" (*danghua*). "Women have revolutionized [short] haircuts; men wear revolutionized Sun Yat-sen suits . . . [we] eat in Sun Yat-sen Restaurant and go for strolls in Sun Yat-sen Park [the new name for Central Park]."

This revolutionary culture or aura clung to the mass organizations promoted by party politicians. Grass-roots activism promised to deepen what appeared to some a merely cosmetic alteration of the city's political and cultural life. Cadres Li Lesan and Zhang Yinqing worked throughout the summer and fall of 1928 to build a network of popular organizations, including labor, peasant, merchant, student, and women's unions and associations, tied to the local party branch and the "Masses Training Committee" (*minxun hui*), which they controlled.[25] The merchants union fought to displace the chamber of commerce. The city's student federation revived under the party tutelage. Women participated in a party-sponsored association. Even peasants from the surrounding suburbs joined an organization directed by Nationalist organizers. Li and Zhang also laid ambitious plans to build a labor movement, the elusive goal of popular organizers since the May Fourth Movement.

Unionism

Within a few months of its founding in June, the citywide Federation of Trade Unions (*zong gonghui*; hereafter FTU) brought over two dozen unions and sixteen thousand members under one organizational umbrella.[26] The FTU drew support from Beijing's small but strategically placed modern utilities, communications, and industrial enterprises. But the body also included rickshaw men, night-soil carriers, barbers, street sweepers, camel drivers, and water carriers. Considering the continued power and prominence of guilds and the growing opposition of national and local-level power-holders to grass-roots organizing, the Beiping union movement did a creditable job of building a base for itself in 1928.

The union movement benefited from the initial clarity and directness of the populist and activist message given out by FTU cadres. In the summer of 1928, as the movement added enterprise after enterprise and trade after trade to its lists, Li Lesan and Zhang Yinqing openly called for class struggle.[27] (Soon afterward they made an about-face and sought to harmonize their position with that of the more conservative Nationalist mainstream.)[28] Cadres of the FTU actively sought out potential union recruits and established a high public profile, which drew workers to the union cause. Shortly after the Nationalists began to operate in the open, streetcar workers contacted party cadres with a view to organizing a union. Zhang Yinqing and another colleague visited the streetcar yard in the Bridge of Heaven district to make arrangements for a solemn inaugural meeting, convened in the predawn hours of June 26.[29]

Once organized, workers quickly moved to press demands for higher wages and better working conditions. Streetcar workers requested more pay and a reduction in working hours.[30] Postal workers demanded shorter hours, as well as two days off per month, an increase in pay, and a guarantee against wages falling into arrears.[31] Unions representing electric company employees, newspaper carriers and deliverers, and printers made demands related to wage and job-security issues.[32] None of these early actions, taken by workers in conjunction with union organizing, led to strikes or violence. In most instances workers quickly won all or most of what they wanted.

Rapid success in establishing a citywide presence for the labor movement led, however, to the FTU's first political crisis. On August 17, 1928, General Yan Xishan, from his headquarters in Taiyuan, ordered union offices closed. In a circular telegram explaining his action, Yan claimed:

Within the last month, two or three party cadres have stirred up the workers, created all kinds of unions, and sparked class conflict.... Disorder is increasing. Plots are being prepared. City residents are apprehensive and fearful, and the wealthy are fleeing. I fear an explosion even worse than what happened in Guangzhou and Wuhan.[33]

By misrepresenting the political and social impact of the union movement on local order and raising the bloody specter of revolution and reaction, Yan apparently hoped to intimidate party cadres and their supporters. But party leaders kept their heads and neutralized Yan's attempted coup by appealing his decision to officials in Nanjing and apparently forging a countermanding order when a satisfactory reply was not forthcoming. In the ensuing confusion, unions resumed their work. Union leaders, who had prudently taken "sick leave," reappeared in public with their FTU badges on.[34] Political deadlock and indecision at the national and local levels prevented an antilabor juggernaut from wiping out the organizational gains made in June and July.

Workers guarded and celebrated their newly won right to free and unmolested participation in citywide political rallies and demonstrations. On July 7, 1928, the local party branch organized a rally to celebrate the victory of the Northern Expedition.[35] The demonstration was scheduled for the morning, and many city services were suspended to allow streetcar workers, telephone operators, and postal workers to attend. A lantern parade was planned for the evening, which government authorities tried to cancel, citing a directive from Nanjing discouraging or banning most public demonstrations. Party officials refused, and the parade went on as scheduled.

Chiang Kai-shek was visiting the city at the time to negotiate with his warlord allies, and a contingent of bodyguards accompanying him decided to participate in the procession. The parade began outside Tianan Gate, with women's organizations in the lead, followed by streetcar workers, the soldiers, and various schools and labor unions. The line of march passed north through Central and Beihai Parks in what must have been a striking nighttime scene of banners and lights winding through the old imperial pavilions and gardens. As the procession reached the north gate of Beihai, some of the women slowed the pace to the point that the soldiers began to complain by shouting, "Faster in front!" Streetcar workers replied that the women were tired from holding meetings all day. The soldiers then began to needle the streetcar men by

suggesting in a ribald way that the workers carry the women if
they were that tired. The workers took offense, and the two sides
began to quarrel. Attempts by parade marshals to mediate failed,
and the soldiers attacked the workers, beating several and
smashing the lanterns they were carrying. Li Lesan and Zhang
Yinqing, who were directing the march, stopped the fight and
ordered pickets under their command to arrest and detain one of
the soldiers. The march resumed its course, turning south past the
Xisi and Xidan intersections and west on Changan Avenue back
toward Tianan Gate. As the procession passed the gate to the
headquarters of the "War Zone Military Command" twenty soldiers and detectives, in apparent retaliation for the arrest of their
comrade, rushed out and grabbed four streetcar workers. When
the marchers saw what was happening, they sprang to the aid of
the four, only to find themselves facing a line of soldiers with rifles
pointed and ready to fire. With the nightmare image of the March
18 Incident no doubt in mind, "the masses withdrew in alarm."
Party officials, the police, and military officials met the following
day to arrange an exchange of prisoners and negotiate a settlement. Meanwhile, workers drove two streetcars emblazoned with
antimilitarist slogans around town to publicize their "powerful
sense of grievance" and to display four wounded workers as proof
of their case against the soldiers. Chiang's representatives finally
agreed to pay the medical bills of workers injured in the fracas and
to prosecute the soldiers involved.

The July 7 celebrations also triggered disputes by workers over
political rights and the more prosaic but deeply contentious issue
of paid holidays. Paid holidays were rare in China in the 1920s.
Workers were usually given time off only at the three major festivals. As a result, political participation came to be seen by workers
as a means of legitimately shortening seven-day workweeks.[36] Employers took a predictably dim view of worker demands for politically related holidays. Bathhouse proprietors threatened to dismiss
barbers in their establishments who continued to take off from
work to attend weekly Sun Yat-sen memorial meetings at their
union headquarters.[37] Postal officials complained that the workers
had taken more holidays in the year since the union was founded
than in the whole previous seventeen years of the Republic.[38] The
Beiping Federation of Factories, newly organized to counter the

growing power of labor unions, claimed that their members would be forced out of business if they continued to give in to demands for "holidays and more holidays with full pay."[39] Eventually a compromise was worked out, recognizing a fixed number of national days to be added to customary days off at festival time.[40]

In addition to wage increases, protection from arbitrary firings, and greater political freedom, unions also provided a limited range of broader social benefits. Electric-company, match-factory, streetcar, and Finance Bureau printing-office unions opened schools for workers or their children.[41] Low-status workers received a new measure of respect. For example, night-soil workers were feted with a tea party at the local party headquarters.[42]

Rebellion in the Ranks

In the course of union struggles in 1928, both the FTU center and individual unions grew stronger. Unions won victories in confrontations with owners and managers, often with the help of FTU leaders and the party. Zhang Yinqing turned out to be a particularly skillful practitioner of labor politics, with a flair for exploiting public opinion and connections to higher-level political and military elites. In October 1928 the FTU targeted the Danhua match factory for union organizing. The plant, which employed over one thousand workers, was notorious for its low wages, unsafe working conditions, and callous use of female and child labor.[43] Zhang Yinqing single-handedly overcame the factory management's opposition to unionization by entering the plant armed only with a portrait of Sun Yat-sen and brushing past a sign that read "Thank you for not visiting." Zhang displayed Sun's portrait in one of the factory workshops and called on the workers to stop work and attend a meeting. A union was organized on the spot, and an executive committee was selected which immediately began drawing up a list of demands. Officials of the FTU wrote a report on conditions in the plant and arranged to have it appear in the local press to publicize the plight of match-factory workers. Cadres directed workers to submit their demands to management the same day the exposé was published to maximize pressure on the firm. By this time, factory workers were in a militant mood. When the company rejected their demands, they wanted to go out on strike; FTU leaders persuaded them to accept a job slowdown and a march on party and government offices instead. In the course of their procession around the city, the Danhua workers managed to interest garrison commander Zhang Yinwu in their cause, and he sent his own representative to participate with party and FTU officials in mediation sessions between the company and the union. After the talks had dragged on for several days, Zhang Yinwu's representative lost his temper over the company's apparent intransigence. He boxed the ears of a company official, punched him in the eye, and then had him spirited away in an automobile. Shortly after the incident, the company agreed to a raise in pay for all categories of workers, including children, and a monthly contribution to a workers' school.[44]

As the union movement consolidated its position in Beijing as a presence in citywide politics and a power in a range of trades and enterprises, party and FTU leaders like Li Lesan and Zhang Yinqing shifted their energies from the task of organizing unions to the problem of managing union affairs and mediating between their constituents and other groups and organizations. In the first flush of organizing and union activism in the summer and fall of 1928, the militancy of workers often left Li and Zhang to play the role of mediator between labor and capital. This was true even when FTU cadres were striking a radical pose, and it was especially the case after they had moderated their rhetoric. At times it appeared that the FTU, despite its initial radicalism, was at least as concerned with administering its realm, like other *fatuan*, as in leading a movement capable of promoting broad reforms in the workplace. At the request of several newspapers the FTU acquiesced in police repression of "bad elements" in the newspaper-carriers union.[45] Cadres of the FTU, led by Zhang Yinqing, persuaded Yanjing carpet-factory workers to end their strike without a settlement in hand even though a "majority of workers were disgruntled" with the compromise.[46] Printers who went out on strike without first accepting FTU leadership were targeted for arrest by the party.[47] The FTU and the local Nationalist party branch favored workers many more times than management or the interests of order. But the tendency of FTU cadres to adopt the rhetoric of legality, convention, and order to check or moderate worker militancy is noteworthy.

Against the spontaneity of much of the labor movement in the summer of 1928, party and FTU cadres tried to maintain control over individual unions and work groups. The FTU waited a month from the time of its founding to call a general meeting of union representatives to elect an executive committee.[48] In the meantime the labor federation functioned as the instrument of Li Lesan and Zhang Yinqing. Even after leaders drawn from member unions took office, the FTU relied heavily on party professionals like Zhang to set policy and expand or limit the scope of conflict between workers and their adversaries. By fall 1928 party organizers had constructed a multitiered apparatus centered on the Masses Training Committee, which supervised both the FTU and member unions. Citing the danger of "extremism," the Masses Training Committee notified the FTU that news of union "disorders" ought to be relayed to it so that cadres could be dispatched to mediate the conflicts.[49] The FTU responded by ordering member unions to seek its permission before carrying out job actions so as to avoid "reckless [or] rash strikes."[50]

To protect themselves and the labor movement from the violence of men like Yan Xishan, deal effectively with other local elites, and mediate conflicts within their own domain, FTU cadres spoke and behaved like responsible urban managers. Their success in creating an organization capable of imposing a degree of control over a large segment of the city's working class made them powerful figures in local politics. However, following a pattern discernable in the careers of other civic activists, like An Disheng and Sun Xueshi, this organizational achievement also made them targets for internal rebellion.

For a time in 1928 it appeared that the leaders of the old *fatuan*, such as the chamber of commerce, might form a partnership with new groups, like the FTU, to manage city affairs on the basis of a consensus fashioned from Nationalist ideology and the practice of informal elite mediation and coordination. For example, on National Day, October 10, 1928, the space outside Tianan Gate was divided and roped off into party, government, military, student, peasant, worker, merchant, and police assembly areas representing Nationalist-style corporatism.[51] Zhang Yinqing and chamber representative Leng Jiayi shared the speakers platform with representatives of other unions, associations, and societies. But alongside joint appearances suggesting a measure of consensus and unity, the chamber and the merchants union had already commenced their bitter contest over control of the merchant community. Based on what appeared to be a firm foundation of mass organizations, party leaders could afford to contemplate expanding their field of operations. Not content to organize the unorganized, party cadres sought to invade the preserves of established elites. Eventually the whole of urban society could be "party-ized" and "revolutionized." Unfortunately for party leaders like Li and Zhang, in late 1928 and 1929 this foundation began to crack and buckle as workers rebelled against the incumbent FTU leadership.

In December 1928 union members from the electric-light company quarreled with FTU leaders over tactics used in the workers' struggles with the utility.[52] The workers were demanding a wage increase, protection against arbitrary firings, equal compensation for job-related injuries for both regular workers and apprentices, and the right to split yearly profits with company stockholders in the form of increased bonuses. Militant workers, led by Li Youguang, apparently planned to cut off electricity to the city if their demands were not met. The FTU, in line with its by then established policy of moderating labor unrest in the interest of preserving social peace, sent its agents to the company to prevent a shutdown. The FTU also convened a meeting of one hundred representatives of member unions to condemn the actions of the electric-light workers. A formal resolution blamed "reactionary elements" that had emerged "from the depths to foment disorder," stripped the electric-light union of its FTU affiliation, and demanded the arrest of Li Youguang and his supporters. Federation leaders then dispatched pickets to the electric-light company, where they "arrested" one of Li's followers. While dissident electric-light workers later claimed that it was the FTU and its followers in the local union which advocated using power cutoffs to wring concessions from the company, the repressive nature of actions taken by FTU leaders in December suggests that grassroots militancy within the local conflicted with the more moderate stance taken by the FTU center. In response to the FTU's attack on the union, two hundred utility workers marched to party headquarters and demanded to talk to federation leaders. Zhang Yinqing came out and spoke to the workers for an hour and succeeded in persuading the crowd that they had been misled. In an eloquent summation of the FTU's position, conveyed with a "heavy heart," Zhang elicited expressions of support from the protesters, and the workers returned to the utility. However, in subsequent weeks, the breach between the FTU and the electric-light workers widened. The workers were unable to win more than nominal concessions from the company, and the FTU did not rescind its censure of the union. Dissident laborers had pamphlets printed up attacking Zhang Yinqing and the FTU and alleging that Zhang, not they, had jeopardized the city's power supply.

In February 1929 a faction in the streetcar-workers union also broke with the FTU. Ironically, the conflict between the federation and the streetcar workers originated in a successful labor action taken by the union in the fall of 1928. Because of the small scale of most enterprises and work groups and the way in which native-place ties often reinforced occupational identity, Beijing workers were capable of displaying impressive zeal in defense of group interests. Militant carriers of water and night soil offered extreme examples of how far workers would go to protect territory and livelihood. Streetcar drivers and conductors had a similarly combative spirit based on professional pride, proletarian consciousness, and exposure to the constant irritant represented by fare cheaters. In November 1928 a fresh spate of incidents involving fights with soldiers who refused to pay their fares and who threatened or attacked conductors and drivers drove the union to take dramatic action to publicize worker grievances.[53] For two days beginning November 21, workers allowed everyone to ride free in order, in the words of a manifesto issued by the union, "to show our misery." Beijing residents, many of whom could not afford regular streetcar travel, crowded onto the cars. Zhang Yinqing joined numerous other mediators from the municipal government and the company in attempts to resolve the conflict. Zhang personally visited the union's headquarters in the Bridge of Heaven district and met with union leaders. The workers agreed to accept mediation and resume selling tickets again "in the interests of social order." The company agreed to compensate workers injured in attacks by soldiers, contribute a monthly sum to the union's school, raise wages, and negotiate with military officials to exert better control over troops in the city.

Although to all outward appearances the streetcar men represented a unified front of workers and union and FTU leaders, three
months later this apparent unity dissolved into factional discord.[54]
On February 14, 1929, half of the streetcar company's work force
met in the Buddhist Iron Mountain Temple in the business district
outside Qian Gate, intending to overthrow the incumbent leadership group. When FTU leaders heard about the meeting, they
sent sixty pickets in cars to break it up. By the time the FTU's men
reached the temple, the dissidents had adjourned, and the next day
two hundred workers marched on the local party headquarters to
formally press their demands. The workers carried a manifesto
suggesting that union leaders had misappropriated bonus money
intended for the workers and had failed to account for funds contributed by the company to the union's school. Moreover, union
leaders selected by the FTU were "illiterate" and "worse than the
militarists." When three workers had gone so far as to question
the policies of union leaders, they were locked up and tortured.
The workers complained that the "company and the union are at
loggerheads. If we go against the company we get suspended. If we
go against the union we are beaten." A party official who agreed to
meet with the workers lectured the crowd on the importance of
observing party discipline and following the proper procedures for
replacing union leaders. The workers responded with chants demanding the ouster of "all of the black sheep" in leadership positions and the publication of union accounts.

The FTU countered that the dissidents were in the thrall of the
former police chief and Anfu clique member Zhu Shen, who was
currently serving as managing director of the streetcar company.
Relations between management and workers had never been ami-
cable enough to make this kind of collusion likely. But if a majority
of workers had been willing to characterize their union leaders as
worse than militarists—the ultimate epithet used by conductors
and drivers who hated soldiers and the brutality they represented
—management might have begun to appear attractive by contrast.
The FTU sent pickets to arrest eight leaders of a "workers club"
organized to replace the union and turned the workers over to
the police with allegations that they were Communists, counter-
revolutionaries, and anti-FTU. In a recognition of the inherent
implausibility of charges that were a pastiche of accusations of

left- and right-wing conspiracies, local courts eventually cleared the men of any wrongdoing.

The charges against Zhang Yinqing made by the electric-light and streetcar workers suggested leadership methods that were dictatorial and a general willingness to run roughshod over rank-and-file opinion.[55] Intrusions by the FTU into basic-level constituencies, by handpicking union leaders and imposing a layer of bureaucracy and patronage over work groups, excited charges of favoritism, undemocratic procedures, and corruption. In their haste to build a formidable union federation in 1928, FTU leaders took little care in fitting the overarching structure of unionism to the needs and preferences of particular groups. Li Lesan and Zhang Yinqing recruited into the FTU apparatus workers who, in some cases, were unrepresentative of their fellows. In the streetcar union, "illiterates" were promoted to leadership positions over workers who prized education and technical competence. In the initial string of organizational and collective-bargaining victories presided over by the FTU, these conflicts remained latent. As the new discipline and leaders imposed by the FTU grated against older norms and habits, tensions suppressed in the interest of class and party unity became manifest. Electrical workers accepted FTU appointees and later declared that "they turned out to be what most workers expected."

While FTU leaders had been active prior to 1928 secretly organizing many of the workers who joined the federation after the arrival of the Northern Expedition, work groups also tended to have their own, separate traditions of solidarity and struggle. The speed with which FTU unions emerged in 1928 was due in part to the fact that streetcar workers, carpet-factory employees, printers, and other laborers were already organized informally. Workers had fought for their rights and interests for years without the protection and guidance of an umbrella body like the FTU, and the result was a fierce sense of independence in their participation in Nationalist labor politics. This strong sense of corporate identity was a characteristic feature of city politics. The chamber of commerce was an often unwieldy coalition of trades, enterprises, and guilds. But when the merchants union challenged its authority, the body warned: "We don't want any third party butting into our affairs." Aggressively modern groups like streetcar workers, as well as low-status workers like rickshaw men and night-soil carriers, developed collective identities that came as close to sub-cultures as the general Chinese concern with consensus permitted. This sense of separateness, reinforced by unique social roles, such as taking tickets or carrying excrement, or by particular ethnic identities, such as hailing from Shandong, heightened both the need for bridges to lessen social isolation and the tendency to see attempts at control by outsiders like FTU and Nationalist politi-cians as a usurpation of established prerogatives.

Factionalism

Nationalist cadres who had performed so effectively in the sum-mer and fall of 1928 in mobilizing support among city residents experienced a spreading plague of constituent revolts and factional struggles by the winter of 1928–29. Zhang Yinqing and his sup-porters were buffeted from above as well as from below. In Nan-jing leftists like Wang Jingwei and Ding Weifen were rapidly losing influence to conservative centralizers like Hu Hanmin and Chen Guofu. In the fall of 1928 Chen, who had been put in charge of the party's organization department, began a systematic effort to re-place leftists and independents in local party branches with right-ists and Chiang Kai-shek loyalists.[56] This rightward swing in party policy provoked a leftist reaction, embodied in a "Society for the Reorganization of the Nationalist Party," or "Reorganizationist Clique," with Wang Jingwei and other nationally prominent party leaders at its core.

Given the growing opposition by national-level politicians in Nanjing to anything that smacked of grass-roots politics, leaders of mass organizations and popular movements naturally gravi-tated toward the Reorganizationists. In December 1928, as a part of the center's purge of leftist elements in the party, the Nationalist Central Executive Committee ordered the recall of five members of the local Beiping party branch, including Li Lesan, and their replacement by individuals sent from Nanjing.[57] The FTU im-mediately called a meeting, presided over by Zhang Yinqing and attended by over two hundred union representatives, to declare its support for the recalled cadres.[58] In public telegrams designed to rally support among party branches in other provinces, the FTU also called for leftist Wang Jingwei's return to power and the expulsion of Chen Guofu and Hu Hanmin. The party branch issued a similar protest citing the record of sacrifice made by the "good comrades" targeted for transfer while they worked underground during the Zhang Zuolin years.[59]

With Li Lesan gone, Zhang Yinqing labored to maintain influence within the party branch and control over the FTU. Pressured by authorities in Nanjing to accept "rectification" of local party organization and by dissension within the union movement, Zhang orchestrated a new FTU election in January 1929 in which he withdrew from direct involvement in federation affairs and placed supporters, like the leader of the rickshaw-pullers union, Han Shiyuan, in key positions.[60] In the spring of 1929, Zhang Yinqing attended a conference of mass organizations in Nanjing, which called for the return of Wang Jingwei from self-imposed exile in Europe.[61] In March, at the Third Congress of the Nationalist party in Nanjing, several Reorganizationist leaders were purged, setting the stage for an alliance in the winter of 1929–30 between leftist party dissidents, like Wang Jingwei, and northern warlords Yan Xishan and Feng Yuxiang. It is reasonable to assume that Zhang Yinqing joined the Reorganizationists in 1929.[62] Since the political alliance between northern warlords like Yan Xishan and Feng Yuxiang, on the one hand, and leftist politicians like Wang Jingwei, on the other, had yet to be cemented, affiliation with the Reorganizationist cause placed local politicians in a difficult position. Without clear support from the militarists, taking a stand against the Nanjing regime and Chiang Kai-shek was likely in the short run to earn one more enemies than friends.

Throughout the remainder of 1929, right-wing cadres tapped by their superiors in Nanjing struggled to reclaim the party apparatus from Zhang Yinqing and the Grand Alliance. Zhang and his associates had made enough enemies among their own constituents within the labor movement to provide these outsiders with a means of organizing a powerful opposition movement. Streetcar and electric-utility workers became the backbone of an insurgent "new faction" in the FTU, which aimed to unseat Zhang Yinqing's "old faction."

The bill of particulars put forward against Zhang by the insurgent FTU "new faction" claimed that he had "put his old friends and acquaintances in key positions in the unions," "clutched the unions in a monopoly grip," and "acted without regard for the opinions of the workers."[63] Playing on these antagonisms, the "rectification" team allied with the conservatives in Nanjing was able by the fall of 1929 to win the backing of seventeen of twenty-one FTU unions active at that time for a drive to replace the federation's leaders. In the bargain, dissident unions won powerful backing for their struggle to drive the old faction out of power. Ironically, the workers who allied with the Nationalist right were among the most "proletarian" in the city in terms of class consciousness and progressive political commitments. With the rectification team acting as a catalyst, an alliance was formed between a pro-Nanjing faction within the party branch and dissident unions.[64] Zhang Yinqing's faction retained the support of only four unions: the rickshaw pullers, road-construction workers, street sweepers, and sewer and drain cleaners.

The weakening of Zhang Yinqing's hold on the FTU through defections to the new faction left him outnumbered by dissident unions but not necessarily outmanned if he could retain the backing of the city's sixty thousand rickshaw men. Rickshaw men offered labor organizers a sea of supporters if a way could be found to appeal to and harness their interests and enthusiasms. In his roles as urban manager and mediator, Zhang Yinqing found being responsible for this turbulent, angry constituency an onerous task. To a politician beset by opponents within and without the FTU, the loyalty of rickshaw men, representing as it did the weight of mass support and a trigger ready to release anarchy and disorder on the city, might be parlayed into a considerable political asset. In the fall of 1929 Zhang and his supporters mobilized rickshaw men to defend their positions in the party and the FTU against attack by rectification cadres and the new faction. Allied with radical party activists against new right cadres and their working-class supporters, rickshaw men turned out to be radical themselves in one respect. They felt that getting to the root of their problems meant destroying their arch competitor, the streetcar. After years of crowding around the edges of politics in supporting roles as audience, claquers, and walk-on reminders of the condition of the city's laboring poor, rickshaw men were about to get a chance, however briefly, to hold center stage for themselves.

Eleven

Machine-Breakers: The Streetcar Riot of October 22, 1929

In *Camel Xiangzi*, moneylender Gao Ma, while giving advice on financial matters to the novel's rickshaw-puller protagonist, muses about the advantages of Xiangzi's profession. "If *I* were a man and pulled a rickshaw...I would do my own pulling and my own singing. In ten thousand things, I would not seek help from anyone. If only I could! I wouldn't switch places with a county magistrate. To pull a rickshaw is a bitter thing. But if I were a man, and had the strength of a band of sworn brothers, I'd pull a rickshaw anyway and not go and be a policeman."[1] Everyone knew how bitter a rickshaw man's life could be. Poor, ordered about by policemen, beaten by soldiers, robbed of customers by streetcars and buses, he was victimized by forces he had little control over and only rudimentary defenses against. In partial recompense he was allowed to lead a freer, more disorderly life, outside the discipline of factory or guild. But it was the freedom of the petty entrepreneur and the hell-raiser or rascal (*liumang*) and not of a political man.

The creation in the fall of 1928 of a rickshaw men's union sponsored by the Federation of Trade Unions (FTU) gave pullers a chance to confound these stereotypical images and claim the political and legal status denied them at mid-decade.[2] The first thing the new union did was to demand to know what had happened to the compensation fund promised pullers in 1924 by the chamber of commerce and the streetcar company. Where was their "factory for poor people"?[3] With Sun Xueshi again president of the chamber, and given the record of bad faith, broken promises, and financial irregularities that ran through the tangled history of chamber, streetcar company, and police involvement in the affair, this was an embarrassing question indeed.[4] As a result of the union's demand, and a similar petition made by the vehicle guild, a new committee composed of municipal, party, FTU, and rickshaw-pullers-union officials was formed to build the factory with funds provided by the chamber.[5] By the fall of 1929 the FTU and party cadres managed to find a site near Xidan Arch in the West City and began limited operations weaving carpets.[6] But with machines still to purchase and install, the project had yet to make a dent in the problem of unemployment and underemployment among rickshaw pullers. Five years after the initial promise of relief and compensation had been made, rickshaw men received their "factory" in token form.

Taken by itself, this latest installment in the sad tale of Beijing's rickshaw men and their precarious livelihood repeated the well-worn theme of elite arbitration and paternalistic gestures. However, other things were happening in the spring and summer of 1929 to give the rickshaw man's role in urban society—in the past passive and combative by turns—a sharper, more independent political focus. In a succession of incidents rickshaw men struck out at many of the institutional and social forces pinning them down as members of the city's class of laboring poor. It was as if rickshaw men as a class had set about to rewrite the street songs that portrayed them in a pathetic light, to contest the dependent roles assigned to them, and to do their "own pulling" and "own singing . . . and in ten thousand things . . . not seek help from anyone." The final act in this new drama was a wild riot on October 22, 1929, in which tens of thousands of rickshaw pullers became machine-breakers in a concerted attack on the streetcar system.

Unions and Crowds

From early spring to mid-autumn of 1929 rickshaw men met, petitioned, marched, protested, fought, and finally rioted in a continuous fashion until they were among the most politically active groups in the city. They drew on the full repertoire of collective and public strategies available to city residents, based on the May Fourth and May Thirtieth legacies, *fatuan* and guild conventions, the framework of mass politics provided by Nationalist cadres, and their own habits of street fighting and confrontation.

Like other aggrieved groups in the city, rickshaw men assembled in crowds to visit the headquarters of government, party, and military officials to submit petitions and demands. Touring processions of petitioners had become a common sight in the city since the arrival of the Northern Expedition. The fragmented nature of the regime decreed a route that wound its way past the mansions and ministries of the Inner City in a "connect-the-dots" exercise, which rarely traced a coherent pattern of political responsibility. On March 21, 1929, four hundred rickshaw union members marched from the local party branch headquarters just inside Xuanwu Gate east to the offices of the municipal government.[7] Led by union officials, the pullers asked the mayor to rescind a new gate tax of four coppers levied on pullers taking fares in and out of the city. In their petition the rickshaw men argued that four coppers was a heavy burden for them. The pullers added that life had been hard since the opening of the streetcar system, and the recent transfer of the capital to Nanjing had made things worse.

Two weeks later another toll, this time on the road from Xizhi Gate to the Western Hills, caused three hundred pullers to descend in protest on police district offices in the northwest corner of the Inner City adjacent to the gate.[8] Police officers promised to refer the issue to higher levels, but when no reply was forthcoming, the rickshaw men marched to the city center to appeal directly to the mayor. They refused to disperse until a deputy of the mayor received a delegation of workers and promised to look into the matter with a view toward abolishing the tax.

By April the rickshaw-pullers union numbered 1,300 members.[9] The union and the FTU submitted a petition to the city government on behalf of "two thousand pullers of the north and west suburbs" outside Xizhi Gate, asking for restrictions on a competing bus service running from the gate to Haidian and the Summer Palace.[10] Visiting tourists were among the most lucrative of fares for rickshaw men, and modernization of transport to suburban tourist attractions was a direct threat to the livelihood of men who specialized in the Haidian and Western Hills trade. Several hundred pullers again assembled at party branch headquarters to parade to city hall. The rickshaw men made specific demands relating to the hours when buses would be permitted to run, the size of fares charged, and the right to pick up passengers between scheduled stops. The petition frankly acknowledged that the buses had improved transportation, but nonetheless it declared the policies of the company unjust. The chief of police convened a meeting of representatives of the FTU, the union, the rickshaw-owners guild, and the bus company. After two months of negotiations, the bus company came to terms that set bus fares at a lower rate than the rickshaw-pullers union had demanded and banned rickshaw men from soliciting at bus stops.

Rickshaw men proved willing to work through representatives and accept the good offices of mediators. A new militancy among pullers, however, also produced spontaneous acts of protest. In early July a policeman on patrol in the western suburbs came upon a group of rickshaw men attempting to "arrest" a fellow puller for violation of union regulations.[11] When the policeman tried to free the man, the other laborers heatedly asserted the right to discipline their own union members. As more pullers converged on the scene the policeman whistled for assistance. A fight broke out in which police arrested four rickshaw men, but not before the pullers seized a policeman as a hostage and carried him off to the nearest union branch office. Ten people were injured, including an FTU official who had taken the side of the workers.

The incident demonstrated a keen desire by rickshaw men to police their own ranks. This preference for self-regulation had long been practised by guilds and was more recently reasserted with the new popularity of paramilitary pickets and guards among a wide range of groups and associations. In general, habits of corporate self-regulation aided the police in keeping the peace. Long hours, few holidays, and for many workers, residence in a shop or attached dormitory meant that order in the workplace, however it was enforced, went a long way toward achieving a more general level of social control. These same practices, of course, threatened to undermine the police department's claim to a monopoly on the use of force in the city. While the action taken by the rickshaw men against the hapless individual who ran afoul of union rules was by no means unusual in this broader context, the police regarded attempts by pullers to disregard or evade police supervision as provocative. Rickshaw men had for years been a prime target and test subject for the police's development of order-keeping tactics and strategies. Attempts in 1929 to challenge these controls grated against the policeman's sense of public order.

During the summer, quarrels between the streetcar company and the rickshaw trade began to slip out of the control of guild, *fatuan*, and party elites and into the rougher world of street-level mobilization. In late June the company had announced plans to increase its ridership with a "round-the-town night car" program.[12] The idea was to add extra cars to the system on summer evenings between six and midnight so that residents could buy discount tickets and take pleasure rides to cool off from the summer heat and humidity. As soon as they heard about the plan, the rickshaw-pullers union objected in protests made through the FTU and the party. At the same time, the owners guild petitioned the government through the chamber of commerce to ban the venture. The police and the city government arranged discussions on the issue, but the guild refused to accept a compromise solution offered by the company.[13] Striking at the company's perennial public relations sore point, the guild added that if the proposed measures were adopted, "the one remaining thread of livelihood of our impoverished compatriots, the rickshaw pullers, will be destroyed."[14] The government took no immediate action on the petition but acknowledged the legitimacy of the rickshaw trade's claim by framing the issue as one of "the prosperity of the city and its communications, on the one hand, and livelihood, on the other."[15]

While negotiations dragged on through July, police reported a new militancy among rickshaw men, reflected in an "extremely tense" atmosphere at gatherings of pullers.[16] Fights began to break out between pullers and streetcar workers.[17] Several of the incidents took place in the northwestern part of the Inner City, which had been the scene of earlier protests over gate taxes and tolls and competition with buses. In an article entitled "Peking Promised Spectacle of Clash Between Tramway Company and Rickshaw

Men," the *North China Standard* noted that the pullers were in a "belligerent mood."[18] Pullers claimed that the "night car" policy threatened the livelihood of "100,000" workers and that they would use force if necessary to stop it.

Streetcar workers, never of a mind to take harassment on the job lightly, were fresh from another clash with Chiang Kai-shek's bodyguards.[19] While Chiang was in the city for another round of meetings with northern militarists and politicians, his soldiers had beaten up and arrested the driver and conductor of a streetcar that had collided with a military vehicle. Within twenty-fours and with the help of the FTU, the workers had extracted an apology from Chiang. Soon after conflicts with rickshaw men began to erupt, streetcar workers held a meeting to demand that the FTU dissolve the rickshaw-pullers union and its branches.[20] The FTU, which was undergoing considerable strain at the time as a result of struggles between the "old" and "new" factions, called a general meeting to work out ground rules for dealing with conflicts involving union members.[21] While continuing to support and represent the rickshaw men as a large and growing element in the labor movement (and the old faction's principal ally), the FTU leadership tried to limit its political and legal liability for pullers' actions.

The night-car service was scheduled to begin operations on the evening of August 5. Ignoring the FTU's official caution about violent confrontations, rickshaw men prepared to use force to stop the cars from running after 10 P.M.

When members of the union of rickshaw coolies heard [that additional cars were about to be put into service], they passed the word round that they should block the progress of the cars. In less than half an hour more than one hundred coolies assembled in the west city and later divided themselves into groups of ten to twenty to guard different stations and watched for the coming of the special trains. The coolies shouted that they would smash the cars at sight.[22]

Drivers and conductors working their normal shifts could not help noticing angry bunches of rickshaw men deployed along their routes. As word of these ominous gatherings spread, streetcar workers hurriedly assembled outside Tianan Gate.[23] The workers sent representatives to the company, threatening a strike unless the service was canceled. This double threat of riot and strike caused the inaugural run of extra cars to be aborted, and the company eventually abandoned the idea of increasing revenues by exploiting the entertainment and recreational value of the streetcar system.

Rickshaw men followed through on their threats of violence later in the month when a minor altercation over parking regulations escalated into a major confrontation with the authorities.[24] On August 31 a rickshaw puller paused in front of the entrance to a public park to solicit a fare in defiance of police regulations. When a policeman on watch ordered the rickshaw man to move, the puller refused and a fight broke out. One report had the rickshaw man knocking down the policeman by himself. Another stated that other pullers in the vicinity had joined in on the attack. Within minutes police and troops converged on the scene to aid the policeman. Because of the proximity of a union branch office, they found themselves facing not one, or several, but thirty or forty laborers. In the ensuing struggle, three rickshaw men were arrested and taken to the district police station. The police force, with the help of troops, was able to use its gridlike deployment throughout the city to contain the conflict.

The initial quarrel and fight were commonplace. Thirty rickshaw pullers coming to the aid of a fellow worker was a little out of the ordinary. What happened next was unprecedented and crumpled the structure of police control. Late on the evening of the thirty-first, policemen in the station holding the arrested rickshaw men were roused by several hundred pullers come to demand the release of their comrades. Again, there were conflicting versions of what followed. One press account stated that the rickshaw men stormed the station, overcame the police, and freed the jailed men. Another suggested that the police gave up their prisoners when the crowd threatened them. After the rescue, the crowd left with a promise to send delegates back to negotiate.

Under these kinds of pressure, some local policemen withdrew from close supervision of rickshaw pullers. On September 3 ten rickshaw men jumped a streetcar as it arrived at the Xidan Arch station and forced all the passengers to get out.[25] Although several of the passengers were jostled, no one was hurt. A district police station was close by, but the police did not intervene. A later police investigation of the incident acknowledged that the officers and men at Xidan had been derelict in their duty and were "truly worn out and useless." Police, accustomed in the past to using superior numbers, organization, and morale to back up the orders they gave to pullers, now found themselves facing rickshaw men with iron in their souls and branch organizations at their beck and call.

Both the police and the FTU were alarmed over the rash of violent incidents involving rickshaw men and policemen, and a conference of union and police officials was called in an effort to defuse tensions.[26] The two sides drew up a document entitled "Measures to Prevent Conflicts Between Rickshaw Men and the Police," which acknowledged that long-standing prejudices had contributed to the worsening of relations between policeman and puller. The police agreed to direct its men not to "look on rickshaw men with disrespect but rather to treat them as the equal of other classes of people." In order to counter disrespect by rickshaw pullers for the authority of the uniform, the FTU would instruct pullers to "strictly uphold the law and do their best to follow the directions of the police." The FTU also agreed to give police the names of branch officials and notify the authorities whenever citywide or branch meetings were to be held. In this way the formal accountability and informal consultation that characterized elite relations at the citywide level might be extended down to the district and neighborhood where recent conflicts had broken out. If a conflict did develop, the district police chief would send for an FTU official to stop it. Whenever rickshaw men felt that police actions were unjustified, they should handle the problem through "lawful procedures" and not "assemble a crowd and make trouble."

By this time, however, assembling in crowds and "making trouble" had become the puller's weapon of choice. On September 5, the day the agreement between the FTU and the police was signed, rickshaw men rallied to right a common wrong done them in their dealings with higher-status passengers. Lone pullers were especially vulnerable to customers who used proximity to home compound and community at the end of a journey to cheat them out of fares. When a group of college students rode rickshaws to their school compound in the West City and then ran through the gate without paying, the rickshaw men tried to follow the students, and school guards clubbed them at the gate.[27] Rickshaw men who witnessed the incident immediately ran to notify the nearby Xidan Arch branch, and a crowd of a hundred pullers was quickly formed to march in protest to the gate of the school. Later in the day another altercation between students and pullers took place nearby, and a rickshaw man was injured. In retaliation, workers dispatched from the Xidan Arch branch abducted one of the students and held him at branch headquarters until the police arranged for his friends to pay compensation.

The combined strength of rickshaw men as an organized, legally recognized group and as a rebellious crowd had a palpable influence on city politics and city life in September 1929. A local newspaper headlined an article on the combativeness of the pullers "Rickshaw Union Power Spreads Throughout the Whole City."[28] The size of the union's membership had quadrupled to over four thousand from spring to summer 1929, making it the largest union in the FTU.[29] Branch offices sprouted throughout the city. The West City, the Xizhi Gate area, the western suburbs, and the Bridge of Heaven, areas with large concentrations of rickshaw men and poor people, produced the most active branches. The union was able to supply not only points around which rickshaw men could rally to defend their interests but also a measure of guild-style social welfare benefits, like money for funerals and weddings.[30] On certain issues, such as the gate and road tolls and competition with bus companies and the streetcar company, the union, working through the FTU and the party, was an effective lobbyist for rickshaw men. Unfortunately, negotiated settlements tended to break down, in part because of the uncompromising nature of the rickshaw pullers' demands. And in the case of the streetcar company's night-car policy, threats of violence proved more effective than negotiations in getting what the pullers wanted.

Controversies that focused attention on the relationship between the rickshaw and the streetcar and between rickshaw men and policemen put the pullers in a "belligerent mood," which was conducive to mediation only in the sense that an ugly demeanor was an added spur to elites to defuse these tensions. Once mobilized by the FTU and union leaders, rickshaw men began to deviate from the rules of conduct laid down for them as union members. The FTU and the pullers' citywide union lost control of branch activities on several occasions as rickshaw men did things no "responsible" individual or organization wanted to take credit for. Local cadres realized the danger represented by the pullers' special brand of radicalism. In early September, the Masses Training Committee issued an open letter to the city's rickshaw men, which began by noting that while workers joined unions to "eradicate individual suffering" and "increase the power of the revolution," pullers must realize that streetcars and buses were a "natural phenomenon" associated with "social advancement."[31] "Workers," the letter continued, "our enemy is not the streetcar or the bus but the feudal power that oppresses the masses." The local party branch sent a notice to the rickshaw-pullers union, observing that many men entering the union had misunderstood the union's purpose and by getting into conflicts with "outsiders" had come to commit "illegal acts."[32] The remedy suggested was a convocation of government, FTU, and union representatives.

The logic of party, FTU, and guild representation required time and patience to turn grievances into legitimate claims. When rickshaw men were ordered about and beaten by policemen, abused or cheated by passengers, or robbed of a fare by a bus or a streetcar, they wanted immediate redress. A government report dated toward the end of September noted with alarm the reflexive, unmediated nature of this street-level activism. "Rickshaw pullers of late have often quarreled with policemen and passengers or have gathered in crowds and acted abusively. . . . In recent days conflicts have broken out between pullers and policemen, pullers and bus company employees, and pullers and streetcar workers."[33]

Beneath the politics organized by labor leaders and convocations of elites, an impassioned social movement emerged among rickshaw men in the summer and early fall of 1929. Rickshaw men took their cues not only from policy makers and leaders but also from social dramas featuring familiar characters, like policemen and long-gowned passengers, and familiar feelings, like anger and resentment.

The twin development of organized politics and spontaneous insurgency gave rickshaw men a range of strategies and tactics to choose from. Pullers could petition, march, distribute leaflets, demonstrate, kidnap members of offending groups, lay siege to police stations, rush streetcars, or fight. Despite their revolutionary rhetoric and a record of radicalism, party leaders tended to channel popular grievances toward a moderate reformist kind of representation and mediation. Pullers could rally to these banners and leaders or they could take an ordinary gripe from their life on the streets, like police harassment, and demand resolution of the issue on the spot. This latter type of direct action and confrontation took place in the familiar setting of the street as an "informal open court." Militancy and new habits of collective action served to pack the court in favor of rickshaw men.

The choice for Nationalist ideology and organization required membership dues, deference to leaders, and acceptance of the risk that victories won, like the 1924 "factory for poor people" settlement, would come to little or nothing. Choosing direct action required a common cast of mind about the rightness or wrongness of a thing, the willingness to break a rule, code, norm, or convention, and the strength or guile to resist or elude forces brought to bear against rule breakers. As autumn approached, the city's rickshaw men moved back and forth between both sets of choices and resisted the efforts of the FTU, the party, the police, and the city government to keep them within institutional boundaries.

Political Consciousness and Class Consciousness

The skirmish line drawn by rickshaw men in the summer of 1929 in the struggles between themselves and their traditional foes suggested a growing radicalism, which pointed toward the October riot. The long record of heat and occasional fire generated by friction between pullers and fellow city residents who patronized, policed and competed, with them provides clues to the emotion and reasoning that lay behind this new, organized combativeness.

Fortuitously, in the midst of the fights, quarrels, and controversies involving rickshaw men in the summer of 1929, social researcher Huang Gongdu surveyed the opinions of one hundred rickshaw men, who also happened to be union members, looking for evidence of "proletarian consciousness."[34] Like many of his fellow intellectuals, Huang was intrigued by the question of whether Chinese workers were capable of performing the radical political role conventionally assigned workers. Huang assumed that modern-minded Chinese workers would be "proletarian," but he wondered whether ordinary workers in Chinese cities were modern-minded. Rickshaw men were to provide a test case.

Writing up his results in December 1929, in the aftermath of the streetcar riot, Huang concluded that the city's rickshaw men were "class conscious to an extent" because "their experience of life makes them aware of their own misery" and "they know that by using collective action and their potential for organization, they can, within certain limits, improve their lives. However, they do not clearly comprehend their surroundings. They have no clear idea of the present political, economic, and social situation, and no understanding of labor movement methods. They have power. But because they do not clearly understand their environment, they lack correct goals and methods. A derailed locomotive can do harm to both passengers and bystanders."[35]

Huang's definition of class consciousness required only that workers be aware of their impoverished state and be willing to act together to seek remedies for their grievances. They did not need to satisfy more rigorous Marxian criteria based on feelings of class solidarity, an understanding of their subordinate social position, and a willingness to use radical means to transcend prevailing social arrangements.[36] As an intellectual with left-wing National-ist sympathies, Huang appears to have been looking for a kind of "proletarian" or modern and forward-looking populism rather than class-conscious political activism.

To his dismay, Huang found that the political and social ideas of many rickshaw men were traditional and specific to their own situation rather than modern and driven by the desire to partici-pate in a movement of global dimensions. He was disappointed by the flat, matter-of-fact responses he received when he asked the pullers "What are labor unions?" Based on the organization-building experiences of recent months, rickshaw men pictured unions in concrete terms. For most, unions were simply groups of workers, the places where workers met, or organizations.[37] Two workers described unions as just another "trade association." Only a few made more proletarian-sounding associations, like "worker government." Expecting responses that evoked a grander sense of labor unions as a special kind of organization, Huang Gongdu equated concreteness with ignorance. In fact, as the city's history of unionism showed, the struggle to achieve a public identity as a "group" (*tuanti*) and find a space to inhabit politically was no mean feat. For two workers, a union constituted "worker territory" (*gonren di dipan*), or a place or sphere of influence taken by force. Not all workers were pleased with the results of this concrete achievement. Five pullers stated that a union was a "place to stir up trouble."

Since "troublemaking," negotiations, and meetings—the activities most associated with unions by pullers—were as much the province of guilds as of unions, Huang's evidence does at first glance suggest that rickshaw men "misunderstood" the larger significance of the question. Judging by their responses, Huang might as well have asked them "What are guilds?" If a labor union was an organization like any other, rickshaw men in joining had succeeded in making a novel organization serve a traditional purpose by winning a place in the city's established social order. Alternatively, they had failed to exploit the full potential of unionism as a movement pitched toward the social transformation of the city along Marxian lines, or the organizational transformation prescribed by Nationalist party principles.

When Huang pressed his one hundred respondents to explain more precisely the aim of labor unions, the additional details they provided reinforced the impression that many workers regarded unions in much the same way they thought of guilds.[38] Half of them believed that unions were principally designed for holding meetings, demonstrating, negotiating, or protecting workers. Traditional guild concerns, like "taking care of workers" and "dealing with misfortune," were as much on the minds of rickshaw men as Sun Yat-sen's Three People's principles, "revolution," overthrowing imperialism and reactionaries, and "helping victims of injustice." Some members expressed annoyance, not uncommon among both guild and union members, at the burdens imposed by way of "collecting union dues" and "poking one's nose into other people's business."

When another social researcher, named Yu Side, collected data on the same question in a survey administered by the FTU and member unions, the answers he received indicated that other Beiping workers tended to make the same kind of basic identification of unions with established conventions of group life and politics.[39] Just as the chamber of commerce was a modern organization constructed on a base of old-fashioned guilds, so modern unionism appeared to depend for its structure and style on craft-guild sentiments and practices. But whereas in Yu's survey, workers, when queried as to the "purpose of labor unions," commonly cited support for Sun's Three People's Principles and loyalty to the revolution, rickshaw men made only passing reference to formal ideology. The two sets of responses also diverged when workers became more specific about union goals. Workers in the general survey saw unions as instruments for achieving higher wages, shorter hours, and educational benefits. When rickshaw pullers got down to specifics they mentioned "overthrowing buses," "overthrowing streetcars," "showing worker anger," and "not allowing workers to be bullied."

Fusion of unionism and guild practice might take either a moderate or a radical form. On the one hand, the traditional guild preference for mediated settlements arranged through go-betweens reinforced the tendency of union leaders to submit to elite threats and blandishments.[40] On the other hand, labor militants could find support for direct action in the habits of conflict and even violence that were also a part of guild politics. The five respondents who saw unions as weapons for attacking buses and streetcars were unlikely to be satisfied with reformist solutions in which social justice was weighed against social order. If the ultimate expression of conventional worker aspirations in Beiping was guild protection or an eight-hour workday, when rickshaw men let their imaginations run away with them they saw city streets free of competitors. The idea of bashing the competition was an old one, as rickshaw men had discovered decades earlier when mule carters had tried to drive them out of business. Joining professional jealousy to an expanded repertoire of modern political techniques and justifications resulted in a more virulent form of group competition.

Huang took the five machine-breaking responses he elicited as evidence that by the summer of 1929 an "extremely small group of rickshaw pullers had already stored up a mad ambition to riot."[41]

Rickshaw men had acquired a political consciousness edged with deep resentment and directed at individuals and institutions with the power to dominate and harass them. This "mad" edge had always been present to a degree in the public behavior of rickshaw men, who lashed out at policemen, passengers, rivals, and anyone else attempting to relegate pullers to the bottom of the social heap. Acting singly or in small groups in random rebellion, these pullers had been classed as "hooligans." Acting together with a public and collective presence enhanced by union organization, politicized pullers constituted a broader challenge to the existing political and social order. As politically conscious city residents, rickshaw men had come to accept and participate in the group-politics milieu of meetings, mediation, and petitions. As actors in a street theater of rebellion building into a social movement in the summer of 1929, pullers began to dwell on the fact of their subordination as a class. This "class consciousness," made possible by participation in their own, miniature social movement, made them aware of the integral nature of the institutions dominating them.[42]

Rickshaw men both operated as petty entrepreneurs trading in personal transportation (hence Gao Ma's envy of Xiangzi's "freedom") and worked for passengers who hired them on a one-time, daily, or monthly basis. Independent entrepreneurship combined with the role of hired laborer put rickshaw men in a "contradictory location" between social classes.[43] Although rickshaw men hawked their services like tradesmen, they were well outside the "traditional petty bourgeoisie" of shopkeepers and independent craftsmen. They toiled like day laborers and yet rarely faced the direct and sustained authority of social and economic superiors as a fixed relationship. Instead, they fought running battles with upper-class passengers, policemen, and more modern rivals. Union organization for men in such circumstances might simply mean enhancing their ability to defend their trade and livelihood in a manner akin to guild politics. But this essentially conservative and defensive posture concealed a mad ambition to strike hard at the "class" of enemies who oppressed or confined them, individuals and organizations whose power was based variously on private capital, social status, or administrative position. Huang Gongdu sensed that deep down, rickshaw pullers know that their enemy is not the garage owner, but rather the buses and streetcars they compete with. Ever since the streetcar and bus services opened, the rickshaw pullers's business clearly felt the effects. Under their antibus and antistreetcar banners, they do not hate the garage owners; they recognize that they are members of the same class.... Deep down, rickshaw pullers know that their opponent is not the garage owner but the machine.[44]

The claims of rickshaw men against machines deployed by "bureaucratic capitalism" and the machinelike administrative power of the police constituted a revolt against the modern wing of the city's established social order.

Rickshaw men were conveniently aided in this rebellion by traditional notions of economic and social justice and a modern revision of the idea of "people's livelihood" (*minsheng*). Like machine-breakers in nineteenth-century Europe, rickshaw men could appropriate natural and customary rights associated with a preindustrial "moral economy."[45]

Eric Hobsbawm and George Rude, in their study of the 1830 "Captain Swing" agricultural uprisings in England against the introduction of threshing machines, note that the "weapons with which the labourers fought were archaic, though their use was sometimes new."[46] Little by way of "social inventiveness" was required, given access to a popular culture richly stocked with ideas and strategies conducive to resisting economic change at the local level. In resisting streetcars and buses, rickshaw men fought with all means available, including unionism and appeals to public opinion, which were modern rather than archaic. This was a sensible approach, given that years of mass movements and association building had added considerably to the urban armory of popular political and social weapons. At the same time, the "archaic" dimension of what rickshaw men were doing and arguing for in defense of their "rice bowls" was more adaptable to modern conditions than the "obsolescent paternalist code" European laborers had to rely on.[47]

The clearest example of the relative suppleness of traditional Chinese notions of economic rights and responsibilities is the ease by which the old notion of "people's livelihood" (*minsheng*) was modernized by Sun Yat-sen as one of his three "People's Principles" along with democracy and nationalism. What Chinese workers lacked by way of an indigenous analogue to the political "rights of the freeborn Englishman" they could make up with Western borrowings.[48] Having won the right to speak and act politically, they then could appropriate for the content of their political message those elements in Chinese political culture, like *minsheng*, which prized harmony and social obligation.

As machine-breakers in the making, the men interviewed by Huang did not exhibit blind faith in the past or implacable hostility to modern ideas.[49] The rickshaw was a machine after all, and rickshaw pulling had emerged after the turn of the century as a junior partner in the partial modernization of the capital's infrastructure. The mix of modern and traditional sentiments reflected in Huang's survey was natural to a class of men who were engaged in a novel occupation while being surrounded by a still vital pre-industrial economy.

Similarly, most rickshaw men strongly identified with China as a modern republic. But many expressed their patriotism in language resonant with the past. Nearly 90 percent professed love for the Republic of China (Zhonghua minguo).[50] When asked what the Republic of China was, the most common replies were "we are!" and "our country."[51] The entire range of answers included traditional clichés, such as "the five lakes and four seas" and "the Yellow Emperor's descendants," which Huang speculated might have come from the opera or from storytellers, and bits of contemporary political rhetoric, such as "land of the Three People's Principles" and "anti-imperialism." The emotional and rhetorical content of the pullers' answers persuaded Huang that "among rickshaw men, very few knew what the 'Republic of China' is" and "rickshaw pullers do not have a national viewpoint" and "have not received a good education."[52] Huang Gongdu was looking for a description of what the Republic of China formally was in 1929: a constitutional government headquartered in Nanjing. What he found was a core of simple patriotism illustrated with images and ideas taken from the operatic stage and mass assemblies outside Tianan Gate.

Huang, as a Nationalist sympathizer, found the pullers' responses to questions about "revolution" even more disturbing. Asked whether revolution was "good or bad," the rickshaw men answered "bad" (45%), "good" (36%), "it isn't clear" (10%), "it doesn't matter" (8%), and "it's better than no revolution" (1%).[53] Huang, who conducted the interviews himself, assumed that his respondents understood revolution to mean political and social changes brought by the Northern Expedition. He explained the predominantly negative responses in the following way:

They [the pullers surveyed]—I deduce—completely relied on a standard of personal advantage and disadvantage in deciding whether or not to endorse the revolution. They endorsed the revolution because afterwards thcy were able to organize a labor union. Their interests were safe-guarded to a degree. They later disapproved of the revolution because the capital was moved south and the rickshaw business was affected.

But the rickshaw men's reservations about revolution in fact went deeper than pique, shared by many Beijing residents, at removal of the capital. For many pullers, revolution meant violence and dis-order bereft of any larger meaning or purpose.[54] Revolution was "making trouble," "anarchy and disorder," "no peace in the world," and "having nothing to eat." Alternatively, revolution represented "equality between men and women," "freedom and equality," "a unified country," "loving China," "unity," and "happiness and well-being." For many, the operative word was to "overthrow" (*dadao*), with one's aim directed variously at Japan, imperialism, foreigners, Zhang Zuolin, "the bad guys," "revolu-tionary cliques," capitalists, "bad things," corrupt officials, war-lords, the Communist party, "evil gentry and local bullies," and Wu Peifu. One rickshaw man imagined revolution to be "everyone overthrowing everyone else."

Many rickshaw men viewed revolution as a power struggle played out on battlefields and between rival elites in a fashion that put the conflict beyond their reach. Others saw revolutionary poli-tics and ideology in more immediate terms with a cast of charac-ters drawn from the puller's own realm of experience. An incident early in October involving a conflict between a rickshaw man and a fare-cheating passenger is emblematic of the kind of immediate and practical meaning some pullers attached to Nationalist revolu-tion.[55] After a rickshaw man pulled a woman to the door of her residence she refused to pay him the agreed-upon fare. At this point the old story of a swindled rickshaw man was given a new twist. The rickshaw man took the money he had been given and threw it after her into the compound, exclaiming, "You take it!" When the head of the household, a man named Zhou, came out to discuss the matter with the puller he noticed that the man was wearing a union badge inside his jacket. The rickshaw man, by way of justifying the fare he had demanded, told Zhou that "today, in the age of the Three People's Principles, [you] ought to pay more." When Zhou balked at paying the money, the rickshaw man pulled his vehicle in front of the doorway to prevent anyone from leaving until he received what he believed to be just compensation.

Rickshaw men, in the course of their labors, had the opportunity to lock horns directly and indirectly with moneyed and propertied individuals, warlords, corrupt officials, cliques, and thugs, or their agents. The FTU was riddled with factions in 1929. Police officials who misappropriated relief funds for rickshaw men, and chamber of commerce leaders who betrayed the pullers' trust by allowing the 1924 agreement to wither away, were arguably corrupt. The street, rickshaw garages, lower-class brothels, and teahouses were well populated with bullies and bad guys. And if rickshaw-garage owners were rarely seen by pullers as "capitalists," the men who financed and ran streetcar and bus companies certainly fit that description. Revolution as a military campaign to unify China was some distance from the life and politics of a rickshaw man. Revolution as intense struggle and as moral retribution was closer to the experience of men who marched against bus companies, harassed streetcars, and stormed police stations with the thought of "overthrowing" their enemies.

This street-level perspective on contemporary Chinese politics was not unreasonable or unrealistic. There was little that was extraordinary or odd about the attitudes and opinions of rickshaw men surveyed by Huang Gongdu unless one measured them against Huang's own, rather rigid sense of orthodoxy and reality. Like their fellow residents, rickshaw men on the whole were patriotic, somewhat cynical about—but not immune to—contemporary ideologies, and driven by aspirations for themselves and their children. In this regard the laboring poor of China in the 1920s resembled the poor of contemporary Third World cities, who have been found by researchers to have the "aspirations of the bourgeoisie, the perseverance of pioneers and the values of patriots."[56] Nearly every rickshaw man queried expressed an interest in improving his own education and sending his children to school.[57] When asked about the advantages of an education, rickshaw men revealed an impressive range of grand and petty ambitions.[58] By studying, one could become wealthy, an official, a teacher, a university student, famous, a military officer, a clerk, "commander-in-chief," and chief of police. One would be able to improve one's livelihood, get a better job, read newspapers and write letters without help, speak foreign languages, avenge grievances, study with women, "establish a false front," and marry freely. One would not be taken advantage of, be swindled, have to "vent one's spleen," or have to rely on others.

Rickshaw men were acutely aware of how their poverty and social inferiority threw up obstacles to achieving the freer and more satisfying and comfortable life represented by these goals. Their aspirations were derived from a common city culture that illuminated an increasingly complex maze of old and new pathways to wealth, power, and status. Seeking economic security by insisting on one's right to livelihood was a perfectly respectable strategy for any aggrieved group in an urban moral economy studded with "rice bowls" liable to be defended to the bitter end. It was the requirements for the rickshaw pullers' defense of their livelihood which made their ambitions appear "mad" and which finally set them off from the rest of the urban community. Their opposition to buses, streetcars, slippery elite mediators, rude soldiers, and officious policemen was shared by other groups to a point. Newspaper reporters, city officials, politicians, streetcar and bus company officials, and chamber of commerce leaders understood what pullers were talking about in the summer of 1929. But they became progressively alarmed and were finally shocked by the lengths rickshaw men proved willing to go to put their point across.

Every group in the city which could manage it organized to stake out their claim to a secure position in the economy and polity. Rickshaw men made considerable progress along these lines in 1929.

Although most feel that their lives are bitter, most also have a kind of "optimistic" attitude. . . . They realize that they have achieved some degree of power in society. Before, when there were no unions, the rickshaw garages could freely increase the rickshaw rent when they wanted to. The bus and streetcar could freely use the lowest rates possible to compete with the rickshaw. Now it's not the same. Rickshaw garages, buses, and streetcars must to some extent take into account the rickshaw puller's side of things.[59]

But rickshaw men did not stop there. Other aggrieved groups marched and demonstrated. Many extended their disagreements into fights and altercations. But only the rickshaw men and their street-worker allies rioted. By early fall 1929, rickshaw pullers had developed habits of confrontation of special intensity and a locomotive force of considerable power. They had marked out as common knowledge among fellow FTU members, the merchant community, and officials and cadres in the government and the party a list of complaints about the way they were treated. In their view, they were too poor, public welfare was inadequate, their fellow citizens did not appreciate their plight, promises to help them had not been kept, police regulations had made it hard to earn a living, and their more modern rivals were too powerful. By themselves, the complaints, like criticisms, pleas, and invective scattered throughout Huang Gongdu's survey, merely evoked a mood of discontent. Seen as a sequence of political statements made in the spring, summer, and fall of 1929, the complaints had a focus and a logic. They constituted a critique of the way the city worked.

Prelude to Riot

By late September the wave of unrest among rickshaw men appeared to subside. Between the flurry of fights and demonstrations involving pullers in August and early September and the riot on October 22 lay a period of weeks in which little was heard from rickshaw men as an organized or mobilized community. Rickshaw men returned to their customary place as the subject of newspaper anecdotes and the object of pity mixed with apprehension. In this vein, the press reported the melancholy, and by now standard, story of a forty-four-year-old rickshaw man found sitting dead in his vehicle near Dongdan Arch.[60] The pullers' capacity for public and collective militancy had not disappeared, however. Three days before the riot, in an altercation between a puller and a soldier over a fare, a crowd of two or three hundred rickshaw men materialized within minutes to back up their comrade.[61] Only the timely arrival of a squad of policemen prevented the rickshaw men from carrying the soldier off to union headquarters. The incident caused local residents, "fearing a great agitation," to flee indoors.

Having "stored up" their "mad ambition" (in Huang Gongdu's phrase) over the summer months, rickshaw men managed to hold on to this radicalism until a turn in the wheel of local politics offered a chance to express their special brand of indignation. These political energies might have dissipated had not factional struggles between Zhang Yinqing and his opponents created a mechanism for transforming rebellious attitudes and habits into open insurgency. Up until the eve of the riot, the FTU had been a hindrance as well as a help to rickshaw men in furthering their more radical aims. Zhang had attempted to moderate and control his rickshaw-puller constituents. This commitment to a politics of social control ended up as a casualty of his final, desperate attempts to deflect FTU and party challenges to his power. In the meantime, as discontent among rickshaw men appeared to soften, peasants, Buddhists, streetcar workers, and the general citizenry took turns in staging mass protests, which had the effect of charging and recharging city politics with conflict and tension.

The degree to which the circle of groups and classes drawn to the language and tactics of mass politics had been widened in 1928 and 1929 was marked out in a dramatic way when, on September 30, five thousand suburban peasants and vegetable brokers marched into the city, waving banners of protest.[62] In the government's search for revenue authorities had decided to abandon the century-old tax rates levied at city gates on produce coming into the city and to sell the right to raise revenue to tax farmers. The entrepreneurs who bought the concession took the name "Benevolent Vegetable Trade Monopoly" and announced new taxes one hundred times the old rates.

The protesters first assembled outside the old Ministry of Agriculture and Commerce building in the West City. The building housed the five Nationalist-led mass organizations, including the Beiping Peasants Association. Party cadre Han Shiyuan, a member of Zhang Yinqing's old faction, exhorted the crowd to "overthrow" the monopoly, which "oppresses us," but warned those assembled to remain orderly: "If order dissolves into disorder (*luan*) and reactionary elements intrude, our petition will not be successful." From there the demonstrators marched four abreast south to Xidan Arch and east to local party headquarters. The crowd carried peasant association banners and posters attacking the monopoly, which "fleeces peasants," and "swearing to death" not to recognize it. At party headquarters, peasant association leaders went in to meet with officials while the crowd waited in anxious anticipation "like wild geese." Party executive committee member Li Hanming, a Nanjing-backed rival of Han Shiyuan for control of the local party apparatus, came out to speak to the crowd and acknowledged that the city government had "received many petitions in the past, but this time the number of people is enormous" and expressed the "earnest hope that you take the preservation of order as important." When Li agreed to communicate the demands to higher levels, the crowd shouted slogans in praise of the local party branch and commenced a march along West Changan Avenue to the offices of the municipal government.

At city hall aides to Mayor Zhang Yinwu, who was out of the office at the time, met with the crowd's representatives for two hours. As the afternoon wore on the demonstrators, who had not had a chance to eat lunch, began to get restless and started to drift out into the avenue, blocking streetcar lines until thirty or forty cars were backed up. Since city residents had come to see disruption of streetcar service as an indicator of political and social disorder on a par with closed gates, the crowd's apparently inadvertent action heightened fears that some larger conflict was brewing. When Zhang Yinwu, a young and dynamic military officer turned politician, finally arrived on his bicycle, he assured the crowd that the monopoly would be abolished, a promise that was met with great shouts of approval.

The presence of demonstrating peasants in the center of the city created alarm among the moneyed and propertied classes. Merchants who remembered the Boxer uprising or were aware of Communist-led peasant insurgencies to the south had reason to look on the mobilization of farmers with trepidation. In response, the chamber of commerce called out its militia.[63] When the police refused to provide the chamber with rifles, the chamber issued wooden clubs and stationed men outside Qian Gate to guard the central business district.

A few days later, as vegetable markets began to return to normal, Buddhist clergy, a group new to mass politics, took to the streets. On October 5 over two thousand priests, monks, and sympathizers paraded in the rain to protest the occupation of Iron Mountain Temple by streetcar workers.[64] The workers had taken over the temple, located about halfway between Qian Gate and the Bridge of Heaven, as a school for their children. The streetcar workers union claimed that the temple was unoccupied and that opium pipes and obscene books had been found on the premises. Buddhist religious officials wrote to the police, demanding that union leaders be punished and the temple returned to religious use. The day before the march, priests and monks held a news conference in Sun Yat-sen Park to state their side of the controversy and distributed propaganda materials to the public. The march itself was orderly. Newspaper photos show robed monks with flags and drums, marching along streetcar track, with several rickshaw pullers looking on. Streetcar workers responded by pasting anti-Buddhist signs and slogans on their cars.

By mounting an anticlerical attack against Buddhists, workers generated support among other self-consciously modernist and iconoclastic groups in the city. The city's student union issued an "antisuperstition declaration" accusing monks of being "unproductive and notorious for their alliances with rotten officials and gentry."[65] This argument, however, was not likely to win broad support in a city where Buddhism had a largely favorable image, especially among ordinary citizens and the poor.[66] Good works had also earned friends for the Buddhists. Twenty-two "workshops for poor people" signed a petition in support of the Buddhists' position.[67] By labeling Buddhists bad and "unproductive," streetcar workers risked making enemies beyond the community of priests and monks who opposed them on the Iron Mountain Temple issue.

Two days after Buddhists marched against the temple occupation, streetcar workers became embroiled in conflict with another group of laborers. On October 7 municipal construction workers repairing a road outside Qian Gate momentarily blocked the passage of streetcars, thus triggering an argument and a fight with conductors and drivers.[68] The police arrived to stop the brawl but not before there were several injuries. When another fight broke out near the same spot five days later, streetcar workers left their posts to march to the FTU's offices in the old Ministry building to demand redress.[69] The police finally dispatched men to move twenty streetcars stalled by the work stoppage. In the settlement that followed, two road-construction workers were dismissed from their jobs.

In winning concessions from the construction laborers, the streetcar men took advantage of the fact that the road workers were in an insecure position within the FTU. The several hundred common laborers employed by the city to maintain roads, sweep the streets, and clean sewers and drains had been organized into three unions. But municipal officials, with the support of the central government, had ruled that as government workers they had no right to organize.[70] Despite this adverse ruling, street-workers' unions managed to retain their affiliation with the FTU. But they lacked the fully legitimate status of groups like the streetcar workers. The streetcar-workers union exploited this vulnerability when they pushed for formal arbitration.

Streetcar workers, well known by now for their political sophistication and independence, evinced considerable skill in using party and mass politics to attack their opponents. During the "Double Ten" national day, streetcar workers succeeded in making issues of particular concern to them a central element in what was supposed to be a festive celebration of unity and equality among all groups.[71] On October 10 an estimated seventy thousand people turned out for a morning rally in the Forbidden City, beneath the elevated platform supporting the emperor's old throne room, presided over by rightist cadres selected by authorities in Nanjing in May 1929 to "rectify" the local party apparatus. Zhang Yinqing had been squeezed out of his customary role as impresario of mass political events. The rectification team had succeeded in taking control of the Masses Training Committee, which had been Zhang's base for exerting influence on party-directed mass politics.[72] The rightist cadres, having discovered that the "roots of the FTU were deep and the branches strong," decided to cleanse the organization by "starting at the bottom and moving toward the top."[73] This strategy and Zhang's partial eclipse presented streetcar workers and other dissident groups with the opportunity to place their demands before politicians eager to build mass support.

The assembly began with a one-hundred-and-one-gun salute ringing through the normally quiet palace, followed by the hoisting of flags and a reading of Sun Yat-sen's will. The crowd bowed three times to a portrait of Sun, and party and government officials gave speeches. A reporter on the scene at the start of the program described the celebrants as participating "with unusual enthusiasm and in perfect order." Zhang Minjing and Li Hanming, both leading members of the pro-Nanjing contingent, were present on the platform. Zhang as the presiding official spoke on the timely topic of unity and factionalism. Arguing that for the first time in the eighteen-year history of the Republic "true unity" had been achieved, he warned that "reactionary cliques were constantly preparing for action." As the speechmaking continued, the streetcar-workers union suddenly approached the platform with resolutions concerning the Iron Mountain Temple affair. They wanted the statements read to the crowd. After Zhang and the others deliberated for a time they agreed to "put [the resolutions] to the masses for a vote." The motions asked the municipal government to convert all temples in the city to schools and vocational centers within one week. The petition to the government took the form of an ultimatum, since, if the municipal authorities refused or delayed, the five mass organizations planned to hold an "All-City Residents Assembly" and unilaterally abolish all places of worship. Finally, the streetcar-workers union specifically asked that title to Iron Mountain Temple be transferred to it and that the monks who had protested the workers' occupation of the building be punished. The resolutions were passed, but only in the face of "considerable commotion." As a result, FTU representatives decided to cancel a march planned for immediately after the rally, for fear of further disorder. Beneath and alongside ritual expressions of mass unity and loyalty to the Nationalist party and movement, turbulence generated by group politics and competition was readily apparent. The streetcar workers' tactics resulted in a spectacular but brittle public relations victory. As Mayor Zhang Yinwu noted later, streetcar workers had succeeded in making themselves into the city's "choicest target" by boldly taking on group after group, ranging from soldiers to Buddhists.[74]

Another sign of discrepancies between the appearance of consensus and the potentially corrosive effects of group politics came when late-arriving telephone workers tried to elbow their way ahead of a contingent of vegetable peddlers to reach what they regarded as their rightful position in the pecking order of unions. When the peddlers refused to yield, the telephone workers attacked them with clubs. Police and FTU officials had to intervene to stop the fighting. Leaders and directors of citywide organizations and events spread broad coverlets of formal consensus over the lumpy and contentious constituencies they were responsible for. If mass nationalism and traditions of elite coordination were efficient machines for producing these coverings, divisions based on class, status, and power were just as active in shredding them to pieces.

Riot

By mid-October 1929, city residents had witnessed the rapid escalation of private quarrels involving groups as diverse as vegetable brokers, peasants, Buddhist monks, and streetcar workers into major public protests. National-day celebrations retained the festive, consensual air characteristic of these gatherings but with an undercurrent of bitter confrontation as party-favored groups like the streetcar workers lashed out at their opponents. Relatively well paid, high-status workers had attempted to push aside lower-status comrades. That the telephone workers had clubs at the ready surprised no one. The impulse to arm and defend oneself in the midst of this general intensification of city politics, a process that had been building momentum since the arrival of the Northern Expedition, was infectious. A few days after the Double Ten rally, the chamber of commerce announced the formation of a seven-thousand-man militia armed with clubs and a few guns.[75]

On October 18 six labor unions drew up a petition highly critical of Zhang Yinqing and his supporters on the FTU executive committee.[76] The document, signed by the postal, electric-light-and-power, waterworks, telegraph, and carriage-driver unions, attacked Zhang's "monopoly control" and "feudal methods." These were the same arguments rebellious electric-light-and-power workers and streetcar men had made individually in past conflicts with the FTU leadership. This time, however, the unions had banded together to demand a new election to vote out the incumbents. The next day a delegation of union leaders presented the petition to pro-Nanjing cadre Li Hanming at the party branch office. Dissident FTU unions found natural allies among these rightist cadres, who were themselves in conflict with Zhang Yinqing and old-line leftists in the party. Li accordingly received the petition and immediately agreed to authorize a meeting of union representatives on October 20 at 2 P.M.

The meeting convened at FTU headquarters in the old Ministry building for the supposed purpose of discussing procedures for holding elections in the near future.[77] Party official Deng Yangzhi was present to represent the rectification team backed by Nanjing. Chen Zixiu and Xu Shequan represented incumbent FTU leaders. The meeting of over two hundred delegates had barely gotten under way when a representative from the telephone company union stood up and moved that the meeting be declared a formal, plenary session of the FTU. Sensing an electoral coup in the making, supporters of the incumbent leadership objected. In the confusion, party official Deng Yangzhi made what were interpreted as intemperate remarks, and he was immediately surrounded and beaten. Other union leaders came forward to mediate and protect Deng. Just as a measure of calm returned to the meeting hall, Li Shouchang, leader of the streetcar-workers union delegation, stormed out with supporters and sympathizers in tow. As Li and the other new-faction delegates left, they were jostled by a crowd of old-faction supporters, including a contingent of construction workers who had their own bone to pick with the streetcar-workers union. The new-faction unionists later claimed that old-faction leader Chen Zixiu had ordered the construction workers to break up the meeting in order to avoid a snap vote.

In the aftermath of the October 20 disorder at FTU headquarters, the local party branch decided to make public the petition it had received from dissident unions criticizing the FTU leadership.[78] The six original signatories, joined by the streetcar-workers union, also took out an advertisement in local newspapers.[79] Entitled "An Urgent Announcement," the notice repeated the charge that a "small number of bad elements" had taken control of the FTU:

They take oppressing workers as their specialty. We unions could not bear it any longer and so we asked the Masses Training Committee [recently purged of Zhang Yinqing's influence] to reform the FTU. These reactionary elements pretended to misunderstand why we called for a plenary session and made false charges against the Masses Training Committee that it was plotting to break up the FTU. They incited road-construction workers and street sweepers to beat up Masses Training Committee representative Deng Yangzhi and streetcar union delegate Li Shouchang.

Asserting that the undersigned unions were not responsible for the disturbance, the statement concluded by complaining that "the fact that this illegal act could happen under the blue and white flag of the Republic is really detestable."

In the aftermath of the disturbances on October 20, only road-construction workers, street sweepers, sewer and drain cleaners, and the Xidan Arch branch of the rickshaw-pullers union remained loyal to the old faction. The three municipal unions stuck with the old faction, and the incumbents in turn supported their claims to legal status in the face of opposition from government authorities and directives from Nanjing. The Xidan Arch rickshaw-pullers branch supported the incumbent FTU leaders as an expression of both heightened militancy and patronage ties. Xidan pullers had been in the thick of the August 5 mobilization against the streetcar company's "night car" policy and the September 9 conflict between policemen and rickshaw pullers over parking regulation. In addition, the poor-factory run by the FTU for rickshaw men was located on Piku Lane just north of Xidan Arch and presumably administered to the needs of Xidan branch pullers with particular care.[80]

On October 21 the seventeen unions opposed to Zhang Yinqing and the incumbent FTU leadership met to plan their next course of action.[81] Reflecting the fact that FTU factionalism had not produced a neat division between rickshaw men and the balance of the FTU membership, several rickshaw-puller branches supported the dissidents. The delegates, with telephone-company union leader Wang Bochao in the chair, established a "Peace Preservation Association" (*weizhi hui*) and a militia armed with bayonets and wooden clubs with ten men each drawn from the streetcar, telephone, postal, and rickshaw-pullers unions. Each militiaman was given thirty cents for expenses, except for rickshaw pullers, who received twenty cents more, perhaps in recognition of the greater sacrifice they would make by not working and of the split loyalties they may have felt with their union divided between rival factions. The meeting lasted over four hours, with the participants resolving to meet the following day to finally decide the question of new elections. With an overwhelming majority of FTU unions and the newly reconstituted party branch in their camp, the dissident unions had good reason to be confident about translating their grievances into electoral victory.

The next day, October 22, the two sides converged on the old Ministry of Agriculture and Commerce building, which contained the offices and legitimating seals and charters coveted by both.[82] The building itself was redolent of the mix of bureaucratic and revolutionary "odors" and auras adhering to official and political Beiping. Once a center of reformist plans and projects under the Qing and early Republic, with the transfer of the capital to Nanjing the building became an archive for government documents relating to agriculture and mining. Since only part of the structure was taken up by document storage, the five party-directed mass organizations, including the FTU, were given permission to move into the unoccupied portion of the old Ministry. The head archivist deeply resented the intrusion and launched a legal and political campaign to oust the labor, women's, student, peasant, and merchant organizations. The unions and associations stood their ground in a conflict between organizers and archivists, which seemed to epitomize the unresolved and ambiguous nature of the city's political identity. Processes of "museumification" and mobilization proceded apace as huge blocks of the official city slipped into curated and catalogued slumber while civil society remained wide awake with the stimulation provided by an intensified group and mass politics.[83]

Shortly before noon on October 22 Zhang Yinqing and Chen Zixiu led two hundred workers from the four loyalist unions in an occupation of FTU offices. The old Ministry building was in turn surrounded by the militia of the dissident unions. Once inside, Zhang and Chen bitterly denounced their opponents. The FTU was threatened by a small number of "aristocratic workers." Leaders of the streetcar, telephone, electric-light-and-power, and postal unions, they declared, were "the ones we hate most." Singled out for special invective was the head of a rickshaw-pullers branch in the western part of the Inner City, who supported the dissidents. They labeled the militia organized by the new faction "idiotic" and "oppressive" as well as illegal. "What right has this small number of aristocratic unions to overthrow the executive committee? What can this small number of streetcar, telephone, postal, and electric-light-and-power unions say to that?" After all, "we represent the vast majority of poor workers" and, moreover, "we are human too." Zhang and Chen assured their followers that they would protect the incumbent executive committee "by legal means" and declared their dedication to Republican and Nationalist ideals. Zhang Yinqing had stirred workers before with his blunt eloquence. Besieged by opponents, Zhang, who had once mobilized an entire factory aided only by a portrait of Sun Yat-sen, sought to use Nationalist ideology as a shield against his attackers.

Since one of the main charges against Zhang Yinqing and his supporters was his allegedly "feudal" and tyrannical style of leadership, his attempt to portray the union dissidents as "aristocratic" and "reactionary" was a shrewd rhetorical device. Not all of the workers allied with the new faction could be characterized as members of a labor aristocracy. Night-soil workers, carriage drivers, and one or more branches of the rickshaw-pullers union supported the dissidents. Still, workers in the city's modern utilities and factory sector led the fight to hold new elections, and there were significant differences in status and income between workers in modern enterprises and unskilled laborers like rickshaw men and street sweepers. This cleavage between "aristocratic workers" and the "vast majority of poor workers" was real enough. It helped produce and intensify conflict between streetcar men and lower-status workers like rickshaw pullers and road-construction laborers. Zhang Yinqing and Chen Zixiu sought to exploit these tensions in defense of the old executive committee.

By one in the afternoon, the crowd of pickets and bystanders outside the old Ministry on Fengsheng Lane had grown to over two thousand.[84] The east end of the lane, opening onto the major north-south-running avenue that connected Xisi and Xidan Arches, was packed with rickshaws. Reporters present noted Buddhist monks in the crowd. Two days before, there had been new protests and disorders at the Iron Mountain Temple over the streetcar workers' continued occupation of the building. The monks had an obvious interest in a conflict likely to place the

streetcar-workers union in a stronger position in the FTU. By 2 : 30
P.M. the confrontation between the two factions had become so
ominous that a group of party cadres decided to try to mediate
the dispute. Leaders of the four mass organizations not directly
involved in the quarrel—peasants, merchants, students, and
women—met to work out a compromise. The groups sympathized
with the dissident unions, agreeing that "the old committee's
behavior shows that it wants unwarranted control" of the FTU
and characterizing as "stubborn adherence to error" the loyalty of
the road-construction workers, street sweepers, sewer and drain
cleaners, and the Xidan Arch rickshaw-pullers branch. But the
mediators also expressed hope that "both sides would take peace
as their principle and together find a solution without relying on
arms." Representatives were dispatched in a successful attempt to
arrange a mediation session for the next day. A special delegation
was sent to the Liulichang offices of the telephone-workers union
to consult with Wang Bochao, the putative leader of the new faction. Up until this point, the sequence of events closely followed
the pattern of factional struggle common to every "circle" in the
city. As the two FTU factions generated what seemed to be an
irreconcilable conflict, a homeostatic impulse within the larger
community of activists and cadres signaled the need to buffer and
mediate the impending clash.

By the time the mediators had concluded their labors it was
seven in the evening. Participants in the day's confrontation began
to leave the old Ministry and environs for home.[85] A large crowd
of pickets, FTU members, and other interested parties, including
reporters and monks, lingered outside. As a contingent of rickshaw men from the Xidan Arch branch walked out of Fengsheng
Lane and turned south for home, a streetcar crowded with passengers happened by. The pullers blocked the track, probably intending to harass the driver and conductor, as had happened so many
times in the past. An FTU official who had been a part of the
mediation team working to resolve the split between the old and
new factions came over to quiet what looked like a minor squabble.
In this instance, as was often the case in street-level conflicts,
playing the role of mediator required literally stepping in between
two hostile parties. Unfortunately for the official, the rickshaw
men, in their anger, mistook him for a streetcar-union official and

knocked him to the ground. They then proceeded to wreck the streetcar.

By the conclusion of this first act of destruction, the pullers had been joined by several hundred municipal workers also allied with the old faction. The excited crowd marched south, attacking every streetcar in their path. In their thoroughness they "did not miss one streetcar along the way."[86] As Eric Hobsbawm has noted, aside from the specific grievances that might cause a crowd to attack modern urban transport, streetcars, "whether in Calcutta or Barcelona, are unusually convenient for rioters."[87] The "large and trackbound vehicles, when burned or overturned, can block streets and disrupt traffic very easily." Within the next three hours, as the crowd streamed south and east along the streetcar tracks, hundreds of rioters were joined by thousands and then tens of thousands of rickshaw pullers. As many as twenty-five thousand people, mostly rickshaw men, took part in the uprising.[88]

The initial attack near the old Ministry flowed directly out of the political struggle for leadership of the FTU. Pullers from the Xidan Arch branch, and the municipal workers who joined them in smashing the first streetcar, were activists completely attuned to the preceding days and weeks of factional conflict. Later accounts of the riot, hostile to Zhang Yinqing and the old faction, claimed that the attack on the streetcars had been ordered by Zhang as an act of revenge for his impending defeat. Some rickshaw men arrested in the riot's aftermath confessed that they had been paid in advance to attack the streetcars.[89] However, since Wang Bochao, leader of the telephone-workers union, was the principal architect of the campaign against the old faction, and the streetcar-workers union was only one of several unions leading the attack against the incumbents, a riot against the streetcar system would seem to have been an oblique and ineffectual line of attack for someone as politically astute as Zhang. Although the riot began as an episode spun out of clashes among a widening circle of Zhang Yinqing's friends and enemies, the transformation of a brawl among hundreds into a movement involving thousands shifted the conflict onto a different plane.

The swelling crowds yelled "Down with the streetcar company!" and "Give every rickshaw man an extra fifty coppers a day!"[90] Slogans shouted by the rioters also denounced the streetcar company for the long delays in creating a fund for the relief of rickshaw men.[91] The crowd turned east at Xidan Arch and marched unopposed along Changan Avenue to the center of the city, past the offices of the city government and the police. The rioters followed the route taken by numerous groups of petitioners in the past year. But this time there was no stopping to seek an audience with the mayor or hear explanations from other officials. For their part, Mayor Zhang Yinwu and his subordinates in the police and military made no immediate attempt to stop the carnival of destruction.[92] The mayor later said that the police failed to intervene at once because the initial conflict was purely a union and party matter.[93] Armed with traditions of corporate self-regulation and the novel idea that the party had the right to override or deflect governmental authority, political activists had made a point of resisting what they regarded as police interference in their affairs. As experience had demonstrated in the last year and a half, policemen risked attack if they disregarded the boundaries and spheres of influence drawn around offices and assemblies. But by backing off from their own responsibility to intervene at the first sign of disorder, the police allowed the first attack to succeed and propel the rioters down the track. Police were later publicly criticized for not having intervened at once.[94] Once the crowd escaped the grid of precinct and district jurisdictions and began sweeping through the city, the rioters became a moving target difficult to contain or neutralize. "Darting in and out of alleyways" adjacent to major avenues, pullers used their knowledge of urban topography to devastating effect.[95]

With the temporary abdication of the police from their responsibility to maintain order, and Zhang Yinwu's delay in calling out troops, rickshaw pullers were able to cast away the rules and regulations imposed on them daily. Consciously or unconsciously, they did something many no doubt had long desired to do: direct traffic. "For some time they were complete masters of the streets, holding up all sorts of traffic, stopping motor cars and searching them, questioning the occupants and refusing passage through certain streets."[96] For a few hours, streetcars, "aristocratic workers," automobiles, upper-class passengers, and policemen were all subordinated to the will of the crowd. This dramatic reversal of roles, the momentary seizure of the street as territory daily contested but never controlled by the pullers, and the destruction of their hated rival all explain the exhilaration of the crowd. In his post mortem on the riot, Mayor Zhang noted that the "great crowd of rickshaw pullers . . . acted as if they were intoxicated."[97]

A moment of riotous protest can be expressive as well as purely instrumental.[98] As the rioters "literally ripped some of the cars to pieces" and "temporarily took charge of the main thoroughfares . . . threatening with their sticks anyone who seemed inclined to disregard their orders," they dramatically expressed the depth of their resentments and discontent. Not all of these feelings could be organized in slogans and ideologies or channeled into rational political activity. Countless social dramas in the past, which had displayed and reinforced the rickshaw man's dependent status, dissolved into a single, dramatic blow delivered against all the political, social, and cultural forms of domination experienced by pullers.

Discovering these emotions did not mean that the rioters had lost their senses. The target of their fury, the streetcar system, imposed a natural structure on the riot as rickshaw men and their allies moved systematically south and east from the disorder's point of origin in the West City. Following the streetcar lines as they wreaked physical destruction on the system also led the rioters to the headquarters of the streetcar company's management and workers. Between nine and ten in the evening, the crowds began to converge on the company offices in the East City and on union headquarters located at the streetcar yard in the Bridge of Heaven district. Reporters explained the size and aggressiveness of the crowd surrounding the union office by noting that rickshaw pullers in the area were already in an "agitated state" because of the occupation of the Iron Mountain Temple and the most recent disturbances between streetcar workers and Buddhists.[99] By the time the rioters reached their twin destinations, sixty of the company's ninety streetcars had been damaged or destroyed. In some cases, rioters had destroyed the motor and the drive mechanism. In others, windows had been broken and wooden slats torn off the sides of the cars. Shelters for passengers at streetcar shops had been pulled down and power lines had been cut. City streets were "paved with broken glass and bits of woodwork from a long line of wrecked cars."[100] Although there were no fatalities, eighteen streetcar workers suffered beatings at the hands of rioters, some of whom wielded iron or wooden clubs.[101] Sixty-five workers later reported the theft or loss of ticket boxes, money bags, or articles of clothing.

As the crowds prepared to rush the two offices, police and troops finally moved in to disperse the crowds. Troops cleared the streets with fixed bayonets. As the soldiers marched, rioters and spectators "melted away."[102] In places where rickshaw pullers put up a fight, troops fired blanks and used rifle butts against the clubs wielded by the demonstrators. Nearly two hundred rioters were arrested.[103] Soldiers and police also managed to trap one thousand rickshaw men near the Drum Tower in the northern part of the Inner City. Many of those arrested claimed they had gathered in support of the dissident unions and had not taken part in the riot. Rickshaw men who had joined the riot at the old Ministry building returned to find their vehicles stolen. When they hurried in to seek help from FTU officials, they found the offices empty. Fearing a "responsibility problem," FTU cadres had deserted their posts.[104]

The next day was relatively free of conflict. Scattered fights broke out between rickshaw men who wanted to declare a general strike and those who sought to resume work.[105] Zhang Yinwu declared martial law in the city, and troops and police occupied the offices of the rickshaw-pullers union and branch offices, as well as the offices of the three municipal unions. Despite the fact that the streetcar company decided to suspend all service because of the damage done by the rioters and fears of further disorder, streetcar workers packed five cars still in working condition, decorated them with signs and slogans, and drove along track that still remained clear of wreckage, celebrating their victory.[106]

Public reaction to the riot focused on the long-standing conflict between the rickshaw pullers and the streetcar company. While struggles within the FTU and between Buddhists and streetcar workers were cited as contributing factors, most reports of the night's violence began with a recognition that rickshaw men had resented the streetcar ever since the company began operations. Under the headline "Tens of Thousands of Rickshaw Laborers Attack Streetcars," the popular daily *Shibao* (Truth Post) noted that "ever since the Beiping streetcar was built, the average rickshaw puller, in his job, has acutely felt the streetcar's impact."[107] Only the pro-Nanjing party branch argued for a conspiracy on the part of Zhang Yinqing and his faction as the "overriding, long-term cause" of the riot.[108]

Police and troops ended up arresting and detaining over one thousand people.[109] Top-level union cadres accused of being ringleaders of the riot were dealt with harshly. While Zhang Yinqing managed to escape the city, reportedly in disguise, several other old-faction members, including his cousin Chen Zixiu, were caught.[110] Chen had been apprehended by plainclothes detectives as he tried to board a train for Tianjin the day after the riot. Two weeks later, Chen and three other union officials were shot by a firing squad at the Bridge of Heaven execution ground. Although he was reported to have been tortured during interrogation, Chen maintained his innocence to the end.[111] Chen's steadfast denial of a conspiracy behind the riot suggests that while he and Zhang Yinqing may have planned to disrupt FTU meetings as a means of holding onto power, they had not ordered their supporters to attack the streetcar system. The three others, all officials of the rickshaw-pullers union, admitted being involved in leading attacks on the streetcars. Although these confessions may have been obtained under duress, the fact that significant numbers of rioters arrested were union committeemen or branch leaders suggests that while the old-faction members at the FTU level were not directly involved in the riot, union officials provided leadership for the crowds of rickshaw men.[112]

Punishment for others arrested in connection with the riot was relatively light, although the first days of detention were filled with uncertainty and suffering. Most of the cases were tried in a temple compound near Beihai Park, which had been turned into a temporary prison. To guard against a rescue attempt or breakout, three machine guns and four ranks of troops were stationed at the main gate.[113] In the days after the riot, families of those accused congregated outside the temple gates in an attempt to make contact with the men and supply them with food.[114] Wives and mothers wept as they asked after their husbands and sons. Family members were both concerned about the fate of those detained and anxious about how they would get by without income brought in by the pullers. Even temporary detention had a punishing effect on the livelihood of rickshaw-puller households. The men arrested were denied food for two days until the police arranged for each detainee to receive one steamed bun. Interrogations proved so time-consuming that investigators resorted to examining the accused rioters in groups of seven. Most of those arrested denied involvement in the disorders and refused to incriminate fellow pullers but promised to cause no further trouble.[115] Thirty-five men received jail sentences ranging from four months to a little over a year.[116] Ninety-eight were released after signing bonds guaranteeing their future good behavior. Most of the others were exiled from the city. Eight hundred and eighty-nine men were taken in three groups six miles outside the city walls, released, and ordered not to come back. This "banishment" was carried out with considerable ceremony by uniformed troops on the same day in columns to the east, west, and north of the city.[117]

Within a week after the riot, new FTU elections were held in circumstances and under new rules that ensured that the "new faction" would dominate the executive committee.[118] The rickshaw-pullers union was given a temporary suspension, and the road-repair, street-sweepers, and sewer-and-drain-cleaners unions were permanently outlawed.[119] With "old-faction" leaders in jail or in hiding and their supporters banned from participation in the election, the results were a foregone conclusion. While the dissident union members, now in control, were undoubtedly pleased, party officials who spoke at the reconvened FTU assembly appeared somewhat shocked by the wild climax to the factional struggles they had been party to. Zhang Minjing, noting that he had been impressed by the "fervent" nature of the Beiping labor movement, also acknowledged that the result "was not what I had imagined."[120] The whole experience proved that the "worker movement must be under the leadership of the party," the leadership ought to be "cleansed," and individuals must not seek private gain. Of course, it was party factionalism emanating from Nanjing which had enabled dissident unions to win their independent struggle for power in the FTU.

The streetcar company claimed that damage done to sixty cars amounted to $400,000.[121] The streetcars began running again at the end of December after gaining permission from the government for a rate increase to compensate for the losses. With the rate hike, and at the cost of executed leaders, imprisoned and exiled comrades, and temporary loss of formal representation in the FTU, rickshaw men had won part of what they had been fighting for. In addition, the city agreed to exempt the company from taxes for three months. Streetcar workers, in a development that must have taken some of the sweetness away from their factional victory in the FTU, were also forced to bear a share of the losses. After a brief dispute, the streetcar workers agreed to forfeit their year-end bonus and take half-pay for a month.[122] Perhaps even worse, the union was also forced to give up control of Iron Mountain Temple.[123] Buddhists had protested again when the workers had begun to demolish a temple wall to expand their school, and fearing trouble, Mayor Zhang Yinwu ordered the Social Welfare Bureau to take control of the building. Months later, Buddhists and the streetcar workers were still engaged in litigation over the matter.[124]

Conclusion

Like other Republican cities, Beiping was the scene of many strikes, demonstrations, rallies, and protest marches. But the attack on the streetcar system was the first large-scale civil disorder in the city since the troop riots of 1912 and the Boxer uprising of 1900. If one classifies the latter two disturbances as, respectively, officially sanctioned looting and the product of an anarchic battle plan, the 1929 streetcar riot is the only example of riotous civil disorder in the city's history from the late Qing to the Tianan Gate Square riot of 1976. Whether one adopts the English dictionary definition of a "wild, violent, public disturbance of the peace" or the term for riot found in contemporary documents—*baodong*, or "to assemble a large number of people to kill, set fires, pillage, and commit other acts of violence, including actions of a political nature"—the streetcar riot stands out as a moment of uncommon and wild, if peculiarly discriminate, disorder.

Rickshaw men took a long time to work themselves up to the deed. In 1924 rickshaw men were prepared to lie down on the tracks to stop the cars from running. Their plan failed at the last moment when their patron, Sun Xueshi, caved in under pressure from the company's powerful protectors. In 1929 pullers found the collective will to riot only after months of experimentation with a range of political tactics and strategies and a dress rehearsal in August.

Recent studies of popular unrest and violence emphasize the importance of emergent values and political experience in explaining riotous behavior. In its report on the causes of riots in American cities in the 1960s, the National Advisory Commission on Civil Disorder concluded that "disorder did not typically erupt without preexisting causes, as a result of a single 'triggering' or 'precipitating' incident. Instead, it developed out of an increasingly disturbed social atmosphere in which typically a series of tension-heightening incidents over a period of weeks or months became linked in the minds of many with a shared network of underlying grievances."[125]

In the case of the Beiping riot, the trigger was pulled when rickshaw men and streetcar workers tangled in proximity to the old Ministry and the factional strife the building housed. Beforehand a disturbed social atmosphere had come to permeate citywide politics through a chain of tension-heightening incidents involving rickshaw men, streetcar workers, municipal laborers, Buddhists, and party and union cadres. Each group developed, partly as a by-product of clashes with each other, an acute sense of shared grievance. When political militancy was added to the natural prickliness of urban residents accustomed to bumping into each other and chafing against each other's prerogatives and interests, the stage was set for the radical escalation of social conflict.

Normally, the city's social order adjusted to these tensions and conflicts by fielding a small army of mediators and go-betweens to buffer and soften the clash of contentious individuals and groups. While the Nationalist political apparatus attempted to mimic these practices in order to win a place for itself in the family of organizations that ruled the city, the ideology and organization of mass politics also contained another track, which favored escalation over mediation. After abortive attempts to promote a politics that encouraged escalation of social tensions by targeting capitalist factory owners and powerful organizations like the chamber of commerce, Nationalist cadres settled down to manage their own affairs in a "responsible" fashion. But in doing so they became the targets of factional opposition and social movements. These attacks were based both on the habits of faction that were part and parcel of the established social order of the city and on the logic of movement politics fostered by Nationalist cadres themselves and patterned after years of marches, protests, and Tianan Gate demonstrations.

In the 1930s Lao She wrote a short story clearly inspired by the streetcar riot, entitled "Black Li and White Li."[126] In the story, he uses the smashing of streetcars to illuminate the differences between two middle-class brothers: one a well-meaning but ineffectual individual, the other a ruthless political operator. The Li brothers, who closely resemble each other except for a mole on the face of "Black" Li (the elder and kindly one), employ a rickshaw man named Wang Wu, who appreciates Black Li's paternalistic concern for his well-being but finds the radical brother's incitement to violence more to the point. The riot takes place as planned, and Li Siye ("White" Li) is hunted as a ringleader. Erye, the apolitical brother, has his mole removed in order to pass as his radical sibling and gives himself up to the police, allowing Siye to escape. Erye and five rickshaw pullers, in imitation of the fate of Chen Zixiu and the three rickshaw-union cadres, are condemned to death, drawn through the streets to the execution ground, and killed.

Lao She offers the reader a choice between the "good" brother, who can only act by sacrificing himself, and the "bad" brother, whose success as a political organizer is based on his cynicism and lack of human feeling. The author makes no comment on whether the riot itself was justified, although Wang Wu is portrayed as a sympathetic character and no one disputes his contention that the streetcar is a direct threat to the rickshaw pullers' livelihood. The radical brother, with his political sophistication, natural rapport with the working poor, shrewd and unsentimental outlook, and ability to cheat the executioner, bears a striking resemblance to Zhang Yinqing. His brother's humanism evokes the debates of the 1920s over the moral dilemmas associated with rickshaw pulling and the frustration many intellectuals experienced in their attempt to find a means of resolving social problems as vexing as the plight of the puller.

Contemporary ideologies helped justify a multitude of questionable political activities, ranging from beating up fellow workers and smashing public utilities to political favoritism and the corrupt use of office. Lao She implies that participation in modern politics kills one's sense of moral responsibility. Even a casual reading of the daily press or participation in public life would have given Lao She impressions of Republican politics of sufficient sordidness and violence to support the "realism" of the bleak picture of mass politics he draws in "Black and White Li," *Camel Xiangzi*, and other works. In *Camel Xiangzi*, Lao She's rickshaw-puller hero begins participating in politics only after his near-complete degeneration as a human being. He "becomes a beast" in Beiping, that most "cultural" of cities.[127] He joins a rickshaw-pullers union at the urging of Yuan Ming, a greedy and unscrupulous former student turned Nationalist labor organizer. "Yuan Ming sold ideas (*sixiang*) for money. Xiangzi accepted ideas for money."[128] Yuan Ming believes in his radical ideology and persuades Xiangzi that it "made complete sense." Both men without hesitation use their beliefs to justify committing evil deeds for personal gain. As a student, Yuan Ming, full of progressive views, had denounced his humanistic teacher, Professor Cao (Xiangzi's kindly employer and the moral twin of Black Li), to the Nationalists as a Communist in revenge for a bad grade. Later, Xiangzi informs on Yuan to the police for sixty dollars, sending the union leader to his death by firing squad at the Bridge of Heaven.

To the degree that Lao She's deft portrayals of politicians like Yuan Ming and Siye resemble the images polemicists created for their adversaries in the 1920s, one can appreciate both the opportunism rampant in city politics and the underlying quest for a moral center present among activists and ordinary citizens. However, Lao She's loathing for modern politics, a sentiment shared by many of his contemporaries who saw politicians as "bureaucratic gangsters" or worse, obscures the points at which popular aspirations, traditional political motifs, and modern ideology fit together in urban China in the 1920s.

Zhang Yinqing's rise to power was directly related to his ability to make Nationalism and the Three People's Principles relevant to the lives of his constituents. For all their railing against "feudalism," political operatives like Zhang were adept at shaping their rhetoric and behavior to fit conventional expectations of how community affairs should be managed. Zhang was a despot or "local emperor" with modern ideas and the knack for posing as the protector of lesser men than he. Nationalist ideology fused the laborer's "rice bowl," Confucian statecraft attention to "people's livelihood" (*minsheng*), and Sun Yat-sen's "Principle of People's Livelihood" in a formula that made the rickshaw man's Luddism at least as modern as it was traditional. Instead of rejecting China's traditional "moral economy," which justified the defense of livelihood as a means of ensuring social harmony, in favor of a "political economy," which protected property and profits, modern Chinese politics as a general rule modernized and reinforced traditional economic rights by linking them to the idea of citizenship. As studies of European machine-breaking have shown, laborers who attacked machines in order to protect their jobs typically enjoyed considerable community support for their actions.[129] But in the contest between the residue of community norms and the solvent power of modern capital, technology, and organization, older values finally dissolved. In the case of China, Nationalist ideology bottled the old wine of *minsheng* in a way that made the mad ambitions of rickshaw men recognizable, if not palatable, to people who applauded and supported the Nationalist "revolution." For those indifferent or hostile to the blue-sky and white-sun label, what the rickshaw men were attempting to do was simply vintage urban politics based on defense of corporate interests. Rickshaw men defended their traditional right to livelihood as citizens and fought modernization by manipulating modern party politics. The mingled atavism and modernism of the riot demonstrates the paradoxical nature of social change in the modern era: the more one resists progress, the more entangled one becomes in the advance of modern capital and modern state power.

Twelve

Order and Movement in City Politics

Displaced Development

In 1928, while still president of the Beijing chamber of commerce, cigarette salesman Wang Wendian resigned as vice-president of the All-China Chamber of Commerce. Wang complained that he, and presumably his firm, Nanyang Brothers Tobacco Company, had wearied of spending thousands of dollars subsidizing the body.[1] Republican China contained organizations labeled "All-China," which were barely local, as well as "presidents," like Cao Kun, whose influence hardly reached beyond the walls of the capital. The "higher" one got or the closer to the "center" one went the greater the likelihood that one would run across these political and organizational shells. Local chambers of commerce, labor federations, and student unions were far stronger, on balance, than their national counterparts, when such parent organizations existed. Nonetheless, the lines of authority running through semifictional hierarchies were drawn in such a way as to make possible a relationship weighted in the other direction once the center had been seized and consolidated and these nation-spanning and citywide networks of organizations were brought under control. By the end of the twenties a substantial proportion of city people in China had reached a level of political consciousness commensurate with their formal status as citizens of a republic. Merchants, workers, students, women, suburban farmers, and assorted professionals entered citywide associations and unions, poised for eventual integration into nationwide systems.

The tendency toward increasing scales of integration had broad support in Chinese urban society. As plants grow toward sunlight, modern Chinese organizations grew toward political authority. Even in the dimly lit Republican polity, movement toward greater unity was detectable in the way city residents allowed themselves to be administered and mobilized by institutions and individuals with claims to national political authority. This centralizing tendency did not spring from craven attitudes toward superiors or from blind obedience. The record of political activity among all groups and classes in Beijing in the 1920s suggests, if anything, a natural combativeness and a willingness to challenge the authority of policemen, employers, politicians, and warlords. Politically conscious Chinese recognized the value of state intervention both in coordinating the production of public goods, like social peace and economic security, and in legitimizing (or delegitimizing) the existing social order.

Following Clifford Geertz, we might say that Chinese appreciate the utility of both "statecraft" (or "governance, in the sense of regnancy, regime, dominion, mastery") and "stateliness" (or "pomp, in the sense of splendor, display, dignity, presence").[2] By dint of their unique vantage point at the center of the Chinese political world, Beijing residents were in a good position to understand the administrative and theatrical elements of politics and their relationship to each other. Traditionally, urban elites had worked within the administrative and normative context provided by the state. Guildsmen and gentry members supervised the fighting of fires, the arrest of thieves, the feeding of the poor, and the orchestration of festivals and rituals designed to make their authority enchanting.[3] They did all this knowing that the soldiers, officials, and courtiers of the emperor were busy at some remove maintaining a coercive, managerial, and normative apparatus to back up, coordinate, and legitimize their local efforts.[4] In the Republican era, city residents, now citizens rather than subjects, faced governments that pretended to assume a greater administrative burden and made equal claims to transcendent political authority based now on modern nationalism. At the same time, government, on the whole, was neither efficient nor enchanting. This was a knotty problem for city people, who demonstrated their willingness to be administered by paying for an expensive police department, and their readiness to be politically enthralled by participating in Tianan Gate demonstrations. Under the circumstances, there was nothing to be done but to wait for the appearance of a state with suitably enlarged capacities. Beijing, unlike revolutionary Paris, could not produce such a beast on its own, although, if the political center could be restored, the city gave every indication of being willing and able to follow its lead. In the meantime, the trenchworks of local politics, including both well-worn guild practices and freshly dug *fatuan*, were maintained and defended against imperfect representations and manifestations of the state, as well as against classes and movements impatient with the status quo.[5] Political failure at the center necessitated displacement of political development from governmental to quasi-governmental institutions, from national to local politics, and from center to periphery.

If, for Mao Zedong, the Chinese people formed a blank page upon which a new text could be written, the Republican city was a prepared canvas, stretched and framed so as to be responsive to political artistry and unforgiving in its resistance to flawed concepts and amateur efforts. While sojourning in Beijing, three Republican political figures—Yuan Shikai, Zhang Xun, and Zhang Zuolin—were tempted to restore the monarchy and reestablish the city as an imperial capital. They were rewarded with mockery and defeat.[6] Sacrifices at the Temple of Heaven proved to be wholly incompatible with the ritual of mass politics performed outside Tianan Gate. In 1928 and 1929, young Nationalist organizers struggled to transform the city according to a model of party rule, with only slightly greater success. Their efforts were undermined by internal conflicts and by the unwillingness of local elites to cede them more than one or two corners of the urban social and political canvas.

Political success on a grand scale required recognition of the reality and potency of citizenship as the base of modern politics; the ability to fill, or at least surround, the political center with a complete and enthralling political vision; and the will and resources to fight through the trenchworks of city politics to reach city residents in their shops, factories, offices, and courtyard residences. Over time, as Republican political projects faltered, the initiative in city politics passed to defenders rather than attackers of the existing social and political order. For outsiders like the warlords, city trenches were an almost unfathomable maze. For Nationalist revolutionaries, they became alternately barriers, which exhausted the capacity of cadres to mobilize mass support, and protection against a center at Nanjing bent on recalling the original marching orders that had sent them on their transformative mission in the first place.

As the histories of the police, the chamber of commerce, and the FTU indicate, Beijing society was plastic enough in its social and political structures to accommodate directed change. At the same time, limits to the plasticity of the city, like the physical limits imposed by city walls, were apparent in the ability of groups to resist external pressures and wall themselves off from outside intervention.

In Beijing, city gates were designed to be at least as impressive as the city walls, and the gated enclosures that groups in the city built around themselves implied both a willingness to open up to outside alliances and administration and an ability to repel intruders. The politics of organizations like the chamber of commerce and the FTU included intramural bloodletting, siege craft against external enemies, and unlocking the gates to allow outsiders in to help one faction trounce another. Paradoxically, the larger the organization and the more extensive its defenses, the more likely that the gates would be opened. Even the night-soil and water-carriers guilds, defended by their "impenetrable military walls," let in police, newspaper reporters, union organizers, and prosecutors when these intrusions coincided with the logic of factional competition. In larger organizations, formed from separate guilds, unions, or student organizations, the relative weakness of communal consciousness and dependence on external ideologies for legitimacy made the admission of outsiders and outside influences even more likely.

The most basic-level units in the city, like labor gangs and groups (*kouzi*), were connected to higher levels indirectly, often through their ability to replicate the dominant model of patriarchal authority internally without actually touching the structure of guild power they nested within. Citywide, legally constituted organizations directly abutted the state. Beijing's gates and walls again seem an apt metaphor. In the 1920s the two most prominent gates in the city were, arguably, Tianan and Qian. Outside Tianan Gate, a minor imperial portal unexpectedly pressed into performing a central role in the political life of the Republic, crowds assembled to create and sustain mass nationalism. Inside lay a museum. Tianan Gate drew a line between the museumified imperial past and the mass political future. The ritual significance of the Forbidden City would only survive as a point of contrast with the new political rituals outside. Qian Gate, which separated the "official" Inner City from the "merchant" Outer City, was remodeled to accommodate increased traffic. In analogous fashion, state and society were directly joined in Republican China in a well-trafficked relationship. Governmental disrepair and disorganization led to broken connections between state and citizenry, at least insofar as politics as a two-way street is concerned, but the habit of formal contact, established through the activities of cadres of all hues, never was suspended.

Politics on the Defensive

In the section of the *Prison Notebooks* where Antonio Gramsci compares the dominant institutions and beliefs of a social order to the "trench-systems of modern warfare," he distinguishes between politics as a "war of movement" and as a "war of position."[7] Movement to actively resist or overthrow the powers-that-be, through a general strike for example, is to be distinguished from passive resistance centering on marginal defense or enlargement of one's social position. Gramsci is interested in the way revolutionary movements, unable to win a clear victory on the battlefield of strike and demonstration, become entangled in positional warfare with the besieged regime. He explains the shift to a politics of position by pointing to the tenacity of the existing social order, represented by the Church, the industrial system, and the dominant culture, which forms "a powerful system of fortresses and earthworks" behind the "outer ditch" of the state.

In the case of a country the size and diversity of China, wars of position and movement could take place simultaneously in different regions and at different levels. The war of position among militarists could be broken by the sudden maneuvering of Zhang Zuolin or the line of march of the Northern Expedition. Cities could explode, as they did in 1919 and 1925, in mass demonstrations and then return to a politics in which groups and classes struggled to consolidate, defend, or marginally expand their gains. Feng Yuxiang's defeat in 1926 rang the curtain on the May Thirtieth Movement in Beijing. The stalemate in 1928 among northern warlords and the Nanjing regime allowed movement politics to reemerge.

As Gramsci points out, the subsiding of movement politics allows one to take the measure (make "an accurate reconnaissance") of nongovernmental institutions. Beijing's essential orderlines can be explained by the "depth" of local institutions and the expert generalship of local elites. One can easily misread the Republican period as a time of unrelieved disintegration and disorder if one fails to look behind the governmental ditch to see An Disheng, Sun Xueshi, Zhou Zuomin, and other locally famous defenders of personal, corporate, and public interests. Even individuals identified ideologically with politics as a war of movement, like Zhang Yinqing, can be seen attempting to join their quadrant of corporate fortifications to the citywide system of trenches. Movements politics, in part, was the existing social order brought outdoors to Tianan Gate in carnival costume for display and legitimation.

This system worked because of the willingness of local elites to incorporate new groups into the social order even at the risk of complicating their own defensive strategies. Of course, the endless elaboration of "responsible" persons, meetings, and assemblies had its point of vulnerability. The political system was far more efficient at social control than in providing solutions to social problems. As Ira Katznelson has pointed out, this is characteristic of city politics when institutions evolve to buffer potentially intense class or ethnic conflicts without redistributing power or wealth.[8] In Beijing the buffering effect was accomplished, not mainly through party politics, as it was in American cities at the turn of the century, but through the modernization of traditional practices like mediation and the deployment of a "cadredom" capable of capping mass unrest and deflecting incursions by predatory political forces.

The image of local elites as mediators, brokers, and experts at positional political warfare helps shed light on a key problem in the study of Republican-era politics: the social basis of regimes.

Was the Nanjing regime, for example, the political crystallization of bourgeois and landlord interests?[9] Or was the Nationalist state "its own constituency," cut off by choice or circumstance from all social forces?[10] The Nationalists' most ardent supporters locally were the mass constituencies mobilized by cadres like Zhang Yinqing. Local elites were decidedly cool in their appreciation of a regime that exacted warlord-style protection costs, on the one hand, and unleashed mass movements against established authority, on the other. Over time local elites made an accommodation with their new political overlords. Given the faction-ridden, politically disorganized nature of the Nationalist regime, maintaining such a working relationship required considerable skill and forebearance. Local elites, and the class interests they represented, were tied to authorities in Nanjing, not as pawns or puppet masters, but as participants in a series of specific transactions in which they brokered local resources and support for higher-level concessions and services. The presence of this stratum of local managers and order-keepers allowed regimes like that based in Nanjing to skate on the surface of Chinese society and to achieve maximum political maneuverability at the cost of minimal day-to-day control over local affairs. It might have served the long-run interests of the Nationalists if they, like the Communists in the countryside, had fallen through the ice. After 1927 hardy plungers and swimmers like Li Lesan and Zhang Yinqing were rare in the Nationalist camp. After 1929 they were practically nonexistent.

Conflict and Cohesion as a Continuous Process

In response to mid- to late-nineteenth-century urban social crises, city elites and organizations had renewed or developed an impressive array of policies and strategies for coping with social conflict and dislocation.[11] Government officials encouraged the formation of militia, soup kitchens, charities, market-regulating mechanisms, and other public endeavors. But the basic tasks of management and control were handled by parapolitical bodies, like guilds. Gathering pressures brought on by rural unrest and uneven industrial development put increasing strain on these traditional institutions. After the turn of the century, the promise and prospect of government intervention in policing, managing, and developing urban society raised expectations among officials and the public that solutions to poverty, disorder, and underdevelopment were at hand.[12] Traditional and modern, governmental and quasi-governmental approaches appeared to reinforce each other.

The partial unraveling of these strands of ideology and organization in the teens and twenties left in doubt the question of how cities would respond to change and dislocation. Hybrid institutions like "factories for the poor," which combined the idea of state-sponsored industrialization with Chinese and Western notions of philanthropy, appeared as gestures designed to pacify the poor and public opinion rather than as solutions to the problems of unemployment and economic insecurity. Gestures artfully made won considerable local political currency as the careers of civic leaders like Sun Xueshi demonstrate. But the unbridged gap between expectations and social realities also led to explosions like the streetcar riot and prepared the way for administered solutions to urban social problems after 1949.

Cities undergoing modernization tend to be disorderly places. According to Louis Chevalier, nineteenth-century Paris was a

sick city, a city perpetually racked by all kinds of crises and conflicts, a city perpetually agitated . . . by disturbances ranging from random street brawls and fights in the workshops to the great revolts, riots and revolutions of the workers, from continual brutalities in workshop and street and the daily settlement of scores to the most formal affray; from personal hatreds to the great hatreds of the people.[13]

Beijing in the 1920s, as a great urban center, contained its share of crises, conflicts, disturbances, brawls, settlements of scores, and personal hatreds. However, the city was not very productive of great revolts and great hatreds. To be sure, slowness of modernization and growth in Beijing lessened the kind of social and demographic pressures Chevalier points to in the case of Paris as principal causes of urban unrest. At the same time, a reading of the Beijing local press provides ample evidence of workshops, streets, and neighborhoods torn by an assortment of intense conflicts.

Nonetheless, conflicts that advanced from a base of individual and group antagonisms to the level of citywide politics with hatreds and antagonisms intact or enhanced, such as the 1929 streetcar riot, were the exceptions to the rule of social order. Somewhere along the way, as issues, and the aggrieved groups and movements attached to them, passed through and along the trenches of city politics, conflicts were buffered and mediated. The resulting image and reality of social peace impressed many visitors and observers for whom Beijing seemed a picture of perpetual calm. A visitor fresh from Shanghai and Nanjing who pronounced the city "placid" was startled upon his arrival by the sudden clang of a streetcar bell in the quiet of the train station and charmed by the solitary movements practitioners of *taijiquan* (the Chinese exercise system of slow, circular movements) in Sun Yat-sen Park.[14] It was not simply that, judging from local sources and documents, beneath this placid surface the city was turbulent and conflict-ridden. Rather, these calm surfaces represented the actual face used in public settings by elites, leaders, managers, and institutions to convey a sense of order in an environment threatened by chaos and disorder. The suddenness with which calm surfaces erupted into political storms, and the urgency with which mediators worked to quiet these waters and political entrepreneurs competed to fish in them, suggests that consensus, conflict, and restoration of order were part of the same continuous process.

Constant references to the importance of social peace, local order, and unity and to the dangers of disorder, troublemaking, and faction in the political statements of diverse institutions and groups reflected hopes and anxieties natural to a disordered age. But this way of talking about city life also followed a definite political logic. Harmony was politically valuable not only as a goal in itself but also as a means of enhancing the impact of conflict and dissension.[15] The ritual display of harmonious relations among chamber of commerce leaders or party cadres set the stage for dramatic clashes between rivals and factions. The idealized picture of leaders fulfilling their fiduciary responsibilities worked in the short run to head off challenges to incumbents, and in the long run to provide leverage for critics and insurgent groups prepared to accuse persons in authority of embezzlement, nepotism, despotism, and betrayal of public trust. Praise ritually bestowed on leaders saddled them with "campaign promises" that could never be kept. Public shows of unity masked factional maneuvering, while open political confrontation presaged reconstruction of group or institutional harmony.

Any attempt to reconstitute a unified Chinese political order would build on and reinforce this obsession with social order and at the same time create the conditions under which factional opposition and social movements could reemerge. The "tallness" of political and social hierarchies made to stretch across a continent and into densely populated, highly stratified cities and towns put considerable tension into relationships between and among national, regional, local, and sublocal levels. Looking ahead in time with this perspective, the consensual nature of politics in China in the 1950s, when the Communist party was able to enforce unity and suppress conflict, stands out as a major anomaly in modern Chinese urban history. The Cultural Revolution, with its multileveled factional struggles, double game of group competition and mass movement, and complex transactions between players at the center and in local arenas, displayed patterns of positional and movement politics already recognizable in the Republican era. While it is unlikely that Chinese cities will return anytime soon to the particular disorders of the twenties or the sixties, political struggles will continue, played out against a framework of jointed hierarchies, pivoting on the behavior and misbehavior of cadredom, and politically conscious social classes and groups.

The modern Chinese urban tradition, which emerged in the 1920s, includes both conflict and consensus as intertwined themes and principles. Chinese cities produced neither a Great Revolution nor a state capable of stopping one from emerging in the countryside. They did contribute to both revolution and state making before and after 1949 by producing, one the one hand, class conflict, political radicalism, modern public opinion, habits of political violence, and the central images and symbols of mass nationalism and, on the other, police forces and other elements of "cadredom," a corporate style of social organization, formal and informal techniques for mediating and controlling social conflict, and a powerful sense of support for social peace and economic security. No city or alliance of city-based forces ever proved capable of ordering these contradictory tendencies into a self-conscious, self-interested urban political order. Instead, cities became storehouses of political technique, strategy, and sentiment open to anyone with the understanding and the will to inventory and exploit them.

Notes

Periodicals that have been cited frequently in the notes have been identified by the following abbreviations:

GSK	*Gendai Shina no kiroku*
JCGB	*Jingshi jingcha gongbao*
NCS	*North China Standard*
North China Herald	*The North-China Herald and*
	Supreme Court and Consular Gazette
STSB	*Shuntian shibao*
XDPL	*Xiandai pinglun*
YSB	*Yishi bao*

Preface

1. See, for example, Andrew J. Nathan, *Peking Politics, 1918–1923: Factionalism and the Failure of Constitutionalism* (Berkeley and Los Angeles: University of California Press, 1976); Ernest Young, *The Presidency of Yuan Shih-k'ai: Liberalism and Dictatorship in Early Republican China* (Ann Arbor: University of Michigan Press, 1976); Chow Tse-tsung, *The May Fourth Movement: Intellectual Revolution in Modern China* (Stanford: Stanford University Press, 1967).

2. Nathan, especially chap. 7, "The Republic Debased, 1923."

3. The question of what is "distinctive" about modern Chinese urbanism has been a focus of recent scholarship on Chinese cities. See Martin K. Whyte and William L. Parish, *Urban Life in Contemporary China* (Chicago: University of Chicago Press, 1984), and William T. Rowe, *Hankow: Commerce and Society in a Chinese City, 1796–1889* (Stanford: Stanford University Press, 1984).

Chapter 1

1. Descriptions of Beijing as a built environment can be found in Yu Qichang and Chen Keming, eds., *Gudu bianqian jilue* (On the transformation of the capital; Beiping: n.p., 1941); Juliet Bredon, *Peking* (New York: Oxford University Press, 1982); and Oswald Siren, *The Walls and Gates of Peking* (London: Lane, 1924).

2. The late-imperial city's rigid attention to the central location of the palace complex, organization along a north-south axis, and a grid pattern of avenues, reflected the restoration of ancient canons on the cosmology of city planning. Arthur Wright, "The Cosmology of the Chinese City," in G. W. Skinner, ed., *The City in Late Imperial China* (Stanford: Stanford University Press, 1977), p. 72.

3. Li Chengyi, *Sanshi nian lai jiaguo* (My home and country in the last thirty years; Hong Kong: Chen hua Press, 1961), pp. 4–5.

4. Praise for the beauty of the Beijing sky is from Chi Tang [pseud.], "Beiping di haohuai" (Beiping's good and bad points), in Tao Kangde, ed., *Beiping yigu* (A glance at Beiping; Shanghai: Yuzhou feng she, 1938), p. 2. Leonardo Benevolo describes eighteenth-century Naples as "a gigantic monumental ensemble unique in all Italy" in *The History of the City*, trans. Geoffrey Culverwell (Cambridge: MIT Press, 1980), p. 701.

5. Peter Quennell, *A Superficial Journey Through Tokyo and Peking* (London: Faber and Faber, 1934), pp. 181–182.

6. Sidney Gamble, *Peking: A Social Survey* (New York: George H. Doran, 1921), p. 62.

7. *Jingwu guize* (Rules of police work; Beijing: Shuntian shibao, 190?), "Jingwu guize," p. 31.

8. Reported by Naito Konan in a 1911 article: "Constitutional Government in China," in Joshua Fogel, ed. and trans., "Naito Konan and the Development of the Conception of Modernity in Chinese History," *Chinese Studies in History* 17:1 (Fall 1983): 61.

9. Marshall Berman, *All That Is Solid Melts into Air: The Experience of Modernity* (New York: Simon and Schuster, 1982), p. 194.

10. Mark Girouard discusses the notion of the European "city as export" in his book *Cities and People* (New Haven: Yale University Press, 1985).

11. Bredon, pp. 133–146.

12. The exception was Duan Qirui's seat of government in Iron Lion Lane east of the Imperial City. Li Chengyi, p. 8.

13. This process of political decay was already apparent earlier in the decade. See Andrew J. Nathan, *Peking Politics, 1918–1923: Factional-*

ism and the Failure of Constitutionalism (Berkeley and Los Angeles: University of California Press, 1976).

14. *NCS*, 17 March 1927, p. 8; 22 March 1927.

15. Gavan McCormack, *Chang Tso-lin in Northeast China, 1911–1925: China, Japan, and the Manchurian Idea* (Stanford: Stanford University Press, 1977), p. 210.

16. See Joseph Levenson's discussion of "the Hung-hsien emperor [Yuan Shikai] as a comic type" in "Volume Two: The Problem of Monarchical Decay," *Confucian China and Its Modern Fate* (Berkeley and Los Angeles: University of California Press, 1968), pp. 3–7.

17. *YSB*, 4 June 1928, p. 2.

18. McCormack, p. 248.

19. *NCS*, 9 June 1928, pp. 1, 12. Bao was captured by Nationalist forces shortly after his departure from Beijing. He and his troops were returned to Beijing, where leading lights of the Peace Preservation Association ensured their favorable treatment. In early July they were allowed to leave for Mukden.

20. Beiping was the name given the city at the beginning of the Ming dynasty. Beiping became Beijing when the capital was moved north in 1409.

21. A directive issued in Nanjing claimed that "corrupt elements" had "usurped" Beijing and continued to pose a threat to the revolution. *YSB*, 7 July 1928, p. 7.

22. *YSB*, 1 July 1928, p. 3.

23. *YSB*, 4 July 1928, p. 3.

24. Ibid.

25. *YSB*, 6 July 1928, p. 7.

26. *YSB*, 4 July 1928, pp. 2–3.

27. *Peking Leader*, 9 July 1929, p. 1.

28. Ibid., 11 July 1929, p. 1.

29. As late as 1925 the foreign ministry continued to function, including the convening of a tariff conference in Beijing. See Yen Hui-ch'ing's account of his tenure as foreign minister in his memoir, *East-West Kaleidoscope, 1877–1946* (New York: St. John's University Press, 1974). But after the Anfu-Zhili war in 1920, the government was progressively debilitated as it failed to meet payrolls. *NCS*, 16 June 1926, pp. 2–3. By mid-decade the degree to which official salaries were in arrears was thought to be worse than at any time since the Taiping Rebellion. *STSB*, 1 January 1927, p. 5.

30. Lu Xun, who worked in the Ministry of Education from 1912 to 1926 under twenty-seven different ministers, conveys this impression in his diaries and fiction. William A. Lyell, *Lu Hsun's Vision of Reality*

(Berkeley and Los Angeles: University of California Press, 1976), p. 125.

31. Informal estimates placed the number of aspirants for official position as high as 100,000. Gamble, *Peking*, p. 101; *NCS*, 18 April 1926, p. 8. A good estimate of the total number of officials and government workers in 1925 is 80,000. L. K. T'ao, "Unemployment Among Intellectual Workers in China," *Chinese Social and Political Science Review* 13 : 3 (July 1929): 3.

32. "Xi Ying" [pseud.], *Xi Ying xianhua* (Idle gossip from Xi Ying; Shanghai: Xinyue shudian, 1928), p. 127.

33. The term is used, for example, in a 1920 newspaper article on the efforts of chamber of commerce leaders to ensure that their organization functions "without the slightest bureaucratic odor" or official interference. *YSB*, 22 April 1920, p. 7.

34. *YSB*, 9 October 1928, p. 7.

35. Qu Zhisheng, *Pingyong ji* (Mediocre writings; Taibei: Taiwan Shangwu yinshu guan, 1958), p. 120.

36. Frederic Wakeman, Jr., *The Fall of Imperial China* (New York: Free Press, 1975), pp. 76–78.

37. In 1926 a police census counted 913,000 residents within the city walls. Thirty percent were natives of the city, 40 percent were from other provinces, and 273,000 were classified as bannermen (*qiren*). *NCS*, 19 November 1926, p. 1. Another 150,000–200,000 persons lived outside the city walls in Beijing's suburbs. The size of the city's population remained slightly above one million throughout the decade. For example, a police census recorded 1,133,541 individuals in the city and suburbs in 1922 and 1,287,516 in 1928. (*China Weekly Review*, 11 March 1922, p. 74; *STSB*, 10 September 1928, p. 7.)

38. The disorders associated with the Boxer Rebellion disrupted payment of stipends. See chapter 4 on the recruitment of impoverished bannermen as policemen.

39. See, for example, late-Qing writer Wu Wo-yao's story "A Bannerman at the Teahouse," trans. Gloria Bien, *Renditions* 4 (Spring 1975).

40. For example, in 1924 payment to bannermen was forty months in arrears, at which time the Ministry of Finance released 40,000 yuan for stipends amounting to only 16–50 coppers per recipient. *NCS*, 11 April 1924, p. 8.

41. *NCS*, 23 October 1929, p. 8. The issue contains an article entitled "The Manchus of Yesterday and Today," by Jermyn Lynn.

42. "Wei Gan" [pseud.], *Beiping yehua* (Evening chats in Beiping; Shanghai: Zhonghua shuju youxian gongsi, 1935), pp. 4–5.

43. *YSB*, 15 April 1924, p. 7.

44. "Chi Tang," *Beiping's Good and Bad Points*, in Tao Kangde,

pp. 2–3.

45. *New York Times*, 1 January 1928, III, p. 7.

46. Peter Quennell, *The Marble Foot* (London: Collins, 1976). Excerpted in the *Times* (London), 4 September 1976, p. 7.

47. George Kates, *The Years That Were Fat* (Cambridge: MIT Press, 1967), p. 87.

48. Guy Alitto, "Rural Elites in Transition: China's Cultural Crisis and the Problem of Legitimacy," in Susan Mann Jones, ed., *Political Leadership and Social Change at the Local Level in China from 1850 to the Present: Select Papers from the Center for Far Eastern Studies*, University of Chicago, vol. 3 (1978–79), pp. 218–275.

49. See William T. Rowe, *Hankow: Commerce and Society in a Chinese City, 1796–1889* (Stanford University Press, 1984). Rowe documents the "rise of a guild-centered, sub-rosa municipal apparatus" in post-Taiping Hankou.

50. Ira Katznelson, *City Trenches: Urban Politics and the Patterning of Class in the United States* (New York: Pantheon, 1981). Katznelson in turn borrows the metaphor of "trench-systems" from Antonio Gramsci. See Gramsci, *Selections from the Prison Notebooks*, Quintin Hoare and Geoffrey N. Smith, eds. and trans. (New York: International Publishers, 1971), pp. 229–239.

Chapter 2

1. Richard Gilman isolates the notion of "falling away or down" from "standards, norms, 'classical' achievements" as the core meaning of decadence. Gilman, *Decadence: The Strange Life of an Epithet* (New York: Farrar, Straus and Giroux, 1979), p. 68.

2. A rough calculation of the number of fares taken by rickshaw men can be made through a comparison of the rickshaw and streetcar businesses. We can determine the average cost of a *streetcar* fare for 1926, a year for which good data on the rickshaw trade are also available:

$$\frac{\text{gross revenues for 1926}}{\text{total fares}} = \text{average fare } \frac{\$727,866}{22,885,299} = \$.03$$

(source: H. O. Kung, "Tramways in Shanghai, Tientsin, and Peiping," *Far Eastern Review* [February 1937]). Based on a sample of journeys using four coppers per *li* as the standard (though highly variable) rate for rickshaws in 1926, riding a rickshaw turns out to be about twice as expensive as the streetcar. Rickshaw and streetcar rates are from *(Shiyong) Beijing zhinan* (A practical guide to Beijing; Shanghai: Commercial Press, 1926), part 6, p. 16. Ignoring for the moment the fact that rickshaw journeys, on the average, were likely to be somewhat shorter than street-car journeys (because of the speed advantage of the streetcar over longer distances), assume that the average rickshaw fare was $.06. Gross earnings in the rickshaw trade can be calculated on the basis of estimates of the average daily income of individual rickshaw men: $.47 ("Economic Study of the Peking Ricsha Puller," *Chinese Economic Monthly* 3:6 [June 1962]: 256); $.54 (L. K. T'ao, *Livelihood in Peking* [Beijing: China Foundation for the Promotion of Education and Culture, 1928], p. 124); and $.66 (Sidney Gamble, *How Chinese Families Live in Peiping* [New York: Funk and Wagnalls, 1933], p. 32). Assuming 60,000 pullers working 331 days a year ("Economic Study of the Peking Ricsha Puller," p. 256), that yields 9.4, 10.7, and 13.1 million dollars a year, respectively, in gross earnings. The total number of fares per day would come to 429,223, 488,584, and 598,173. These figures suggest an average of between 7 and 10 fares a day per rickshaw man. The average puller spent about four or five hours a day actually pulling. Li Jinghan, "Beijing renli chefu xianzhuang di diaocha" (An investigation of conditions among rickshaw pullers in Beijing), *Shehui xue zazhi* (Journal of Sociology) 2:4 (April 1925). This puts the average ride between thirty and forty minutes for a distance of two or three miles, plausible averages given the distances involved in travel around Beijing.

3. Li Jinghan, "An investigation of conditions," p. 1.

4. Harry A. Franck, *Wandering in Northern China* (New York: Century Co., 1923), p. 197. Contemporary photographs bear out this impression. See, for example, street scenes in Heinz v. Perckhammer, *Peking* (Berlin: Albertus-Verlag, 1928).

5. Tan Shih-hua, *A Chinese Testament*, as told to S. Tretiakov (New York: Simon and Schuster, 1934), p. 235.

6. Peter Quennell, *A Superficial Journey Through Tokyo and Peking* (London: Faber and Faber, 1934), p. 187.

7. Yi-tsi Feuerwerker, "The Changing Relationship Between Literature and Life," in Merle Goldman, ed., *Modern Chinese Literature in the May Fourth Era* (Cambridge: Harvard University Press, 1977), p. 302. See also Jonathan Spence's discussion of the genre in his book *The Gate of Heavenly Peace: The Chinese and Their Revolution* (New York: Viking, 1981), pp. 194–195, 397–398.

8. Spence, pp. 194–195.

9. Huang Gongdu, "Duiyu wuchan jieji shehui taidu di yige xiao-xiao ceyan" (A short test for proletarian consciousness), *Shehui xue jie* (Sociological World) 4 (June 1930): 158.

10. For a brief account of Lao She's early life, see Ranbir Vohra, *Lao She and the Chinese Revolution* (Cambridge: Harvard East Asian Research Center, 1974), pp. 5–9.

11. Lao She, *Lao niu poche* (Old ox and a broken cart; Hong Kong: Yuzhou shudian, 1981), p. 48, cited and translated in Vohra, p. 70.

12. See, for example, "Liu's Court" and "Black Li and White Li," in Wang Chi-chen, ed. and trans., *Contemporary Chinese Short Stories* (New York: Columbia University Press, 1944).

13. Lao She, "Wo zenyang xie *Luotou Xiangzi*" (How I wrote *Luotou Xiangzi*), in Hu Xieqing, ed., *Lao She shenghuo yu chuangzuo zishu* (An account of Lao She's life and creative work in his own words; Hong Kong: Sanlian shudian, 1981), p. 66.

14. Ibid., pp. 67–68.

15. Ibid., p. 68.

16. Tsuchida Mitsufumi, "Rickshaw," *Kodansha Encyclopedia of Japan*, vol. 6 (Tokyo: Kodansha, 1983), p. 311; Joseph I. C. Clarke, *Japan at First Hand: Her Islands, Their People, the Picturesque, the Real* (New York: Dodd, Mead and Co., 1920), p. 182; and John R. Black, *Young Japan*, vol. 2 (London: Trubner, 1881), p. 312.

17. "Economic Study of the Peking Ricsha Puller," p. 253.

18. Edward T. C. Werner, "Peking in the Eighties," in E. T. C. Werner, *Autumn Leaves: An Autobiography with a Sheaf of Papers, Sociological, Philosophical, and Metaphysical* (Shanghai: Kelly and Walsh, 1928), p. 167.

19. Hattori Unokichi, *Pekin rōjō nikki*, Ōyama Azusa, ed. (Tokyo: Heibonsha, 1965), pp. 199–200.

20. Ibid.

21. Li Jinghan, "An investigation of conditions," p. 1.

22. *Chinese Economic Bulletin*, 10 October 1925, pp. 209–210; 2 January 1926, p. 11; 11 April 1925, p. 212; 23 April 1927, p. 211.

23. A former Minister of Justice quoted in *Millard's Review*, 8 November 1919, p. 408.

24. The number of rickshaws and rickshaw pullers in Beijing were as follows:

year (and month)	public	private	total	pullers
1915				20,859
1923 (September)	24,000	6,941	30,941	
1923			41,553	70,000
1924 (April)	29,000	7,500	36,500	70,000
1924			44,200	60,000
1925 (June)	18,937	6,940	25,877	
1925 (September)	18,899			
1929 (February)	30,252			
1930	38,600	4,300		

The figures are from T'ao, *Livelihood*, p. 106; "Economic Study of the

Peking Ricksha Puller," p. 253; *China Weekly Review*, 8 September 1923, p. 68; Li Jinghan, "An investigation of conditions," p. 1; *STSB*, 17 April 1924, p. 7; and Lou Xuexi, Chi Zehui, and Chen Wenxian, eds. and comps., *Beiping shi gongshang ye gaikuang* (A survey of industry and commerce in the city of Beiping; Beiping: Beiping shi shehui ju, 1932), p. 638.

25. *Chinese Economic Bulletin*, 27 February 1926, p. 11.

26. Li Jinghan, "Beiping zuidi xiandu di shenghuo chengdu di taolun" (A discussion of the lowest standard of living in Beijing), *Shehui xue jie* 3 (September 1929). These were families earning less than 200 yuan a year. Three-quarters of the households spent less than two dollars a year. In poor and working-class families, 60 to 70 percent of income went for food, making transportation a definite luxury. In higher income brackets, the amount of money and percentage of income spent on travel by rickshaw, automobile, streetcar, and train rose steeply. Sidney Gamble, *How Chinese Families Live in Peiping* (New York: Funk and Wagnalls, 1933), pp. 170–171.

27. The term "walking city" was coined by Sam B. Warner in his book *Streetcar Suburbs: The Process of Growth in Boston, 1870–1900* (Cambridge: Harvard University Press, 1962).

28. *Beijing zhinan* (Guide to Beijing; Shanghai: Zhonghua shudian, 1917), part 6, p. 5.

29. H. Y. Lowe [Lu Xingyuan], *The Adventures of Wu: The Life Cycle of a Peking Man*, vol. 2 (Princeton: Princeton University Press, 1983), p. 24.

30. *XDPL*, 3:64 (27 February 1926): 230.

31. Zhang Youyu, "Wodi huiyi" (My reminiscences), *Wenshi ziliao xuanbian* 9 (A compendium of historical materials; Beijing: Beijing chuban she, 1981), p. 5.

32. Li Jinghan, "Lowest standard of living," p. 3.

33. Ibid., p. 6.

34. Ibid., p. 2.

35. Li Jinghan, "Beijing lache di kugong" (The hard life of Beijing's pullers), *XDPL*, 3:62 (13 February 1926): 5. The survey of one thousand pullers found the following distribution by native place and former occupation:

Beijing	53	banner	25
Metropolitan District	31	peasant	24
Zhili	9	worker	18
Shandong	5	peddler	13
other	2	soldier	5
		none	15

36. Lao She, *Luotou Xiangzi* (Camel Xiangzi; Hong Kong: Nanhua shudian, n.d.), p. 39.

37. Wang Cifan, "Nongcun dizhu yu dushi pinmin" (A village landlord and the urban poor), *Duli pinglun* (Independent Review) 106 (1934): 6.

38. Li Jinghan, "Lowest standard of living."

39. Li Jinghan, "Hard life," p. 5. Six percent more pullers were working in Beijing in the winter than in the summer.

40. *China Weekly Review*, 3 March 1934, p. 24.

41. *Chinese Economic Bulletin*, 1 January 1927, p. 9.

42. In Chengdu, a smaller-scale version of Beijing's combination of administrative and commercial functions, almost all of the city's 7–8,000 rickshaw men were drawn from the urban unemployed. Ibid., 23 April 1927, p. 212.

43. Li Hua, "Qianyan" (Preface), Li Hua, ed. and comp., *Ming Qing yilai Beijing gongshang huiguan beike xuan bian* (Selected stele of industrial and commercial guilds in Ming and Qing Beijing; Beijing: Wenwu chuban she, 1980), p. 14.

44. Niida Noboru, "The Industrial and Commercial Guilds of Peking and Religion and Fellow Countrymanship and Elements of Their Coherence," *Folklore Studies* (1950).

45. *Luotou Xiangzi*, p. 2.

46. "Economic Study of the Peking Ricsha Puller," p. 256.

47. *YSB*, 26 January 1923, p. 7; 13 August 1923, p. 7.

48. For example, municipal records for 1930 show that during the year 2,278 businesses closed and 2,838 opened; 118 old teahouses went out of business, and 136 new ones opened their doors; 106 coal stores closed, and 119 opened, and so forth. *Beiping shi gongbao* 80 (19 January 1931).

49. *NCS*, 3 May 1925, p. 8.

50. Chu Chi-ch'ien and Thomas Blaisdell, Jr., *Peking Rugs and Peking Boys: A Study of the Rug Industry in Peking* (Beijing: Chinese Social and Political Science Association, 1924), p. 30.

51. Li Jinghan, "Hard life," p. 6.

52. *Chinese Economic Bulletin*, 2 June 1928, pp. 274–276.

53. Ibid., 21 April 1928, pp. 196–198.

54. T'ao, *Livelihood*, p. 48.

55. *YSB*, 9 January 1921, p. 5; 28 May 1921, p. 7; 11 February 1925, p. 7; 31 July 1921, p. 7.

56. "Tun Tu" [pseud.], "Beiping di yang chefu" (Beiping rickshaw men), in Tao Kangde, ed., *Beiping yigu* (A glance at Beiping; Shanghai: Yuzhou fengshe, 1938), pp. 165.

57. Ye Dezun, "Shehui shenghuo (renli che)" (Social livelihood [The rickshaw]), *Xin Zhongguo za* (New China) 1:1 (September 1919): 123.

58. *XDPL*, 3:64 (27 February 1926): 9.

59. "Lao Xuan" [pseud.], *Shibao fenghua* (Gibberish from the *Truth Post*; Beiping: Shibao chuban she, 1935), pp. 116–117.

60. Zhang Houzai, "Renli che wenti" (The rickshaw question), *Xin Zhongguo za* 1:1 (September 1919): 113.

61. *YSB*, 28 January 1921, p. 5.

62. *YSB*, 26 January 1921, p. 5.

63. *YSB*, 17 June 1921, p. 7.

64. Zhang Houzai, p. 112.

65. *XDPL*, 3:64 (27 February 1926): 230.

Chapter 3

1. Li Jinghan, "Beijing renli chefu xianzhuang di diaocha" (An investigation of conditions among Beijing rickshaw pullers), *Shehui xue zazhi* (Journal of Sociology) 2:4 (April 1925): 15.

2. "Economic Study of the Peking Ricsha Puller," *Chinese Economic Monthly* 3:6 (June 1926): 256.

3. Lao She, *Luotou Xiangzi* (Hong Kong: Xuelin youxian gongsi, n.d.), p. 7.

4. Wu Guang, "Yi Beiping gong qingtuan dixia douzheng pianduan" (Reminiscences of the underground struggles of the Communist Youth League in Beiping), *Hongqi piaopiao* (The Red Flag Waves; Beijing: n.p., 1957): 131.

5. *YSB*, 15 October 1929, p. 7 (a rickshaw man run over by a herd of cattle); and 25 December 1924 (a puller whose vehicle was damaged in a collision with a horse-drawn carriage).

6. Ibid., 20 July 1922, p. 7.

7. "Tun Tu" [pseud.], "Beiping di yangchefu" (Beiping rickshaw men), *Beiping yigu* (A glance at Beiping; Shanghai: Yuzhou fengshe, 1938), p. 164.

8. *YSB*, 16 May 1929, p. 7.

9. L. K. T'ao, *Livelihood in Peking: An Analysis of the Budgets of Sixty Families* (Beijing: China Foundation for the Promotion of Education and Culture, 1928), p. 125.

10. *Huabei ribao*, 10 September 1929, p. 6.

11. *JCGB*, 5 April 1928, p. 3.

12. A death typically attributed to *feipao* is reported in *YSB*, 19 October 1920, p. 5. The police attempt to crack down on the practice is reported in *YSB*, 26 October 1920, p. 5.

13. Listed here are some average rickshaw fares in the years between 1911 and 1940:

year	per month	per day	per hour	per mile (li)
1911			25 cents	
1917	$20.00	$1.30	20 cents	2 coppers
1920			16 cents	
1926	$18.00	$1.00	10 cents	4 or 5 coppers
1940				4 coppers

The rates for 1911, 1917, 1920, 1926, and 1940 are drawn respectively from Emil S. Fischer, *Guide to Peking and Its Environs Near and Far* (Beijing: Tientsin Press, 1925), p. 11; *Beijing zhinan* (Guide to Beijing; Shanghai: Zhonghua shudian, 1917), part 6, p. 5; Sidney Gamble, *Peking: A Social Survey* (New York: George H. Doran, 1921), p. 63; *(Shiyong) Beijing zhinan* (A practical guide to Beijing; Shanghai: Commercial Press, 1926), part 6, p. 16; and *Pekin annai ki* (A guide to Beijing; Tokyo: Shimin inshōkan, 1940), p. 342. The 1911 and 1920 rates are for foreigners and thus are somewhat higher than average. The rise in the copper rate is explained by the radical devaluation of copper currency in the 1920s.

14. Ellen N. La Motte, *Peking Dust* (New York: Century Co., 1920), p. 20. La Motte compares the slow and measured pace of the Tokyo puller with the frenetic speed of young rickshaw men in Beijing and attributes the difference to greater competition.

15. "Tun Tu," p. 161.

16. *JCGB*, 22 January 1928, p. 3.

17. Li Jinghan, "An investigation of conditions," p. 1.

18. Lao She, *Luotou Xiangzi*, p. 3.

19. Ibid., p. 2.

20. George Kates, *The Years That Were Fat* (Cambridge: MIT Press, 1967), p. 99.

21. Qu Zhisheng, "Beiping shehui diaocha suo" (The Beiping Social Research Institute), in Qu Zhisheng, *Pingyong ji* (Mediocre writings; Taibei: Taiwan shangwu yinshu guan, 1958), p. 119.

22. *JCGB*, 6 January 1928.

23. Xi Ying [pseud.], *Xi Ying xianhua* (Idle gossip from Xi Ying; Shanghai: Xinyue shudian, 1928), p. 351.

24. *YSB*, 3 August 1920, p. 5. A rickshaw man sold his eight-year-old daughter to a "flesh merchant" for twenty-five dollars while his wife looked on and wept.

25. *New York Times*, 28 January 1928, III, p. 1.

26. *NCS*, 1 January 1928, p. 11.

27. *Beijing Ruifuxiang* (Ruifuxiang of Beijing), Ziben zhuyi jingji gaizao yanjiu shi, Zhongguo kexue yuan jingji yanjiu suo (Research Office for the Transformation of the Capitalist Economy, Chinese Academy of Sciences Economic Research Institute), ed., (Beijing: Sanlian shudian, 1959), pp. 20–23.

28. *Chinese Economic Monthly* 2:8 (May 1925).

29. *NCS*, 18 April 1924, p. 1.

30. Li Jinghan, "Beijing lache di kugong" (The hard life of the Beijing puller), *XDPL* 3:62 (13 February 1926): 5.

31. Kates, p. 253.

32. T'ao, *Livelihood in Peking*, p. 103.

33. Ye Dezun, "Shehui shenghuo (ren liche)" (Social life [The rickshaw]), *Xin Zhongguo za* 1:1 (September 1919): 127–128.

34. Lao She, *Luotou Xiangzi*, p. 79.

35. In Wang Chi-chen, ed. and trans., *Contemporary Chinese Short Stories* (New York: Columbia University Press, 1944), p. 67.

36. Gamble, *Peking*, pp. 272, 486. In these areas the percentage of the "very poor" was two to ten times greater than the average.

37. Ibid., p. 39.

38. T'ao, *Livelihood*, p. 39.

39. Li Jinghan, "Hard life," p. 5.

40. *YSB*, 1 November 1921, p. 7.

41. Wu Guang, "Reminiscences," p. 131.

42. In Shanghai, Chengdu, Guangzhou, and Fuzhou middlemen rented rickshaws from garages and sublet them to pullers. These brokers took the risk of loss or damage but also passed on the cost of this service to the rickshaw man. *Chinese Economic Bulletin* 216 (11 April 1925): 212; and "The Ricksha in Shanghai and Peking," *Chinese Economic Monthly* 2:8 (May 1925): 38.

43. See the case of an owner named Wang Ziyi who was praised in the press for his compassionate treatment of rickshaw men. *YSB*, 24 June 1921, p. 7.

44. Lao She, *Luotou Xiangzi*, p. 42.

45. *YSB*, 4 November 1924, p. 7.

46. *XDPL*, 3:64 (27 February 1926): 231.

47. Li Jinghan, "An investigation of conditions," p. 14.

48. Wu Guang, p. 31.

49. Lao She, *Luotou Xiangzi*, p. 1.

50. *JCGB*, 9 January 1928, p. 3.

51. *JCGB*, 17 January 1928, p. 3.

52. *YSB*, 28 February 1925, p. 7.

53. *YSB*, 29 September 1920, p. 5.

54. *YSB*, 14 May 1921, p. 7.

55. *YSB*, 2 September 1929.

56. *JCGB*, 1 January 1928.

57. *YSB*, 8 February 1925, p. 7.

58. On at least one occasion the police proposed, without effect, a fixed schedule of rates for rickshaw travel by the day, hour, and minute. *YSB*, 17 April 1921, p. 3.

59. *YSB*, 12 May 1928, p. 3. In this case the offender was jailed for two days.

60. *YSB*, 15 February 1928, p. 3. A policeman was especially offended when a passenger struck a rickshaw man in full view of him.

61. *JCGB*, 3 February 1928, p. 3; 3 April 1928, p. 3; 7 June 1928, p. 3; *YSB*, 14 October 1919, p. 6.

62. *JCGB*, 13 June 1928, p. 3.

63. Wu Guang, p. 134.

64. *YSB*, 18 March 1925, p. 7.

65. Kinchen Johnson, *Folksongs and Children-Songs from Peiping* (Taibei: Dongfang wenhua shuju, 1971), pp. 149–150.

66. Lao She, *Wo jeiyi beizi* (My life; Shanghai: Huiqun chuban she, n.d.), p. 23. Also noted and discussed in Michael Duke, "The Urban Poor in Lao She's Pre-War Short Stories," *Phi Theta Papers* 12 (1970): 92.

67. *Jingshi jingcha faling huizuan* (A compilation of police ordinances; Beijing: n.p., 1915).

68. *JCGB*, 7 January 1928, p. 3, and *New York Times*, 6 February 1927, p. 23, report enforcement of the rules concerning clothing.

69. *YSB*, 28 September 1922, p. 7.

70. Lao She, *Luotou Xiangzi*, pp. 265–66.

71. *JCGB*, 13 July 1928, p. 3.

72. *YSB*, 30 May 1923, p. 7.

73. Wu Guang, p. 130.

74. *YSB*, 6 April 1921, p. 7.

75. Huang Gongdu, "Duiyu wuchan jieji shehui taidu di yige xiao-xiao ceyan" (A short test for proletarian consciousness), *Shehui xue jie* (Sociological World) 4 (June 1930): 177.

76. Ibid., p. 173.

77. *XDPL*, 3:64 (27 February 1926): 232.

78. Huang Gongdu, p. 169.

79. Ye Dezun, "Social livelihood," pp. 121–122.

80. Lao She, *Luotou Xiangzi*, p. 51.

81. "Tun Tu," p. 164.

82. *XDPL*, 3:64 (27 February 1926): 230.

83. Kates, p. 97.

84. Lao She, *Luotou Xiangzi*, p. 3.

85. Vera Vishnyakova-Akimova, *Two Years in Revolutionary China, 1925–27*, trans. Stephen Levine (Cambridge: Harvard East Asian Research Center, 1971), p. 29.

86. In one case a group of rickshaw men engaged in a cat-and-mouse game with the police in an effort to maintain their hold over a lucrative spot outside a popular bathhouse. *JCGB*, 15 February 1928, p. 3.

87. *YSB*, 8 August 1923, p. 7.

88. *YSB*, 9 July 1923, p. 7.

89. *XDPL*, 3:64 (27 February 1926): 232.

90. Zhang Houzai, "Renli che wenti" (The rickshaw question), *Xin Zhongguo za* 1:1 (September 1919).

91. *Industrial Labour in Japan*, International Labour Office (Geneva: P. S. King, 1933), pp. 48, 88–89; and Jon Halliday, *A Political History of Japanese Capitalism* (New York: Pantheon, 1975), pp. 68–69, 93.

92. Jean Chesneaux, *The Chinese Labor Movement, 1919–1927* (Stanford: Stanford University Press, 1968), p. 41. Outstanding examples of rickshaw-puller militancy in China include a riot against the Shanghai streetcar company in 1918, a strike in Nanjing in 1925 to protest introduction of buses, and a riot in Hangzhou in 1929 over competition with a local bus company. Chesneaux, p. 128; *NCS*, 11 April 1925, p. 8; and *China Weekly Review*, 13 April 1929, p. 275.

93. *China Weekly Review*, 26 October 1929, p. 316. When the rent in Beiping was 30 coppers a day, the rates were 36–52 in Shanghai, 66 in Wuhu, 80 in Nanchang, 88–100 in Hankou, and 62 in Changsha.

94. Wu Guang, p. 134.

95. Li Jinghan, "An investigation of conditions," p. 19.

96. Ibid.

97. *STSB*, 1 February 1924, p. 7.

98. Some garage owners actively solicited the aid of pullers by giving the men in their establishments a five-day rent holiday. *YSB*, 4 February 1924, p. 7.

99. Ibid.

100. *YSB*, 29 April 1924, p. 7.

101. *NCS*, 24 July 1924, p. 8.

102. *Jingshi zong shanghui hangming lu* (Membership roster of the Metropolitan Chamber of Commerce; Beijing: n.p., 1925). Li Jinghan's data suggest that a larger number (385) attended guild meetings at least occasionally. Li, "An investigation of conditions," p. 19.

103. Kates, p. 15.

104. Lao She, *Luotou Xiangzi*, pp. 6–7.

Chapter 4

1. Huang Gongdu, "Duiyu wuchan jieji shehui taidu di yige xiao-xiao ceyan" (A short test for proletarian consciousness), *Shehui xue jie* (Sociological World) 4 (June 1930): 176–177.

2. Allan Silver makes the distinction between a police state and a policed society in "The Demand for Order in Civil Society: A Review of Some Themes in the History of Urban Crime, Police, and Riot," in David J. Bordua, ed., *The Police: Six Sociological Essays* (New York: John Wiley, 1967).

3. The most complete account of city administration and order-keeping in pre-twentieth-century Beijing is Alison Dray-Novey, "Policing Imperial Peking: The Ch'ing Gendarmerie, 1650–1850" (Ph.D. dissertation, Harvard University, 1981).

4. Dray-Novey, p. 15; *The China Yearbook*, 1923 ed., pp. 596–597.

5. Yu Qichang and Chen Keming, eds., *Gudu bianqian jilue* (On the transformation of the capital; Beiping: n.p., 1941), pp. 3–4.

6. *North China Herald*, 12 April 1907, p. 90.

7. Dray-Novey, p. 142.

8. Imahori Seiji, *Pekin shimin no jichi kōsei* (The self-governing organizations of the citizens of Beijing) (Tokyo: Bunkyudo, 1947).

9. For a discussion of the decisive importance of the New Policy reforms, see Mary B. Rankin, *Elite Activism and Political Transformation in China: Zhejiang Province, 1865–1911* (Stanford: Stanford University Press, 1986), chap. 6.

10. The city seemed to some a "veritable desert." Bertram L. Simpson, *Indiscreet Letters from Peking* (New York: Dodd, Mead, 1907), p. 309.

11. Robert M. Duncan, *Peiping Municipality and the Diplomatic Quarter* (Beiping: Peiyang Press, 1933), pp. 122–124.

12. Marius Jansen, *The Japanese and Sun Yat-sen* (Cambridge: Harvard University Press, 1967), pp. 137–138.

13. Kuzuu Yoshihisa, *Tōa senkaku shishi kiden* (Pioneers and patriots in East Asia; Tokyo: Kokuryū-kai shuppan-bu, 1935), vol. 2, p. 273.

14. Yano Jin'ichi, "Zadankai: rokujūnen no omoide—Yano Jin'ichi hakase o kakonde" (Discussion: memories of sixty years concerning Yano Jin'ichi), with Miyazaki Ichisada and Hagiwara Junpei, *Tōhōgaku* (Eastern Studies) 28 (July 1964): 143. During the Boxer disorders Kawashima and the Japanese had sheltered Prince Su, and Kawashima later adopted a daughter of the prince.

15. Shen Yunlong, "Xu Shichang pingzhuan" (Biography of Xu Shichang), *Zhuanji wenxue* (Biographical Literature) 13:3 (1968): 34.

16. Kuzuu, p. 285.

17. Stephen R. MacKinnon, *Power and Politics in Late Imperial China: Yuan Shi-kai in Beijing and Tianjin, 1901–1908* (Berkeley and Los Angeles: University of California Press, 1980), pp. 151–163.

18. Shen, p. 34.

19. Duncan, p. 2.

20. Kuzuu, pp. 277–281. On the decline of the gendarmerie, see Dray-Novey, pp. 201–202.

21. Ishii Ryōsuke, *Japanese Legislation in the Meiji Era* (Tokyo: Pan-Pacific Press, 1958), pp. 241–262, 459–470, 555–557.

22. Lao She, *Wo jeiyi beizi* (My life; Shanghai: Huiqun chubanshe, n.d.), p. 25.

23. Kuzuu, p. 276.

24. Shen, p. 34.

25. *North China Herald*, 13 October 1905, p. 67.

26. Ibid., 6 October 1905, p. 15.

27. Ibid., 1 December 1905, p. 521.

28. Philip J. Stead, "The New Police," in David Bayley, ed., *Police and Society* (Beverly Hills: Sage, 1977), p. 80.

29. Shen.

30. *Jingshi neicheng xunjing zongting dierci tongji shu* (The second book of statistics of the Inner City Metropolitan Police Office; Beijing: Inner City Metropolitan Police Office, 1907), pp. 33–35.

31. Stead, p. 81.

32. *North China Herald*, 12 April 1907, p. 90.

33. Frank Ki Chun Yee, "The Police in Modern China," Ph.D. dissertation, University of California, Berkeley, 1942, p. 11.

34. Yee, p. 36.

35. Fu-mei Chang Chen, "Local Control of Convicted Thieves in Eighteenth Century China," in Frederic Wakeman, Jr., and Carolyn Grant, eds., *Conflict and Control in Late Imperial China* (Berkeley and Los Angeles: University of California Press, 1975), p. 124.

36. *New York Times*, 30 December 1928, III, p. 7.

37. Dray-Novey, pp. 201–202.

38. *YSB*, 11 June 1924, p. 7; 21 March 1925, p. 7; 17 April 1920, p. 6; 22 October 1928, p. 7.

39. Sidney Gamble, *Peking: A Social Survey* (New York: George H. Doran, 1921), p. 29.

40. Raymond Fosdick, *European Police Systems* (New York: Century Co., 1915), pp. 100, 111, 130.

41. Duncan, p. 42.

42. *NCS*, 14 January 1920, p. 1.

43. *NCS*, 23 October 1929, p. 8, "6,000 of 9,000." Another article on the police from 1928 states that 90 percent of the police were Manchu. *New York Times*, 30 December 1928, III, p. 7.

44. Lao She, *My life*, p. 24.

45. Ibid., p. 23.

46. Gamble, *Peking: A Social Survey*, p. 406, and Duncan, p. 51.

47. Heinz v. Perckhammer, *Peking* (Berlin: Albertus-Verlag, 1928).

48. *Jingwu guize* (Rules of police work; Beijing: Shuntian shibao, 190?). Besides the enduring practicality of joining traditional rhetoric to modern organization, the ideas contained in the lectures would have been carried well into the Republican period by officers and men whose careers began in the last decade of the Qing and continued into the thirties. As late as 1932, one-third of the officers and men at the district level and below had joined the force before 1907. Duncan, p. 42.

49. *Jingwu guize*, "Jingwu guize" (The rules of police work), p. 1.

50. Ibid., p. 3.

51. Ibid., p. 12.

52. Ibid., p. 50.

53. I am indebted to Guy S. Alitto for the idea of the reformed policeman as modern *junzi*. See his book *The Last Confucian: Liang Shu-ming and the Chinese Dilemma of Modernity* (Berkeley and Los Angeles: University of California Press, 1979) for an appreciation of the applicability of Confucian ideas to twentieth-century China.

54. Yoshikawa Kōjirō, "Chūgoku no keisatsu (The police of China), *Yoshikawa Kōjirō zenshū* (Complete works), vol. 16 (Tokyo: Chikuma shobō, 1974).

55. *Jingshi jingcha faling huizuan* (A compilation of police ordinances; Beijing: n.p., 1915), pp. 107–108.

56. *YSB*, 1 April 1924, p. 7.

57. *YSB*, 1 July 1921, p. 7; 6 July 1921, p. 7.

58. *YSB*, 12 February 1925, p. 7; 18 June 1924, p. 7.

59. *YSB*, 25 May 1929, p. 11.

60. Lao She, *The Yellow Storm* (New York: Harcourt, Brace, 1951), p. 38.

61. *YSB*, 24 February 1925, p. 7.

62. Erving Goffman, *The Presentation of Self in Everyday Life* (New York: Doubleday, 1959).

63. Ibid., pp. 34–35.

64. Thomas Metzger, *Escape from Predicament: Neo-Confucianism and China's Evolving Political Culture* (New York: Columbia University Press, 1977), pp. 170, 187–188.

65. *Jingwu guize*, "Rules of police work," pp. 20–21.

66. Ibid., p. 24.

67. *JCGB*, 16 February 1928.

68. *JCGB*, 14 January 1928.

69. *JCGB*, 25 February 1928.

70. *JCGB*, 18 January 1928.

71. *Jingwu guize*, "Rules of police work," pp. 26–27. My emphasis.

72. *JCGB*, 10 June 1928.

73. I am indebted to William Ker Muir, Jr., for pointing out the similarity between mediation techniques as practiced by Republican-era police in Beijing and more recent experiments in the United States with mediation and "arrest avoidance." See his book *Police: Streetcorner Politicians* (Chicago: University of Chicago Press, 1979) for an illuminating discussion of the relationship between moral development and police professionalism.

74. *YSB*, 21 October 1920.

75. *Jingwu guize*, "Rules of police work," p. 66.

76. *JCGB*, 13 January 1928.

77. *YSB*, 3 April 1929, p. 7.

78. *YSB*, 16 April 1929, p. 11.

79. *YSB*, 15 July 1928, p. 3. The paper reported a story in which a policeman on watch has to run back to the precinct office to fetch the key to open a pallisade.

80. *YSB*, 2 May 1922, p. 7. A street of merchants take these steps.

81. *Beiping shi gongbao* 37 (March 1930), "Gongan baogao" (Police report): 26.

82. Silver, p. 6.

83. Ibid., p. 14.

84. Stead, p. 76. "General Instructions" issued in 1829.

85. *Jingwu guize*, "Rules of police work," p. 12.

86. Ibid., pp. 45–46.

87. Ibid.

88. Political development in an urban context includes deployment of an expanding cadre of service personnel, such as police officers, social workers, and teachers, who represent bureaucratic authority and deal with residents on a personal level on the street, in schools and neighborhoods, and within the home. The novel role of these "street-level bureaucrats" is discussed in Douglas Yates, *The Ungovernable City: The Politics of Urban Problems and Policy Making* (Cambridge: MIT Press, 1977), pp. 20–21.

89. A. M. Kotenev, *Shanghai: Its Municipality and the Chinese* (Shanghai: North-China Daily News and Herald, 1927), pp. 448–451.

90. *XDPL*, 2 May 1925.

91. The phrase is from Richard Cobb, *The Police and the People* (Oxford: Oxford University Press, 1970).

92. Li Dazhao, "Beijing shimin yinggai yaoqiu di xin shenghuo" (The new life which the people of Beijing ought to demand), *Li Dazhao xuanji* (Beijing: Remin chuban she, 1962), pp. 239–241.

93. *YSB*, 22 August 1924, p. 7.

94. The role of "streetcorner magistrate" in Beijing can be compared to the observed tendency of U.S. police officers to behave like "streetcorner politicians." Muir, pp. 270–271.

95. Philip Kuhn, "Local Self-Government Under the Republic," in Frederic Wakeman, Jr., and Carolyn Grant, eds., *Conflict and Control in Late Imperial China* (Berkeley and Los Angeles: University of California Press, 1975), p. 262.

96. In April 1923 policemen besieged the Ministry of Finance building until the government agreed to borrow $500,000 to pay back wages. *NCS*, 11 April 1923, p. 8. In June policemen joined the garrison troops of Feng Yuxiang in a strike for back pay which, through Feng, had strong political overtones. James Sheridan, *Chinese Warlord: The Career of Feng Yü-hsiang* (Stanford: Stanford University Press, 1966), p. 127.

97. *STSB*, 8 April 1923, p. 7; *NCS*, 23 March 1923, p. 7.

98. *YSB*, 6 January 1922, p. 7; 9 July 1921, p. 7.

99. *YSB*, 8 December 1924.

100. *NCS*, 29 June 1927, p. 6; 30 June 1927, p. 8.

101. Lei Jihui, *Beiping shuizhuan kaolue* (A brief examination of taxes in Beiping; Beiping: Peiping shehui diaocha suo, 1933), p. 75.

102. *Shuihui* constituted a minor example of a major trend in the rise of civic activism in late-nineteenth-century China. See Rankin, especially chap 4.

103. Susan Mann Jones, "The Organization of Trade at the County Level: Brokerage and Tax Farming in the Republican Period," in Susan Mann Jones, ed., *Political Leadership and Social Change at the Local Level in China from 1850 to the Present: Select Papers from the Center for Far Eastern Studies* (Chicago: Center for Far Eastern Studies, University of Chicago, 1979), p. 79. The term "cadredom" was coined by Philip Kuhn.

Chapter 5

1. Shirley S. Garrett, "The Chambers of Commerce and the YMCA," in Mark Elvin and G. William Skinner, *The Chinese City Between Two Worlds* (Stanford: Stanford University Press, 1974), p. 218.

2. Marie-Claire Bergère, "The Role of the Bourgeoisie," in Mary Wright, ed., *China in Revolution: The First Phase, 1900–1913* (New Haven: Yale University Press, 1968), p. 249. Susan Mann, *Local Merchants and the Chinese Bureaucracy, 1750–1950* (Stanford: Stanford University Press, 1987), pp. 152–155.

3. Ibid.

4. William Rowe, *Hankow: Commerce and Society in a Chinese City, 1796–1889* (Stanford: Stanford University Press, 1984).

5. Bergère, p. 249.

6. Ibid., p. 241.

7. Ibid., p. 249.

8. Li Hua, ed. and comp., *Ming Qing yilai Beijing gongshang huiguan beike xuan bian* (Selected stele of industrial and commercial guilds in Ming and Qing Beijing; Beijing: Wenwu chuban she, 1980), p. 172.

9. Ibid., pp. 173–175.

10. Ibid., p. 172.

11. Ibid.

12. Edward J. M. Rhoads, "Merchant Associations in Canton, 1895–1911," in Elvin and Skinner, p. 106.

13. Joseph Esherick, *Reform and Revolution in China: The 1911 Revolution in Hunan and Hubei* (Berkeley and Los Angeles: University of California Press, 1976), p. 186, and Bergère, pp. 260, 263.

14. Bergère, p. 263.

15. John Fincher, "Political Provincialism and the National Revolution," in Wright, p. 216.

16. *YSB*, 14 May 1919, p. 3.

17. Bergère, p. 282.

18. *YSB*, 22 April 1920, p. 7.

19. Biographical information on An is from *Who's Who in China: Biographies of Chinese Leaders* (Shanghai: China Weekly Review Press, 1925), pp. 1–2, and *Gendai Chūka minkoku Manshūkoku jinmeikan* (Biographical dictionary of the contemporary Chinese Republic and Manchukuo; Tokyo: Gaimusho johobu, 1923), p. 1.

20. Sixty-four silver-and-gold-refining shops belonged to the chamber in 1919, and only 15 in 1928. The number of gold-and-silver shops fell from 29 to 12. The number of jewelry stores rose from 100 to 167. Sidney Gamble, *Peking: A Social Survey* (New York: George H. Doran, 1921), pp. 461–462; and *STSB*, 30 December 1928, p. 7.

21. Madeline Chi, "Bureaucratic Capitalists in Operation: Ts'ao Julin and his New Communications Clique, 1916–1919," *Journal of Asian Studies* 34:3 (May 1975): 679.

22. *Peking Leader*, 7 June 1918, p. 4.

23. *NCS*, 28 December 1919, p. 8.

24. *YSB*, 6 May 1919, p. 6.

25. *YSB*, 22 May 1919, p. 3.

26. Gamble, *Peking*, pp. 163, 461–462.

27. Men elected president during this period included An Disheng (1918 and 1920), banker Yuan Baosan (1920), restaurateur Sun Xuexi (1922, 1924, 1926, and 1928), wine merchant Gao Jinzhao (1926), banker Zhou Zuomin (1926), and tobacco-company executive Wang Wendian (1927).

28. *STSB*, 26 February 1920, p. 11.

29. *YSB*, 8 August 1920, p. 3; 21 September 1920, p. 3; 1 October 1920, p. 3.

30. *STSB*, 20 March 1920, p. 11; 22 March 1920, p. 11.

31. *YSB*, 11 September 1920, p. 5.

32. Garrett, p. 221.

33. *YSB*, 17 September 1920, p. 3.

34. *STSB*, 7 April 1920, p. 11.

35. Andrew J. Nathan, *Peking Politics, 1918–1923: Factionalism and the Failure of Constitutionalism* (Berkeley and Los Angeles: University of California Press, 1976), p. 250.

36. Chi, p. 685.

37. *STSB*, 7 April 1920, p. 11.

38. *YSB*, 22 April 1920, p. 7.

39. *YSB*, 20 August 1920, p. 3.

40. *YSB*, 14 May 1919, p. 3.

41. *STSB*, 8 March 1920, p. 3.

42. *YSB*, 18 September 1929, p. 5. Since the chamber and Police Chief Wu had cooperated during the May Fourth Movement in an effort to moderate the potentially violent confrontation between government and students, Wu's motives in the case may have been more complex than An's accusation suggested. During the May Fourth Movement Wu had taken a relatively soft line toward student protesters and had nearly been sacked. The chamber supported Wu and helped save his job. Chow Tse-tsung, *The May Fourth Movement: Intellectual Revolution in Modern China* (Stanford: Stanford University Press, 1967), p. 146.

43. *YSB*, 8 August 1920, p. 3.

44. *STSB*, 8 March 1920, p. 7.

45. *YSB*, 8 March 1920, p. 3.

46. Ibid.

47. *YSB*, 18 September 1920, p. 5.

48. *STSB*, 8 March 1920, p. 7.

49. *STSB*, 24 March 1920, p. 11.

50. *YSB*, 19 August 1920, p. 3.

51. *YSB*, 1 September 1920, p. 5.

52. Ibid.

53. *YSB*, 17 September 1920, p. 5.

54. Ibid.

55. *YSB*, 27 February 1921, p. 5.

56. *YSB*, 31 October 1920, p. 3.

57. Ibid.

58. *STSB*, 12 January 1922, p. 7.

59. Biographical information on Zhou is from *Gendai Chūka min-koku Manshūkoku jinmeikan*, p. 219, and Howard L. Boorman and Richard C. Howard, eds., *Biographical Dictionary of Republican China*, vol. 2 (New York: Columbia University Press, 1968), pp. 427–429.

60. Lou Xuexi, Chi Zehui, and Chen Wenxian, eds. and comps., *Beiping shi gongshang ye gaikuang* (A survey of industry and commerce in the city of Beiping; Beiping: Beipingshi shehui ju, 1932), p. 559.

61. *NCS*, 5 November 1921, p. 8.

62. *STSB*, 22 April 1921, p. 7.

63. *YSB*, 17 November 1921, p. 7.

64. *NCS*, 30 November 1921, p. 1.

65. *NCS*, 20 November 1921, p. 1; 22 November 1921, p. 1.

66. *NCS*, 22 November 1921, p. 1.

67. *NCS*, 25 November 1921, p. 1.

68. *YSB*, 26 February 1921, p. 3.

69. *YSB*, 16 August 1922, p. 7. By summer 1922 there were over forty.

70. *YSB*, 8 August 1922, p. 7.

71. *STSB*, 12 January 1922, p. 7.

72. *YSB*, 8 February 1922, p. 3.

73. *STSB*, 4 February 1922, p. 7.

74. *STSB*, 10 February 1922, p. 7.

75. *STSB*, 12 February 1922, p. 7.

76. *STSB*, 18 March 1922, p. 7.

77. *STSB*, 12 February 1922, p. 7.

78. Ibid.

79. *YSB*, 8 August 1922, p. 7.

80. Gao was arrested on charges of having taken bribes in connection with the sending of a delegation to the Philadelphia Exposition. *NCS*, 28 September 1926, p. 4.

81. *NCS*, 3 March 1927, p. 8; 4 March 1927, p. 5.

82. John S. Burgess, *The Guilds of Peking* (New York: Columbia

University Press, 1928), pp. 119–121; *STSB*, 30 December 1928, p. 7.
    83. *STSB*, 12 May 1927, p. 7.
    84. *STSB*, 9 July 1927, p. 7; *NCS*, 10 July 1927, p. 1.

Chapter 6

1. The first electric streetcar on Chinese soil began operations in Hong Kong in 1888. The diffusion of streetcar technology in the period from the 1890s to 1930 was limited to Hong Kong, Shanghai, Tianjin, Beijing, and four cities in the northeast (Shenyang (Mukden), Dairen, Harbin, and Fushun). See Nagano Akira, *Development of Capitalism in China* (Tokyo: Japan Council of the Institute of Pacific Relations, 1931?), p. 73; *Chinese Economic Bulletin*, 11 September 1926, p. 156.

2. John P. McKay, *Tramways and Trolleys: The Rise of Urban Mass Transport in Europe* (Princeton: Princeton University Press, 1976), pp. 38, 47–51.

3. Ibid., pp. 67–70.

4. Ibid., p. 244.

5. Naito Konan, "Constitutional Government in China," in Joshua A. Fogel, ed. and trans., "Naito Konan and the Development of the Conception of Modernity in Chinese History," *Chinese Studies in History* 17:1 (Fall 1983): 61.

6. C. F. Remer, *Foreign Investments in China* (New York: Macmillan, 1933), p. 626.

7. For the text of the treaty and annexes describing the Beijing concessions, see John V. A. MacMurray, ed. and comp., *Treaties and Agreements with and Concerning China, 1894–1919*, vol. 2 (New York: Oxford University Press, 1921), pp. 1055–1066.

8. When the BIC went bankrupt in the summer of 1921, the French newspaper *Liberté* noted that "the event has considerable importance considering the Industrial Bank's influence. It means [abandoning] the great public works in Peking which would have made the Chinese capital city a city of French influence" (*New York Times*, 1 July 1921, p. 15).

9. "Beijing shimin yinggai yaoqiu di xinshenghuo," *Li Dazhao xuanji* (Selected works; Beijing: Renmin chuban she, 1962), pp. 239–241.

10. Ibid., p. 240.

11. *NCS*, 22 June 1921, p. 1.

12. The Paris office's speculations in the European arms trade and in commodity-shipping ventures had gone awry. While rumors in Paris about the bank's mismanaged portfolio triggered massive withdrawals between June and December of 1920, private interests and the French government tried to keep the BIC afloat by a variety of means, includ-

ing ordering the French embassy in Beijing to corroborate the local BIC branch's contention that the banking empire was still sound. *Peking and Tientsin Times*, 27 March 1922; *China Yearbook* (Tianjin: Tientsin Press, 1923), pp. 289–291.

13. *NSC*, 22 June 1921, p. 1.

14. *NSC*, 1 July 1921, p. 1; *STSB*, 1 July 1921, p. 7. The *Beijing Times* speculated that Beijing and Shanghai bankers had conspired to buy up the shares and resell them at a profit to favored customers.

15. *STSB*, 1 July 1921, p. 7.

16. *NCS*, 1 July 1921, p. 1.

17. Ibid.

18. *STSB*, 14 June 1921, p. 7.

19. *New York Times*, 1 July 1921, p. 15.

20. *STSB*, 12 July 1921, p. 3.

21. *STSB*, 12 January 1922, p. 7.

22. *China Weekly Review*, 27 October 1923, p. 308; *New York Times*, 25 December 1921, p. 3; *China Yearbook* (1923), pp. 289–291. In late 1921 the Chinese government suggested to the French that Boxer indemnity monies be used to rehabilitate the BIC. Payments that had been forgiven during the First World War were scheduled to resume in December 1922, and France agreed in principle to the diversion of funds for this purpose. By March 1922 backers of the BIC were in a position to answer the streetcar company's first call for capital. The promise of the indemnity money, one of the few solid securities left in the realm of government finance, was sufficient to maintain French participation in the streetcar project and resurrect the BIC as the Sino-French Industrial Bank (*Zhonghua shiye yinhang*). *YSB*, 11 August 1928, p. 7.

23. Liu Yifeng, "Beijing dianche gongsi jianwen huiyi" (An eyewitness account of the Beijing streetcar company), *Wenshi ziliao xuanji* (A compilation of historical materials), vol. 31, (Beijing: Wenshi ziliao chuban she, 1980), p. 265.

24. Ibid.

25. Ibid., p. 268.

26. Ibid.

27. Ibid.

28. Imahori Seiji, *Pekin shimin no jichi kōsei* (The self-governing organizations of the citizens of Beijing; Tokyo: Bunkyudo, 1947).

29. *YSB*, 23 May 1923, p. 7; 1 June 1923, p. 7; 25 July 1923, p. 7; 13 September 1923, p. 7.

30. Alexander Eckstein, *China's Economic Development: The Interplay of Scarcity and Ideology* (Ann Arbor: University of Michigan Press, 1975), pp. 131–132.

31. A nineteenth-century example is the Daoguang emperor's reluctance to shift the transport of tribute grain from the Grand Canal to a more efficient and reliable sea route at the cost of depriving hundreds of thousands of canal workers of their livelihoods. Susan Mann Jones and Philip A. Kuhn, "Dynastic Decline and the Roots of Rebellion," *Cambridge History of China*, vol. 10: *Late Ch'ing, 1800–1911*, John K. Fairbank, ed. (New York: Cambridge University Press, 1978), pp. 125–126.

32. For example, during the 1922 spring famine the police were alarmed by the sudden rapid rise in the number of pullers on the street as "harmful to *minsheng*." *YSB*, 6 March 1922, p. 7, and 8 March 1922, p. 7.

33. *Beiping shi gongbao* (Beiping Municipal Gazette) 7 (1929), "Municipal government," pp. 1–2. This document contains an account of the earlier controversy.

34. E. P. Thompson, "The Moral Economy of the English Crowd," *Past and Present* 50 (1971). Thompson's article introduced the concept to scholarly debate on this issue.

35. *YSB*, 7 December 1920, p. 5.

36. *YSB*, 21 October 1920, p. 3.

37. *STSB*, 27 November 1928, p. 7.

38. *STSB*, 1 July 1923, p. 7.

39. *Beiping shi gongbao* 7 (1929), "Municipal government," p. 1.

40. *NCS*, 28 November 1923, p. 1; 13 December 1923.

41. *NCS*, 13 December 1923.

42. *NCS*, 5 January 1924, p. 8; 18 January 1924, p. 8.

43. Liu Yifeng, p. 268.

44. *NCS*, 18 January 1924, p. 3.

45. *NCS*, 5 January 1924, p. 8.

46. *STSB*, 26 January 1924, p. 7.

47. Ibid.

48. *STSB*, 24 February 1924, p. 7.

49. See a later account of the events of 1924 in *YSB*, 5 November 1928, p. 7.

50. The following account of the events of December 1924 is from Liu Yifeng, pp. 268–270.

51. *China Perspectives* 1:3 (October 1978).

52. *YSB*, 20 December 1924, p. 7.

53. Liu Yifeng, p. 270.

54. *Beiping shi gongbao* 7 (1929), p. 1.

55. *YSB*, 5 November 1928, p. 7.

56. *YSB*, 20 December 1924, p. 7.

57. *YSB*, 21 December 1924, p. 7.

58. *YSB*, 27 December 1924.

59. *YSB*, 24 December 1924, p. 7.

60. *YSB*, 13 January 1925, p. 7.

61. *YSB*, 5 January 1925, p. 7.

62. *YSB*, 28 December 1924.

63. *STSB*, 17 April 1924, p. 7, and Li Jinghan, "Beijing renli chefu xianzhuang di diaocha" (An investigation of conditions among rickshaw pullers in Beijing), *Shehui xue zazhi* (Journal of Sociology) 2:4 (April 1925): 1.

64. Li Jinghan, "An investigation of conditions," p. 20.

65. *YSB*, 5 January 1925, p. 7.

66. *YSB*, 30 December 1924.

67. *YSB*, 9 January 1925, p. 7.

68. H. O. Kung, "Tramways in Shanghai, Tientsin, and Peiping," *Far Eastern Review*, February 1937, 62. From 1926 to 1929, as the company expanded to provide citywide service, it averaged 62,195 to 71,531 fares a day and $727,866 to $1,002,281 in gross revenues. Based on 1924 and 1926 estimates of the incomes of individual rickshaw pullers and the numbers of pullers, the rickshaw trade was an industry of over ten million *yuan* a year, or more than ten times the size of the streetcar business. (See chap. 2, n. 2.)

69. By February 1929 there were 30,252 public rickshaws registered in Beijing, slightly more than before the opening of the streetcar system. *STSB*, 2 February 1929, p. 7.

70. Kung, p. 62: 22,885,299 fares in 1926, 21,059,586 in 1930, and 22,249,280 in 1934.

71. McKay.

72. Fully three-quarters of all households in the city spent two dollars or less on transportation per year. Li Jinghan, "Beiping zuidi xiandu di shenghuo chengdu di taolun" (A discussion of the lowest standard of living in Beiping), *Shehui xue jie* (Sociological World) 3 (September 1929).

73. *(Shiyong) Beijing zhinan* (A practical guide to Beijing; Shanghai: Commercial Press, 1926), part 6, pp. 2–16.

74. Ibid., p. 11.

75. *NCS*, 24 October 1926, p. 2.

76. Kung, p. 62.

77. Liu Yifeng, p. 271.

78. Ibid., p. 270.

79. Ibid., p. 272. Many electric-company users refused to pay their bills. (*YSB*, 23 March 1925, p. 7).

80. Liu Yifeng, p. 273.

81. *YSB*, 30 January 1925, p. 7; 2 February 1925, p. 7.

82. Walter Benjamin, "Moscow," in *Reflections: Essays, Aphorisms, Autobiographical Writings*, trans. Edmund Jephcott (New York: Harcourt Brace Jovanovich, 1978), p. 111.

83. Zhang Yuanro, "Beijing yu Shanghai" (Beijing and Shanghai), *XDPL*, 6:150 (22 October 1927): 13.

84. *YSB*, 11 February 1925, p. 7.

85. *YSB*, 17 January 1925, p. 7.

86. *YSB*, 14 March 1925, p. 7.

87. *YSB*, 1 May 1925, p. 7.

88. *YSB*, 9 March 1925, p. 7.

89. *YSB*, 6 April 1925, p. 8; 7 April 1925, p. 7.

90. For a sensitive account of a comparable progression, see Henry Smith's discussion of "Streetcar Tokyo" in his article "Tokyo as an Idea: An Exploration of Japanese Urban Thought Until 1945," *Journal of Japanese Studies* 4:1 (Winter 1978). This article inspired my own approach to "Streetcar (and Rickshaw) Beijing."

Chapter 7

1. Tao Menghe, ed., *Diyici Zhongguo laodong nianjian* (China Labor Yearbook, no. 1), vol. 2 (Beiping: Institute of Social Research, 1928), p. 198; *YSB*, 30 January 1925, p. 7.

2. Jurgen Kuczynski, *The Rise of the Working Class*, C. T. A. Ray trans. (New York: McGraw-Hill, 1967), p. 51.

3. Peng Zeyi, ed., *Zhongguo jindai shougong ye shi ziliao, 1840–1949* (Materials on the history of modern Chinese handicrafts), vol. 4 (Beijing: Sanlian shudian, 1957). *Beijing gongye shiliao* (Historical materials on Beijing industry), Zhongguo renmin daxue gongye jingji xi (Industrial Economics Department of Chinese People's University), ed. (Beijing: Beijing chuban she, 1960), pp. 1–2.

4. James P. Harrison, *The Long March to Power: A History of the Chinese Communist Party, 1921–1972* (New York: Praeger, 1972), p. 22.

5. Wang Qinghua, "Gao Junyu tongzhi shengping shiji" (Comrade Gao Junyu's life story), in *Wenshi ziliao xuanbian* (A compendium of historical materials), vol. 14 (Beijing: Beijing chuban she, 1982), p. 11.

6. Wei Wei and Qian Xiaohui, *Deng Zhongxia zhuan* (A biography of Deng Zhongxia; Beijing: Renmin chuban she, 1981), pp. 45–49.

7. Ibid., p. 54.

8. *Laodong jie* (World of Labor), 21 November 1920.

9. *Chen bao*, 2 May 1921, p. 2.

10. Jean Chesneaux, *The Chinese Labor Movement, 1919–1927* (Stanford: Stanford University Press, 1968), pp. 174–175.

11. *Chen bao*, 2 May 1921, p. 2.

12. "A Brief History of the Communist Party," in C. Martin Wilbur and Julie Lien-ying How, *Documents on Communism, Nationalism, and Soviet Advisers in China, 1918–1928* (New York: Columbia University Press, 1956), p. 50.

13. Xiao Chaoran, "Guanyu Beijing gongchan dang xiaozu di jianli yu huodong" (Concerning the founding and activities of the Beijing Communist party small group), *Wenshi ziliao xuanbian* (Compendium of Historical Materials), vol. 11 (Beijing: Beijing chuban she, 1981), p. 60.

14. *Chen bao*, 2 May 1921, p. 3.

15. Wilbur and How, p. 50.

16. Chesneaux, p. 192.

17. *NCS*, 25 August 1922, p. 1; 26 August 1922, p. 8; 27 August 1922, p. 1; 12 September 1922, p. 8.

18. Chesneaux, p. 12. Chesneaux records the "paradoxical solidarity" displayed by bosses and workers (p. 81), the active role of craft guilds in the May Fourth Movement (p. 153), and the fact that powerful worker organizations in Guangzhou "still bore the marks of the old guild system" (p. 202).

19. Gail Hershatter, *The Workers of Tianjin, 1900–1949* (Stanford: Stanford University Press, 1986), p. 139.

20. Tso Shih-kan (Sheldon), *The Labor Movement in Peking* (Shanghai: n.p., 1928), pp. 68–69.

21. Sidney Gamble, *How Chinese Families Live in Peiping* (New York: Funk and Wagnalls, 1933), p. 8; Sidney Gamble and T. P. Meng, "Peking Prices, Wages, and Standard of Living," *Chinese Social and Political Science Review* 10:3 (1926): 99 and 106.

22. Gamble and Meng, pp. 105–106.

23. Lou Xuexi, Chi Zehui, and Chen Wenxian, eds. and comps., *Beiping shi gongshang ye gaikuang* (A survey of industry and commerce in the city of Beiping; Beiping: Beiping shi shehui ju, 1932), p. 147.

24. John S. Burgess, *The Guilds of Peking* (New York: Columbia University Press, 1928), pp. 94, 96.

25. Ibid., p. 95.

26. For example, labor bosses led leatherworkers in their 1925 campaign for higher wages. *YSB*, 8 February 1925, p. 7.

27. *YSB*, 10 March 1925, p. 7. A wage increase was proposed by 62 labor bosses and discussed by 127 guild representatives.

28. *STSB*, 31 March 1923, p. 7.

29. *YSB*, 30 March 1924, p. 7.

30. *YSB*, 29 March 1925, p. 7.
31. *YSB*, 31 March 1925, p. 7.
32. *YSB*, 2 April 1925, p. 7.
33. *YSB*, 20 November 1923, p. 7.
34. *YSB*, 20 April 1925, p. 7.
35. *YSB*, 14 March 1925, p. 7.
36. Sidney Gamble, *Peking: A Social Survey* (New York: George H. Doran, 1921), p. 121; *Chinese Economic Bulletin* 9 (3 July 1926), pp. 350–352.
37. *YSB*, 2 October 1924, p. 7.
38. Ibid.
39. By the summer of 1925, a water-trade guild was in evidence. *Chen bao*, 16 June 1925, p. 3.
40. *YSB*, 25 March 1925, p. 7.
41. Lou Xuexi et al., p. 660; *YSB*, 16 May 1929, p. 7.
42. *YSB*, 20 December 1924, p. 7.
43. Tao Menghe, *China Labor Yearbook, no. 1*, p. 217.
44. *YSB*, 8 May 1925, p. 7.
45. *YSB*, 15 July 1924, p. 7.
46. *YSB*, 16 July 1924, p. 7.
47. *YSB*, 17 July 1924, p. 7.
48. *YSB*, 27 July 1924, p. 7.
49. *YSB*, 19 June 1924, p. 7; 22 June 1924, p. 7.
50. *YSB*, 7 July 1924, p. 7.
51. *YSB*, 27 August 1924, p. 7.
52. *YSB*, 23 February 1925, p. 7.
53. *YSB*, 5 December 1924.
54. Lu Zhui and Li Heping, "Jiu Zhongguo Beijing di falang ji gongren zhuangkuang" (The Beijing enamel industry and the condition of workers in old China), *Beijing gongyun shiliao* (Historical materials on the Beijing labor movement), vol. 1, Beijingshi zonggonghui gongren yundong shi yanjiuzu (The Labor Movement History Research Group of the Beijing Municipal Trade Union Federation) ed., (Beijing: Gongren chuban she, 1981), p. 26.
55. *YSB*, 10 May 1925, p. 7.
56. *YSB*, 29 April 1924, p. 7.
57. *YSB*, 27 February 1925.
58. *YSB*, 1 March 1925, p. 7.
59. *YSB*, 4 March 1925, p. 7.
60. *YSB*, 8 March 1925, p. 7; 11 March 1925, p. 7.
61. *YSB*, 9 June 1924, p. 7.
62. *YSB*, 29 July 1924, p. 7.
63. *YSB*, 24 June 1924, p. 7; 26 June 1924, p. 7.

64. *STSB*, 26 March 1920, p. 11.

65. Tao Menghe, *China Labor Yearbook, no. 1*, p. 187; *YSB*, 24 March 1925, p. 7.

66. *YSB*, 8 May 1925, p. 7.

67. Chesneaux, p. 80.

68. *YSB*, 4 February 1925, p. 7.

69. *YSB*, 3 May 1925, p. 7.

70. *YSB*, 19 December 1924, p. 7.

71. Chu Chi-ch'ien and Thomas Blaisdell, Jr., *Peking Rugs and Peking Boys: A Study of the Rug Industry in Peking* (Beijing: Chinese Social and Political Science Association, 1924), pp. 19–20.

72. *YSB*, 22 October 1928, p. 7.

73. *YSB*, 24 March 1922, p. 7.

74. *JCGB*, 7 January 1928; *YSB*, 3 April 1929, p. 7.

75. *YSB*, 28 August 1924, p. 7.

76. Peter Stearns, "National Character and European Labor History," in Peter Stearns and Daniel J. Walkowitz, eds., *Workers in the Industrial Revolution: Recent Studies of Labor in the United States and Europe* (New Brunswick, N. J.: Transaction Books, 1974), p. 18.

77. See Eric Hobsbawm, "Notes on Class Consciousness," in his *Workers: Worlds of Labour* (New York: Pantheon, 1984), p. 21, for a discussion of the persistence of guild-based "consciousness of status."

78. *NCS*, 27 September 1922, p. 1; 28 September 1922, p. 1.

79. E. P. Thompson, "The Crime of Anonymity," in Douglas Hay, Peter Linebaugh, John G. Rule, E. P. Thompson, and Cal Winslow, eds., *Albion's Fatal Tree: Crime and Society in Eighteenth Century England* (New York: Pantheon, 1975), p. 255.

80. *YSB*, 26 March 1925, p. 7.

81. Liu Jiantang, "Huiyi *Xiangdao zhoukan* zai Beijing yinxing di jingguo" (Reminiscences of the process of publishing the *Guide Weekly* in Beijing), in Zhang Jinglu, ed., *Zhongguo xiandai chuban shiliao* (Historical materials on modern Chinese publishing; Beijing: Zhonghua shuju chuban, 1959).

82. *STSB*, 24 March 1925, p. 7; *NCS*, 25 March 1925, p. 1; 26 March 1925, p. 8.

83. Lynda Shaffer, "Mao Zedong and the October 1922 Changsha Construction Workers' Strike," *Modern China* 4:4 (October 1978): 397.

84. Hershatter, pp. 113–14.

85. Ma Chaojun, *Zhongguo laogong yundong shi* (A history of the Chinese labor movement; Taibei: Zhongguo laogong fuli she, 1959), vol. 1, p. 487.

86. Ibid.

Chapter 8

1. F. W. Mote, "The Transformation of Nanking," in G. W. Skinner, ed., *The City in Late Imperial China* (Stanford: Stanford University Press, 1977, p. 114).

2. G. W. Skinner, "Introduction: Urban Social Structure in Ch'ing China," in Skinner, *The City in Late Imperial China*, p. 522. Skinner makes the useful observation that Chinese cities tended to have two nuclei—one gentry, the other merchant—around which the management of community affairs was organized.

3. Richard Sennett, *The Fall of Public Man* (New York: Knopf, 1977). Sennett believes that the height of commitment to political expression in public occurred in the transitional phase of the late precapitalist European city when the convention of public display of status was turned to the task of advertising and expressing modern politics. While Sennett has been criticized for romaticizing this threshold period by way of criticizing the privatized state of contemporary culture (Marshall Berman, "Facades at Face Value," *Nation*, 6 August 1977, pp. 118–121), his insight into the mutually supportive roles of tradition and modern politics helps explain the vitality of public life in partially modernized cities like Beijing.

4. For a discussion of the growing importance of a public (*gong*) sphere in late-nineteenth-century China, see Mary Rankin, *Elite Activism and Political Transformation in China: Zhejiang Province, 1865–1911* (Stanford: Stanford University Press, 1986), pp. 15–27 and chaps. 3 and 4.

5. Jürgen Habermas, "The Public Sphere: An Encyclopedia Article," *New German Critique* 1:3 (1974), summarized and discussed in Richard R. Weiner, *Cultural Marxism and Political Sociology* (Beverly Hills: Sage, 1981), pp. 105–109.

6. I have benefited from discussions with William T. Rowe on the distinctions to be made among *guan, gong,* and *si* in the late imperial and early Republican periods. See also Rankin.

7. Ralf Dahrendorf, *Class and Class Conflict in Industrial Society* (Stanford: Stanford University Press, 1959), pp. 183–189. Dahrendorf details the preconditions of group formation in politics.

8. *Chen bao* estimated in 1925 that there were 80 dailies, 30 evening papers, and 120 news agencies in Beijing. Cited in *NCS*, 4 October 1925, p. 1; *China Weekly Review*, 8 November 1930, p. 359.

9. Lou Xuexi, Chi Zehui, and Chen Wenxian, eds. and comps., *Beiping shi gongshang ye gaikuang* (A survey of industry and commerce in the city of Beiping; Beiping: Beiping shi shehui ju, 1932), pp. 621–625.

10. Tan Shih-hua, *A Chinese Testament* (New York: Simon and Schuster, 1934), pp. 278–279. Tan describes the efforts he and fellow provincials made to publish a literary magazine on credit and by offering commissions on sales to bookstores willing to carry the journal.

11. Jun Ke Choy, *My China Years, 1911–1945: Practical Politics in China After the 1911 Revolution* (Hong Kong: Peninsula Press, 1974), p. 55. Central Park was described in 1916 as the "popular rendezvous of the fashionable public," who came to "watch the parade of fashion and discuss political gossip." A later account by a foreign journalist noted the presence of "the minor lights of the various ministries, the entire Chinese newspaper fraternity, and the fashionable ne'er-do-wells." *North China Herald*, 4 September 1920, p. 604.

12. *YSB*, 4 November 1929, p. 8. These bath gardens (*yuan*) should be distinguished from the more primitive working-class baths (*zaotang*) that dominated the trade before the new-style houses became popular.

13. Lou et al., pp. 686–687.

14. Jermyn Lynn [Lin Jihong], *The Social Life of the Chinese* (Beijing: China Booksellers, 1928), p. 34.

15. John S. Burgess, "The Problem of Prostitution," *Shehui xue za* (Journal of Sociology) 2:4 (April 1925): 4.

16. Yen Ching-yueh, "Crime in Relation to Social Change in China," Ph.D. dissertation, University of Chicago, 1934, p. 86.

17. Li Hua, "Qingyan" (Preface), in Li Hua, ed. and comp., *Ming Qing yilai Beijing gongshang huiguan beike xuan bian* (Selected stele of industrial and commercial guilds in Ming and Qing Beijing; Beijing: Wenwu chuban she, 1980), p. 20. See also Ho Ping-ti, *Zhongguo huiguan shi lun* (On the history of Landsmannshaften in China; Taibei, 1966).

18. *YSB*, 2 February 1921, p. 5.

19. *NCS*, 7 January 1921, p. 2; *STSB*, 25 January 1921, p. 7; 30 March 1921, p. 7; 8 May 1921, p. 7.

20. *YSB*, 18 February 1929, p. 7.

21. *NCS*, 8 September 1922, p. 8; 17 October 1922, p. 7; Su Ru-chiang, "Birth Control in China," Ph.D. dissertation, University of Chicago, 1946, pp. 142–143.

22. Su Ru-chiang, pp. 142–143.

23. *STSB*, 13 January 1922, p. 7.

24. *NCS*, 13 October 1923, p. 1.

25. *NCS*, 18 July 1924.

26. *STSB*, 24 March 1925, p. 7.

27. *YSB*, 16 December 1928, p. 2.

28. *YSB*, 3 May 1919, p. 3; *Wusi aiguo yundong* (The May Fourth

patriotic movement), vol. 1. Zhongguo shehui kexue yuan jindai shi yan-jiu suo (The Chinese Academy of Social Sciences Contemporary History Research Institute), ed. (Beijing: Zhongguo shehui kexue chuban she, 1979), p. 505.

29. For a discussion of the origins of interest group politics in the Republican era, see Joseph Fewsmith, "From Guild to Interest Group: The Transformation of Public and Private in Late Qing China," *Comparative Studies in Society and History* 25:4 (October 1983): 617–618.

30. *YSB*, 7 May 1919, p. 2.

31. Chow Tse-tsung, *The May Fourth Movement: Intellectual Revolution in Modern China* (Stanford: Stanford University Press, 1967), p. 106.

32. Peng Ming, *Wusi yundong zai Beijing* (The May Fourth movement in Beijing; Beijing: Beijing chuban she, 1979), p. 137.

33. Chow Tse-tsung, p. 108.

34. *YSB*, 8 May 1919, p. 2.

35. *YSB*, 22 May 1919, p. 6.

36. *YSB*, 23 May 1919, p. 6.

37. *YSB*, 3 March 1920, p. 2.

38. Huang Di, "'Wusi' yilai zhi Zhongguo xuechao" (Student unrest in China since "May Four"), *Shehui xue jie* (Sociological World) 6 (1932), contains an analysis of student protest in Beijing and other cities, showing the wide range of causes of unrest in the 1920s. Fees, examinations, opposition to particular teachers and administrators, and factional struggles among students fueled a considerable proportion of university unrest.

39. *YSB*, 25 October 1920, p. 5.

40. In 1920 Wu Peifu called for the convening of a national assembly. Ibid.

41. *YSB*, 1 August 1920.

42. *YSB*, 1 March 1920, p. 2.

43. Ibid.

44. *YSB*, 5 May 1920, p. 2. The police allowed a rally attended by 10,000 people on Beijing University's campus.

45. *YSB*, 8 August 1922, p. 7. The original inaugural date for municipal self-government was September 1, 1922.

46. *YSB*, 16 August 1922, p. 7.

47. *YSB*, 13 November 1921, p. 7.

48. Ibid.

49. *YSB*, 16 August 1922, p. 7.

50. *YSB*, 4 February 1921, p. 5.

51. Philip Kuhn, "Local Self-Government Under the Republic," in

Frederic Wakeman, Jr., and Carolyn Grant, eds., *Conflict and Control in Late Imperial China* (Berkeley and Los Angeles: University of California Press, 1975), p. 280.

52. Andrew Nathan has pointed to the deep ambivalence that modern Chinese have felt about suggestions that democracy or constitutionalism might require acceptance of state and individual interests as opposing forces rather than the assumption of essential harmony between official, public, and private realms. Nathan, *Chinese Democracy* (New York: Knopf, 1985).

53. *YSB*, 8 August 1922, p. 7.

54. Ibid.

55. *YSB*, 8 August 1922, p. 7.

56. *YSB*, 12 August 1922, p. 7; 29 August 1922, p. 7.

57. *YSB*, 2 September 1922, p. 7.

58. *YSB*, 20 May 1924, p. 7.

59. *YSB*, 13 November 1921, p. 7.

60. *YSB*, 10 August 1922, p. 7.

61. *YSB*, 10 October 1924.

62. *YSB*, 11 January 1923, p. 7.

63. *YSB*, 15 November 1924, p. 7.

64. For a concise account of the political events associated with the May Thirtieth Movement, see C. Martin Wilbur, "The Nationalist Revolution: From Canton to Nanking, 1923–1928," *Cambridge History of China*, vol. 12, *Republican China, 1912–1949*, part 1 (New York: Cambridge University Press, 1983), pp. 548–549.

65. The number of private colleges increased from twelve to twenty-nine. Ling Ping, "Survey of College, Middle School and Primary School Education in Peking During 1922–24," reported in *NCS*, 14 August 1924, p. 7. A partial census of Beijing universities and colleges in 1926 found ten government schools with 4,500 students and sixteen private schools with almost 8,000 students. *NCS*, 10 October 1926, p. 2.

66. *Beijing ribao*, 2 June 1925, p. 2.

67. Ibid., 3 June 1925, p. 2.

68. *NCS*, 15 May 1925, p. 1; 16 May 1925, p. 1; 23 May 1925, p. 1; 28 May 1925, p. 1. In response to police attempts to suppress student protests in May, the Beijing Student Union split on the question of whether to call a strike on the eve of final examinations. Students also quarreled over an impending agreement between France and China on the release of impounded customs receipts.

69. *NCS*, 8 May 1925.

70. *YSB*, 7 May 1925, p. 7.

71. *NCS*, 23 May 1925, p. 1.

72. *NCS*, 14 May 1925, p. 1.

73. *Chen bao*, 4 June 1925, p. 3; *Beijing ribao*, 4 June 1925, p. 2; *NCS*, 4 June 1925, p. 1; *Times* (London), 4 June 1925, p. 12.

74. *Chen bao*, 5 June 1925, p. 2; 7 June 1925, p. 2.

75. Ibid., 11 June 1925, p. 3.

76. *Peking Leader*, 8 October 1919, p. 4.

77. *NCS*, 4 May 1926, p. 1.

78. The Communist party branch at the Agricultural University had been active in mobilizing peasants in the western suburbs in the vicinity of the school. See Yue Tianyu, as told to Zhao Gengji and Liang Xianghan, "Wo suo zhidao di Zhonggong Beijing diwei zaoqi di geming huodong" (What I know about the Chinese Communist party Beijing committee's early period of revolutionary activity), *Wenshi ziliao xuanbian* (A compendium of historical materials), vol. 11 (Beijing: Beijing chuban she, 1981), pp. 17–18.

79. *STSB*, 13 June 1925, p. 7.

80. *NCS*, 23 June 1925, p. 1.

81. *STSB*, 27 June 1925, p. 7; *Chen bao*, 26 June 1925, p. 3.

82. *NCS*, 3 April 1925, p. 8; *STSB*, 4 May 1925, p. 7.

83. *Chen bao*, 16 June 1925, p. 3.

84. *STSB*, 23 June 1925, p. 7.

85. Ibid.

86. *NCS*, 25 June 1925, p. 8.

87. See Yue Tianyu's detailed account of early Communist activity in Beijing.

88. James P. Harrison, *The Long March to Power: A History of the Chinese Communist Party, 1921–1972* (New York: Praeger: 1972), p. 50.

89. For example, Li Dazhao arranged for contingents of Feng's men to provide protection at rallies and processions. *Li Dazhao zhuan* (A biography of Li Dazhao; Beijing: Renmin chuban she, 1979), p. 170.

90. Police Chief Zhu Shen was Duan Qirui's agent, and the Beijing garrison commander, Lu Zhonglin, was Feng Yuxiang's man.

91. *YSB*, 1 January 1925, p. 2.

92. *YSB*, 20 January 1925, p. 2.

93. *NCS*, 14 January 1925, p. 8; 8 May 1925, p. 1.

94. *NCS*, 12 May 1925, p. 1; 19 July 1925, p. 1.

95. Ch'ien Tuan-sheng, *The Government and Politics of China, 1912–1949* (Stanford: Stanford University Press, 1970), pp. 91–92. The group, known thereafter as the Western Hills faction, was expelled from the party in 1926.

96. *STSB*, 23 November 1925, p. 7.

97. An account of the fall 1925 demonstrations told from the Communist side, which captures the increasingly violent and factional tone of mass politics, can be found in Luo Jing, "Beijing minzhong fanDuan yundong yu Guomindang youpai pohuai yinmou" (The Beijing masses' anti-Duan movement and the destructive plot of the Nationalist right wing), *Xiangdao zhoubao* (Guide Weekly) 140 (30 December 1925): 1275.

98. *STSB*, 12 March 1926, p. 7; 13 March 1926, p. 7.

99. *STSB*, 18 March 1926, p. 7.

100. For accounts of the March 18 Incident, see Yue Tianyu, pp. 30–41, and *STSB*, 19 March 1926, p. 7; *NCS*, 19 March 1926, pp. 1, 5.

101. *STSB*, 2 May 1926, p. 7.

102. *NCS*, 2 December 1925, p. 8.

103. The slogan of the London Corresponding Society was "That the number of our Members be unlimited." E. P. Thompson, *The Making of the English Working Class* (New York: Vintage, 1966, p. 21. Thompson notes: "Today we might pass over such a rule as a commonplace; and yet it is one of the hinges upon which history turns. It signified an end to any notion of exclusiveness, of politics as the preserve of any hereditary *elite* or property group."

Chapter 9

1. The idea of a sequence of openings and closings affecting the way the communities are organized is derived from G. W. Skinner, "Chinese Peasants and the Closed Community: An Open and Shut Case," *Comparative Studies in Society and History* 13:3 (1971).

2. Lao She, *Luotou Xiangzi* (Hong Kong: Xuelin youxian gongsi, n.d.), p. 15.

3. *NCS*, 25 October 1925, p. 8.

4. *NCS*, 6 October 1925, p. 8.

5. *NCS*, 14 November 1925, p. 8.

6. *NCS*, 21 October 1925, p. 1.

7. Dimitrii I. Abrikossow, *Revelations of a Russian Diplomat*, ed. George A. Lensen (Seattle: University of Washington Press, 1964), pp. 168–169. Lao She describes a similar scene in a novella depicting a poor boy executed for stealing a pair of shoes. Cited in Michael Duke, "The Urban Poor in Lao She's Pre-war Short Stories," *Phi Theta Papers* 12 (1970), p. 93.

8. Henry Pu Yi, *The Last Manchu: The Autobiography of Henry Pu Yi*, ed. Paul Kramer (New York: Putnam, 1967), p. 90.

9. *STSB*, 19 November 1925, p. 7.

10. Zhu Shen was a member of the Anfu Club and a key supporter of Duan Qirui; Lu Zhonglin was a subordinate of Feng Yuxiang's. Zhu had a long history, dating back to 1912, of involvement in the Beijing police and court systems and also played a role in developing and managing several economic enterprises in the city. Data on Zhao is from *Peking Leader*, 15 April 1926.

11. Bao Yong had been active, with An Disheng, in prefectural-level self-government and reform groups. *STSB*, 12 January 1922, p. 7; 24 April 1922, p. 7.

12. Zhang Tiezheng, "Beiping liangshi gaikuang" (Food supply conditions in Beiping), *Shehui kexue zazhi* 8:1 (March 1937): 121–150.

13. *NCS*, 14 October 1925, p. 8; 18 October 1925, p. 1.

14. Yen Ching-yueh, "Crime in Relation to Social Change in China," Ph.D. dissertation, University of Chicago, 1934, p. 56. At a minimum, the figures compiled for the years 1919–1927 show an intensification of police activity during the months of the winter defense.

15. Y. L. Tong, "Social Conditions and Social Service Endeavor in Peking," *Chinese Social and Political Science Review* 7:3 (1923): 85.

16. *NCS*, 23 October 1925, p. 8.

17. *NCS*, 17 November 1925, p. 8.

18. *NCS*, 5 January 1926, p. 5; 20 January 1926, p. 8.

19. *STSB*, 18 December 1925, p. 7.

20. *NCS*, 8 January 1926.

21. There could be, however, a "spring famine" among peasants whose food supply from the previous year's harvest had run out.

22. *Peking Leader*, 21 March 1926, p. 7.

23. Ibid., 18 March 1926, p. 6.

24. *STSB*, 1 January 1927, p. 5.

25. *STSB*, 28 March 1926, p. 7.

26. *NCS*, 30 March 1926, p. 1.

27. *NCS*, 13 March 1926, p. 8.

28. *NCS*, 28 March 1926, p. 7.

29. *NCS*, 27 March 1926, p. 8.

30. *NCS*, 1 April 1926, p. 1.

31. *STSB*, 28 March 1926, p. 7.

32. *NCS*, 24 March 1926, p. 1.

33. *Chinese Economic Bulletin*, 12 February 1924, p. 7.

34. *STSB*, 28 March 1926, p. 7.

35. *NCS*, 5 May 1920. Yang must have had a special interest and expertise in military affairs. He became involved in organizing merchant corps again in 1929. *NCS*, 12 September 1929.

36. *NCS*, 3 April 1926, p. 1.

37. *New York Times,* 3 April 1926, p. 6; 4 April 1926, p. 5; 6 April 1926, p. 5.

38. *NCS,* 8 April 1926, p. 8; 9 April 1926; *Peking Leader,* 7 April 1926.

39. *Peking Leader,* 4 April 1926, p. 9.

40. Ibid., p. 1.

41. Ibid., 9 April 1926, p. 6; *NCS,* 9 April 1926, p. 5.

42. *NCS,* 8 April 1926, p. 8.

43. *NCS,* 20 April 1926, p. 8. This was five to six times the number found during the worst months of the winter defense.

44. *NCS,* 18 April 1926, p. 8.

45. Ibid., 11 April 1926, p. 8.

46. *Peking Leader,* 15 April 1926, p. 1; *NCS,* 15 April 1926, p. 8.

47. *Peking Leader,* 16 April 1926; *STSB,* 16 April 1926, p. 7; *China Weekly Review,* 17 April 1926, p. 185.

48. *NCS,* 16 April 1926, p. 1; 1 May 1926, p. 5.

49. *Peking Leader,* 17 April 1926, p. 1.

50. Ronald Suleski, "The Rise and Fall of the Fengtien Dollar, 1917–1928: Currency Reform in Warlord China," *Modern Asian Studies* 13 (1979): 643–660.

51. *NCS,* 20 April 1926, p. 1.

52. *NCS,* 21 April 1926, p. 1.

53. *NCS,* 22 April 1926, p. 1.

54. Ibid.

55. *NCS,* 22 April 1926, p. 1; 24 April 1926, p. 8.

56. *NCS,* 23 April 1926, p. 1.

57. *NCS,* 21 April 1926, p. 8.

58. *NCS,* 5 June 1926.

59. *NCS,* 7 April 1926, p. 1.

60. *NCS,* 27 April 1926, p. 1.

61. *The Yellow Storm,* trans. Ida Pruitt (New York: Harcourt Brace, 1951), p. 3.

62. *NCS,* 25 April 1926, p. 1.

63. *NCS,* 1 May 1926, p. 5.

64. *NCS,* 2 May 1926, p. 5.

65. *NCS,* 2 May 1926, p. 1.

66. *NCS,* 11 May 1926, p. 8.

67. Frederick Lane, *Venice and History* (Baltimore: Johns Hopkins Press, 1966), p. 383.

68. See C. Martin Wilbur, "Military Separatism and the Process of Reunification Under the Nationalist Regime, 1922–1937," in Ping-ti Ho and Tang Tsou, eds., *China in Crisis,* vol. 1 (Chicago: University of Chi-

cago Press, 1968), pp. 203–263.

69. *YSB*, 3 June 1928, p. 2.

70. *YSB*, 4 June 1928, p. 2.

71. *NCS*, 22 June 1928, p. 12.

72. *STSB*, 14 November 1928, p. 7; *NCS*, 15 November 1928, p. 12.

73. The others were student, worker, peasant, and women's organizations.

74. *NCS*, 3 November 1928, p. 12.

75. Joseph Fewsmith, *Party, State, and Local Elites in Republican China: Merchant Organizations and Politics in Shanghai 1890–1930* (Honolulu: University of Hawaii Press, 1985).

76. *NCS*, 15 November 1928, p. 12; *STSB*, 14 November 1928, p. 7.

77. *NCS*, 18 November 1928, p. 1.

78. *NCS*, 8 November 1928, p. 12.

Chapter 10

1. For example, in October 1927 ten workers and students were executed for attempting to organize a labor federation. *NCS*, 30 October 1927, p. 1. Thirteen alleged Communists were killed in May 1928 shortly before Fengtian forces evacuated the city. *YSB*, 18 May 1928, 7. Between April 1926 and May 1928, at the Bridge of Heaven execution ground alone, 946 "Communists, robbers, and hold-up men" were put to death. *NCS*, 31 August 1928, p. 12.

2. *YSB*, 19 July 1928, p. 3. By 1930 the Nationalists had relegated party activists and mobilizers to a minor role and so made mass mobilization of support for the regime virtually impossible. Lloyd Eastman, *Seeds of Destruction: Nationalist China in War* (Stanford: Stanford University Press, 1984), pp. 216–217; and Hsi-sheng Ch'i, *Nationalist China at War* (Ann Arbor: University of Michigan Press, 1982), pp. 184–186. The devaluation of the role of the party in Nationalist politics is also an important theme in Joseph Fewsmith's book *Party, State, and Local Elites in Republican China: Merchant Organizations and Politics in Shanghai, 1870–1930* (Honolulu: University of Hawaii Press, 1985).

3. Robert M. Duncan, *Peiping Municipality and the Diplomatic Quarter* (Beiping: Peiyang Press, 1933).

4. *YSB*, 27 June 1928, p. 3.

5. Duncan.

bureau	1929–30 budget	employees
public security	1,863,600	10,000
public works	373,153	953
social affairs	140,653	83

finance	105,814	176
education	42,739	—
public utilities	33,880	—
public health	19,662	—
land	30,597	—

6. Deng Haoming, "'Benshe' shimo" (The whole story of the "Foundation Society"), *Wenshi ziliao xuanbian* (A compendium of historical materials), vol. 9 (Beijing: Beijing chuban she, 1981), p. 86. Deng notes the continued underground activity of Communists in Beijing in 1928 and 1929.

7. *YSB*, 7 June 1928, p. 3.

8. *YSB*, 8 June 1928, p. 3.

9. *YSB*, 25 July 1928, p. 7. An informal party history claimed that "untold numbers" had been executed.

10. Ibid.

11. Howard L. Boorman and Richard C. Howard, *Biographical Dictionary of Republican China* (New York: Columbia University Press, 1970), vol. 3, pp. 276–278.

12. Zhong Dediao, "Yijiu erba nian shiyi yue Danhua huochai chang gongren daigong di qianqian houhou" ([The story] of the November 1928 slowdown [strike] at the Danhua match factory), in *Beijing gongyun shiliao* (Historical materials on the Beijing labor movement), vol. 2, Beijing shi zong gonghui gongren yundong shi yanjiu zu, ed. (Beijing: Gongren chuban she, 1981), p. 243. See also Deng Haoming, p. 91.

13. *YSB*, 25 July 1928, p. 7.

14. *YSB*, 28 June 1928, p. 3.

15. *Zhongguo guomin dang ge shengshi zong deng ji he ge dangyuan zongji* (General statistics on registered and qualified provincial and municipal members of the Chinese Nationalist party), Zhongguo guomin dang zhongyang zhixing weiyuan hui zongji chu (Statistical Office of the Central Executive Committee of the Chinese Nationalist Party; n.p., 1929). Of 1,770 members of the Beiping municipal party branch in 1929, three-quarters were in their twenties. Over 90 percent were men. Half had been to university, and 90 percent had at least a middle-school education.

16. Ibid. A large minority of party members were Hebei province and Beiping natives (33%). But the central and southern provinces of Hunan (11%) and Guangdong (7%) and neighboring Shandong (9%) and Shanxi (8%) also contributed sizable contingents.

17. Ibid. Three-quarters of the group had a "barely adequate" income (55%) or had "not enough to make ends meet" (19%).

18. Zhong Dediao, p. 243.

19. Boorman and Howard, vol. 3, p. 277. At this time Ding's followers captured key party posts in a number of other localities as well. Deng Haoming, p. 91.

20. Official figures for 1929 recorded 1,700 party members affiliated with the municipal branch. The press in 1928 reported 2,900 members in the city. *YSB*, 28 September 1928, p. 7.

21. *YSB*, 16 December 1928, p. 7.

22. *YSB*, 6 November 1928, p. 7.

23. *NCS*, 4 December 1928; 26 January 1929, p. 11; 31 January 1929, p. 12.

24. *YSB*, 14 May 1929, p. 7.

25. Zhong Dediao, p. 243.

26. *STSB*, 25 October 1929, p. 7; Yu Side, "Beiping gonghui diaocha" (An investigation of Beiping unions), *Shehui xue jie* (Sociological World) 4 (1930): 125.

27. *STSB*, 24 June 1928, p. 7; *NCS*, 24 June 1928, p. 2.

28. Local party cadres throughout the country faced this kind of pressure. See Fewsmith (1985), p. 102.

29. *YSB*, 27 June 1928, p. 7.

30. Wu Bannong, "Hebei sheng ji pingjin liangshi laozi zhengyi di fenxi" (An analysis of labor disputes in Hebei province and the cities of Beiping and Tianjin), *Shehui kexue likan* (Social Sciences Quarterly) 4:3, 4 (July and December 1929): 39; *NCS*, 29 June 1928, p. 1.

31. Wu Bannong, p. 39; *NCS*, 30 June 1928, p. 3; *YSB*, 5 July 1928, p. 7.

32. Wu Bannong, p. 40; *NCS*, 17 July 1928, p. 1; *China Weekly Review*, 18 August 1928, p. 404.

33. Ma Chaojun, *Zhongguo laogong yundong shi* (A history of the Chinese labor movement; Taibei: Zhongguo laogong fuli she, 1959), p. 831.

34. *NCS*, 18 August 1928, p. 12.

35. *NCS*, p. 40; *NCS*, 8 July 1928, p. 1; *YSB*, 9 July 1928, p. 2.

36. Carpet workers at the huge Yanjing factory were given permission to attend the July 7 rally but went on strike when the head labor boss refused to provide meals customarily due them. *NCS*, 10 July 1928, p. 1; Wu Bannong, p. 40; *YSB*, 10 July 1928, p. 7; 11 July 1928, p. 7.

37. *YSB*, 10 January 1929, p. 12.

38. *NCS*, 2 July 1929, p. 1; Wu Bannong, p. 61.

39. *NCS*, 21 December 1928, p. 3.

40. *NCS*, 4 February 1929, p. 14.

41. Tao Menghe, ed., *Dier ci Zhongguo laodong nianjian* (Second Chinese Labor Handbook), (Beiping: Institute of Social Research, 1932)

3:4:133.

42. *NCS*, 26 October 1928, p. 9.

43. Zhong Dediao, *Beijing gongyun shiliao*, p. 245; *YSB*, 21 October 1928, p. 7.

44. Wu Bannong, p. 42.

45. *STSB*, 14 October 1928, p. 7.

46. *NCS*, 11 July 1928, p. 1.

47. Wu Bannong, p. 39; *NCS*, 8 July 1928, p. 1.

48. *YSB*, 28 July 1928, p. 7.

49. *YSB*, 19 October 1928, p. 2.

50. *YSB*, 20 October 1928, p. 7.

51. *YSB*, 10 October 1928, p. 3.

52. Wu Bannong, p. 49; *STSB*, 10 December 1928, p. 7; 28 December 1928, p. 7; *YSB*, 10 December 1928, p. 7.

53. Wu Bannong, p. 46; *NCS*, 21 November 1928, p. 11; *YSB*, 18 November 1928, p. 7; 20 November 1928, p. 7; 23 November 1928, p. 7; 24 November 1928, p. 7.

54. *YSB*, 16 February 1929, p. 7; Wu Bannong, p. 54; *STSB*, 16 February 1929, p. 7; 17 February 1929, p. 1; 6 March 1929, p. 7; *NCS*, 17 February 1929, p. 1; 21 February 1929, p. 11.

55. *STSB*, 3 July 1929, p. 7. The electric-light workers repeated many of the streetcar-worker charges against Li and Zhang in their list of grievances.

56. Tien Hung-mao, *Government and Politics in Kuomintang China, 1927–1937* (Stanford: Stanford University Press, 1972), p. 52. Chen Guofu belonged to the "C. C. clique," which was trying to convert the party into a pliant tool for Chiang Kai-shek.

57. *NCS*, 23 December 1928, pp. 3, 16.

58. *STSB*, 24 December 1928, p. 7; *YSB*, 24 December 1928, p. 3.

59. *YSB*, 23 December 1928, p. 2.

60. "Peipin ni okeru densha bōdō jiken" (The streetcar riot in Beiping), *Gaiji keisatsuhō* 89 (November 1929): 120; *YSB*, 18 January 1929, p. 7.

61. *YSB*, 19 April 1929, p. 7.

62. Li Fuhai, "Renli che gongren za dianche shijian shimo" (The full story of the smashing of the streetcars by rickshaw workers), in *Wenshi ziliao xuanbian* (A compendium of historical materials), vol. 13 (Beijing: Beijing chuban she, 1982), p. 178; Deng Haoming recalled that Li Lesan and the whole Grand Alliance group in Beiping joined the Reorganizationists (p. 96).

63. *STSB*, 25 October 1929, p. 7.

64. "The streetcar riot in Beiping," p. 120.

Chapter 11

1. Lao She, *Luotou Xiangzi* (Camel Xiangzi; Hong Kong: Xuelin youxian gongsi, n.d.), p. 91.

2. Yu Side, "Beiping gonghui diaocha" (An investigation of Beiping unions), *Shehui xue jie* (Sociological World) 4 (1930): 121. In November 1928, the rickshaw-pullers union became the twenty-sixth group of workers in the city to organize and affiliate with the FTU.

3. *YSB*, 1 November 1928, p. 7; *STSB*, 7 November 1928, p. 7.

4. See the chamber's public statement, *YSB*, 6 November 1928, p. 7.

5. *YSB*, 22 December 1928, p. 7.

6. *YSB*, 16 October 1929, p. 7; *Huabei ribao*, 25 October 1929.

7. *NCS*, 23 March 1929, p. 10; *STSB*, 22 March 1929, p. 7.

8. *NCS*, 3 April 1929, p. 12.

9. *NCS*, 23 March 1929, p. 10; *STSB*, 22 March 1929, p. 7.

10. *STSB*, 10 May 1929, p. 7; 15 May 1929, p. 7; *NCS*, 26 May 1929, p. 12; 7 July 1929, p. 14.

11. *NCS*, 10 July 1929, p. 1.

12. *STSB*, 11 July 1929, p. 7; *NCS*, 12 July 1929, p. 12.

13. *Beiping shi gongbao* (Beiping Municipal Gazette) 4 (1929), "Public utilities," p. 3.

14. Ibid., 3 (1929), "Public security," p. 8.

15. Ibid., 4 (1929), "Public utilities," p. 3.

16. Ibid., 3 (1929), "Public security," p. 7.

17. *NCS*, 12 July 1929, p. 12; *STSB*, 11 July 1929, p. 7.

18. *NCS*, 12 July 1929, p. 12.

19. *Da gongbao* (Impartial Daily), 29 June 1929, p. 1; *NCS*, 29 June 1929, p. 1.

20. *STSB*, 11 July 1929, p. 7.

21. *STSB*, 25 July 1929, p. 7.

22. *NCS*, 7 August 1929, p. 1.

23. *Peking Leader*, 7 August 1929, p. 1.

24. *STSB*, 1 September 1929, p. 7; *NCS*, 1 September 1929, p. 15.

25. *Beiping shi gongbao* 13 (1929), "Public security," pp. 2–3.

26. Ibid.

27. *STSB*, 7 September 1929, p. 7.

28. *STSB*, 20 September 1929, p. 7.

29. *STSB*, 25 July 1929, p. 7.

30. *STSB*, 25 October 1929, p. 7. A rickshaw man explained that dues of about 40 coppers a month created a fund that members could draw on for special personal or family emergencies.

31. *Huabei ribao*, 6 September 1929, p. 7.

32. Ibid., 9 September 1929, p. 7.

33. *Beiping shi gongbao* 14 (1929), "Social affairs," p. 5.

34. Huang Gongdu, "Duiyu wuchan jieji shehui taidu di yige xiao-xiao ceyan" (A short test for proletarian consciousness), *Shehui xue jie* (Sociological World) 4 (June 1930). By design all the men he polled were married, had children, and belonged to the rickshaw-pullers union.

35. Ibid., p. 179.

36. Joan M. Nelson, *Access to Power: Politics and the Urban Poor in Developing Nations* (Princeton: Princeton University Press, 1979), p. 156.

37. Huang, "Proletarian consciousness," p. 163.

38. Ibid., pp. 163–165.

39. Yu Side, "Beiping unions," pp. 119–120.

40. For the tendency of unionism to support the established social order by "setting the terms on which workers will submit to the managers' authority," see Jeremy Brecher, *Strike!* (Boston: South End Press, 1972), p. 255.

41. Huang, "Proletarian consciousness," p. 173.

42. For a formal model describing how political consciousness can lead to class consciousness through participation in a social movement, see Richard R. Weiner, *Cultural Marxism and Political Sociology* (Beverly Hills: Sage, 1981).

43. Erik Olin Wright, *Class, Crisis, and the State* (London: NLB, 1978), pp. 61–63.

44. Huang, "Proletarian consciousness," p. 166.

45. E. P. Thompson, "The Moral Economy of the English Crowd in the Eighteenth Century," *Past and Present* 50 (1971).

46. E. J. Hobsbawm and George Rude, *Captain Swing: A Social History of the Great English Agricultural Uprising of 1830* (New York: W. W. Norton, 1975), p. 17.

47. Ibid., p. 550.

48. Ibid., p. 16.

49. E. J. Hobsbawm, *Labouring Men: Studies in the History of Labour* (New York: Basic Books, 1964), p. 7. Hobsbawm notes that machine-breakers typically showed "no special hostility to machines as such."

50. Huang, "Proletarian consciousness," p. 174.

51. Ibid., p. 172–173.

52. Ibid., p. 173–174.

53. Ibid., p. 176.

54. Ibid., pp. 176–177.

55. *YSB*, 9 October 1929, p. 7.

56. Janice Perlman, *The Myth of Marginality: Urban Poverty and Politics in Rio de Janeiro* (Berkeley and Los Angeles: University of California Press, 1976), p. 243.

57. Huang, "Proletarian consciousness," p. 178. Ninety-three wished to study, and ninety-five wanted their children to have an opportunity to go to school.

58. Ibid., p. 178.

59. Ibid., p. 162.

60. *YSB*, 19 September 1929, p. 7.

61. *YSB*, 19 October 1929, p. 7.

62. *STSB*, 1 October 1929, p. 7; 5 October 1929, p. 7; *Huabei ribao*, 30 September 1929, p. 6; 1 October 1929, p. 6; 2 October 1929, p. 6; 4 October 1929, p. 6.

63. *STSB*, 1 October 1929, p. 7.

64. *STSB*, 6 October 1929, p. 7; *NCS*, 5 October 1929, p. 4; *China Weekly Review*, 19 October 1929, p. 283; *Huabei ribao*, 4 October 1929, p. 6; 6 October 1929, p. 6.

65. *NCS*, 15 October 1929, p. 10.

66. Niu Naiou, "Beiping yiqian erbai pinhu zhi yanjiu" (An investigation of 1,200 poor households in Beiping), *Shehui xue jie* (Sociological World) 7 (1932): 157. Ninety-three percent of those surveyed professed to be Buddhists. The authors explained Buddhism's popularity, relative to Confucianism, Daoism, Islam, and Christianity, by noting that "according to Beiping custom, a 'Buddhist' is thought to be a 'good person'."

67. *Huabei ribao*, 6 October 1929, p. 6.

68. *STSB*, 8 October 1929, p. 7; *YSB*, 8 October 1929, p. 7.

69. *STSB*, 14 October 1929, p. 7; 15 October 1929, p. 7; 17 October 1929, p. 7; *Huabei ribao*, 13 October 1929, p. 6.

70. *NCS*, 2 August 1929, p. 11.

71. *NCS*, 12 October 1929; *STSB*, 10 October 1929, p. 7; 12 October 1929, p. 7; *YSB*, 12 October 1929, p. 3; *Peking Leader*, 12 October 1929, p. 12.

72. *Shibao* (Truth Post), 23 October 1929, p. 1.

73. *Beiping shi gongbao* 18 (14 November 1929), "Municipal affairs," pp. 1–2.

74. Ibid.

75. *NCS*, 15 October 1929, p. 9.

76. "Peipin ni okeru densha bōdō jiken" (The Beiping streetcar riot), *Gaiji keisatsuhō* 89 (November 1929): 123–124.

77. *Xin chenbao* (New Morning Post), 21 October 1929 (*GSK*, October 1929, pp. 250–252).

78. Ibid.

79. *Shibao*, 21 October 1929, p. 1.

80. *Huabei ribao*, 25 October 1929.

81. "Beiping streetcar riot," pp. 126–127; *Huabei ribao*, 22 October 1929.

82. "Beiping streetcar riot," p. 128; *STSB*, 23 October 1929, p. 7; *Huabei ribao*, 23 October 1929.

83. *Huabei ribao*, 5 October 1929, p. 6. For a discussion of the notion of "museumification" of China's past, see Joseph Levenson, *Confucian China and Its Modern Fate* (Berkeley and Los Angeles: University of California Press, 1968), vol. 3, pp. 113–115; and Frederic Wakeman's "Foreword" to Levenson, *Revolution and Cosmopolitanism: The Western Stage and the Chinese Stages* (Berkeley and Los Angeles: University of California Press, 1971), p. xiv.

84. *STSB*, 23 October 1929, p. 7; *Huabei ribao*, 24 October 1929 (*GSK*, October 1929, p. 299).

85. *Xin Chenbao*, 23 October 1929 (*GSK*, October 1929, pp. 286–287); *YSB*, 23 October 1929, p. 2; *Peking Leader*, 23 October 1929, p. 1.

86. *YSB*, 23 October 1929, p. 2.

87. E. J. Hobsbawm, *Revolutionaries* (London: Weidenfield and Nicolson, 1973), p. 221.

88. Local documents and newspapers mention "thousands" and "tens of thousands." Foreign wire services gave the figure of 25,000. *Times* (London), 24 October 1929, p. 16, and *New York Times*, 24 October 1929, p. 10.

89. *STSB*, 25 October 1929, p. 7.

90. "Beiping streetcar riot," pp. 121, 130.

91. *NCS*, 23 October 1929, p. 1.

92. Sensitivity to the party's responsibility to police its own ranks cannot account for the fact that Mayor Zhang waited a full three hours after the first attack began to call up troops to clear the streets. As a subordinate of Yan Xishan and as such soon to become part of the Reorganizationist challenge to the Nanjing regime, Zhang Yinwu may have allowed the riot to develop as a means of embarrassing the central government's allies in the local apparatus and aiding leftist politicians like Zhang Yinqing who either were or were about to become Reorganizationists. If that was the case, he miscalculated the ferocity of the disorder he initially appeared to condone.

93. *NCS*, 24 October 1929, p. 1.

94. *Peking Leader*, 23 October 1929, p. 1.

95. *YSB*, 23 October 1929, p. 2.

96. *Peking Leader*, 23 October 1929, p. 11.

97. *Beiping shi gongbao* 18 (14 November 1929), "Municipal government," pp. 1–2.

98. Taken too far, of course, this approach risks what Charles Tilly has criticized as a "hydraulic" explanation of riot and protest in which the "angry individual acts as a reservoir of resentment, a conduit of tension, a boiler of fury," instead of as a "thinking, political man acting on principle." Tilly, "Food Supply and Public Order in Modern Europe," in Tilly, ed., *The Formation of National States in Western Europe* (Princeton: Princeton University Press, 1975), pp. 390–391.

99. *Huabei ribao*, 24 October 1929 (*GSK*, October, p. 299).

100. *Peking Leader*, 23 October 1929, p. 1.

101. *Huabei ribao*, 25 October 1929, p. 5.

102. *NCS*, 24 October 1929, p. 11.

103. *YSB*, 24 October 1929, p. 2.

104. Ibid.

105. *NCS*, 24 October 1929, p. 11.

106. *NCS*, 25 October 1929, p. 2.

107. *Shibao*, 23 October 1929, p. 1.

108. *STSB*, 25 October 1929, p. 7.

109. *NCS*, 25 October 1929, p. 1.

110. Peking Leader, 27 October 1929, p. 12.

111. *NCS*, 29 October 1929, p. 11.

112. *Huabei ribao*, 26 October 1929. Of 1,143 individuals arrested, 925 were workers, 80 committeemen, and 243 group leaders.

113. Ibid., 25 October 1929, p. 5.

114. *Peking Leader*, 25 October 1929, p. 1.

115. *Huabei ribao*, 29 October 1929.

116. *NCS*, 27 November 1929, p. 1.

117. "Beiping streetcar riot," p. 152.

118. *STSB*, 30 October 1929, p. 7.

119. *YSB*, 26 October 1929, p. 7.

120. *Huabei ribao*, 31 October 1929, p. 7.

121. *China Weekly Review*, 7 December 1929, p. 26.

122. *NCS*, 6 November 1929, p. 12.

123. *NCS*, 30 October 1929, p. 12.

124. *NCS*, 26 February 1930, p. 2.

125. Quoted in Anthony Oberschall, *Social Conflict and Social Movements* (Englewood Cliffs, N. J.: Prentice Hall, 1973), p. 111.

126. Translated by Wang Chi-chen in Wang, ed., *Contemporary Chinese Short Stories* (New York: Columbia University Press, 1944).

127. Lao She, *Luotou Xiangzi*, p. 290.

128. Ibid., p. 304.

129. E. J. Hobsbawm, "The Machine Breakers," in Hobsbawm, *Labouring Men: Studies in the History of Labour* (New York: Basic Books, 1964), and Hobsbawm and George Rude, *Captain Swing* (New York: Pantheon, 1968).

Chapter 12

1. *NCS*, 7 January 1928, p. 12.

2. Clifford Geertz, *Negara: The Theatre State in Nineteenth-Century Bali* (Princeton: Princeton University Press, 1980), p. 121.

3. Ibid. Geertz demonstrates in the case of the traditional Balinese state how an "exemplary center" devoted to theatrical representation of societal values can make elements of the social order valued by both kings and landlords, like hierarchy and inequality, "enchanting." In the Balinese case, the state did little else, since most of the "statecraft" functions of governance were handled by local elites and organizations. In traditional China, the state worked to combine statecraft and stateliness in a formula that promoted the sharing of managerial and order-keeping functions between the state and nongovernmental elites and the maintenance of an "exemplary center," which served the state but also legitimized the authority of local power-holders.

4. See Ray Huang's vivid discussion of the structure and function of imperial statecraft and stagecraft in *1587: A Year of No Significance* (New Haven: Yale University Press, 1981).

5. My use of "trenchworks" as a metaphor for urban institutions is taken from Ira Katznelson's application of Antonio Gramsci's insights to urban politics. See Katznelson, *City Trenches: Urban Politics and the Patterning Class in the United States* (New York: Pantheon, 1981).

6. See again Joseph Levenson's characterization of "The Hung-hsien Emperor as a Comic Type," in *Confucian China and Its Modern Fate: The Problem of Monarchical Decay* (Berkeley and Los Angeles: University of California Press, 1968), pp. 3–7.

7. Antonio Gramsci, *Selections from the Prison Notebooks*, Quintin Hoare and Geoffrey N. Smith, eds. and trans. (New York: International Publishers, 1971), pp. 229–239.

8. Katznelson, pp. 188–189.

9. Harold Isaacs suggests the affirmative in his classic *Tragedy of the Chinese Revolution* (Stanford: Stanford University Press, 1961). For a criticism of Isaacs' suggestion of close ties between Chiang Kai-shek and Chinese capitalists, based on evidence of conflict and hostility between state and social class, see Parks Coble, *The Shanghai Capitalists and the*

Nationalist Government, 1927–1937 (Cambridge: Harvard Council of East Asian Studies, 1980). In *The Politics of Cotton Textiles in Kuomintang China* (New York: Garland, 1982), Richard Bush describes a mix of conflict and cooperation in relations between the Nanjing regime and lower Yangzi River industrialists.

10. Lloyd Eastman has made the case for this depiction of state-society relations under the Nationalists. Eastman, *The Abortive Revolution: China Under Nationalist Rule, 1927–1937* (Cambridge: Harvard University Press, 1974). Bradley Geisert argues that connections between the Nanjing regime and local classes and groups were much more complex than Eastman's formulation suggests. See his article "Toward a Pluralist Model of KMT Rule," *Chinese Republican Studies Newsletter* 7:2 (February 1982).

11. William T. Rowe. *Hankow: Commerce and Society in a Chinese City, 1796–1889* (Stanford: Stanford University Press, 1984).

12. In a forthcoming volume on nineteenth-century Hankou, *An Early Modern Chinese City: Conflict and Community in Nineteenth-Century Hankow* (Stanford: Stanford University Press), William Rowe examines the tension between the not inconsiderable capacity of urban institutions to meet social crises and the increasing severity of these challenges toward the end of the Qing.

13. Louis Chevalier, *Laboring Classes and Dangerous Classes* (Princeton: Princeton University Press, 1973), p. 11.

14. Wei Gan [pseud.], *Beiping yehua* (Evening chats in Beiping; Shanghai: Zhonghua shuju youxian gongsi, 1935).

15. The classic discussion of the functional tie between conflict and consensus can be found in Georg Simmel, *Conflict and the Web of Group-Affiliations* (New York: Free Press, 1955). For the notion that concern for consensus can heighten sensitivity to conflict, see Takie Sugiyama Lebra, "Nonconfrontational Strategies for the Management of Interpersonal Conflicts," in Ellis S. Krauss, Thomas P. Rohlen, and Patricia G. Steinhoff, eds., *Conflict in Japan* (Honolulu: University of Hawaii Press, 1984). According to Lebra, "When we focus on conflict, we seem to accept the conflict model and reject the harmony model as if the two were mutually exclusive. This is an oversimplified dichotomy that fails to capture reality. In fact, the logic of bipolarization may well be reversed: the more harmony-oriented, the more conflict-sensitive."

Bibliography

Abrikossow, Dimitrii. *Revelations of a Russian Diplomat*. Edited by George A. Lensen. Seattle: University of Washington Press, 1964.

Alitto, Guy S. *The Last Confucian: Liang Shu-ming and the Chinese Dilemma of Modernity*. Berkeley and Los Angeles: University of California Press, 1979.

———. "Rural Elites in Transition: China's Cultural Crisis and the Problem of Legitimacy." In Susan Mann, ed., *Proceedings of the Center for Far Eastern Studies Modern China Project*. Chicago: University of Chicago Center for Far Eastern Studies, 1979.

Beijing gongye shiliao (Historical materials on Beijing industry). Edited by Zhongguo renmin daxue gongye jingji xi (Industrial Economics Department of Chinese People's University). Beijing: Beijing chuban she, 1960.

Beijing gongyun shiliao (Historical materials on the Beijing labor movement). 4 vols. Edited by Beijing shi zong gonghui gongren yundong shi yanjiu zu (Worker Movement Historical Research Group of the Beijing Federation of Trade Unions). Beijing: Gongren chuban she, 1981.

Beijing ribao (Beijing Daily). Beijing, 1925.

Beijing Ruifuxiang (Ruifuxiang of Beijing). Edited by Ziben zhuyi jingji gaizao yanjiu shi, Zhongguo kexue yuan jingji yanjiu suo (Research Office for the Transformation of the Capitalist Economy, Chinese Academy of Sciences Economic Research Institute). Beijing: Sanlian shudian, 1959.

Beijing zhinan (Guide to Beijing). Shanghai: Zhonghua shudian, 1917.

Beiping shi gongbao (Beiping Municipal Gazette). Beiping, biweekly. 1928–1930.

Benevolo, Leonardo. *The History of the City*. Translated by Geoffrey Culverwell. Cambridge: MIT Press, 1980.

Benjamin, Walter. *Reflections: Essays, Aphorisms, Autobiographical Writings*. Translated by Edmund Jephcott. New York: Harcourt Brace Jovanovich, 1978.

Berman, Marshall. *All That Is Solid Melts into Air: The Experience of Modernity*. New York: Simon and Schuster, 1982.

———. "Facades at Face Value." *Nation* (6 August 1977).

Black, John R. *Young Japan*. Vol. 2. London: Trubner, 1881.

Boorman, Howard L., and Richard C. Howard. *Biographical Dictionary of Republican China*. 4 vols. New York: Columbia University Press, 1967, 1968, 1970, 1971.

Brecher, Jeremy. *Strike!* Boston: South End Press, 1972.

Bredon, Juliet. *Peking*. New York: Oxford University Press, 1982.

Burgess, John S. *The Guilds of Peking*. New York: Columbia University Press, 1928.

———. "The Problem of Prostitution." *Shehui xue zazhi* (Journal of sociology) 2:4 (April 1925).

Bush, Richard C. *The Politics of Cotton Textiles in Kuomintang China*. New York: Garland, 1982.

Chen bao (Morning Post). Beijing, daily.

Chesneaux, Jean. *The Chinese Labour Movement, 1919–1927*. Stanford: Stanford University Press, 1968.

Chevalier, Louis. *Laboring Classes and Dangerous Classes*. Princeton: Princeton University Press, 1973.

Ch'i, Hsi-sheng. *Nationalist China at War*. Ann Arbor: University of Michigan Press, 1982.

Chi, Madeline. "Bureaucratic Capitalists in Operation: Ts'ao Ju-lin and His New Communications Clique, 1916–1919." *Journal of Asian Studies* 34:3 (May 1975).

Ch'ien Tuan-sheng. *The Government and Politics of China, 1912–1949*. Stanford: Stanford University Press, 1970.

China Perspectives. St. Paul, Minn., semiannual.

China Weekly Review. Shanghai, weekly. 1918–1930.

The China Yearbook. Edited by H. G. W. Woodhead. 1915 through 1926–27. London: George Routledge, 1916–1921; Tianjin: Tientsin Press, 1921–1928.

Chinese Economic Bulletin. Beijing, weekly. 1921–1927.

Chinese Economic Monthly. Beijing.

Chow Tse-tsung. *The May Fourth Movement: Intellectual Revolution in Modern China*. Stanford: Stanford University Press, 1967.

Choy, Jun Ke. *My China Years, 1911–1945: Practical Politics in China*

After the 1911 Revolution. Hong Kong: Peninsula Press, 1974.

Chu Chi-ch'ien and Thomas Blaisdell, Jr. *Peking Rugs and Peking Boys: A Study of the Rug Industry in Peking.* Beijing: Chinese Social and Political Science Association, 1924.

Clarke, Joseph I. C. *Japan at First Hand: Her Islands, Their People, the Picturesque, the Real.* New York: Dodd, Mead, 1920.

Cobb, Richard. *The Police and the People.* Oxford: Oxford University Press, 1970.

Coble, Parks. *The Shanghai Capitalists and the Nationalist Government, 1927–1937.* Cambridge: Harvard Council of East Asian Studies, 1980.

Dagong bao (Impartial Daily). Tianjin.

Dahrendorf, Ralf. *Class and Class Conflict in Industrial Society.* Stanford: Stanford University Press, 1959.

Deng Haoming. "'Benshe' shimo" (The full story of the "Foundation Society"). *Wenshi ziliao xuanbian* (A compendium of historical materials). Vol. 9. Beijing: Beijing chuban she, 1981.

Dray-Novey, Alison. "Policing Imperial Peking: The Ch'ing Gendarmerie, 1650–1850." Ph. D. dissertation, Harvard University, 1981.

Duke, Michael. "The Urban Poor in Lao She's Pre-war Short Stories." *Phi Theta Papers* 12 (1970).

Duncan, Robert M. *Peiping Municipality and the Diplomatic Quarter.* Beiping: Peiyang Press, 1933.

Eastman, Lloyd. *The Abortive Revolution: China Under Nationalist Rule, 1927–1937.* Cambridge: Harvard University Press, 1974.

———. *Seeds of Destruction: Nationalist China in War.* Stanford: Stanford University Press, 1984.

Eckstein, Alexander. *China's Economic Development: The Interplay of Scarcity and Ideology.* Ann Arbor: University of Michigan Press, 1975.

Elvin, Mark, and G. William Skinner, eds. *The Chinese City Between Two Worlds.* Stanford: Stanford University Press, 1974.

Esherick, Joseph W. *Reform and Revolution in China: The 1911 Revolution in Hunan and Hubei.* Berkeley and Los Angeles: University of California Press, 1976.

Feuerwerker, Yi-tsi. "The Changing Relationship Between Literature and Life." In Merle Goldman, ed., *Modern Chinese Literature in the May Fourth Era.* Cambridge: Harvard University Press, 1977.

Fewsmith, Joseph. "From Guild to Interest Group: The Transformation of Public and Private in Late Qing China." *Comparative Studies in Society and History* 25:4 (October 1983).

———. *Party, State, and Local Elites in Republican China: Merchant*

Organizations and Politics in Shanghai, 1890–1930. Honolulu: University of Hawaii Press, 1985.

Fischer, Emil S. *Guide to Peking and Its Environs Near and Far*. Beijing: Tientsin Press, 1925.

Fosdick, Raymond. *European Police Systems*. New York: Century Co., 1915.

Franck, Harry A. *Wandering in Northern China*. New York: Century Co., 1923.

Gamble, Sidney. *How Chinese Families Live in Peiping*. New York: Funk and Wagnalls, 1933.

————. *Peking: A Social Survey*. New York: George H. Doran, 1921.

Gamble, Sidney, and Li Jinghan. "Ershiwu nian lai Beijing zhi wujia gongzu ji shenghuo chengdu" (Prices, wages and standards of living in Beijing in the last twenty-five years). *Shehui kexue qikan* (Social Science Review) 4:1 and 2 (October 1925 and March 1926).

Gamble, Sidney, and T. P. Meng. "Peking Prices, Wages, and Standard of Living." *Chinese Social and Political Science Review* 10:3 (1926).

Geertz, Clifford. *Negara: The Theatre-State in Nineteenth-Century Bali*. Princeton: Princeton University Press, 1980.

Geisert, Bradley. "Toward a Pluralist Model of KMT Rule." *Chinese Republican Studies Newsletter* 7:2 (February 1982).

Gendai Chūka minkoku Manshūkoku jinmeikan (Biographical dictionary of the contemporary Chinese Republic and Manchukuo). Tokyo: Gaimusho jōhōbu, 1932.

Gendai Shina jinmeikan (Biographical dictionary of men of contemporary China). Tokyo: Gaimusho jōhōbu, 1928.

Gendai Shina no kiroku (Records of contemporary China). Compiled by Hatano Ken'ichi. Monthly, 1924–1929.

Gilman, Richard. *Decadence: The Strange Life of an Epithet*. New York: Farrar, Straus and Giroux, 1979.

Girouard, Mark. *Cities and People*. New Haven: Yale University Press, 1985.

Goffman, Erving. *The Presentation of Self in Everyday Life*. New York: Doubleday, 1959.

Gramsci, Antonio. *Selections from the Prison Notebooks of Antonio Gramsci*. Translated and edited by Quintin Hoare and Geoffrey N. Smith. New York: International Publishers, 1971.

Halliday, Jon. *A Political History of Japanese Capitalism*. New York: Pantheon, 1975.

Harrison, James P. *The Long March to Power: A History of the Chinese Communist Party, 1921–1972*. New York: Praeger, 1972.

Hattori Unokichi. *Pekin rōjō nikki.* Ōyama Azusa, ed. Tokyo: Heibon-sha, 1965.

Hershatter, Gail. *The Workers of Tianjin, 1900–1949.* Stanford: Stanford University Press, 1986.

Hobsbawn, E. J. *Labouring Men: Studies in the History of Labour.* New York: Basic Books, 1964.

———. *Revolutionaries.* London: Weidenfield and Nicolson, 1973.

———. *Workers: Worlds of Labour.* New York: Pantheon, 1984.

Hobsbawm, E. J., and George Rude. *Captain Swing: A Social History of the Great English Agricultural Uprising of 1830.* New York: Pantheon, 1968.

Huabei ribao (North China Daily). Beiping, 1929.

Huang Di. "'Wusi' yiali zhi Zhongguo xue chao" (Student unrest in China since "May Four"). *Shehui xue jie* (Sociological World) 6 (1932).

Huang Gongdu. "Duiyu wuchan jieji shehui taidu di yige xiaoxiao ceyan" (A short test for proletarian consciousness). *Shehui xue jie* (Sociological World) 4 (1930).

Huang, Ray. *1587: A Year of No Significance.* New Haven: Yale University Press, 1981.

Imahori Seiji. *Pekin shimin no jichi kōsei* (The self-governing organizations of the citizens of Beijing). Tokyo: Bunkyudo, 1947.

Industrial Labour in Japan. International Labour Office. Geneva: P. S. King, 1933.

Isaacs, Harold. *The Tragedy of the Chinese Revolution.* Stanford: Stanford University Press, 1961.

Ishii Ryōsuke. *Japanese Legislation in the Meiji Era.* Translated by William J. Chambliss. Tokyo: Pan-Pacific Press, 1958.

Jansen, Marius B. *The Japanese and Sun Yat-sen.* Cambridge: Harvard University Press, 1967.

Jingshi jingcha faling huizuan (A compilation of metropolitan police ordinances). Beijing, n.p., 1915.

Jingshi jingcha gongbao (Metropolitan Police Gazette). Beijing, daily. 1927–1929.

Jingshi neicheng xunjing zongting dierci tongji shu (The second book of statistics of the inner city metropolitan police office). Beijing: Jingshi neicheng xunjing zongting, 1907.

Jingshi zong shanghui hangming lu (Membership roster of the metropolitan chamber of commerce). Beijing: n.p., 1925.

Jingwu guize (Rules of police work). Beijing: Shuntian shibao, 190?.

Johnson, Kinchen. *Folksongs and Children-Songs from Peiping.* Taibei:

Dongfang wenhua shuju, 1971.

Jones, Susan Mann. "The Organization of Trade at the County Level: Brokerage and Tax Farming in the Republican Period." In Susan Mann Jones, ed., *Political Leadership and Social Change at the Local Level in China from 1850 to the Present: Select Papers from the Center for Far Eastern Studies Modern China Project.* Chicago: University of Chicago Center for Far Eastern Studies, 1979.

Jones, Susan Mann, and Philip A. Kuhn. "Dynastic Decline and the Roots of Rebellion." *Cambridge History of China.* Vol. 10, *Late Ch'ing, 1800–1911.* Edited by John K. Fairbank. New York: Cambridge University Press, 1978.

Kates, George. *The Years That Were Fat.* Cambridge: MIT Press, 1967.

Katznelson, Ira. *City Trenches: Urban Politics and the Patterning of Class in the United States.* New York: Pantheon, 1981.

Kotenev, A. M. *Shanghai: Its Municipality and the Chinese.* Shanghai: North-China Daily News and Herald, 1927.

Kung, H. O. "Tramways in Shanghai, Tientsin, and Peiping." *Far Eastern Review* (February 1937).

Kuczynski, Jurgen. *The Rise of the Working Class.* Translated by C. T. A. Ray. New York: McGraw-Hill, 1967.

Kuzuu Yoshihisa. *Tōa senkaku shishi kiden* (Pioneers and patriots in East Asia). Vol. 2. Tokyo: Kokuryū-Kaishuppan-bu, 1935.

La Motte, Ellen N. *Peking Dust.* New York: Century Co., 1920.

Lane, Frederick. *Venice and History.* Baltimore: Johns Hopkins Press, 1966.

Lao She. "Black and White Li." In Wang Chi-chen, trans. and ed., *Contemporary Chinese Short Stories.* New York: Columbia University Press, 1944.

———. *Lao She shenghuo yu chuangzuo zishu* (An account of Lao She's life and creative work in his own words). Edited by Hu Xieqing. Hong Kong: Sanlian shu dian, 1981.

———. *Luotou Xiangzi* (Camel Xiangzi). Hong Kong: Xuelin youxian gongsi, n.d.

———. *The Yellow Storm.* Translated by Ida Pruitt. New York: Harcourt, Brace, 1951.

———. *Wo jeiyi beizi* (My life). Shanghai: Huiqun chuban she, n.d.

Lao Xuan [pseud.] *Shibao fenghua* (Gibberish from the *Truth Post*). Beiping: Shibao chuban she, 1935.

Laodong jie (World of Labor). Beijing, 1920.

Lebra, Takie Sugiyama. "Nonconfrontational Strategies for Management of Interpersonal Conflicts." In Ellis S. Krauss, Thomas P. Rohlen, and Patricia Steinhoff, eds. *Conflict in Japan.* Honolulu: University of Hawaii Press, 1984.

Lei Jihui. *Beiping shuizhuan kaolue* (A brief examination of taxes in Beiping). Beiping: Beiping shehui diaocha suo, 1933.

Levenson, Joseph. *Confucian China and Its Modern Fate: A Trilogy.* Berkeley and Los Angeles: University of California Press, 1968.

———. *Revolution and Cosmopolitanism: The Western Stage and the Chinese Stages.* Berkeley and Los Angeles: University of California Press, 1971.

Li Chengyi. *Sanshi nian lai jiaguo* (My home and country in the last thirty years). Hong Kong: Chenhua, 1961.

Li Dazhao. *Li Dazhao xuanji* (Selected works of Li Dazhao). Beijing: Renmin chuban she, 1962.

Li Dazhao zhuan (A biography of Li Dazhao). Beijing: Renmin chuban she, 1979.

Li Fuhai. "Renliche gongren za dianche shijian shimo" (The full story of the smashing of streetcars by the rickshaw workers). *Wenshi ziliao xuanbian* (A compendium of historical materials). Vol. 13. Beijing: Beijing chuban she, 1982.

Li Hua, ed. and comp. *Ming Qing yilai Beijing gongshang huiguan beike xuan bian* (Selected stele of industrial and commercial guilds in Ming and Qing Beijing). Beijing: Wenwu chuban she, 1980.

Li Jinghan. "Beijing renli chefu xianzhuang di diaocha" (An investigation of conditions among rickshaw pullers in Beijing). *Shehui xue zazhi* (Journal of Sociology) 2:4 (April 1925).

———. "Beiping zuidi xiandu di shenghuo chengdu di taolun" (A discussion of the lowest standard of living in Beiping). *Shehui xue jie* (Sociological World) 3 (September 1929).

Liu Jiantang. "Huiyi *Xiangdao zhoukan* zai Beijing yinxing di jingguo" (Reminiscences of the process of publishing the *Guide Weekly* in Beijing). In Zhang Jinglu, ed., *Zhongguo xiandai chuban shiliao* (Historical materials on modern Chinese publishing). Beijing: Zhonghua shuju chuban, 1959.

Liu Yifeng. "Beijing dianche gongsi jianwen huiyi" (An eyewitness account of the Beijing streetcar company). *Wenshi ziliao xuanji* (A compilation of historical materials). Vol. 31. Beijing: Wenshi xiliao chuban she, 1980.

Lou Xuexi, Chi Zehui, and Chen Wenxian, eds. and comps. *Beiping shi gongshang ye gaikuang* (A survey of industry and commerce in the city of Beiping). Beiping: Beiping shi shehui ju, 1932.

Lowe, H. Y. [Lu Xingyuan]. *The Adventures of Wu: The Life Cycle of a Peking Man.* Vol. 2. Princeton: Princeton University Press, 1983.

Luo Jing. "Beijing minzhong fanDuan yundong yu Guomindang youpai pohuai yinmou" (The Beijing masses' anti-Duan movement and the destructive plotting of the Nationalist right wing). *Xiangdao zhoubao* (Guide Weekly) 140 (30 December 1925).

Lyell, William A. *Lu Hsun's Vision of Reality*. Berkeley and Los Angeles: University of California Press, 1976.

Lynn, Jermyn [Lin Jihong]. *The Social Life of the Chinese*. Beijing: China Booksellers, 1928.

Ma Chaojun. *Zhongguo laogong yundong shi* (A history of the Chinese labor movement). Taibei: Zhongguo laogong fuli she, 1959.

McCormack, Gavan. *Chang Tso-lin in Northeast China, 1911–1925: China, Japan, and the Manchurian Idea*. Stanford: Stanford University Press, 1977.

McKay, John P. *Tramways and Trolleys: The Rise of Urban Mass Transport in Europe*. Princeton: Princeton University Press, 1976.

MacKinnon, Stephen R. *Power and Politics in Late Imperial China: Yuan Shi-kai in Beijing and Tianjin, 1901–1908*. Berkeley and Los Angeles: University of California Press, 1980.

MacMurray, John V. A., ed. and comp. *Treaties and Agreements with and Concerning China, 1894–1919*. Vol. 2. New York: Oxford University Press, 1921.

Mann, Susan. *Local Merchants and the Chinese Bureaucracy, 1750–1950*. Stanford: Stanford University Press, 1987.

Metzger, Thomas. *Escape from Predicament: Neo-Confucianism and China's Evolving Political Culture*. New York: Columbia University Press, 1977.

Millard's Review (see *China Weekly Review*).

Mitsufumi Tsuchida. "Rickshaw." *Kodansha Encyclopedia of Japan*. Vol. 6. Tokyo: Kodansha, 1983.

Muir, William Ker, Jr. *Police: Streetcorner Politicians*. Chicago: University of Chicago Press, 1979.

Nagano Akira. *Development of Capitalism in China*. Tokyo: Japan Council of the Institute of Pacific Relations, 1931.

Naitō Konan. "Naitō Konan and the Development of the Conception of Modernity in Chinese History." Translated and edited by Joshua A. Fogel. *Chinese Studies in History* 17:1 (Fall 1983).

Nathan, Andrew J. *Chinese Democracy*. New York: Knopf, 1985.

———. *Peking Politics, 1918–1923: Factionalism and the Failure of Constitutionalism*. Berkeley and Los Angeles: University of California Press, 1976.

Nelson, Joan. *Access to Power: Politics and the Urban Poor in Developing Nations*. Princeton: Princeton University Press, 1979.

New York Times. New York, daily. 1900–1930.

Niida Noboru. "The Industrial and Commercial Guilds of Peking and Religion and Fellow Countrymanship and Elements of Their Coherence." *Folklore Studies* (1950).

Niu Naiou. "Beiping yiqian erbai pinhu zhi yanjiu." (An investigation of 1,200 poor households in Beiping). *Shehui xue jie* (Sociological World) 7 (1932).

The North-China Herald and Supreme Court and Consular Gazette. Shanghai, Weekly. 1900–1930.

North China Standard. Beijing, daily. 1919–1929.

Oberschall, Anthony. *Social Conflict and Social Movements.* Englewood Cliffs, N. J.: Prentice-Hall, 1973.

"Peipin ni okeru densha bōdō jiken" (The Beiping streetcar riot). *Gaiji keisatsuhō* 89 (November 1929).

Pekin annai ki (A guide to Beijing). Tokyo: Shimin inshōkan, 1940.

Peking Leader. Beijing, daily. 1919, 1926, 1928–1929.

Peng Ming. *Wusi yundong zai Beijing* (The May Fourth movement in Beijing). Beijing: Beijing chuban she, 1979.

Peng Zeyi, ed. *Zhongguo jindai shougong ye shi ziliao, 1840–1949* (Materials on the history of modern Chinese handicrafts). Beijing: Sanlian shudian, 1957.

Perckhammer, Heinz v. *Peking.* Berlin: Albertus-Verlag, 1928.

Perlman, Janice. *The Myth of Marginality: Urban Poverty and Politics in Rio de Janeiro.* Berkeley and Los Angeles: University of California Press, 1976.

Pu Yi, Henry. *The Last Manchu: The Autobiography of Henry Pu Yi, Last Emperor of China.* Edited by Paul Kramer. New York: G. P. Putnam's Sons, 1967.

Qu Zhisheng. *Pingyong ji* (Mediocre writings). Taibei: Taiwan shangwu yinshu guan, 1958.

Quennell, Peter. *A Superficial Journey Through Tokyo and Peking.* London: Faber and Faber, 1934.

Rankin, Mary. *Elite Activism and Political Transformation in China: Zhejiang Province, 1865–1911.* Stanford: Stanford University Press, 1986.

Remer, C. F. *Foreign Investments in China.* New York: Macmillan, 1933.

Rowe, William T. *An Early Modern Chinese City: Conflict and Community in Nineteenth-Century Hankow.* Stanford: Stanford University Press. Forthcoming.

———. *Hankow: Commerce and Society in a Chinese City, 1796–1889.* Stanford: Stanford University Press, 1984.

Sennett, Richard. *The Fall of Public Man.* New York: Knopf, 1977.

Shaffer, Lynda. "Mao Zedong and the October 1922 Changsha Construction Workers' Strike." *Modern China* 4:4 (October 1978).

Shen Yunlong. "Xu Shichang pingzhuan" (Biography of Xu Shichang). *Zhuanji wenxue* (Biographical Literature) 13:3 (September 1968).

Sheridan, James. *China in Disintegration: The Republican Era in Chinese History, 1912–1949.* New York: Free Press, 1975.

———. *Chinese Warlord: The Career of Feng Yü-hsiang.* Stanford: Stanford University Press, 1966.

Shibao (Truth Post). Beiping, daily. 1928–1930.

(Shiyong) Beijing zhinan (A practical guide to Beijing). Shanghai: Commercial Press, 1926.

Shuntian shibao (Beijing Times). Beijing, daily. 1919–1929.

Silver, Allan. "The Demand for Order in Civil Society: A Review of Some Themes in the History of Urban Crime, Police, and Riot." In David J. Bordua, ed., *The Police: Six Sociological Essays.* New York: Free Press, 1967.

Simmel, Georg. *Conflict and the Web of Group-Affiliations.* New York: Free Press, 1955.

Simpson, Bertram L. *Indiscreet Letters from Peking.* New York: Dodd, Mead, 1907.

Siren, Oswald. *The Walls and Gates of Peking.* London: Lane, 1924.

Skinner, G. William. "Chinese Peasants and the Closed Community: An Open and Shut Case." *Comparative Studies in Society and History* 13:3 (1971).

———, ed. *The City in Late Imperial China.* Stanford: Stanford University Press, 1977.

Smith, Henry D. "Tokyo as an Idea: An Exploration of Japanese Urban Thought Until 1945." *Journal of Japanese Studies* 4:1 (Winter 1978).

Spence, Jonathan. *The Gate of Heavenly Peace: The Chinese and Their Revolution.* New York: Viking, 1981.

Stauffer, Milton T., ed. *The Christian Occupation of China.* Shanghai: China Continuation Committee, 1922.

Stead, Philip J. "The New Police." In David Bayley, ed., *Police and Society.* Beverly Hills: Sage, 1977.

Stearns, Peter, and Daniel J. Walkowitz, eds. *Workers in the Industrial Revolution: Recent Studies of Labor in the United States and Europe.* New Brunswick, N.J.: Transaction Books, 1974.

Su Ru-chiang. "Birth Control in China." Ph.D. dissertation, University of Chicago, 1946.

Suleski, Ronald. "The Rise and Fall of the Fengtien Dollar, 1917–1928: Currency Reform in Warlord China." *Modern Asian Studies* 13 (1979).

Tan Shih-hua. *A Chinese Testament.* As told to S. Tretiakov. New York: Simon and Schuster, 1934.

Tao Kangde, ed. *Beiping yigu* (A glance at Beiping). Shanghai: Yuzhou feng she, 1938.

T'ao, L. K. (Tao Menghe). *Livelihood in Peking: An Analysis of the Budgets of Sixty Families.* Beijing: China Foundation for the Promotion of Education and Culture, 1928.

————. "Unemployment Among Intellectual Workers in China." *Chinese Social and Political Science Review* 13:3 (July 1929).

Tao Menghe, ed. *Dier ci Zhongguo laodong nianjian* (China Labor Yearbook, no. 2). Beiping: Institute of Social Research, 1932.

————. *Diyi ci Zhongguo laodong nianjian* (China Labor Yearbook, no. 1). Beiping: Institute of Social Research, 1928.

Thompson, E. P. "The Crime of Anonymity." In Douglas Hay, Peter Linebaugh, E. P. Thompson, and Cal Winslow, eds., *Albion's Fatal Tree: Crime and Society in Eighteenth Century England.* New York: Pantheon, 1975.

————. *The Making of the English Working Class.* New York: Vintage, 1966.

————. "The Moral Economy of the English Crowd in the Eighteenth Century." *Past and Present* 50 (1971).

Tien Hung-mao. *Government and Politics in Kuomintang China, 1927–1937.* Stanford University Press, 1972.

Tilly, Charles. "Food Supply and Public Order in Modern Europe." In Charles Tilly, ed., *The Formation of National States in Western Europe.* Princeton: Princeton University Press, 1975.

————. *From Mobilization to Revolution.* Menlo Park, Calif.: Addison-Wesley, 1978.

Tong, Y. L. "Social Conditions and Social Service Endeavor in Peking." *Chinese Social and Political Science Review* 7:3 (1923).

Tso Shi-kan [Sheldon]. *The Labor Movement in Peking.* Shanghai: n.p., 1928.

Vishnyakova-Akimova, Vera. *Two Years in Revolutionary China, 1925–27.* Translated by Stephen Levine. Cambridge: Harvard University East Asian Research Center, 1971.

Vohra, Ranbir. *Lao She and the Chinese Revolution.* Cambridge: Harvard East Asian Research Center, 1974.

Wakeman, Frederic, Jr. *The Fall of Imperial China.* New York: Free Press, 1975.

Wakeman, Frederic, Jr., and Carolyn Grant, eds. *Conflict and Control in Late Imperial China.* Berkeley and Los Angeles: University of California Press, 1975.

Wang Chi-chen, ed. and trans. *Contemporary Chinese Short Stories.* New York: Columbia University Press, 1944.

Wang Cifan. "Nongcun dizhu yu dushi pinmin" (A village landlord and the urban poor). *Duli pinglun* (Independent Review) 106 (1934).

Wang Qinghua. "Gao Junyu tongzhi shengping shiji" (Comrade Gao Junyu's life story). *Wenshi ziliao xuanbian* (A compendium of historical materials). Vol. 14. Beijing: Beijing chuban she, 1982.

Warner, Sam B. *Streetcar Suburbs: The Process of Growth in Boston, 1870–1900.* Cambridge: Harvard University Press, 1962.

Wei Gan [pseud.]. *Beiping yehua* (Evening chats in Beiping). Shanghai: Zhonghua shuju youxian gongsi, 1935.

Wei Wei and Qian Xiaohui. *Deng Zhongxia zhuan* (A biography of Deng Zhongxia). Beijing: Renmin chuban she, 1981.

Weiner, Richard R. *Cultural Marxism and Political Sociology.* Beverly Hills: Sage, 1981.

Werner, Edward T. C. *Autumn Leaves: An Autobiography with a Sheaf of Papers, Sociological, Philosophical, and Metaphysical.* Shanghai: Kelly and Walsh, 1928.

Who's Who in China: Biographies of Chinese Leaders. Shanghai: China Weekly Review Press, 1925.

Whyte, Martin K. and William L. Parish. *Urban Life in Contemporary China.* Chicago: University of Chicago Press, 1984.

Wilbur, C. Martin. "Military Separatism and the Process of Reunification Under the Nationalist Regime, 1922–1937." In Ping-ti Ho and Tang Tsou, eds., *China in Crisis*, vol. 1. Chicago: University of Chicago Press, 1968.

———. "The Nationalist Revolution: From Canton to Nanking, 1923–1928." *Cambridge History of China.* Vol. 12, *Republican China, 1912–1949*, part 1. New York: Cambridge University Press, 1983.

Wilbur, C. Martin, and Julie Lien-ying How. *Documents on Communism, Nationalism, and Soviet Advisers in China, 1918–1928.* New York: Columbia University Press, 1956.

Wright, Erik Olin. *Class, Crisis, and the State.* London: NLB, 1978.

Wright, Mary, ed. *China in Revolution: The First Phase, 1900–1913.* New Haven: Yale University Press, 1968.

Wu Bannong. "Hebei sheng ji ping jin liangshi laozi zhengyi di fenxi" (An analysis of labor disputes in the province of Hebei and the cities of Beiping and Tianjin). *Shehui kexue likan* (Social Science Quarterly) 4:3,4 (July and December 1929).

Wu Guang. "Yi Beiping gong qingtuan dixia douzheng pianduan" (Reminiscences of the underground struggles of the Communist Youth League in Beiping). *Hongqi piaopiao* (The Red Flag Waves). Beijing: n.p., 1957.

Wusi aiguo yundong (The May Fourth patriotic movement). Vol. 1. Edited by Zhongguo shehui kexue yuan jindai shi yanjiu suo (The Chinese Academy of Social Sciences Contemporary History Research Institute). Beijing: Zhongguo shehui kexue chuban she, 1979.

Wu Wo-yao. "A Bannerman at the Teahouse." Translated by Gloria Bien. *Renditions: A Chinese-English Translation Magazine* 4 (Spring 1975).

Xi Ying [pseud.]. *Xi Ying xianhua* (Idle gossip from Xi Ying). Shanghai: Xinyue shudian, 1928.

Xiandai pinglun (Contemporary Affairs). Beijing, weekly.

Xiao Chaoran. "Guanyu Beijing gongchan dang xiaozu di jianli yu huodong" (Concerning the founding and activities of the Beijing Communist party small group). *Wenshi ziliao xuanbian* (Compendium of historical materials). Vol. 11. Beijing: Beijing chuban she, 1981.

Yano Jin'ichi. "Zadankai: rokujūnen no omoide—Yano Jin'ichi hakase o kakonde" (Discussion: Memories of sixty years concerning Yano Jin'ichi). With Miyazaki Ichisada and Hagiwara Junpei. *Tōhōgaku* (Eastern Studies) 28 (July 1964).

Yates, Douglas. *The Ungovernable City: The Politics of Urban Problems and Policy Making.* Cambridge: MIT Press, 1977.

Ye Dezun. "Shehui shenghuo (renli che)" (Social life [The rickshaw]). *Xin Zhongguo za* (New China) 1:1 (September 1919).

Yee, Frank Ki Chun. "The Police in Modern China." Ph.D. dissertation, University of California, Los Angeles, 1942.

Yen Ching-yueh. "Crime in Relation to Social Change in China." Ph.D. dissertation, University of Chicago, 1934.

Yen Hui-ching. *East-West Kaleidoscope, 1877–1946.* New York: St. John's University Press, 1974.

Yishi bao (Social Welfare). Beijing, daily. 1919–1929.

Yoshikawa Kōjirō. "Chūgoku no keisatsu" (The police of China). *Yoshikawa Kōjirō zenshū* (The complete works of Yoshikawa Kōjirō). Vol. 16. Tokyo: Chikuma shobō, 1974).

Young, Ernest. *The Presidency of Yuan Shih-k'ai: Liberalism and Dictatorship in Early Republican China.* Ann Arbor: University of Michigan Press, 1976.

Yu Qichang and Chen Keming, eds. *Gudu bianqian jilue* (On the transformation of the capital). Beiping: n.p., 1941.

Yu Side. "Beiping gonghui diaocha" (An investigation of Beiping unions). *Shehui xue jie* (Sociological World) 4 (1930).

Yue Tianyu (as told to Zhao Gengji and Liang Xianghan). "Wo suo zhidao di Zhonggong Beijing diwei zaoqi di gemeng huodong" (What I know about the Chinese Communist party Beijing committee's early period of revolutionary activity). *Wenshi ziliao xuanbian* (A compendium of historical materials). Vol. 11. Beijing: Beijing chuban she, 1981.

Zhang Houzai. "Renli che wenti" (The rickshaw question). *Xin Zhongguo za* (New China) 1 : 1 (September 1919).

Zhang Tiezheng. "Beiping liangshi gaikuang" (Food supply conditions in Beiping). *Shehui kexue zazhi* (Social Science Quarterly) 8 : 1 (March 1937).

Zhang Youyu. "Wodi huiyi" (My reminiscences). *Wenshi ziliao xuanbian* (Compendium of historical materials). Vol. 9. Beijing: Beijing chuban she, 1981.

Zhongguo geyao ziliao (Chinese folksong materials). Compiled by Zhongguo minjian wenyi yanjiu hui (Chinese Popular Literature and Art Research Association). Beijing: Beijing daxue, 1959.

Zhongguo guomin dang ge shengshi zong dengji he ge dangyuan zongji (General statistics on registered and qualified provincial and municipal members of the Chinese Nationalist party). Zhongguo guomin dang zhongyang zhixing weiyuan hui zongji chu (Statistical Office of the Central Executive Committee of the Chinese Nationalist Party). N.p., 1929.

Zhou Shuzhen, comp. *Zhou Zhian (Xuexi) xiansheng zhuan* (Biography of Mr. Zhou Zhian [Xuexi]). Beiping, n.p., 1948.

Zhu Bingnan and Yan Regeng. "Beiping shi zhi caizheng" (Beiping municipal finance). *Shehui kexue zazhi* (Social Science) 5 : 4 (December 1934).

Index

Compositor: Asco Trade Typesetting Ltd.
      Text: 11/13 pt. Sabon
   Display: Sabon
   Printer: Braun-Brumfield, Inc.
    Binder: Braun-Brumfield, Inc.